Something's Wrong With Us

NATSUMI ANDO

CHAPTER 1
Reunited ———————— 3

CHAPTER 2
Sweets for a Ceremony ———— 47

CHAPTER 3
Marriage ———————— 79

CHAPTER 4
Kogetsuan ———————— 109

CHAPTER 5
An Order From a Regular ———— 137

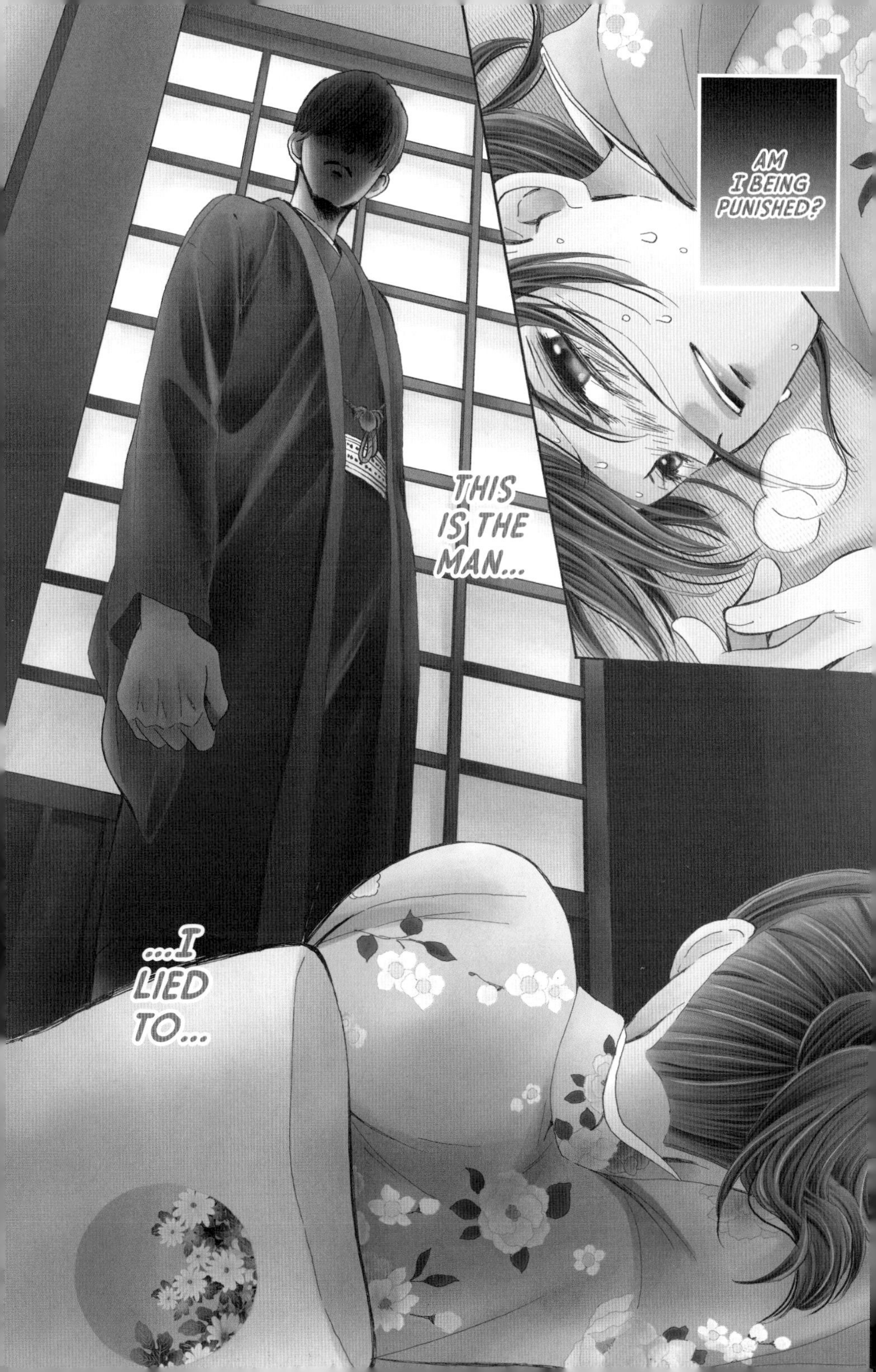
AM I BEING PUNISHED?
THIS IS THE MAN...
...I LIED TO...

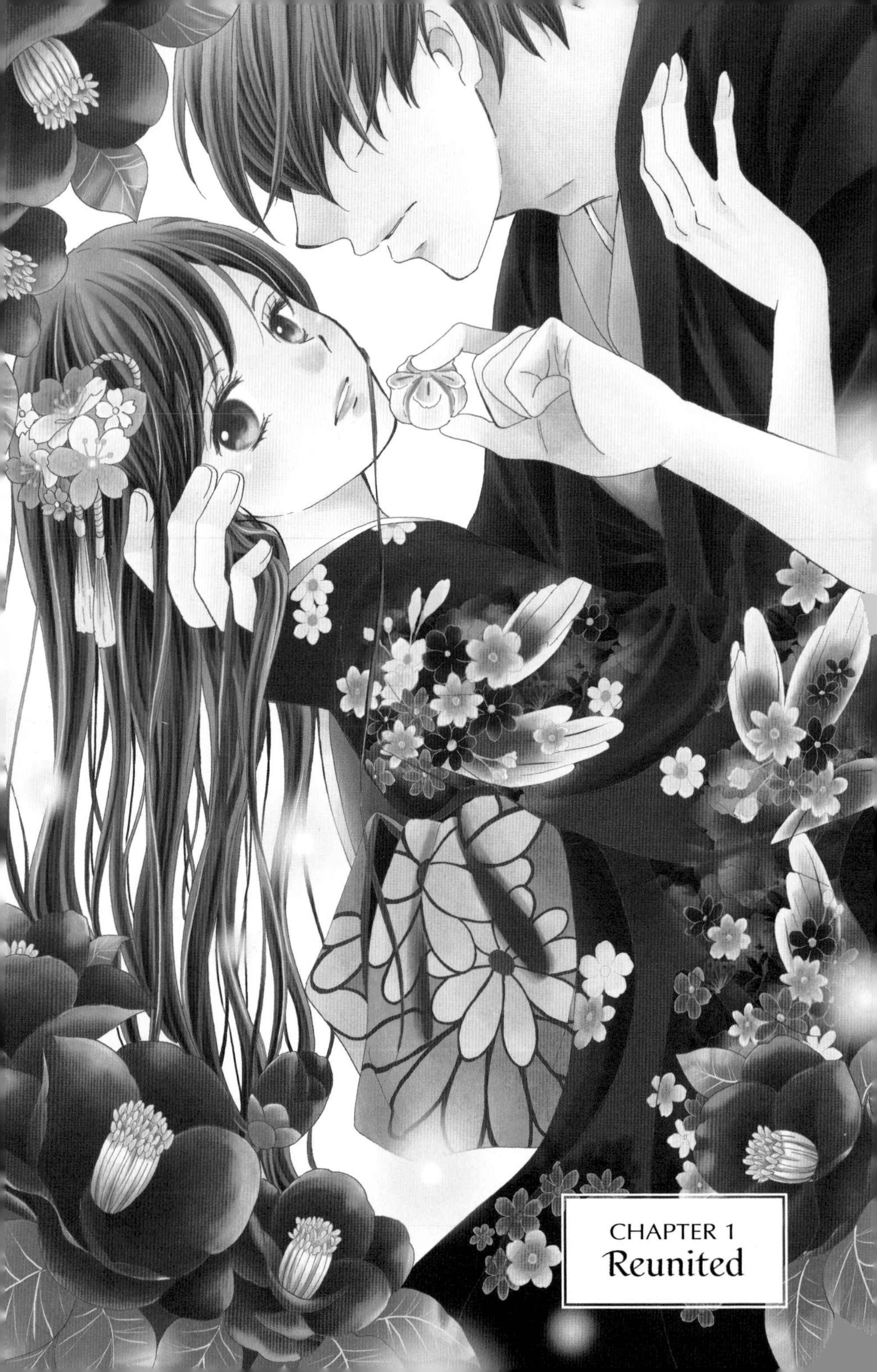

CHAPTER 1
Reunited

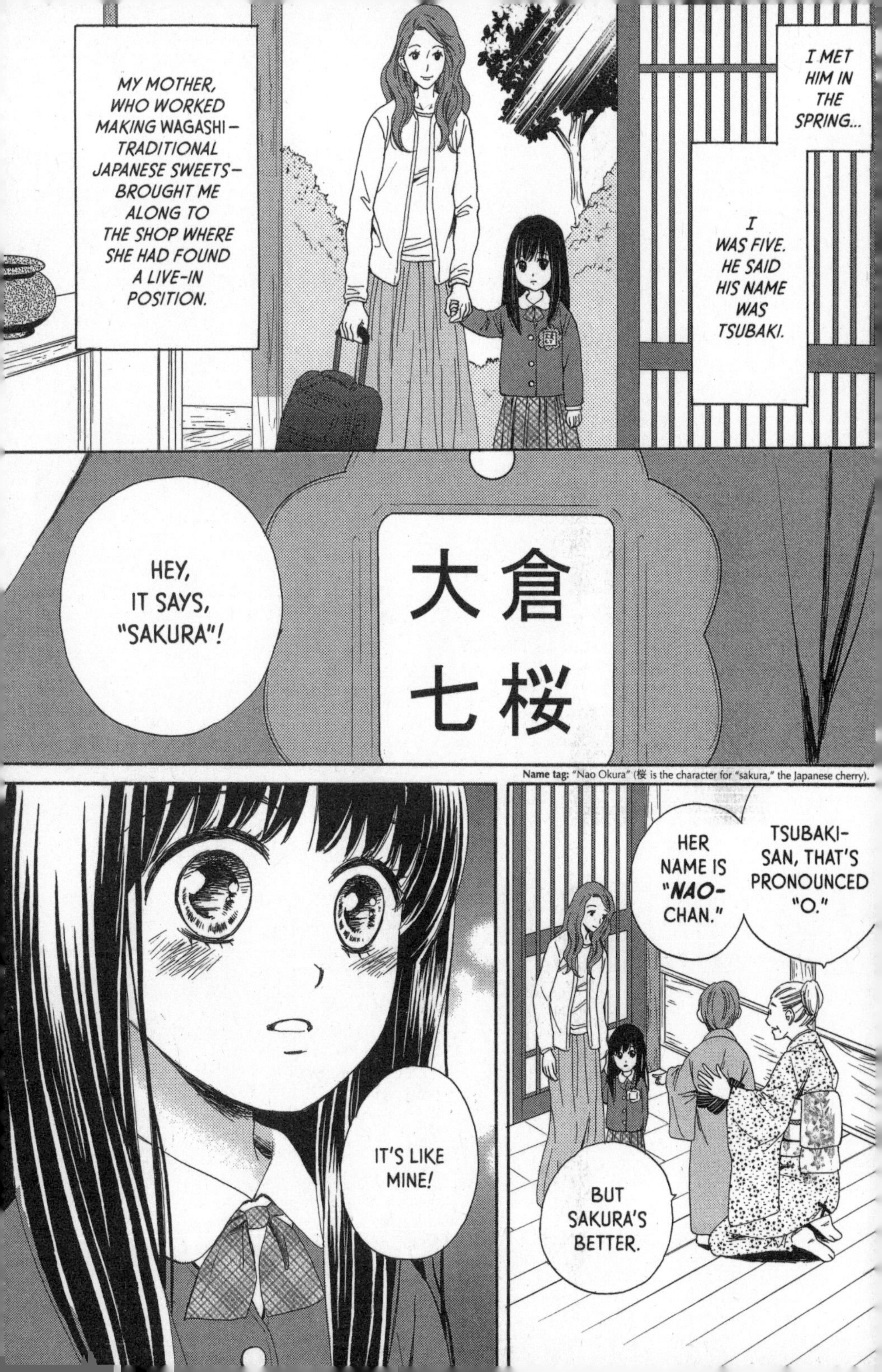
I MET HIM IN THE SPRING...
I WAS FIVE. HE SAID HIS NAME WAS TSUBAKI.
MY MOTHER, WHO WORKED MAKING WAGASHI—TRADITIONAL JAPANESE SWEETS—BROUGHT ME ALONG TO THE SHOP WHERE SHE HAD FOUND A LIVE-IN POSITION.
大倉
七桜
HEY, IT SAYS, "SAKURA"!
TSUBAKI-SAN, THAT'S PRONOUNCED "O."
HER NAME IS "*NAO*-CHAN."
BUT SAKURA'S BETTER.
IT'S LIKE MINE!

Name tag: "Nao Okura" (桜 is the character for "sakura," the Japanese cherry).

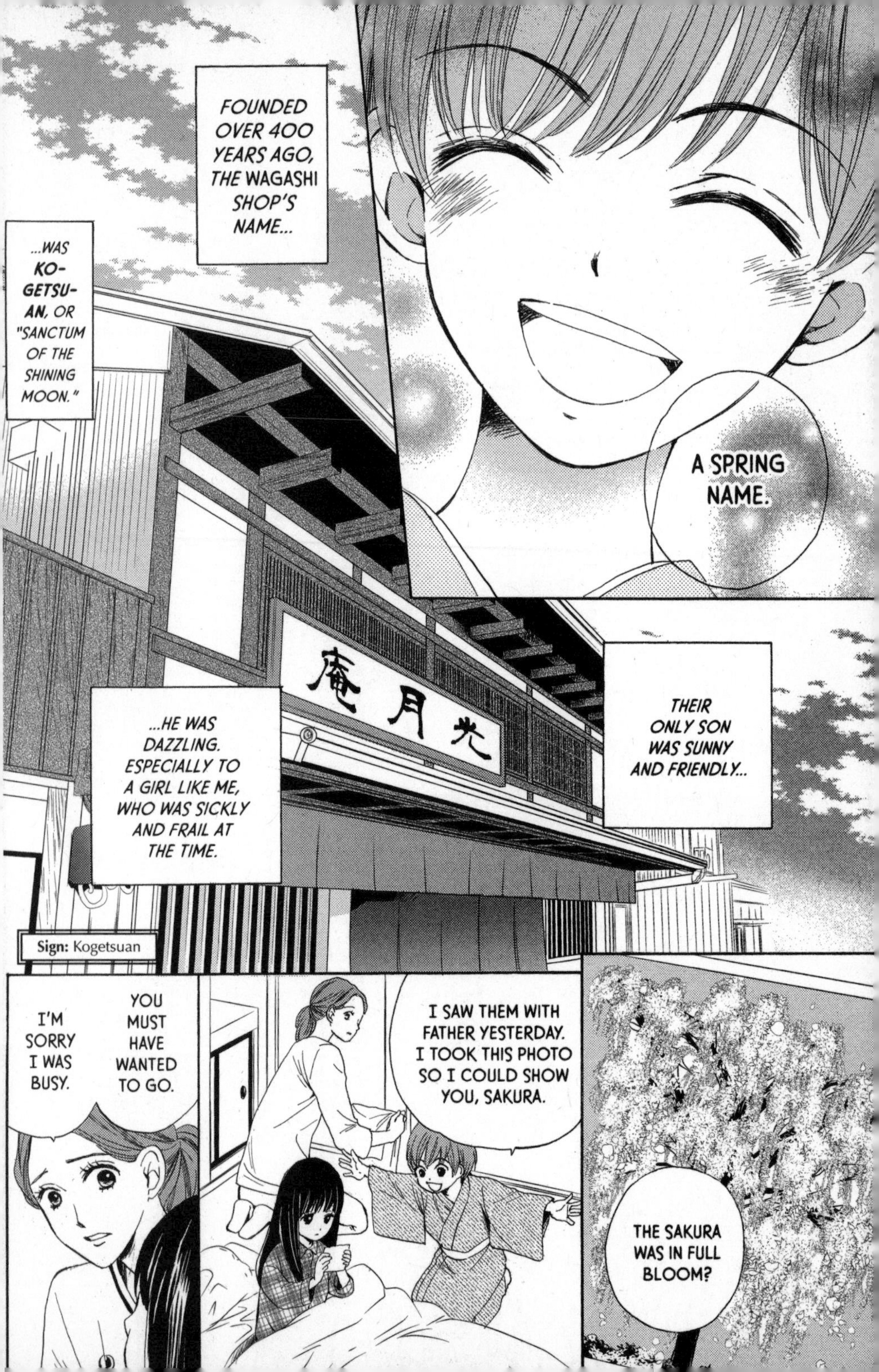
A SPRING NAME.
FOUNDED OVER 400 YEARS AGO, THE WAGASHI SHOP'S NAME...
...WAS KO-GETSU-AN, OR "SANCTUM OF THE SHINING MOON."
THEIR ONLY SON WAS SUNNY AND FRIENDLY...
...HE WAS DAZZLING. ESPECIALLY TO A GIRL LIKE ME, WHO WAS SICKLY AND FRAIL AT THE TIME.
光月庵
Sign: Kogetsuan
THE SAKURA WAS IN FULL BLOOM?
I SAW THEM WITH FATHER YESTERDAY. I TOOK THIS PHOTO SO I COULD SHOW YOU, SAKURA.
YOU MUST HAVE WANTED TO GO.
I'M SORRY I WAS BUSY.

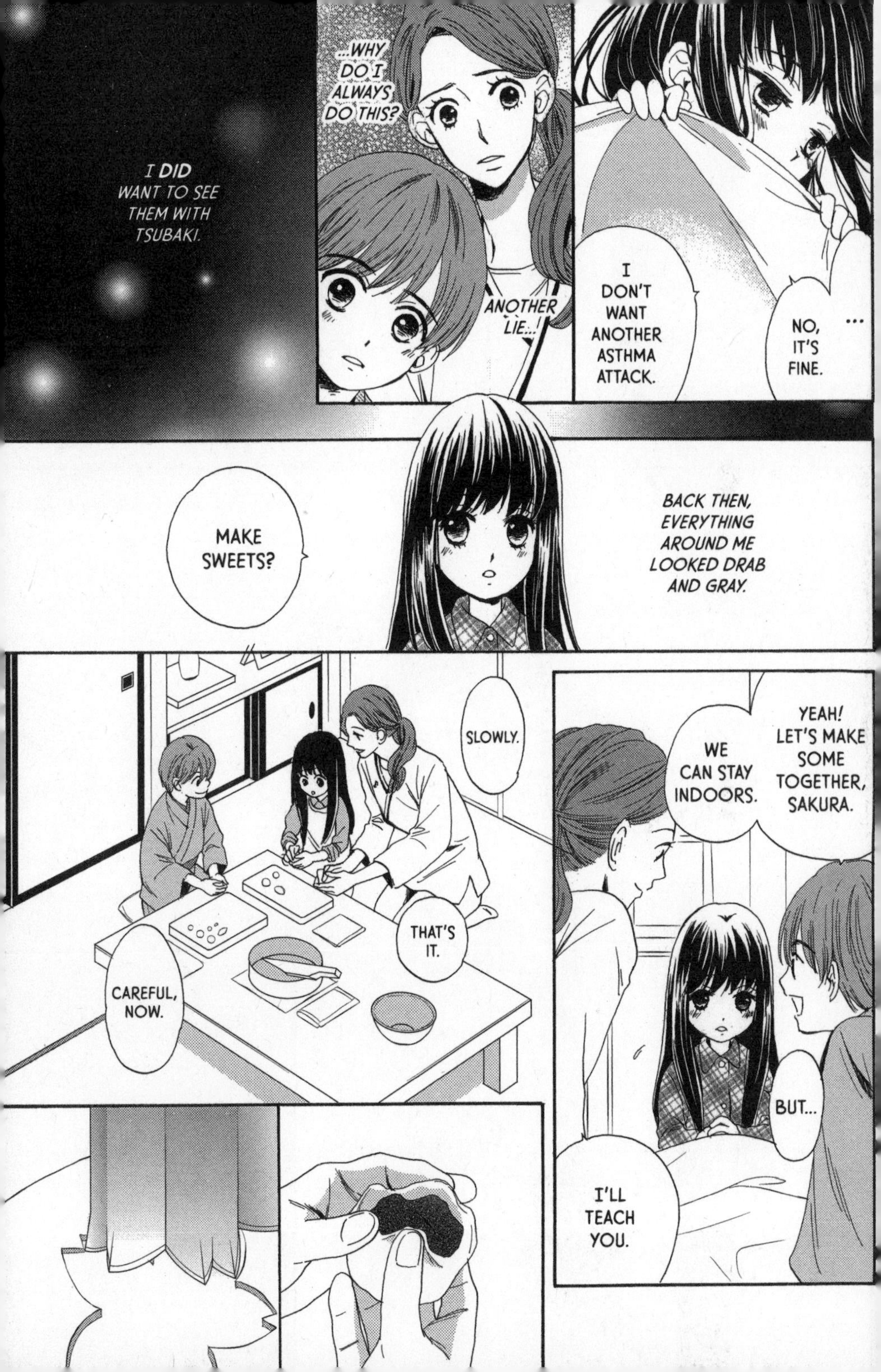
...
NO, IT'S FINE.
I DON'T WANT ANOTHER ASTHMA ATTACK.
...WHY DO I ALWAYS DO THIS?
ANOTHER LIE...
I DID WANT TO SEE THEM WITH TSUBAKI.
BACK THEN, EVERYTHING AROUND ME LOOKED DRAB AND GRAY.
MAKE SWEETS?
YEAH! LET'S MAKE SOME TOGETHER, SAKURA.
WE CAN STAY INDOORS.
BUT...
I'LL TEACH YOU.
SLOWLY.
THAT'S IT.
CAREFUL, NOW.

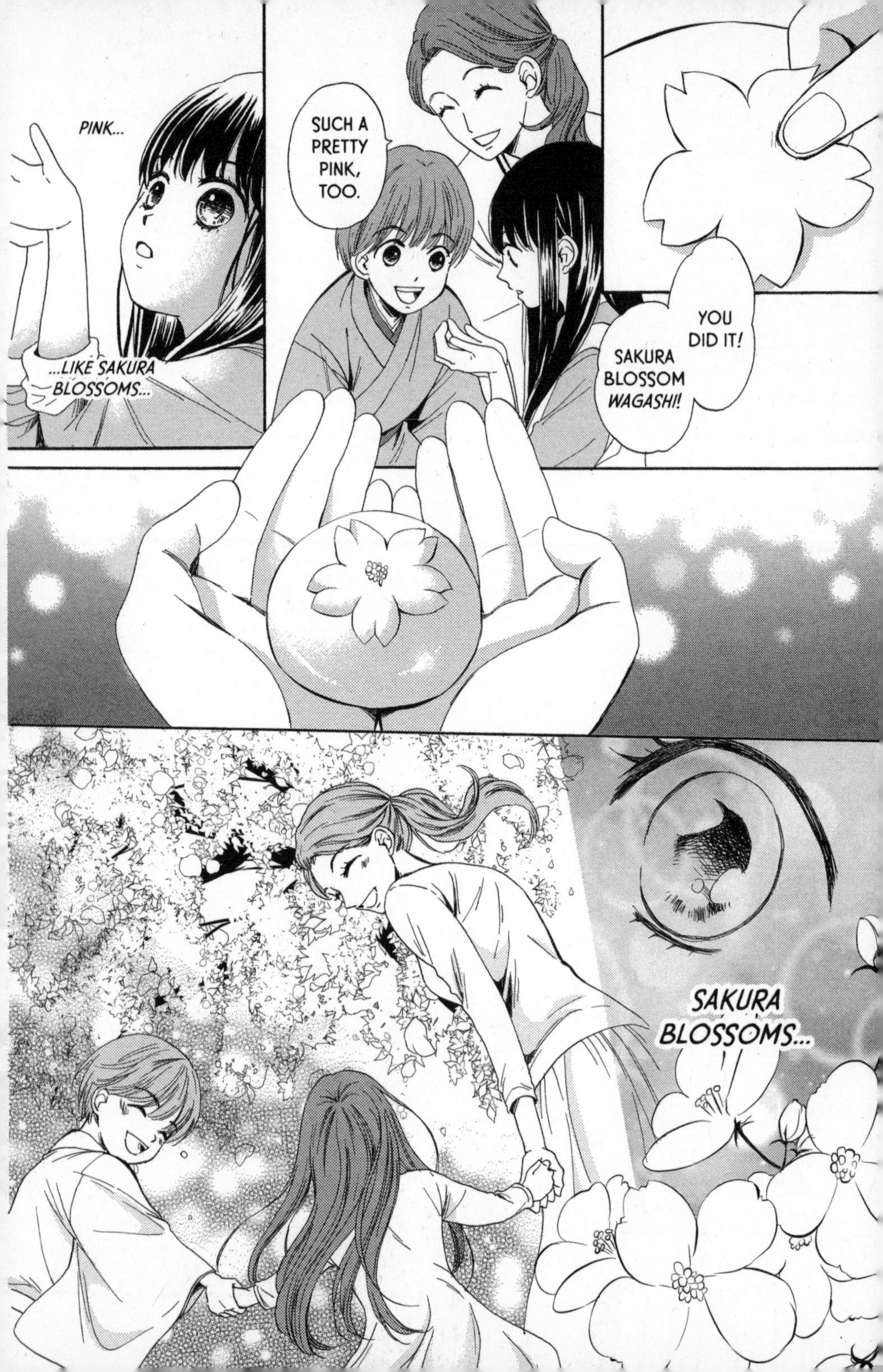
YOU DID IT! SAKURA BLOSSOM WAGASHI!
SUCH A PRETTY PINK, TOO.
PINK...
...LIKE SAKURA BLOSSOMS...
SAKURA BLOSSOMS...

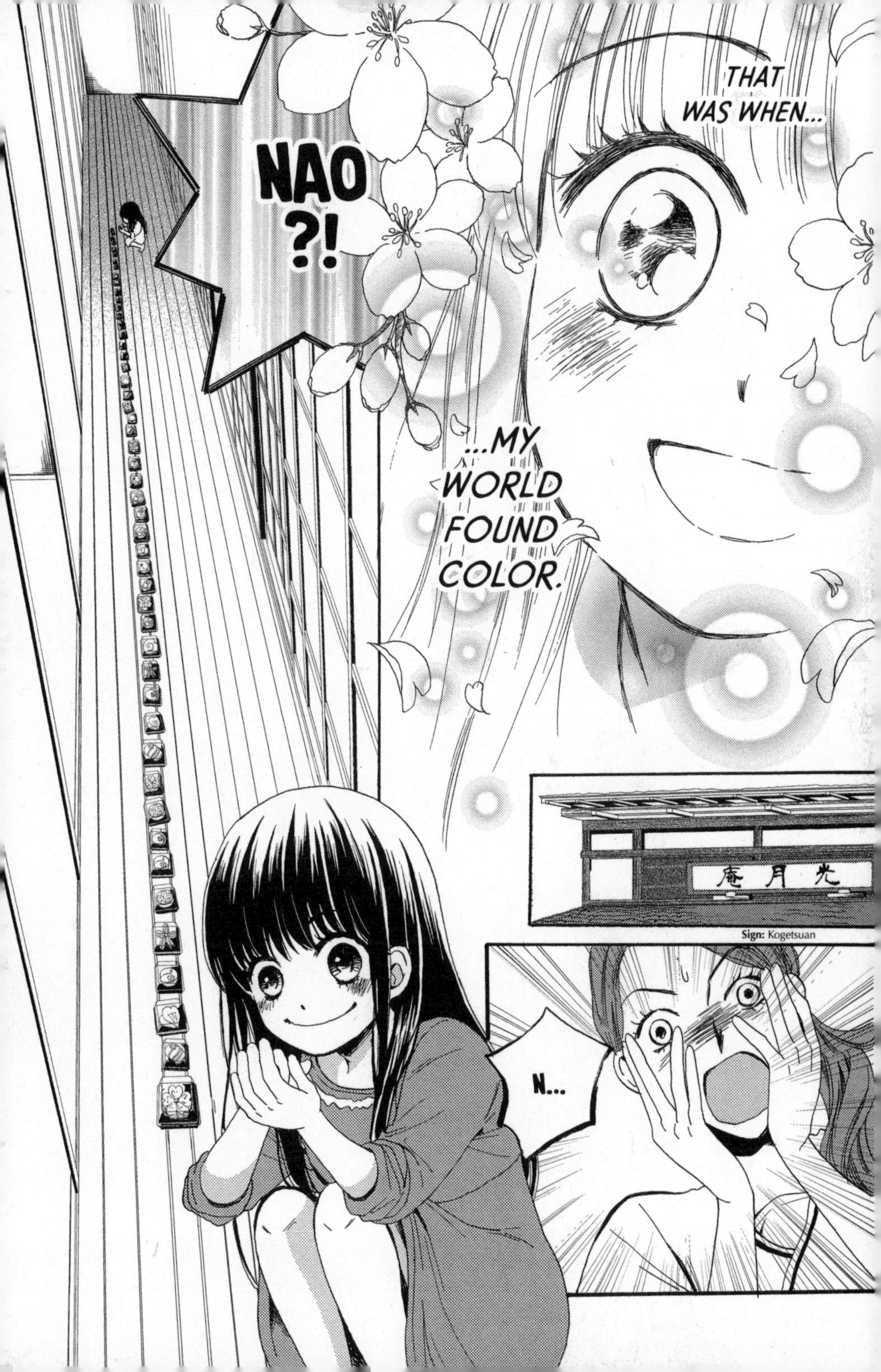
THAT WAS WHEN...
...MY WORLD FOUND COLOR.
光月庵
Sign: Kogetsuan
N...
NAO ?!

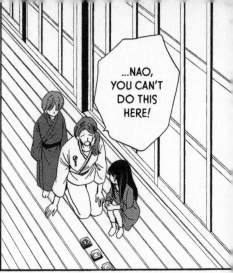

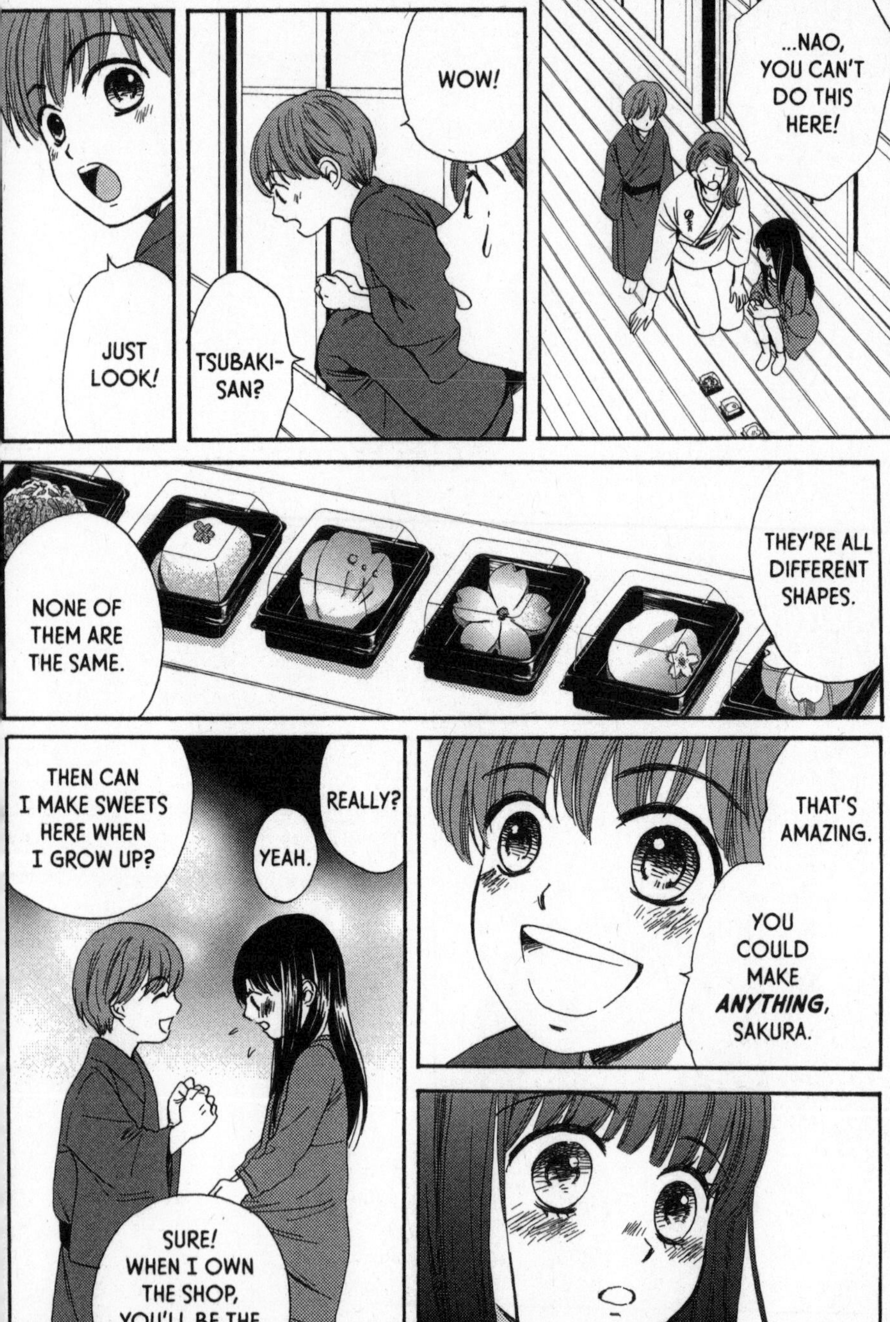
...NAO, YOU CAN'T DO THIS HERE!
WOW!
TSUBAKI-SAN?
JUST LOOK!
THEY'RE ALL DIFFERENT SHAPES.
NONE OF THEM ARE THE SAME.
THAT'S AMAZING.
YOU COULD MAKE ***ANYTHING***, SAKURA.
REALLY?
YEAH.
THEN CAN I MAKE SWEETS HERE WHEN I GROW UP?
SURE! WHEN I OWN THE SHOP, YOU'LL BE THE HEAD CONFEC-TIONER.

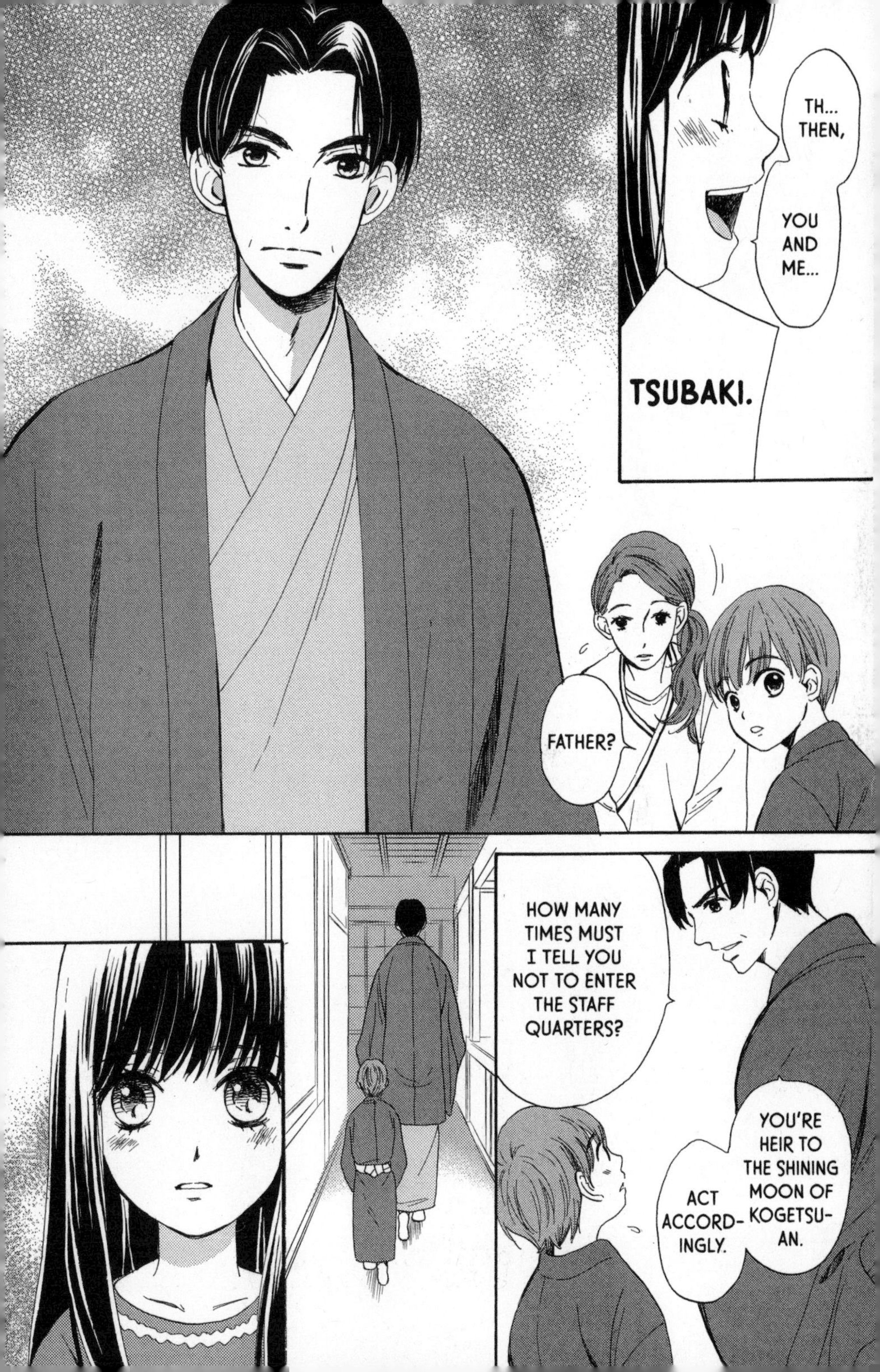
TH... THEN,
YOU AND ME...
TSUBAKI.
FATHER?
HOW MANY TIMES MUST I TELL YOU NOT TO ENTER THE STAFF QUARTERS?
YOU'RE HEIR TO THE SHINING MOON OF KOGETSU-AN.
ACT ACCORD-INGLY.

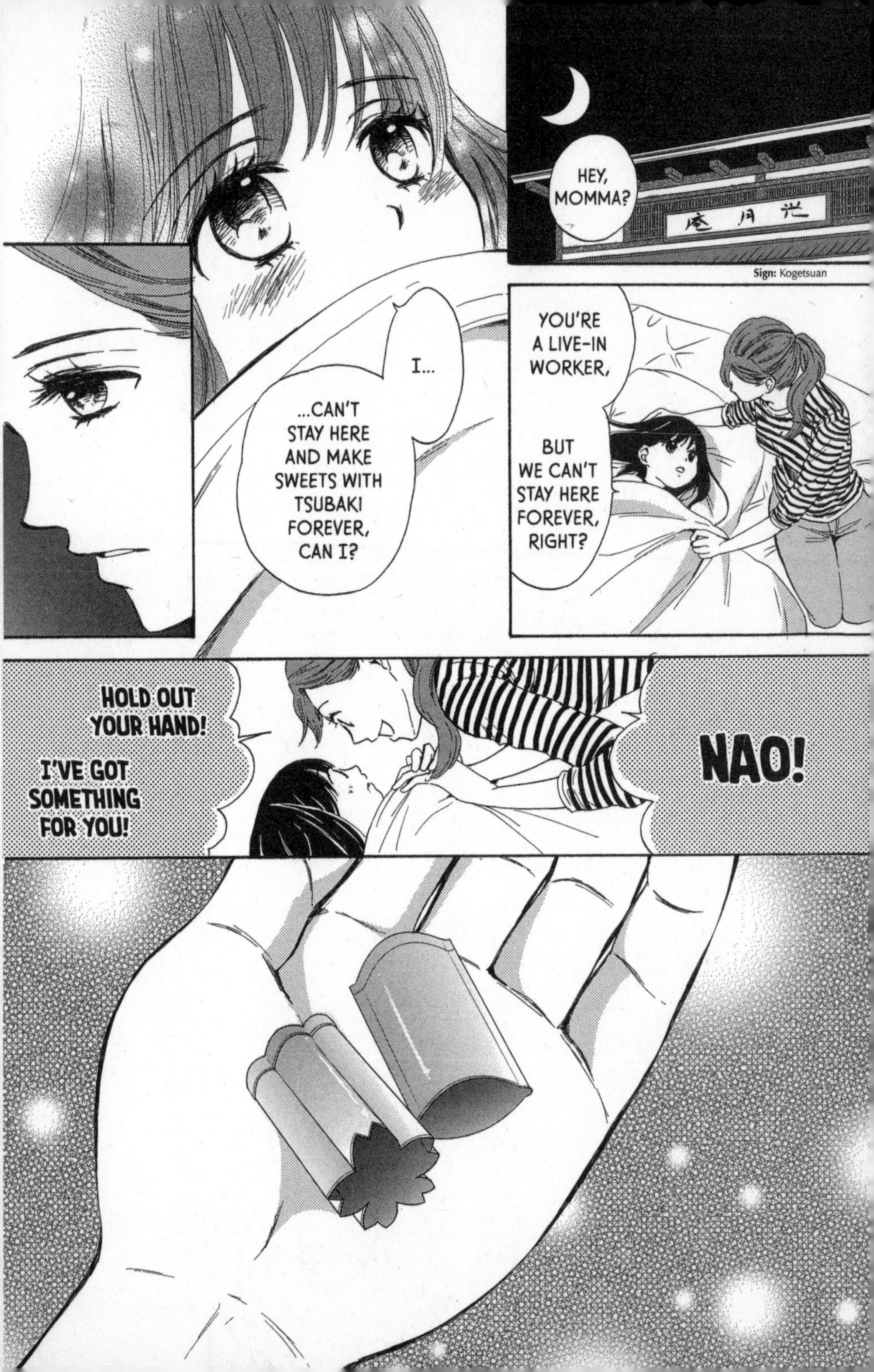
HEY, MOMMA?
Sign: Kogetsuan
YOU'RE A LIVE-IN WORKER,
BUT WE CAN'T STAY HERE FOREVER, RIGHT?
I...
...CAN'T STAY HERE AND MAKE SWEETS WITH TSUBAKI FOREVER, CAN I?
NAO!
HOLD OUT YOUR HAND!
I'VE GOT SOMETHING FOR YOU!

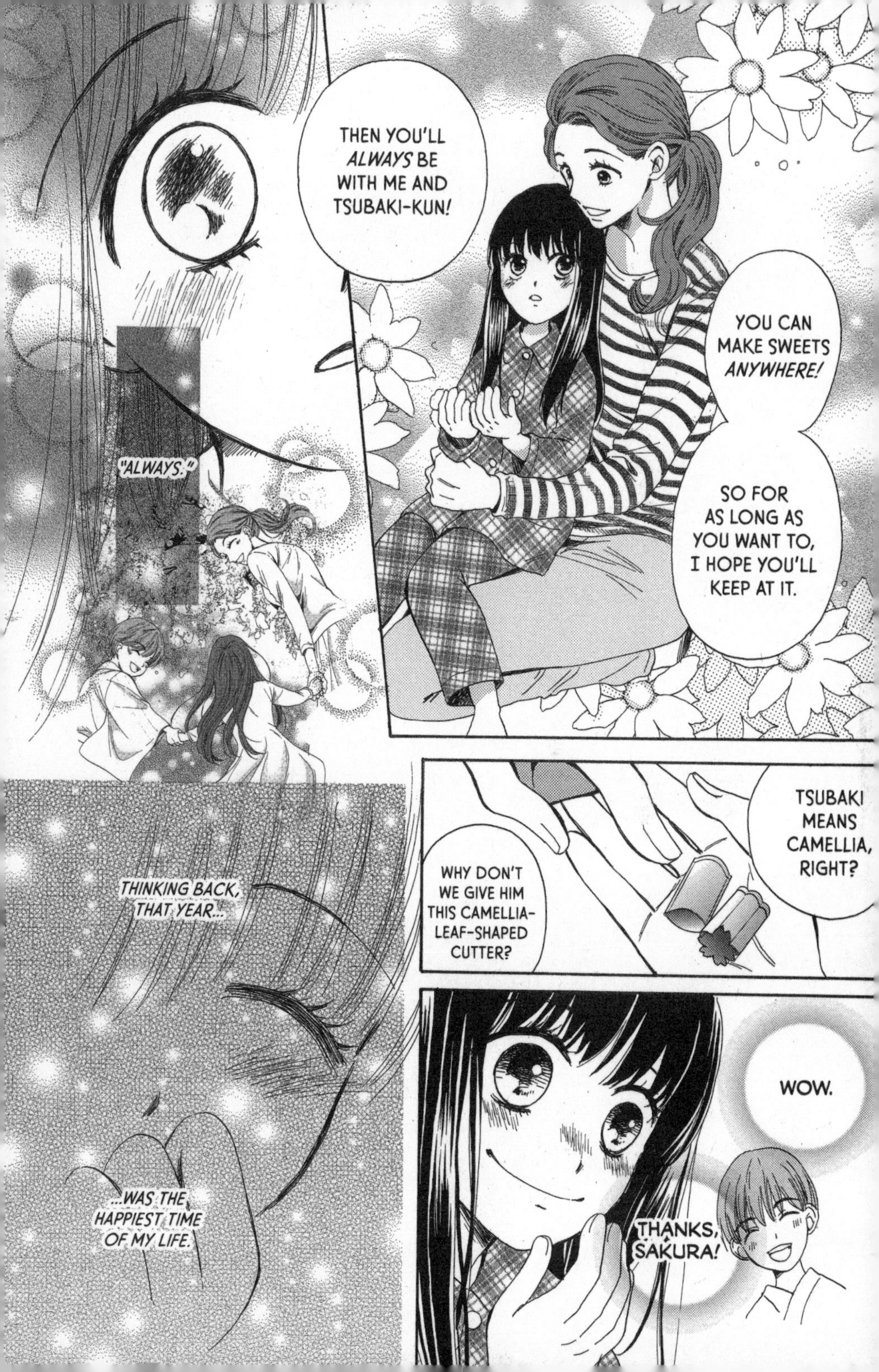
YOU CAN MAKE SWEETS *ANYWHERE!*
SO FOR AS LONG AS YOU WANT TO, I HOPE YOU'LL KEEP AT IT.
THEN YOU'LL *ALWAYS* BE WITH ME AND TSUBAKI-KUN!
TSUBAKI MEANS CAMELLIA, RIGHT?
WHY DON'T WE GIVE HIM THIS CAMELLIA-LEAF-SHAPED CUTTER?
WOW.
THANKS, SAKURA!
"ALWAYS."
THINKING BACK, THAT YEAR...
...WAS THE HAPPIEST TIME OF MY LIFE.

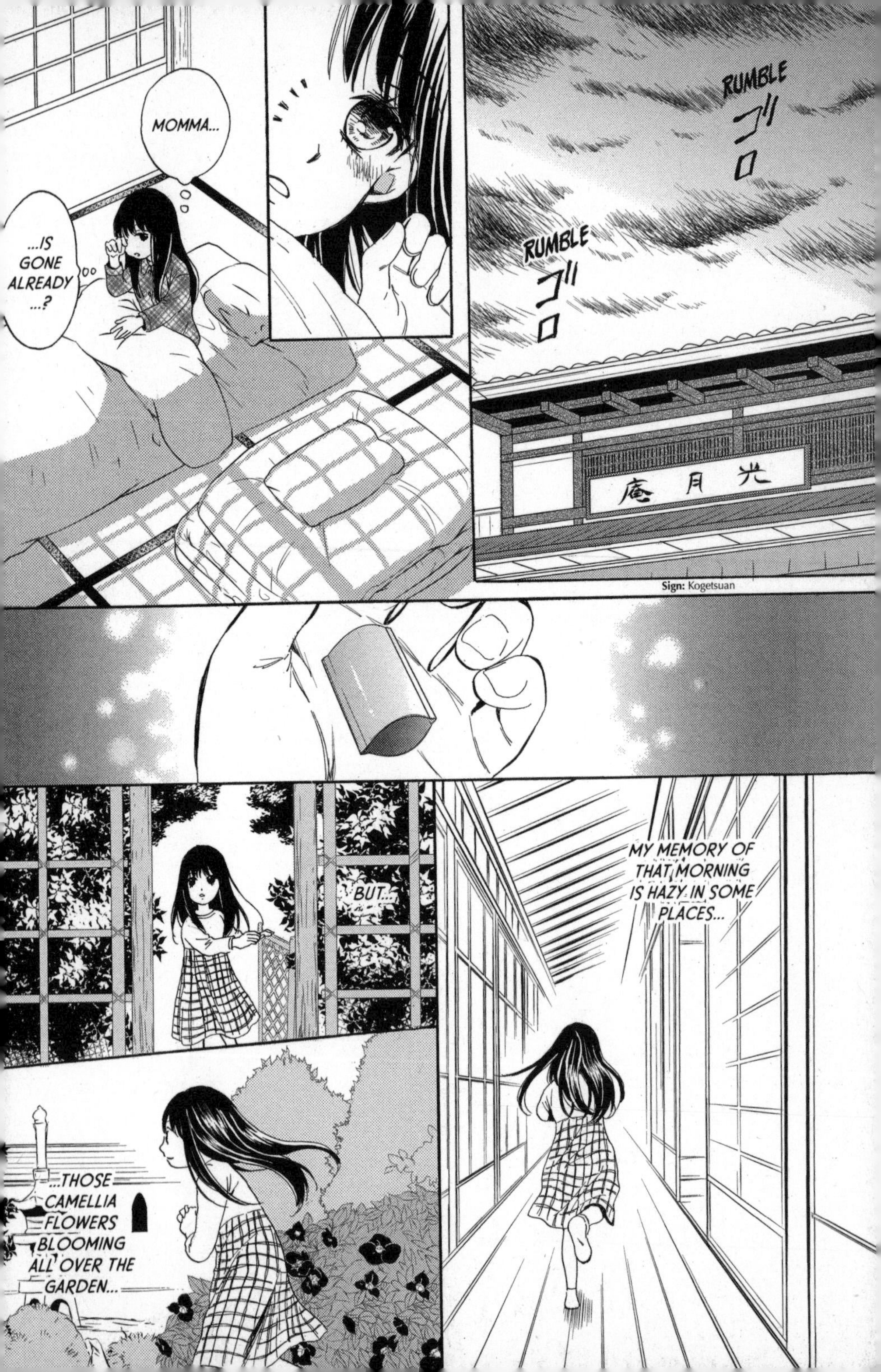
RUMBLE
ゴロ
RUMBLE
ゴロ
光月庵
Sign: Kogetsuan
MOMMA...
...IS GONE ALREADY ...?
MY MEMORY OF THAT MORNING IS HAZY IN SOME PLACES...
BUT...
...THOSE CAMELLIA FLOWERS BLOOMING ALL OVER THE GARDEN...

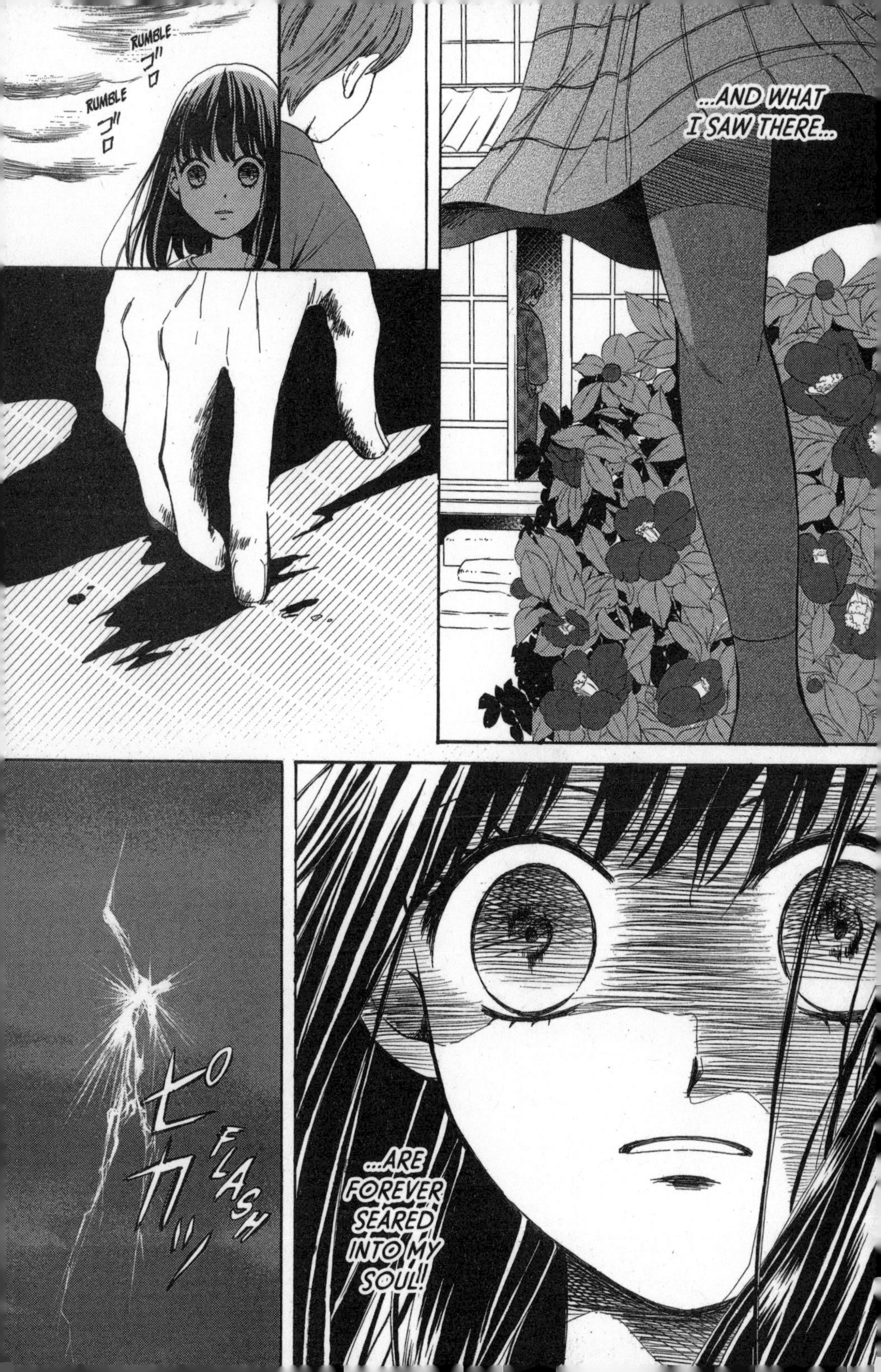
...AND WHAT I SAW THERE...
RUMBLE
ゴロ
RUMBLE
ゴロ
...ARE FOREVER SEARED INTO MY SOUL!
ピカッ
FLASH

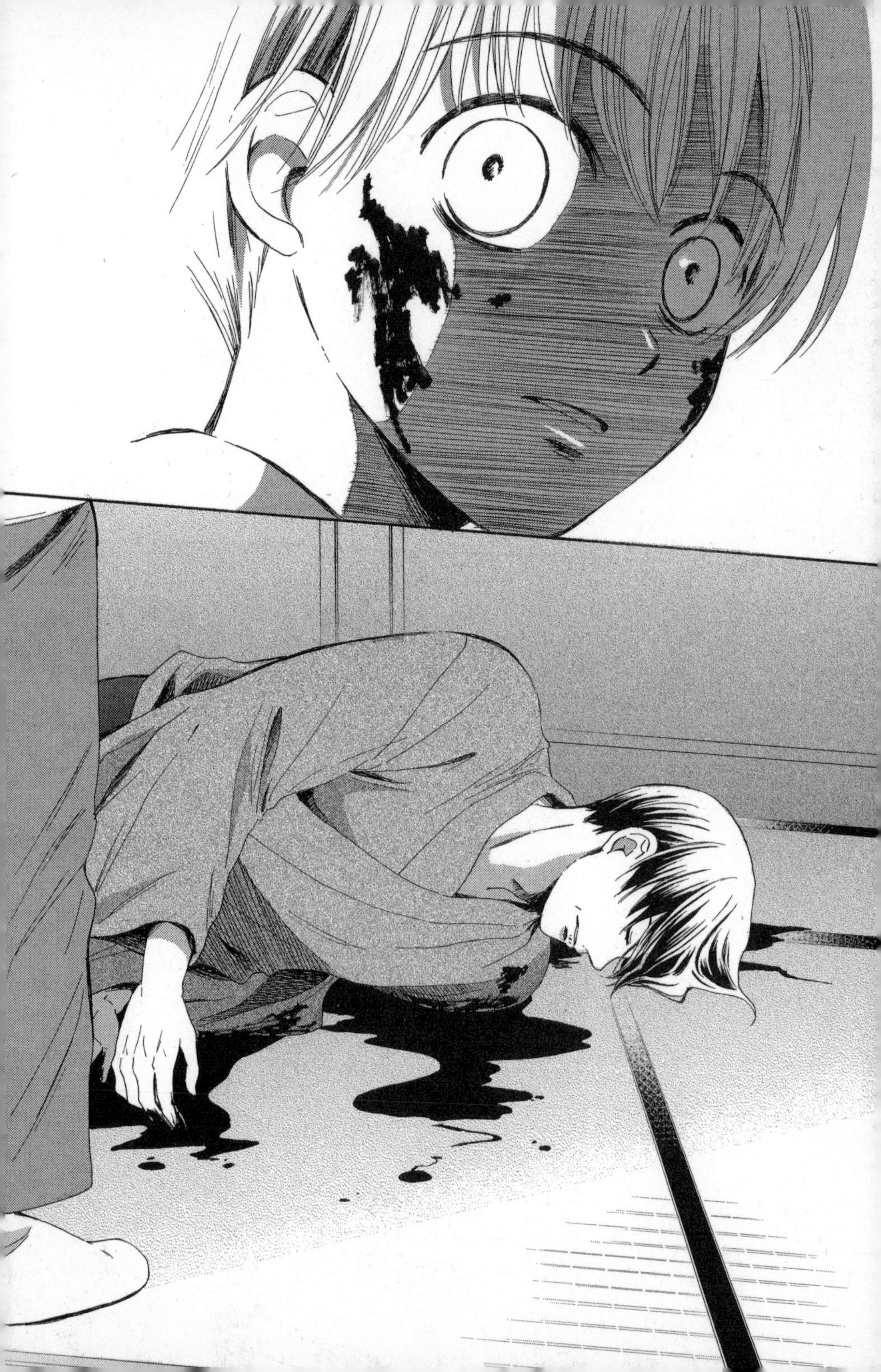

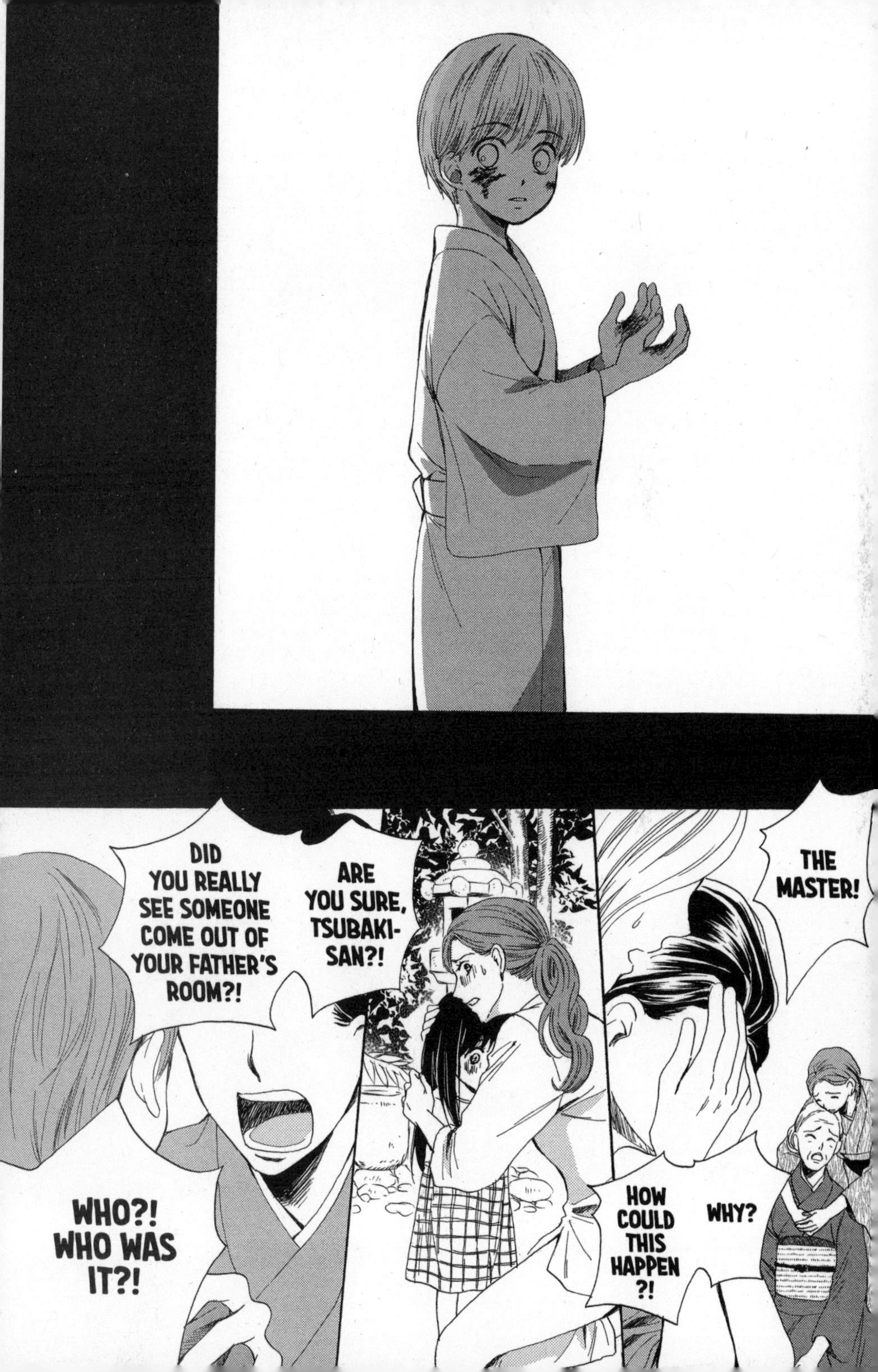
THE MASTER!
WHY?
HOW COULD THIS HAPPEN?!
ARE YOU SURE, TSUBAKI-SAN?!
DID YOU REALLY SEE SOMEONE COME OUT OF YOUR FATHER'S ROOM?!
WHO?! WHO WAS IT?!

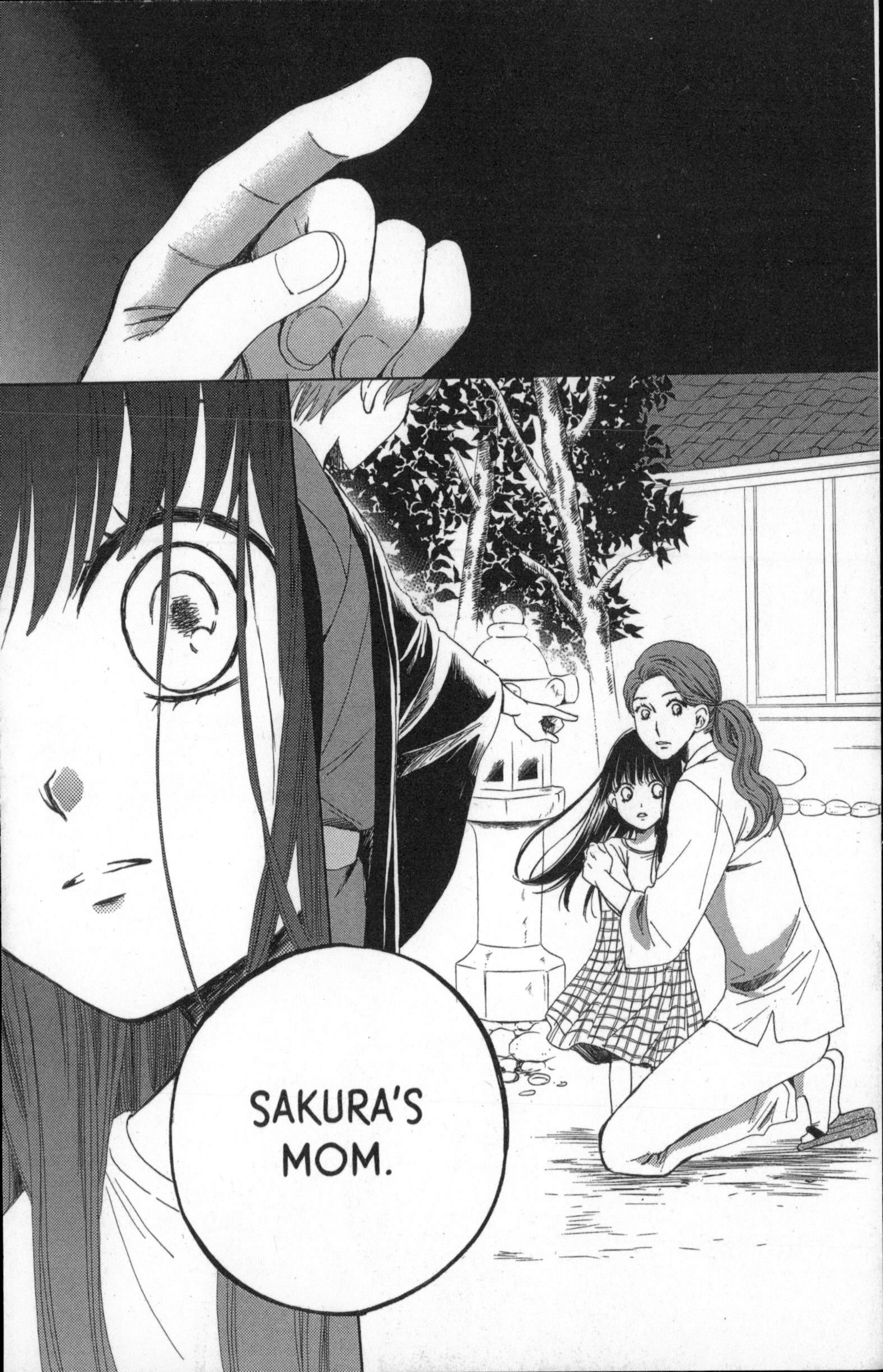
SAKURA'S MOM.

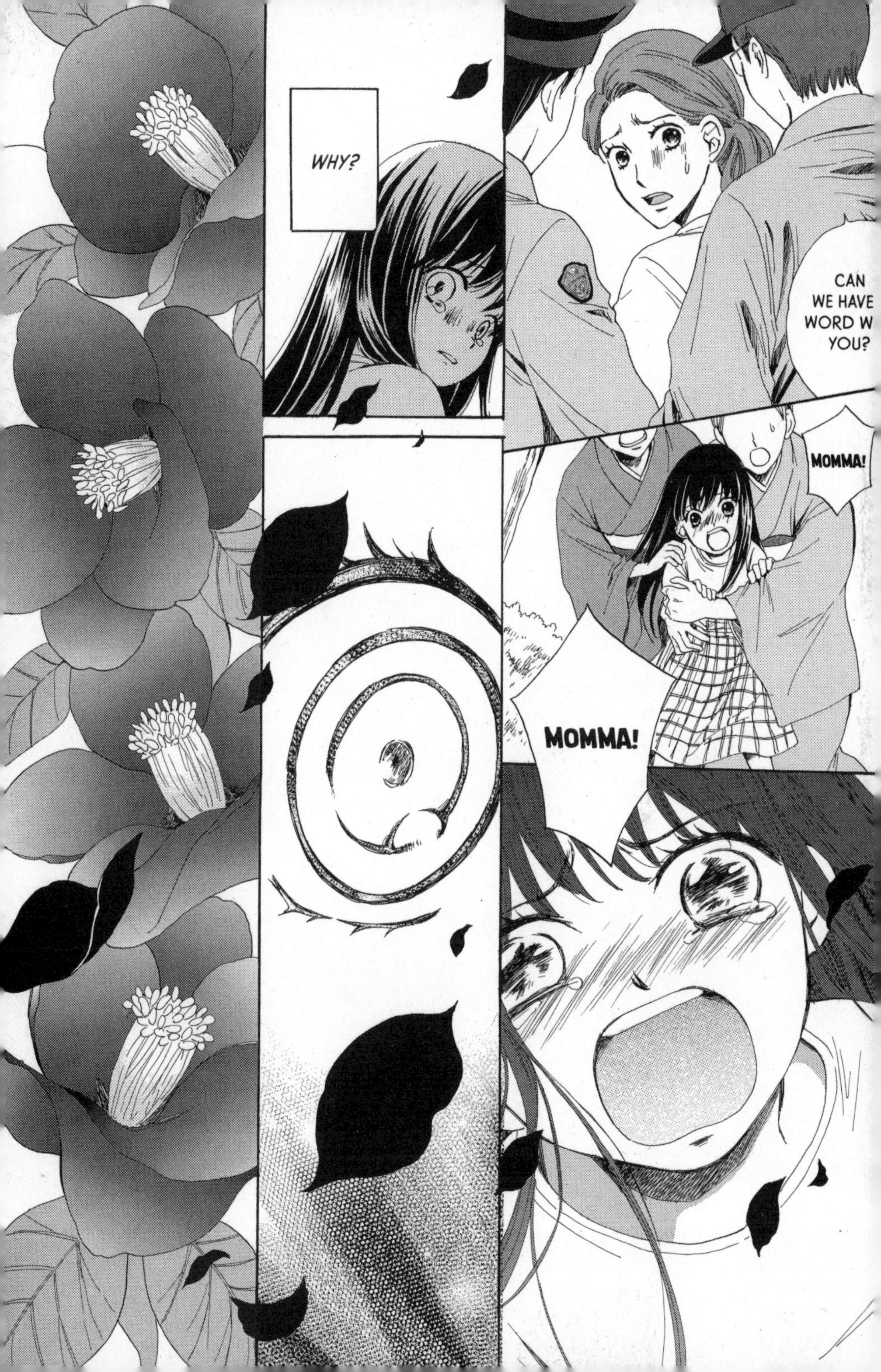
CAN WE HAVE WORD W YOU?
MOMMA!
MOMMA!
WHY?

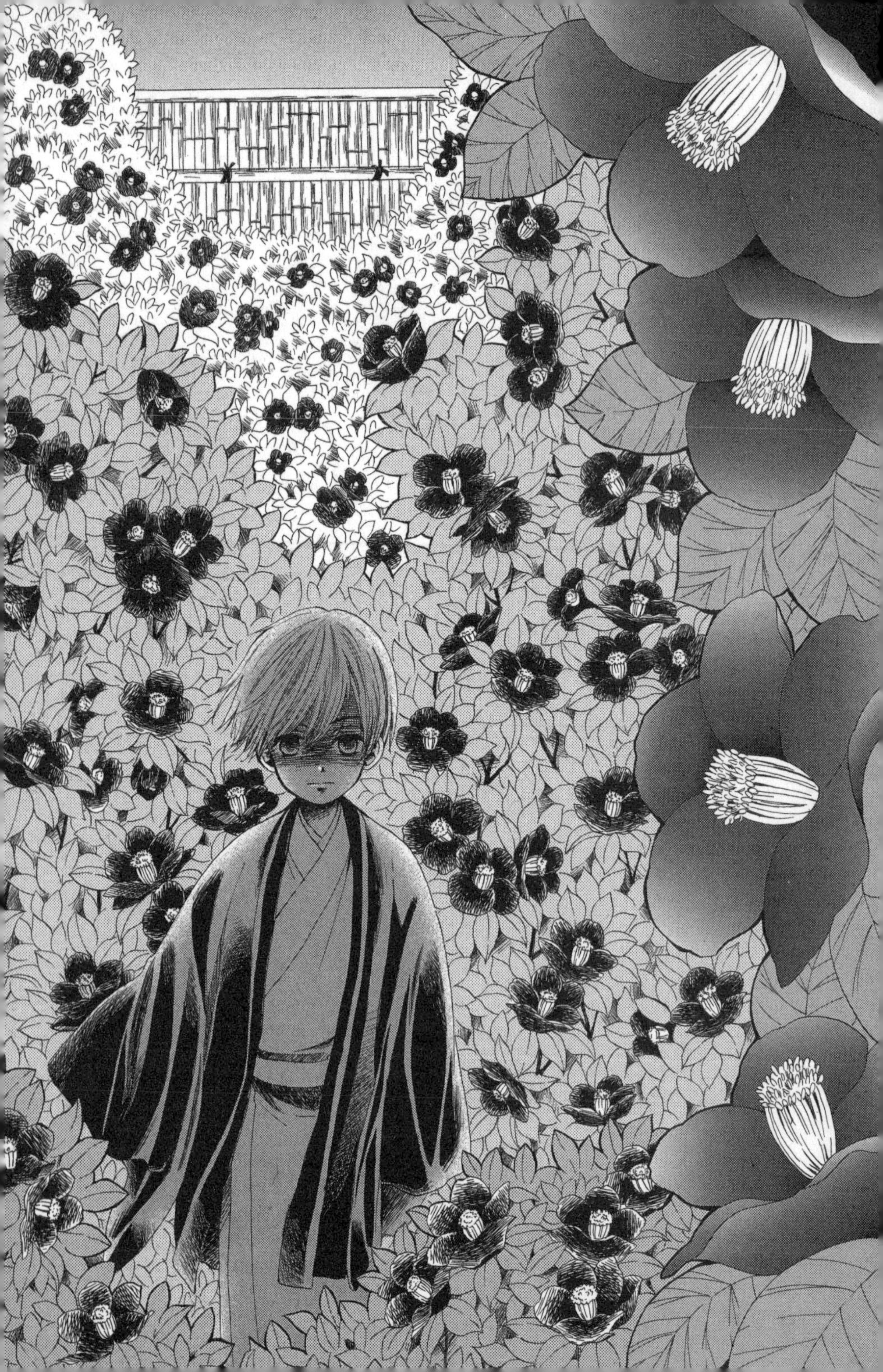

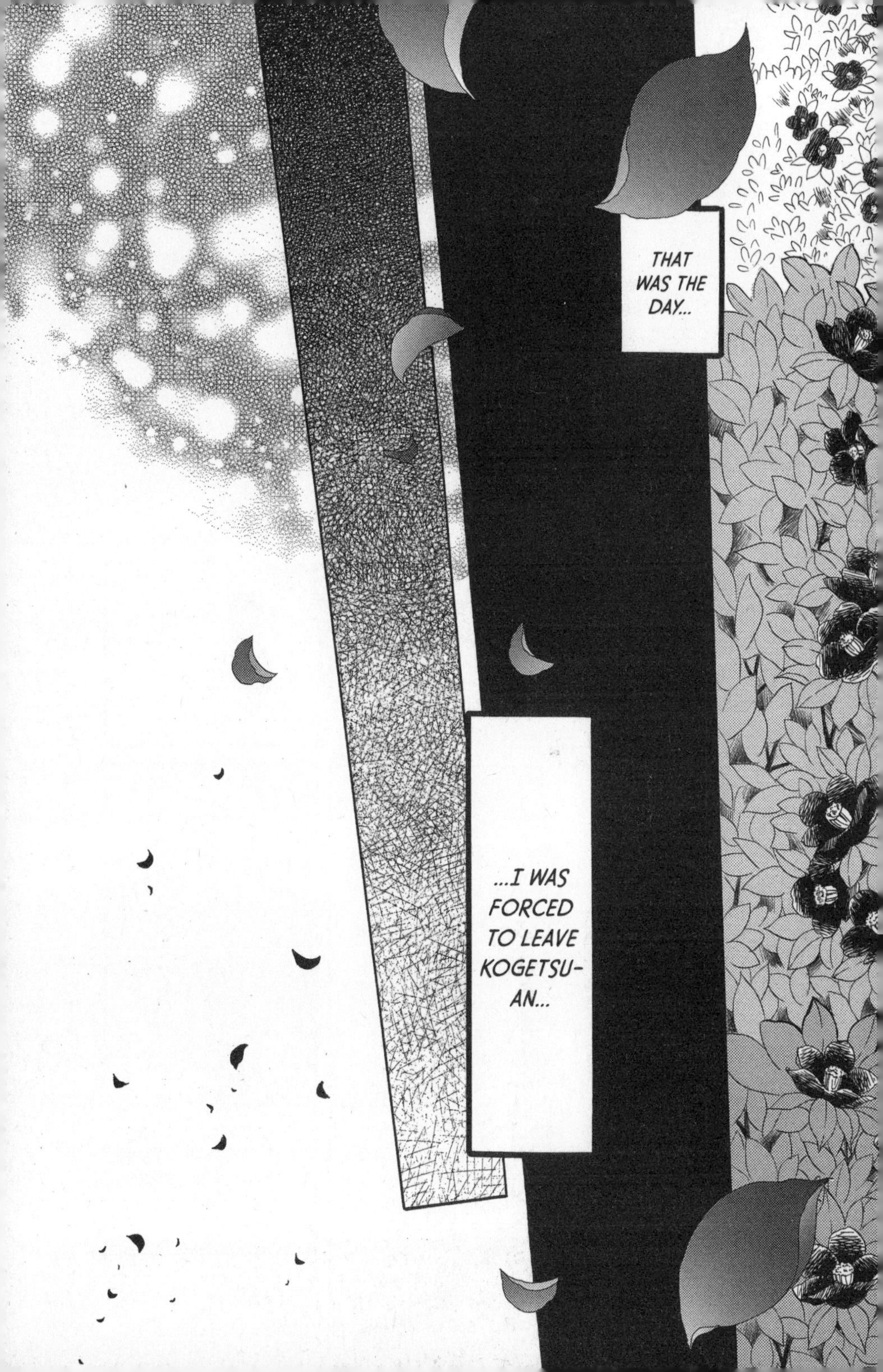
THAT WAS THE DAY...
...I WAS FORCED TO LEAVE KOGETSU-AN...

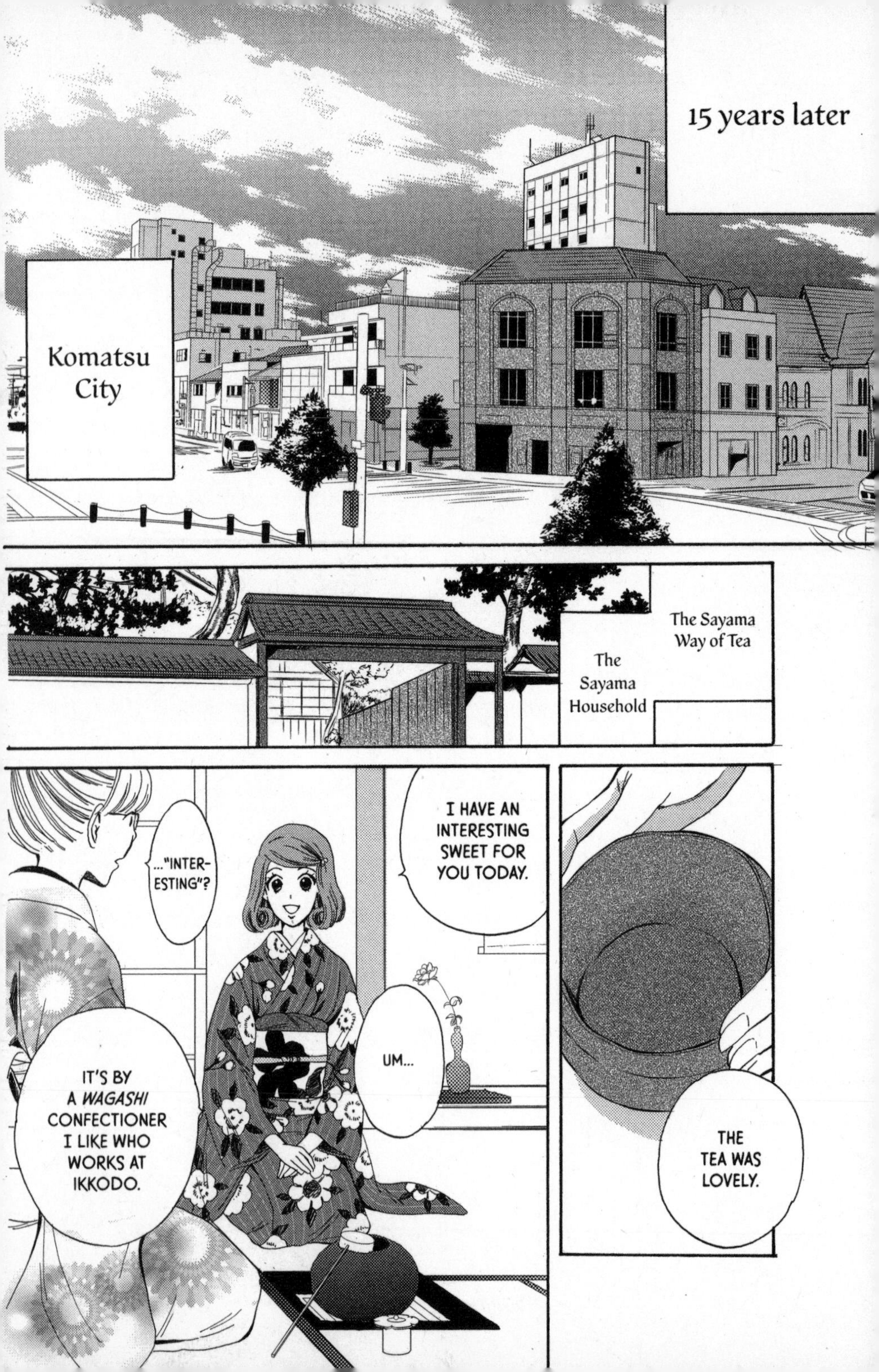
15 years later
Komatsu City
The Sayama Way of Tea
The Sayama Household
THE TEA WAS LOVELY.
I HAVE AN INTERESTING SWEET FOR YOU TODAY.
..."INTERESTING"?
UM...
IT'S BY A *WAGASHI* CONFECTIONER I LIKE WHO WORKS AT IKKODO.

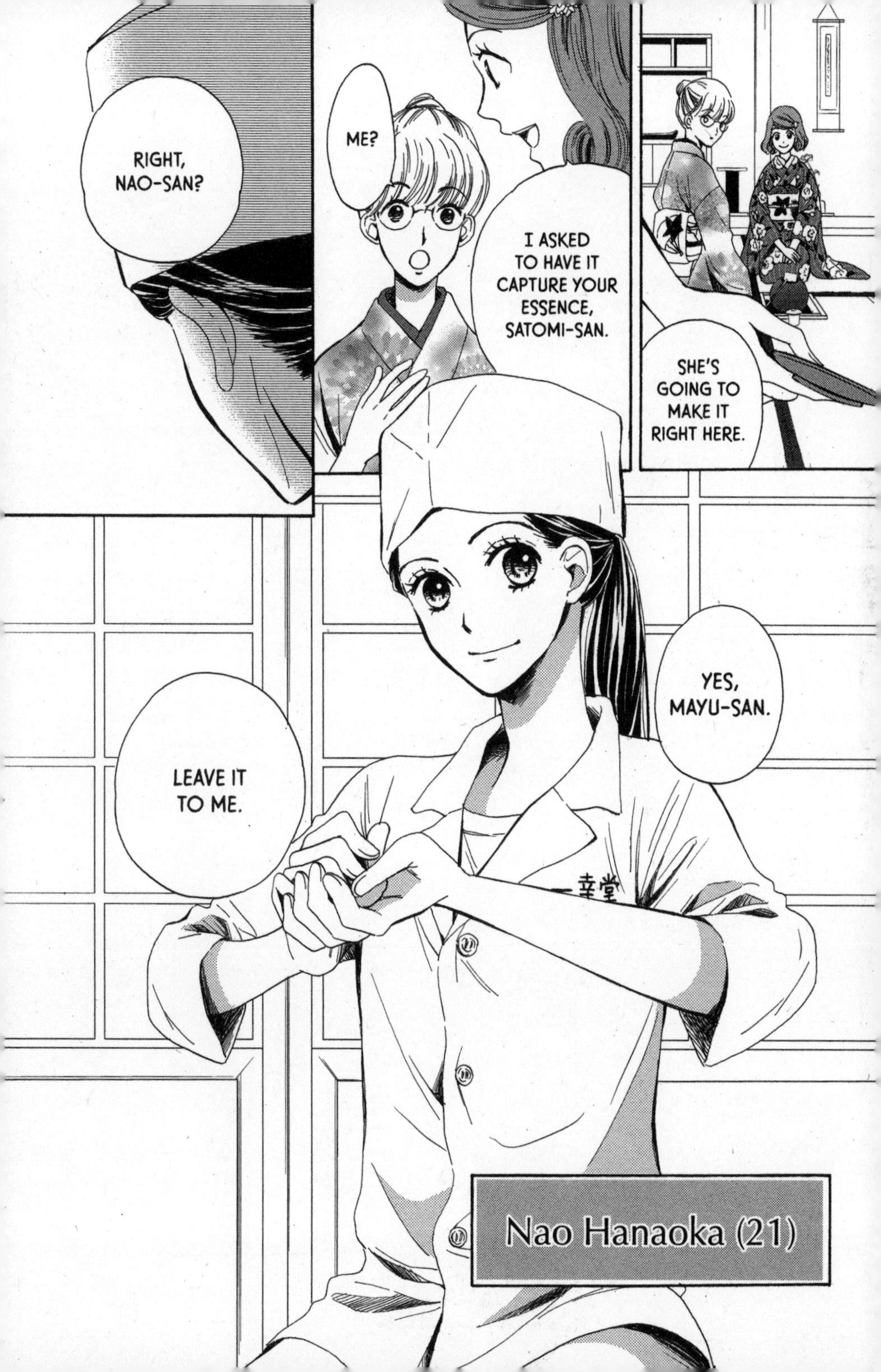
SHE'S GOING TO MAKE IT RIGHT HERE.
I ASKED TO HAVE IT CAPTURE YOUR ESSENCE, SATOMI-SAN.
ME?
RIGHT, NAO-SAN?
YES, MAYU-SAN.
LEAVE IT TO ME.
Nao Hanaoka (21)

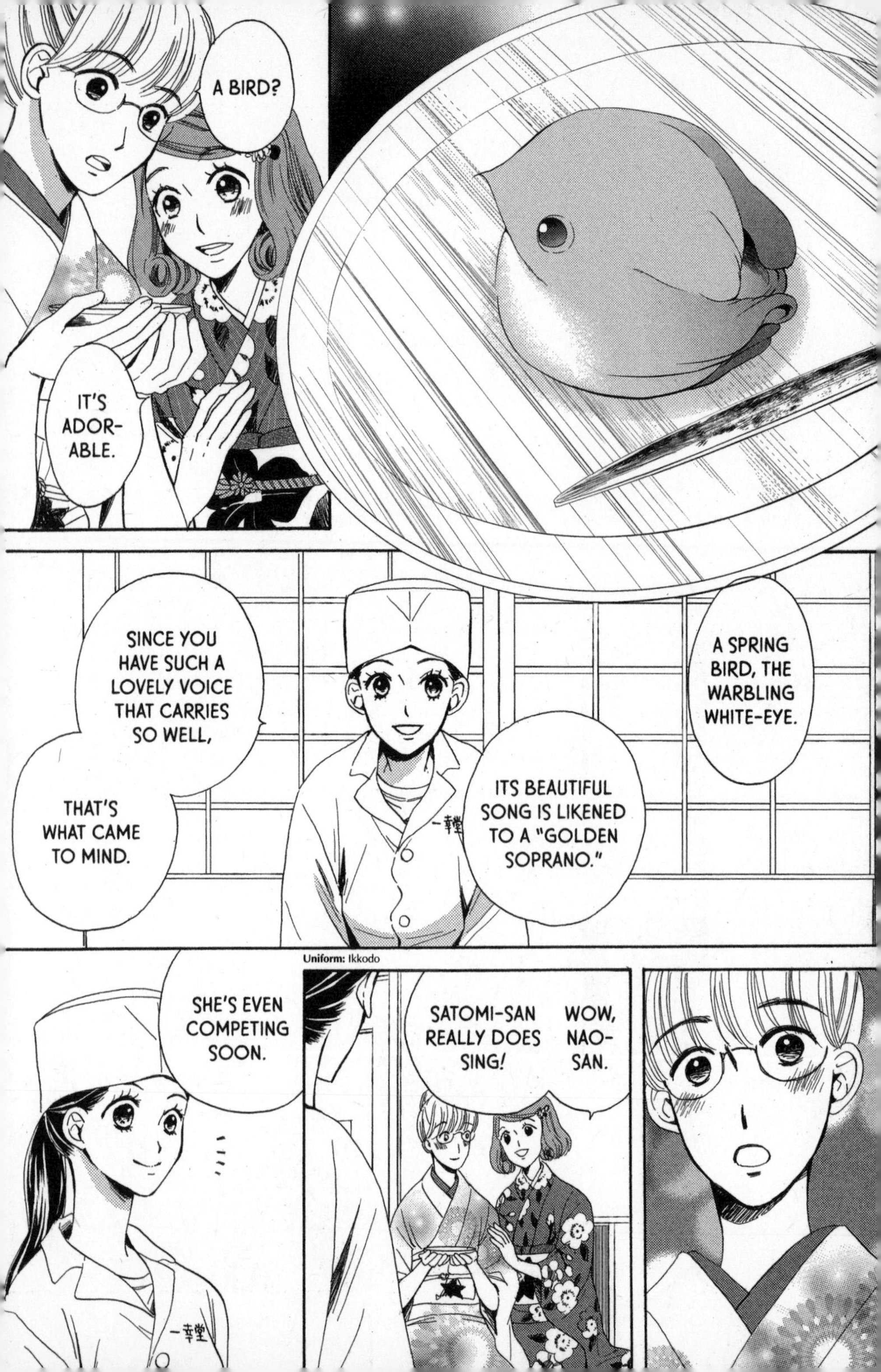
A BIRD?
IT'S ADORABLE.
A SPRING BIRD, THE WARBLING WHITE-EYE.
ITS BEAUTIFUL SONG IS LIKENED TO A "GOLDEN SOPRANO."
SINCE YOU HAVE SUCH A LOVELY VOICE THAT CARRIES SO WELL,
THAT'S WHAT CAME TO MIND.
Uniform: Ikkodo
WOW, NAO-SAN.
SATOMI-SAN REALLY DOES SING!
SHE'S EVEN COMPETING SOON.
...

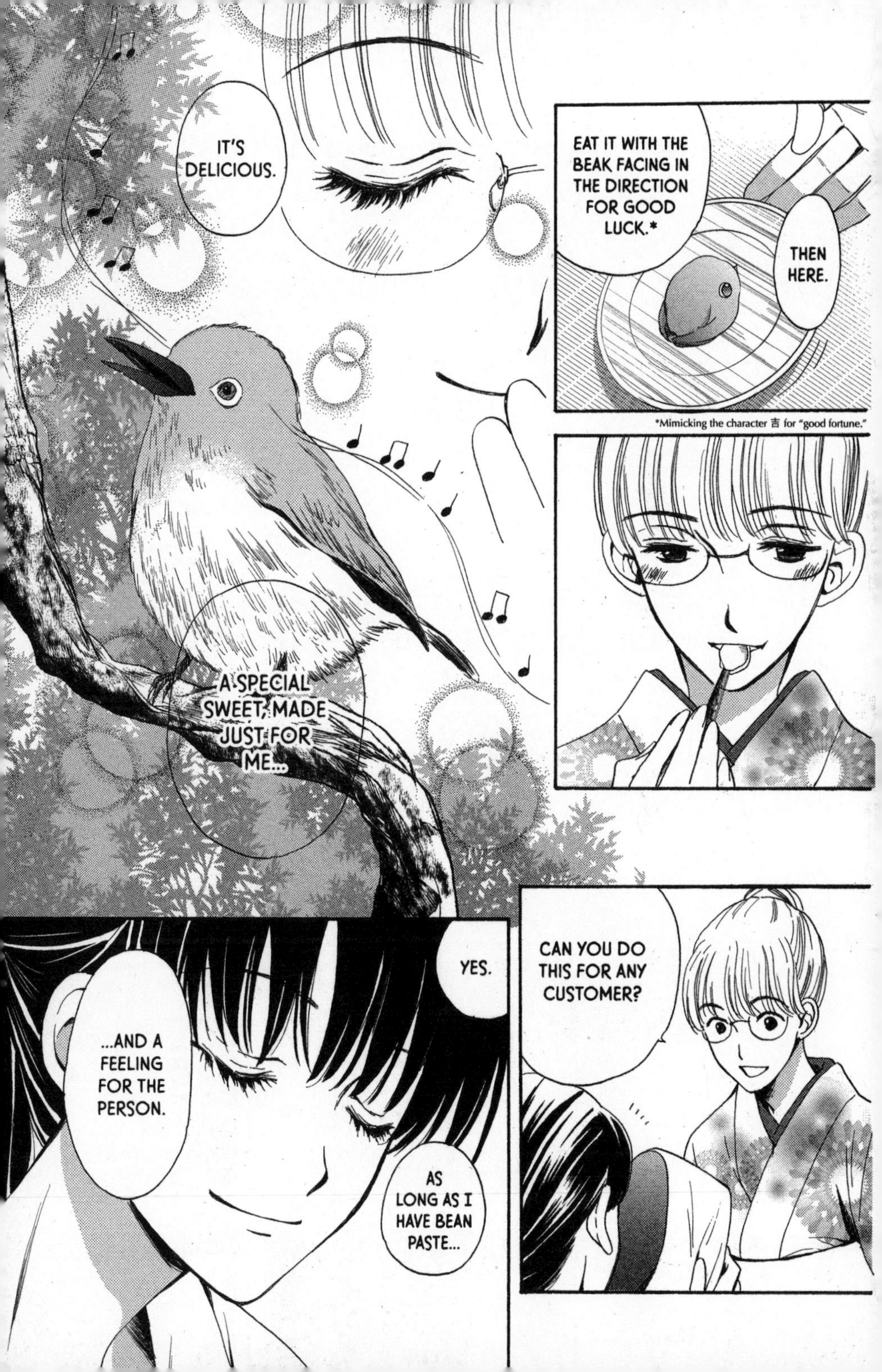
THEN HERE.
EAT IT WITH THE BEAK FACING IN THE DIRECTION FOR GOOD LUCK.*
IT'S DELICIOUS.
A SPECIAL SWEET, MADE JUST FOR ME...
CAN YOU DO THIS FOR ANY CUSTOMER?
YES.
AS LONG AS I HAVE BEAN PASTE...
...AND A FEELING FOR THE PERSON.
*Mimicking the character 吉 for "good fortune."

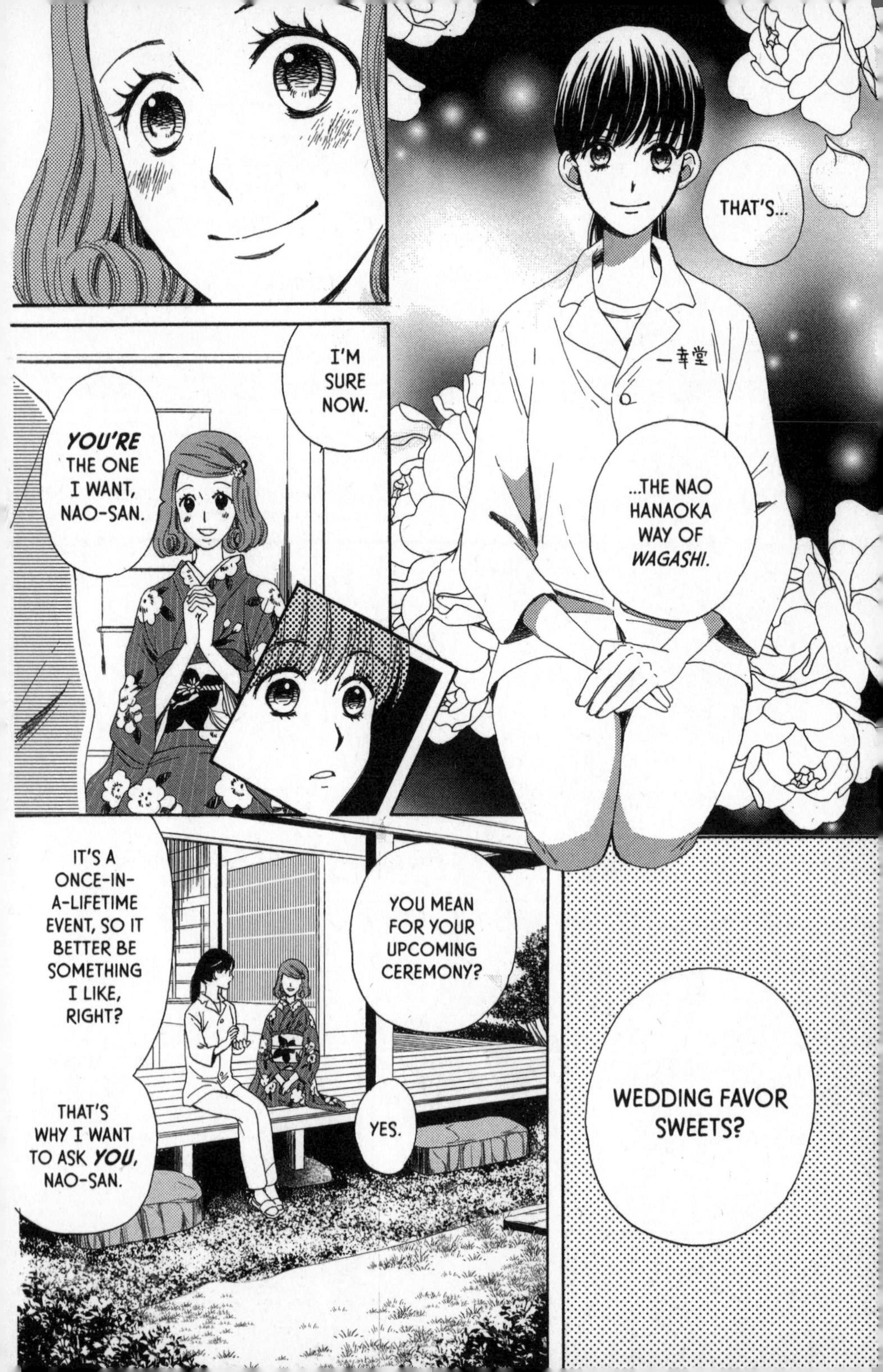
THAT'S...
...THE NAO HANAOKA WAY OF *WAGASHI*.
I'M SURE NOW.
YOU'RE THE ONE I WANT, NAO-SAN.
WEDDING FAVOR SWEETS?
YOU MEAN FOR YOUR UPCOMING CEREMONY?
YES.
IT'S A ONCE-IN-A-LIFETIME EVENT, SO IT BETTER BE SOMETHING I LIKE, RIGHT?
THAT'S WHY I WANT TO ASK ***YOU***, NAO-SAN.

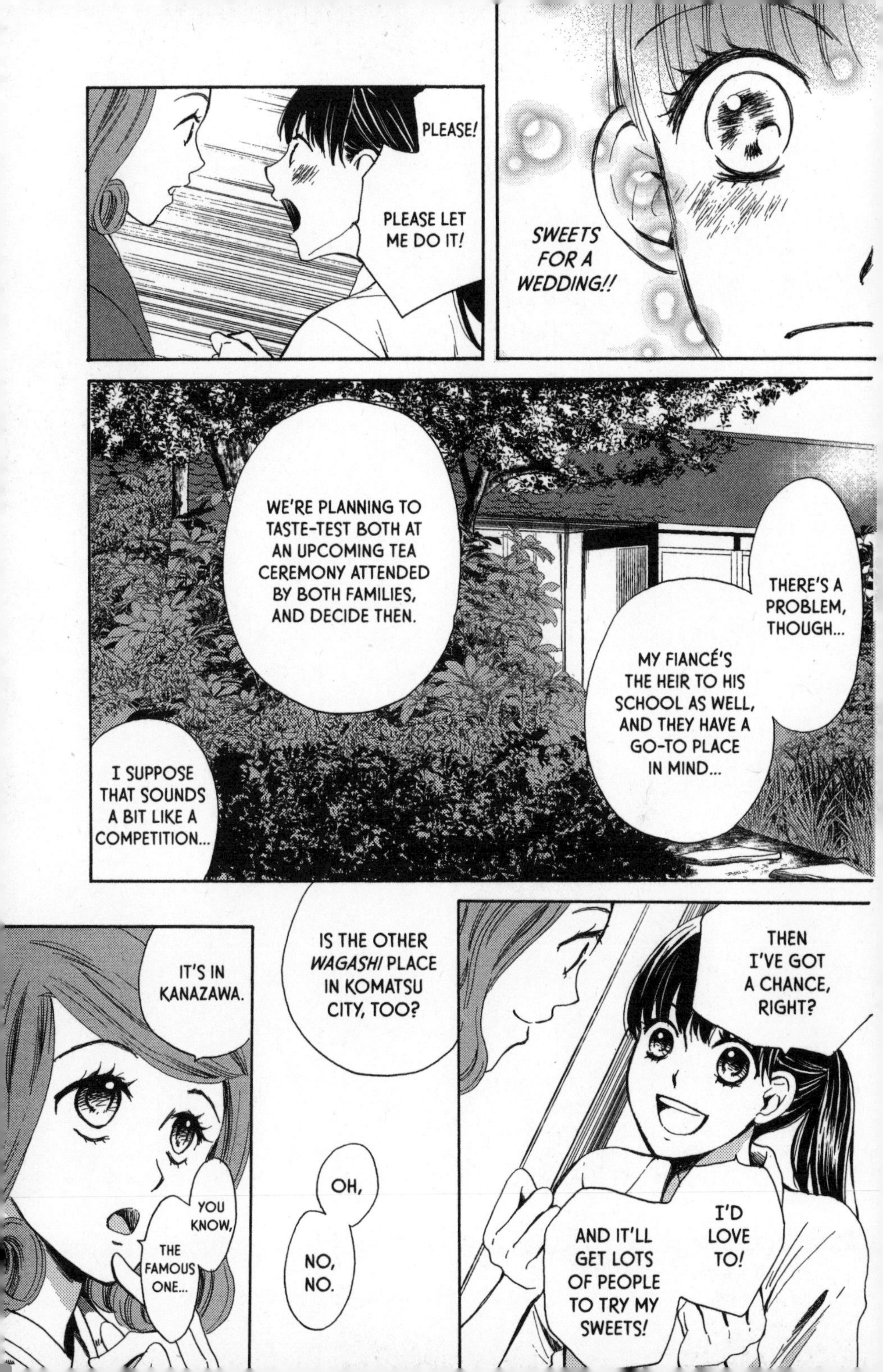
SWEETS FOR A WEDDING!!
PLEASE!
PLEASE LET ME DO IT!
THERE'S A PROBLEM, THOUGH...
MY FIANCÉ'S THE HEIR TO HIS SCHOOL AS WELL, AND THEY HAVE A GO-TO PLACE IN MIND...
WE'RE PLANNING TO TASTE-TEST BOTH AT AN UPCOMING TEA CEREMONY ATTENDED BY BOTH FAMILIES, AND DECIDE THEN.
I SUPPOSE THAT SOUNDS A BIT LIKE A COMPETITION...
THEN I'VE GOT A CHANCE, RIGHT?
I'D LOVE TO!
AND IT'LL GET LOTS OF PEOPLE TO TRY MY SWEETS!
IS THE OTHER *WAGASHI* PLACE IN KOMATSU CITY, TOO?
OH,
NO, NO.
IT'S IN KANAZAWA.
YOU KNOW, THE FAMOUS ONE...

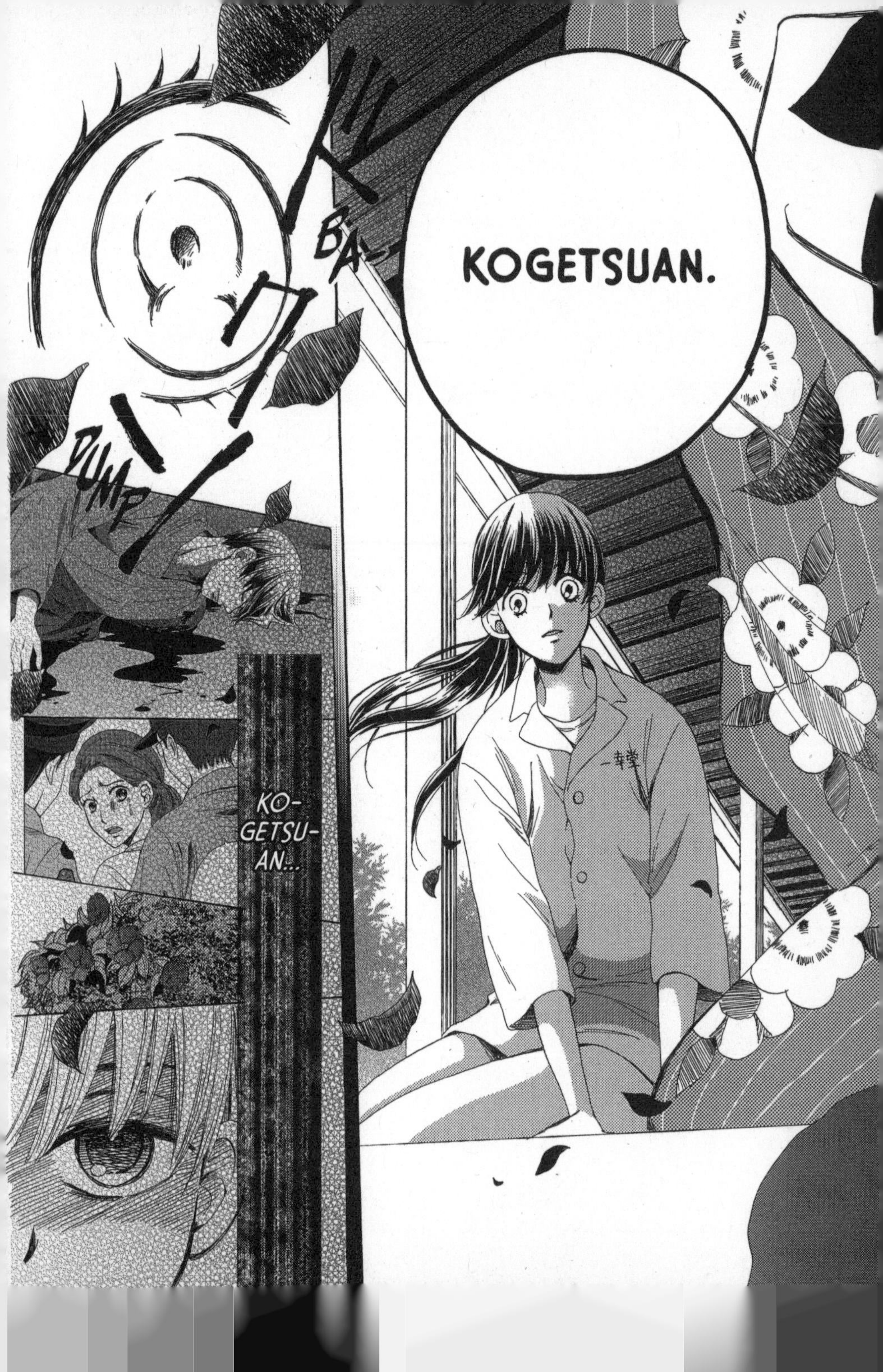
KOGETSUAN.
BA-
DUMP
KO-GETSU-AN...

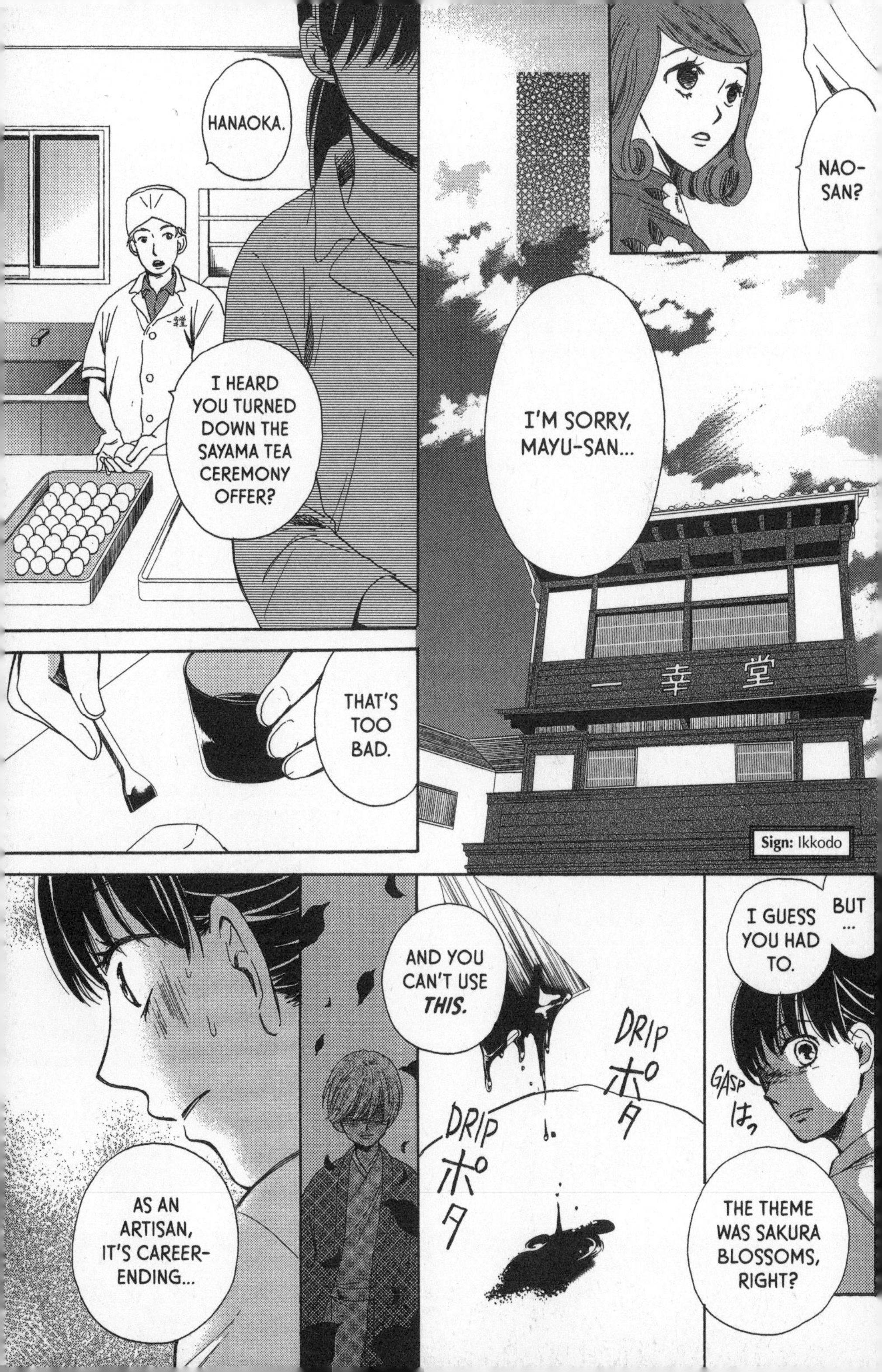
NAO-SAN?
I'M SORRY, MAYU-SAN...
Sign: Ikkodo
一幸堂
HANAOKA.
I HEARD YOU TURNED DOWN THE SAYAMA TEA CEREMONY OFFER?
THAT'S TOO BAD.
BUT ...
I GUESS YOU HAD TO.
GASP はっ
THE THEME WAS SAKURA BLOSSOMS, RIGHT?
AND YOU CAN'T USE *THIS.*
DRIP ポタ
DRIP ポタ
AS AN ARTISAN, IT'S CAREER-ENDING...

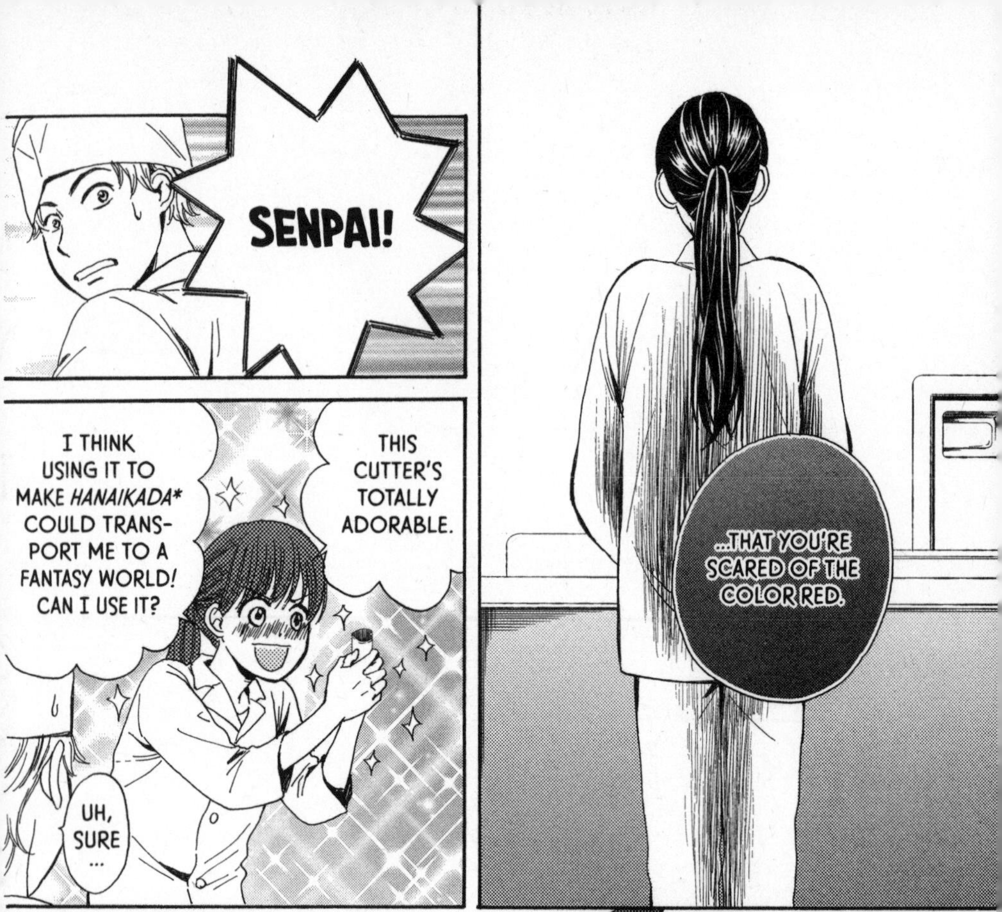
...THAT YOU'RE SCARED OF THE COLOR RED.
SENPAI!
THIS CUTTER'S TOTALLY ADORABLE.
I THINK USING IT TO MAKE *HANAIKADA** COULD TRANSPORT ME TO A FANTASY WORLD! CAN I USE IT?
UH, SURE ...

*A confection shaped like a flower raft.

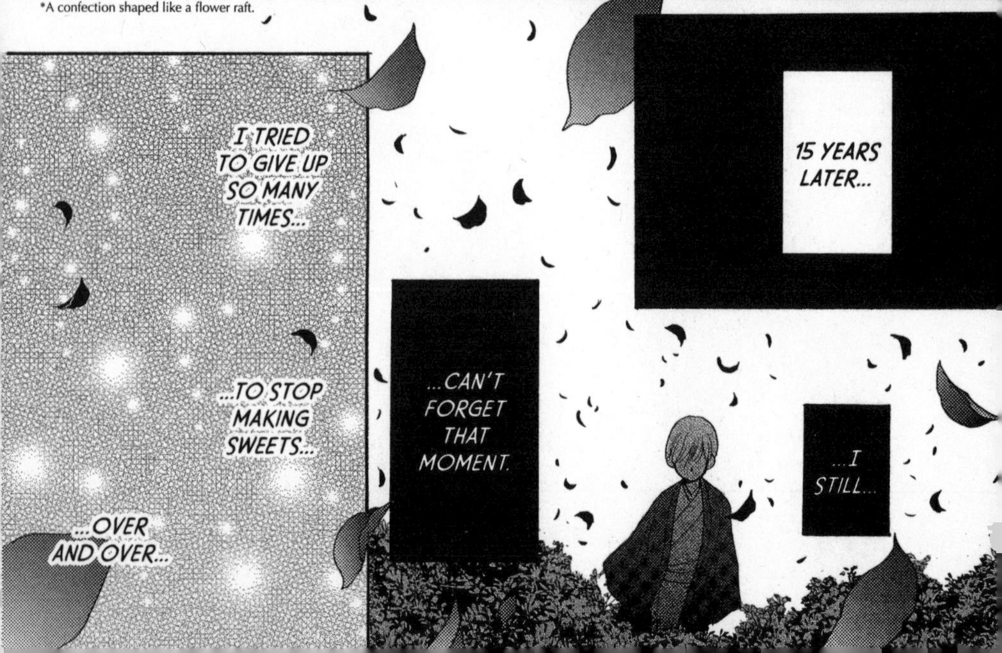
15 YEARS LATER...
...I STILL...
...CAN'T FORGET THAT MOMENT.
I TRIED TO GIVE UP SO MANY TIMES...
...TO STOP MAKING SWEETS...
...OVER AND OVER...

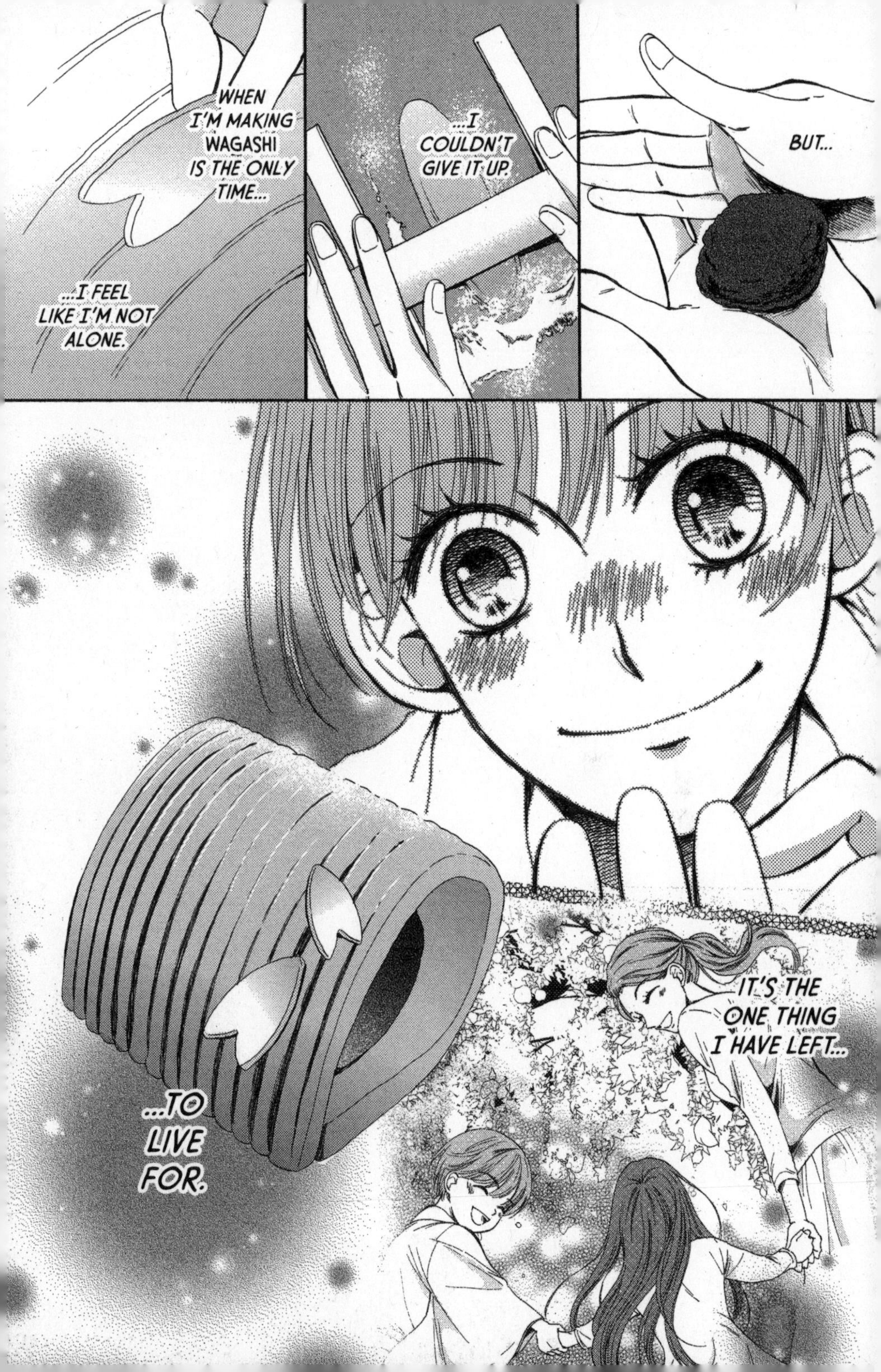
BUT...
...I COULDN'T GIVE IT UP.
WHEN I'M MAKING WAGASHI IS THE ONLY TIME...
...I FEEL LIKE I'M NOT ALONE.
IT'S THE ONE THING I HAVE LEFT...
...TO LIVE FOR.

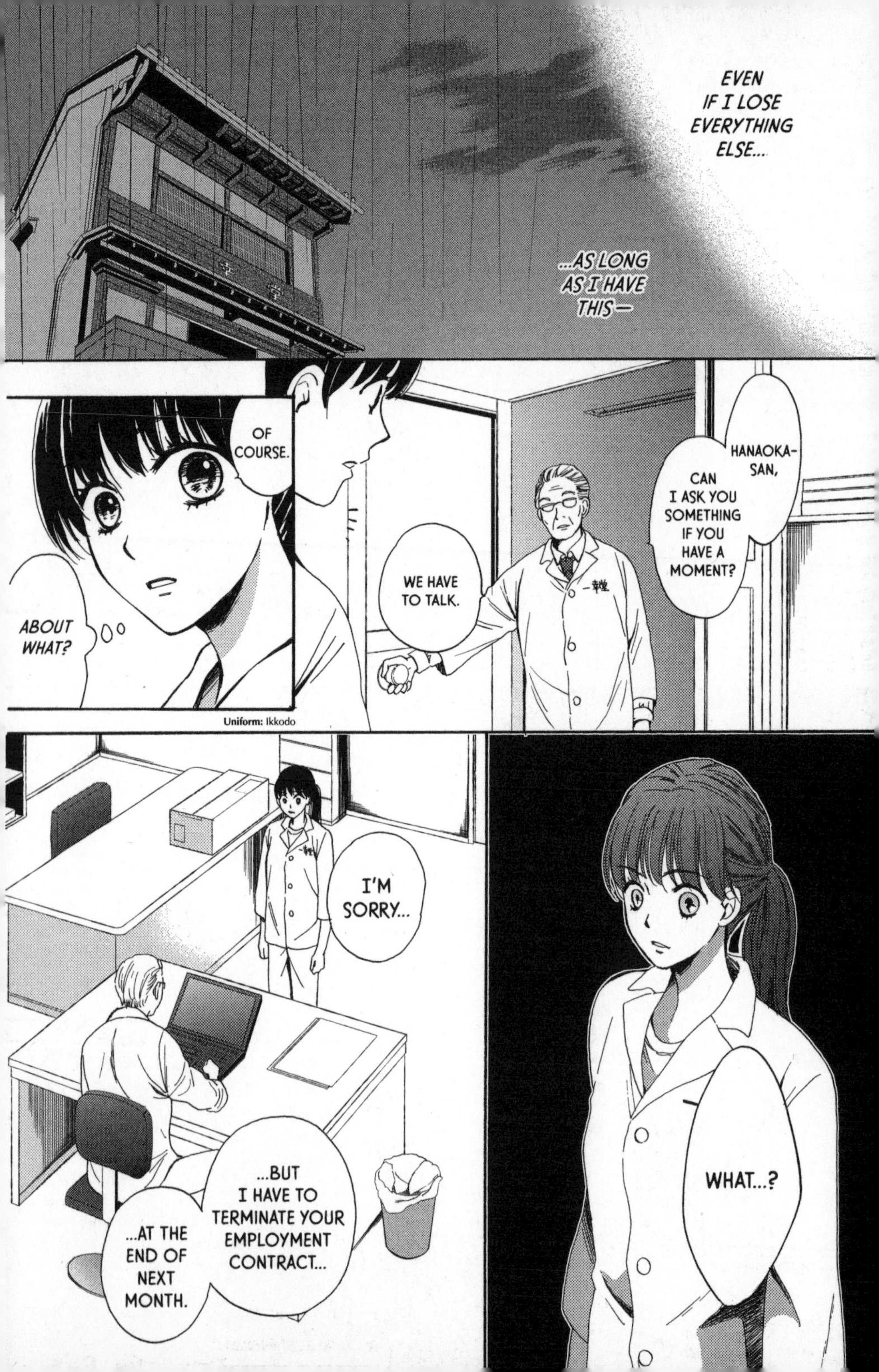
EVEN IF I LOSE EVERYTHING ELSE...
...AS LONG AS I HAVE THIS—
HANAOKA-SAN,
CAN I ASK YOU SOMETHING IF YOU HAVE A MOMENT?
WE HAVE TO TALK.
OF COURSE.
ABOUT WHAT?
Uniform: Ikkodo
WHAT...?
I'M SORRY...
...BUT I HAVE TO TERMINATE YOUR EMPLOYMENT CONTRACT...
...AT THE END OF NEXT MONTH.

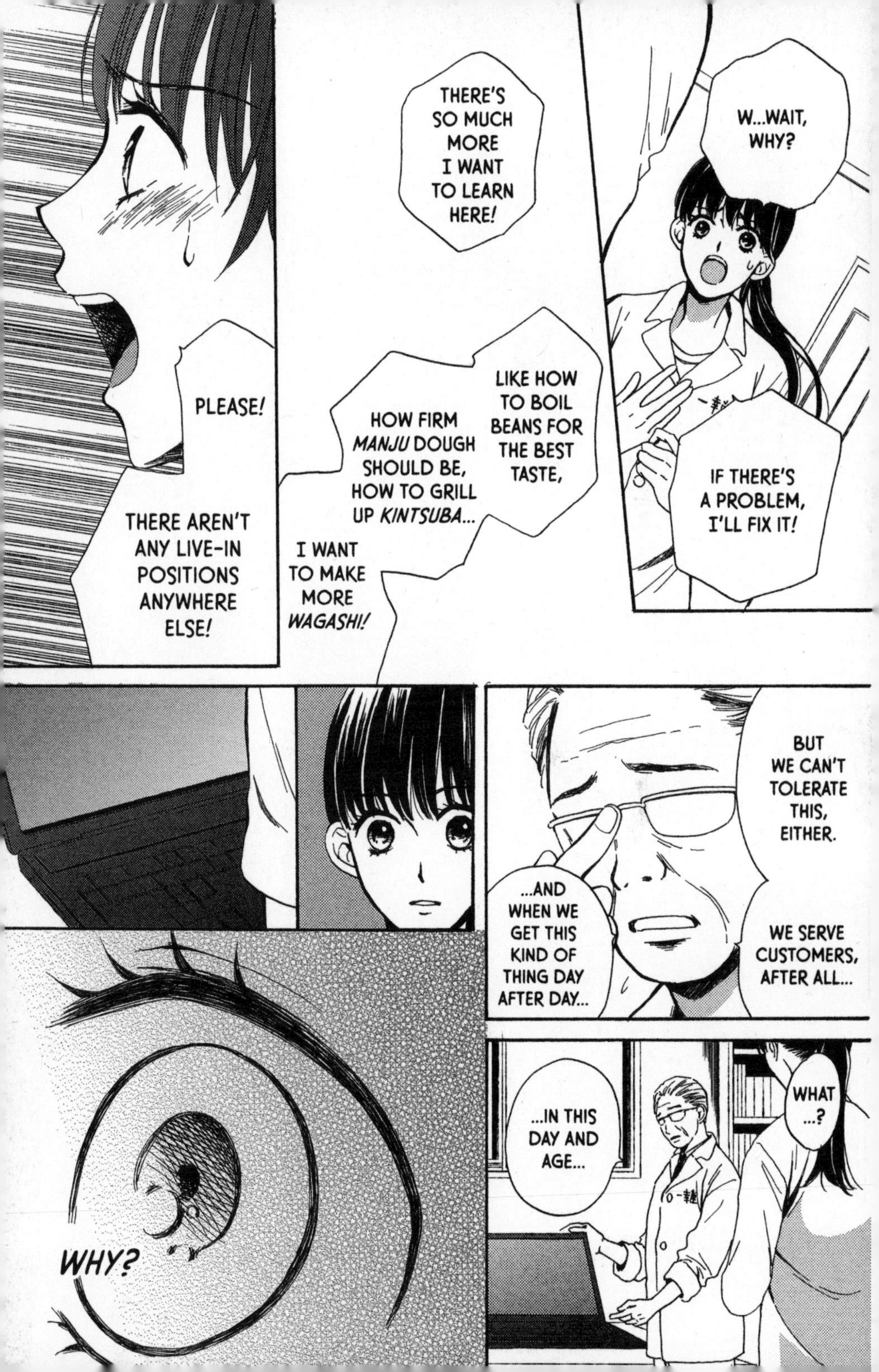
W...WAIT, WHY?
IF THERE'S A PROBLEM, I'LL FIX IT!
THERE'S SO MUCH MORE I WANT TO LEARN HERE!
LIKE HOW TO BOIL BEANS FOR THE BEST TASTE,
HOW FIRM *MANJU* DOUGH SHOULD BE, HOW TO GRILL UP *KINTSUBA*...
I WANT TO MAKE MORE *WAGASHI!*
PLEASE!
THERE AREN'T ANY LIVE-IN POSITIONS ANYWHERE ELSE!
BUT WE CAN'T TOLERATE THIS, EITHER.
WE SERVE CUSTOMERS, AFTER ALL...
...AND WHEN WE GET THIS KIND OF THING DAY AFTER DAY...
WHAT ...?
...IN THIS DAY AND AGE...
WHY?

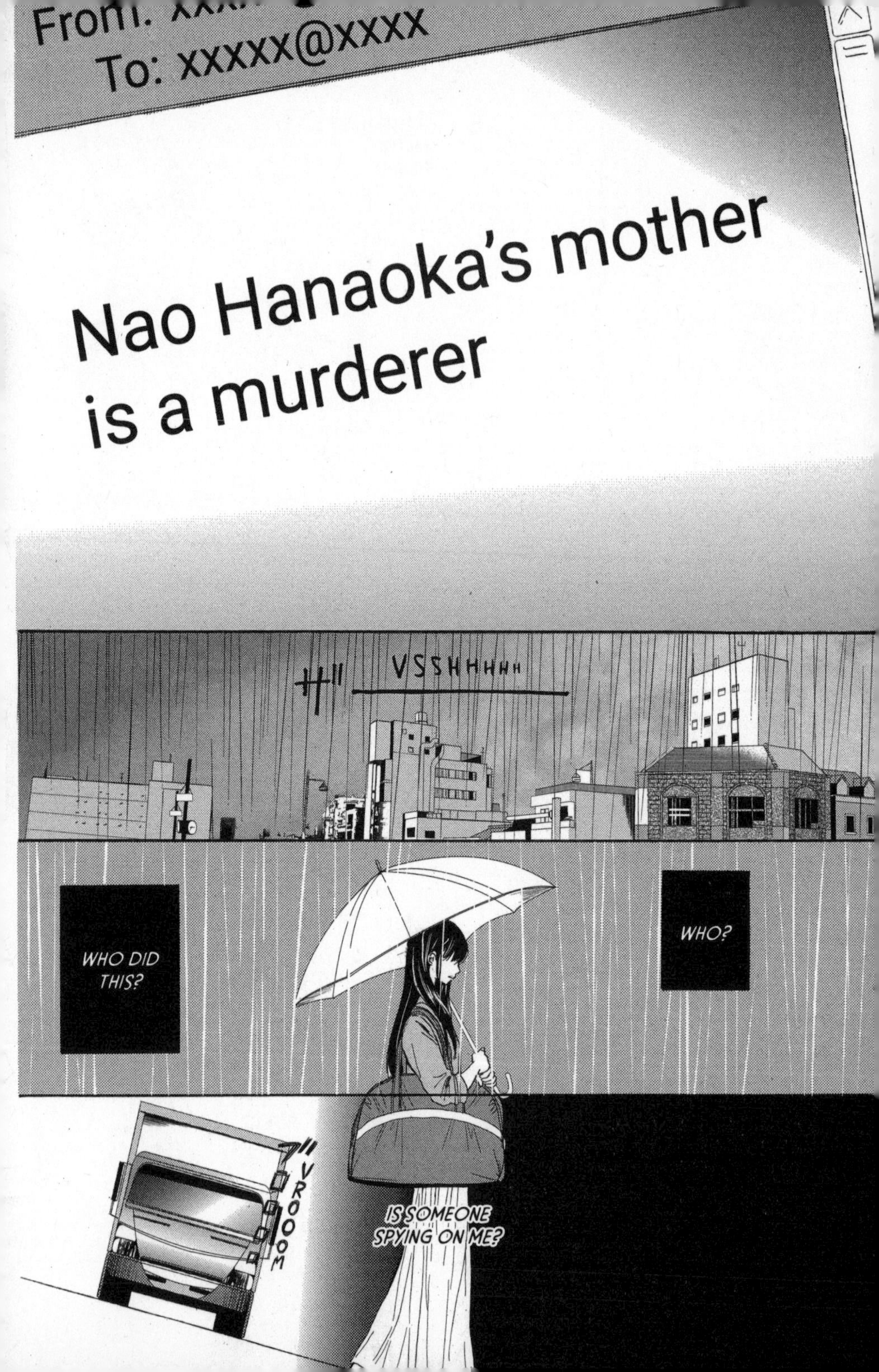
From:
To: xxxxx@xxxx
Nao Hanaoka's mother is a murderer
VSSHHHHH
WHO?
WHO DID THIS?
IS SOMEONE SPYING ON ME?
VROOOOM

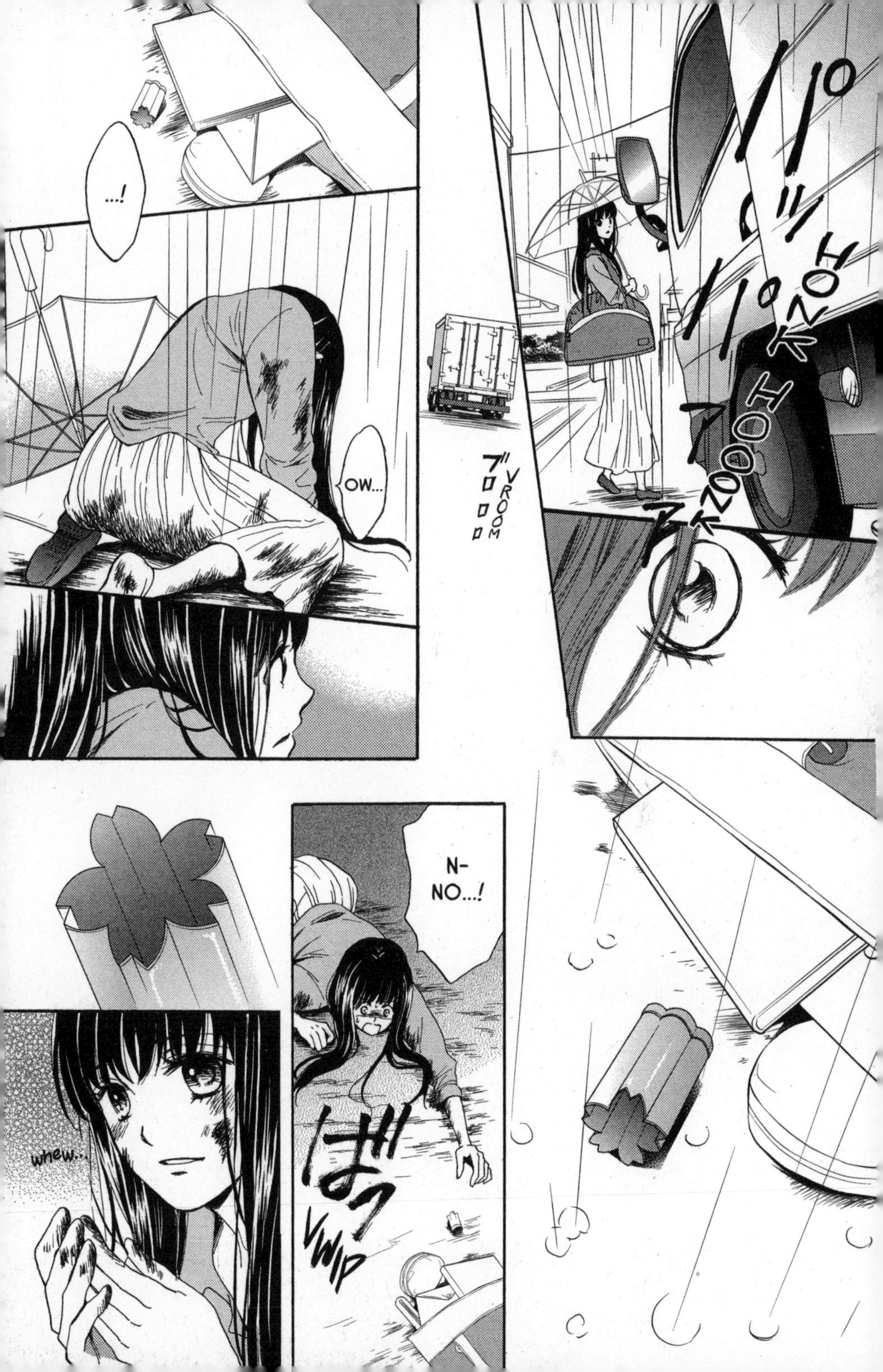
HONK HONK
ブロロロ
VROOM
...!
OW...
N-
NO...!
ぱっ
VWIP
whew...

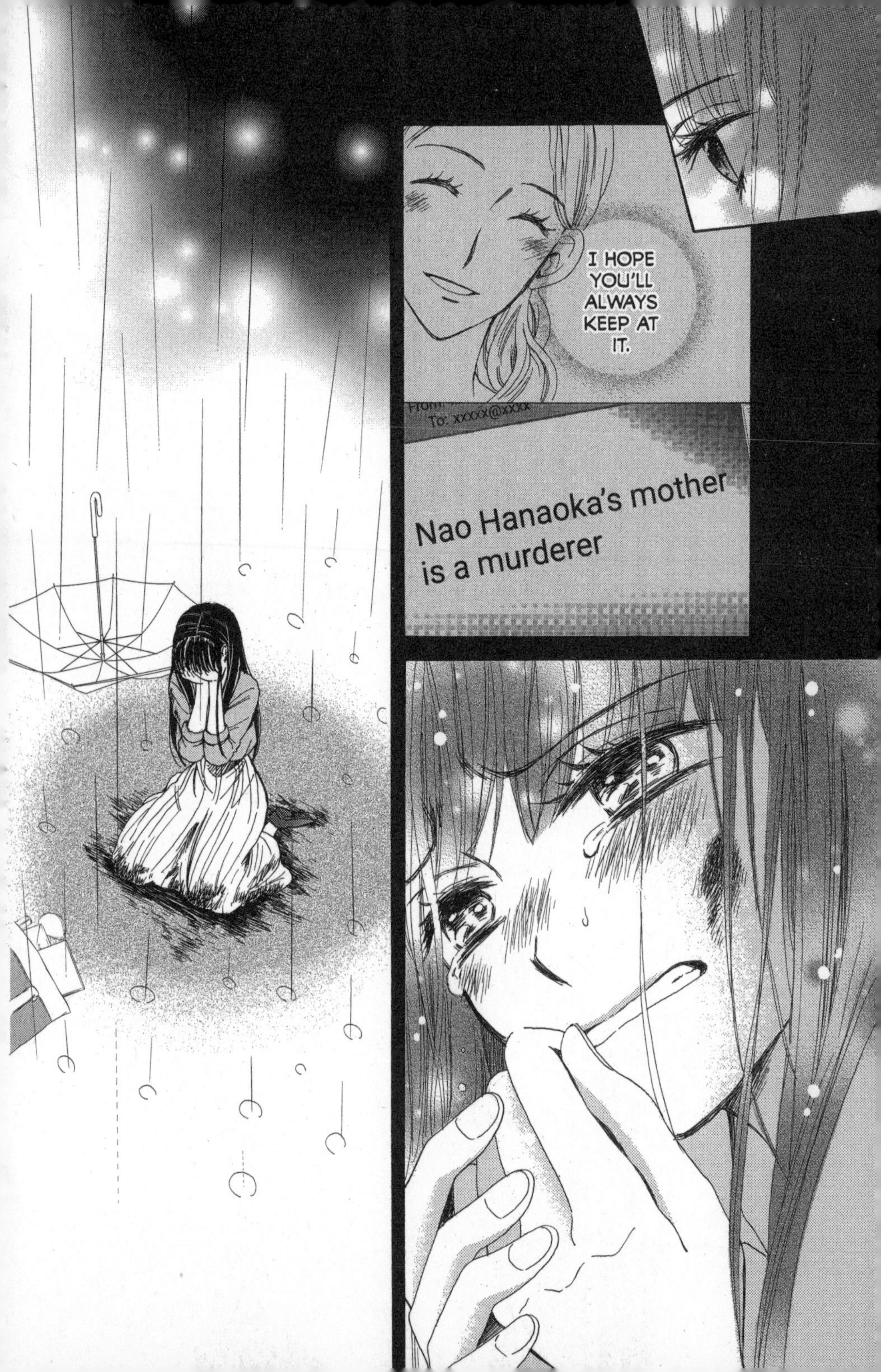
I HOPE YOU'LL ALWAYS KEEP AT IT.
To: xxxxx@xxxx
Nao Hanaoka's mother is a murderer

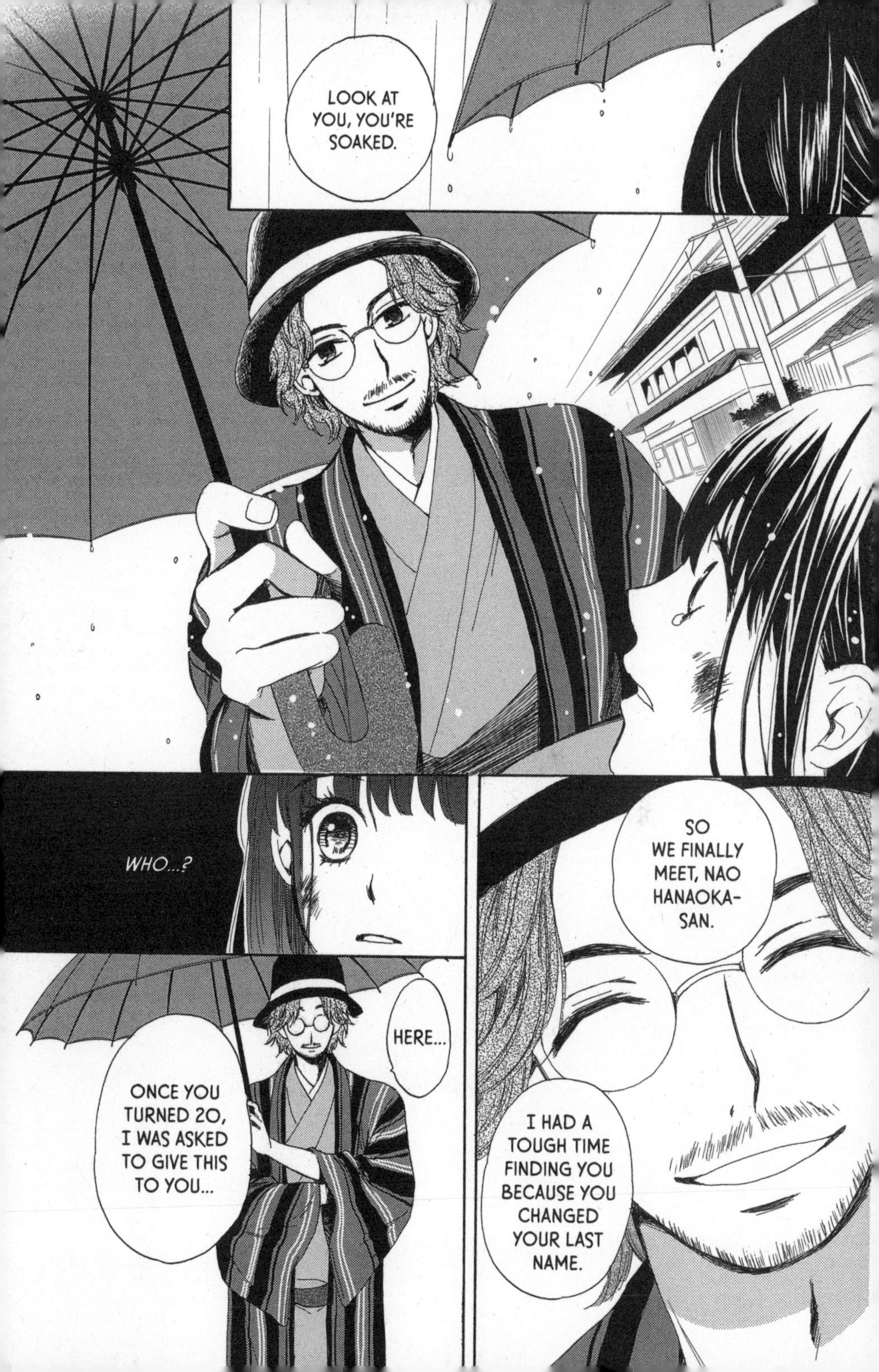
LOOK AT YOU, YOU'RE SOAKED.
SO WE FINALLY MEET, NAO HANAOKA-SAN.
I HAD A TOUGH TIME FINDING YOU BECAUSE YOU CHANGED YOUR LAST NAME.
WHO...?
HERE...
ONCE YOU TURNED 20, I WAS ASKED TO GIVE THIS TO YOU...

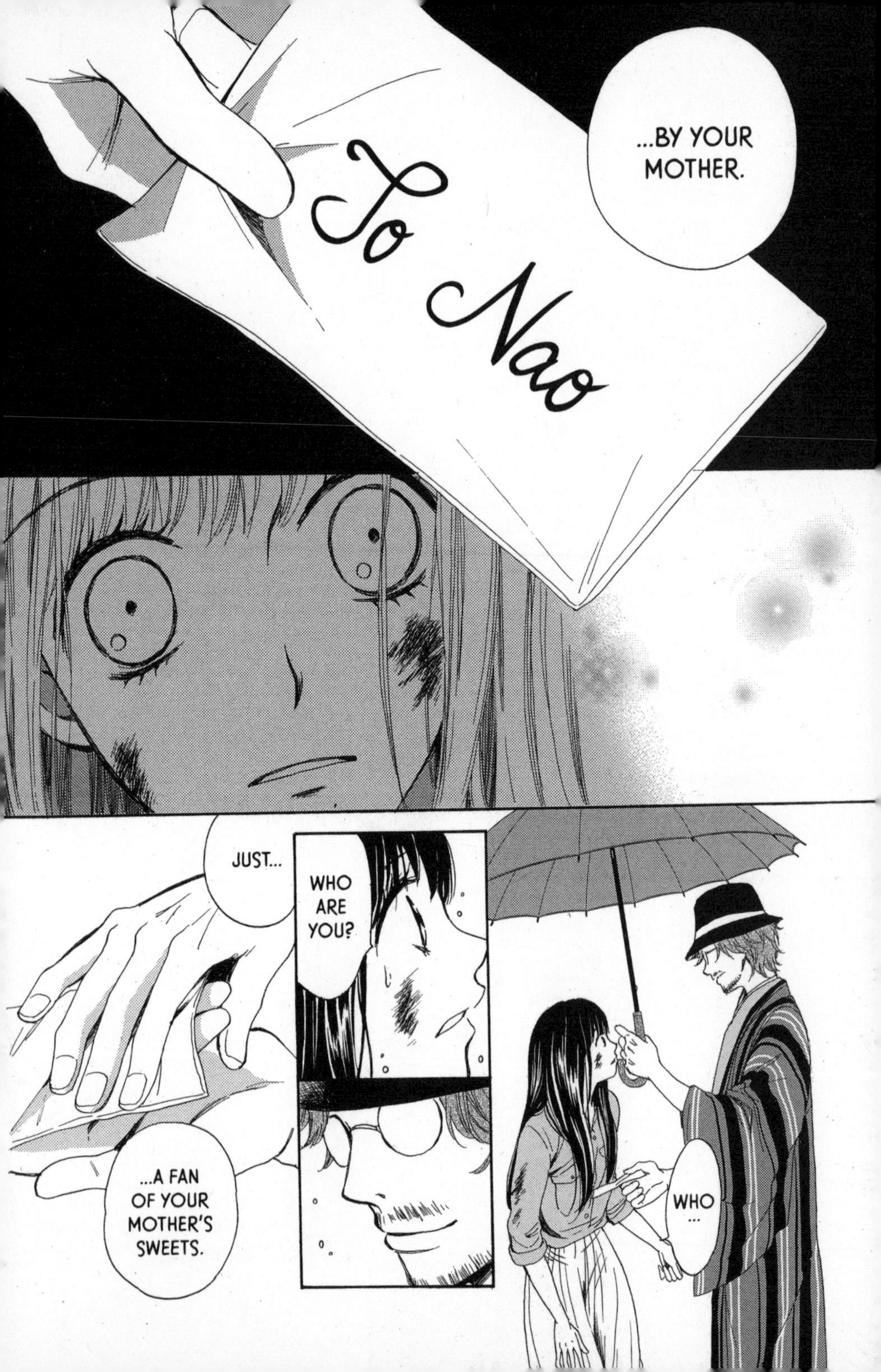
...BY YOUR MOTHER.
To Nao
WHO ...
WHO ARE YOU?
JUST...
...A FAN OF YOUR MOTHER'S SWEETS.

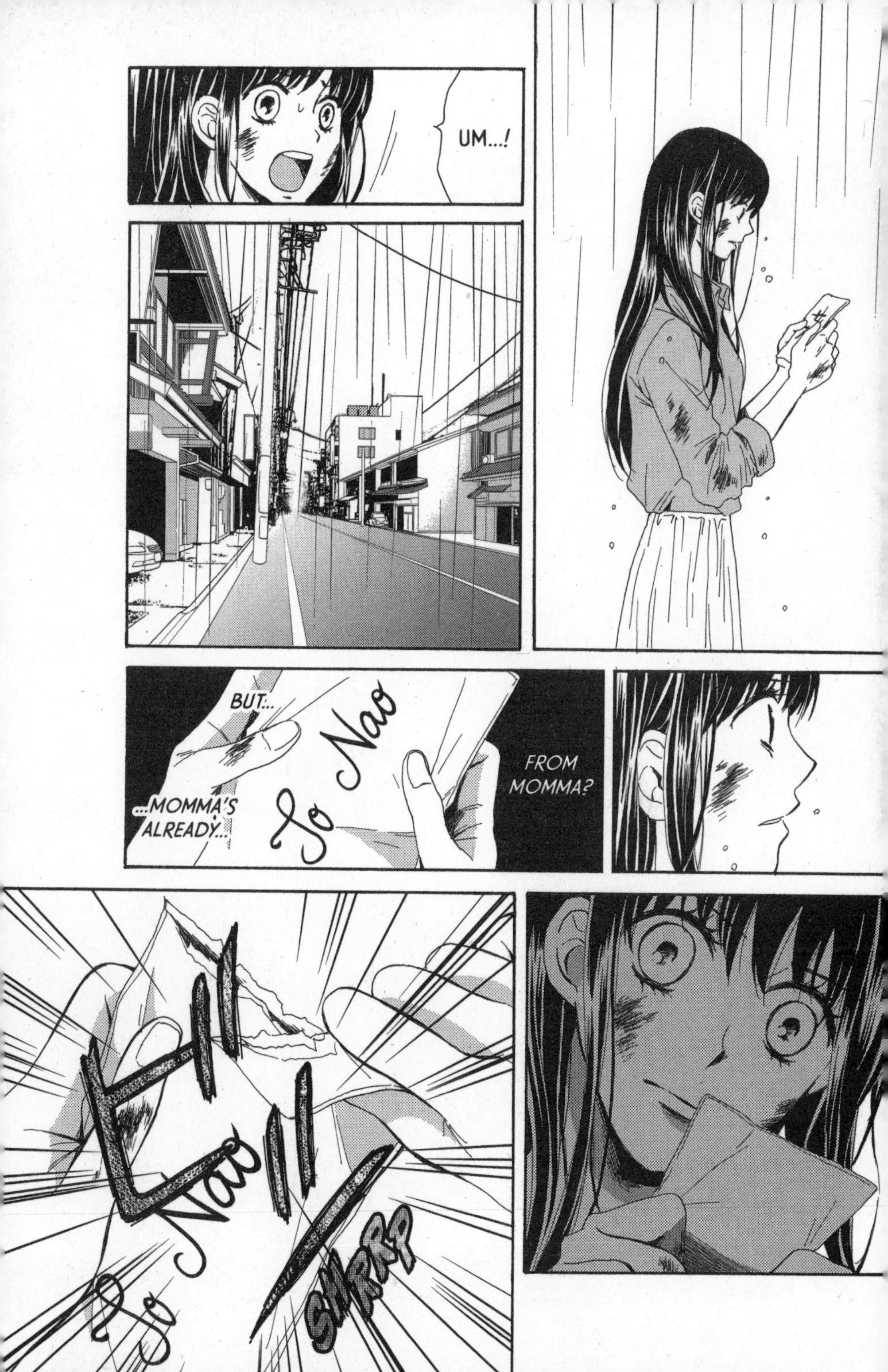
UM...!
FROM MOMMA?
BUT...
...MOMMA'S ALREADY...
To Nao
To Nao
SHRRP

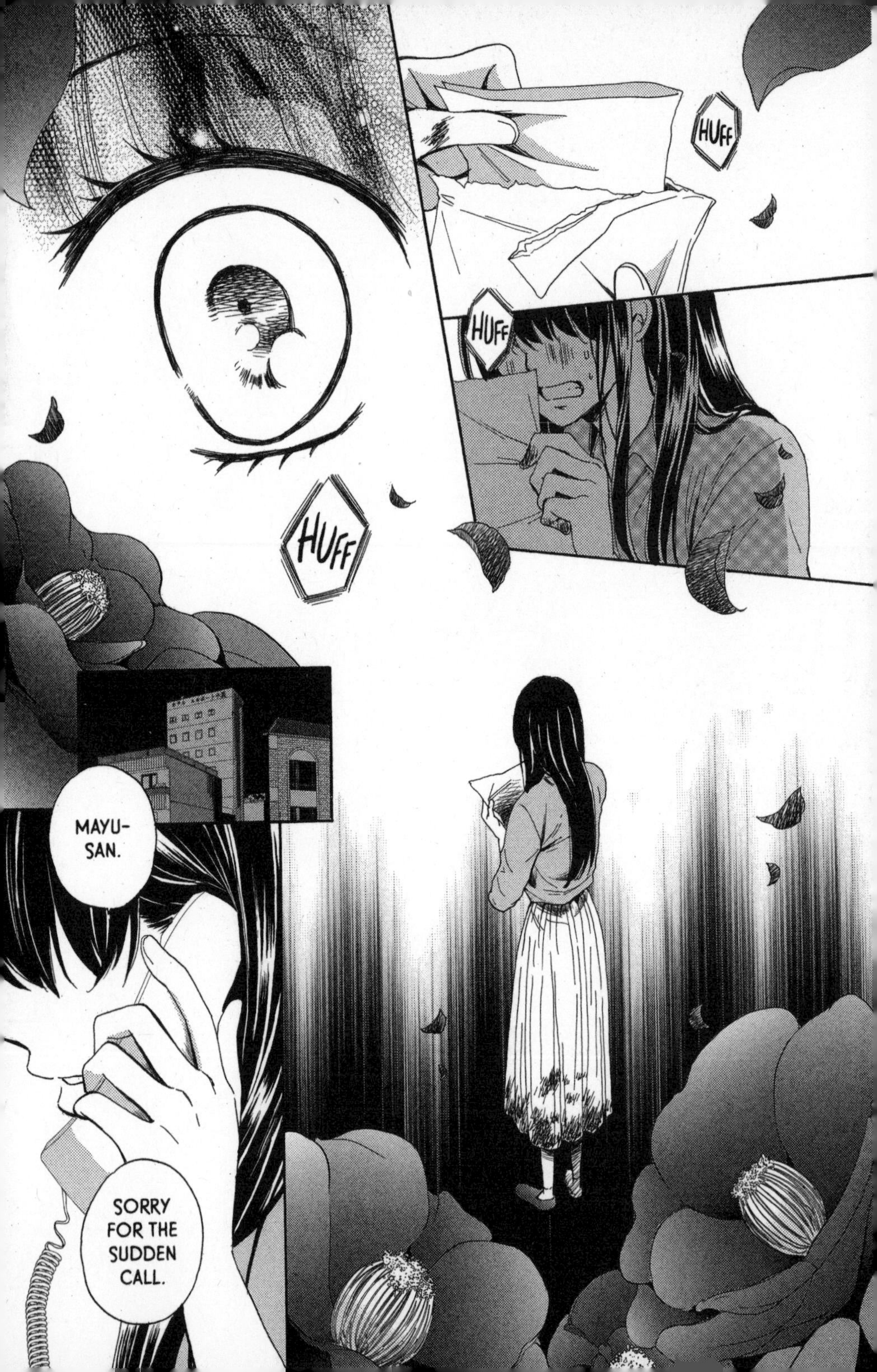
HUFF
HUFF
HUFF
MAYU-SAN.
SORRY FOR THE SUDDEN CALL.

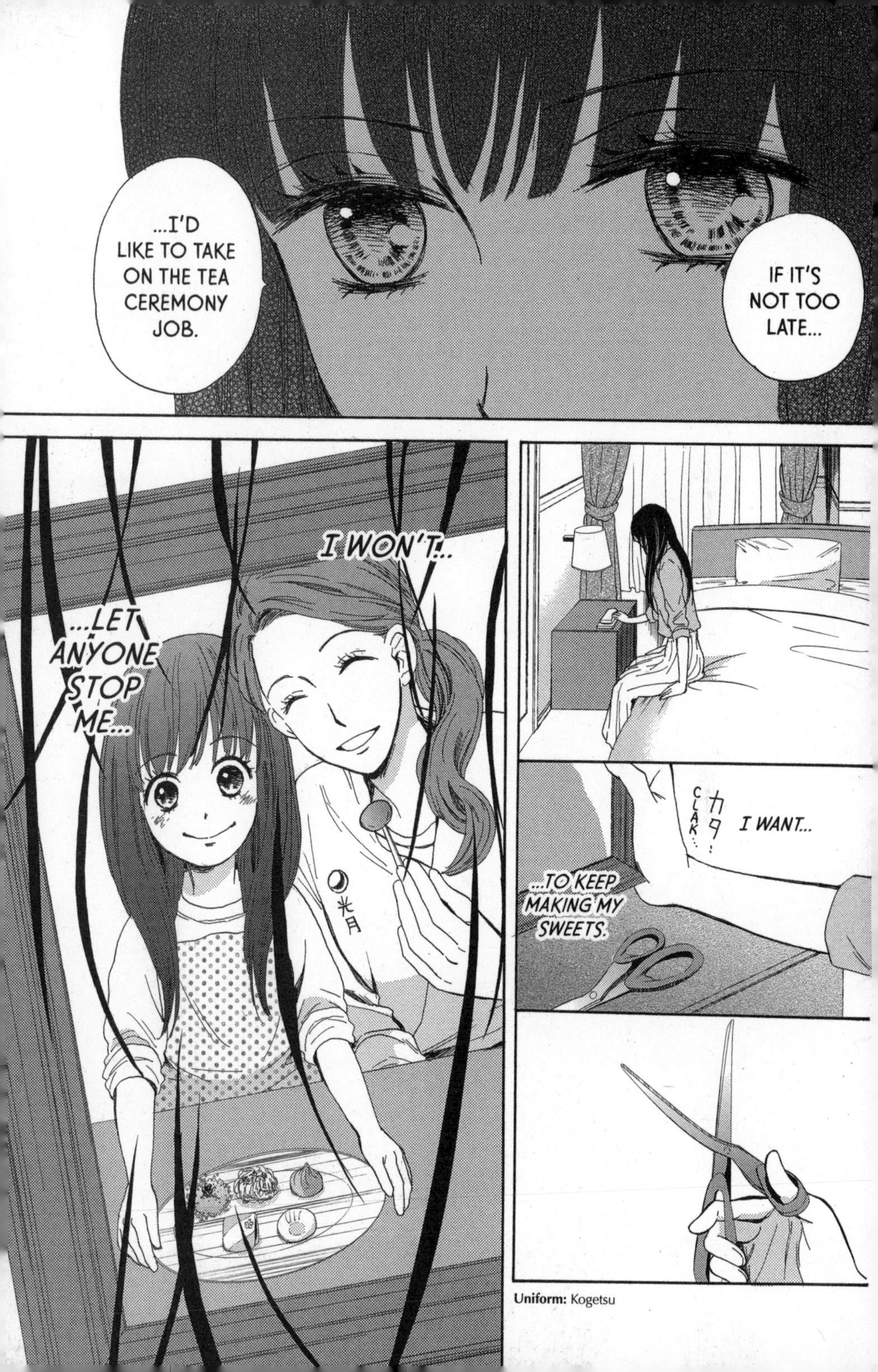
IF IT'S NOT TOO LATE...
...I'D LIKE TO TAKE ON THE TEA CEREMONY JOB.
カタ
CLAK...
I WANT...
...TO KEEP MAKING MY SWEETS.
I WON'T...
...LET ANYONE STOP ME...
光月

Uniform: Kogetsu

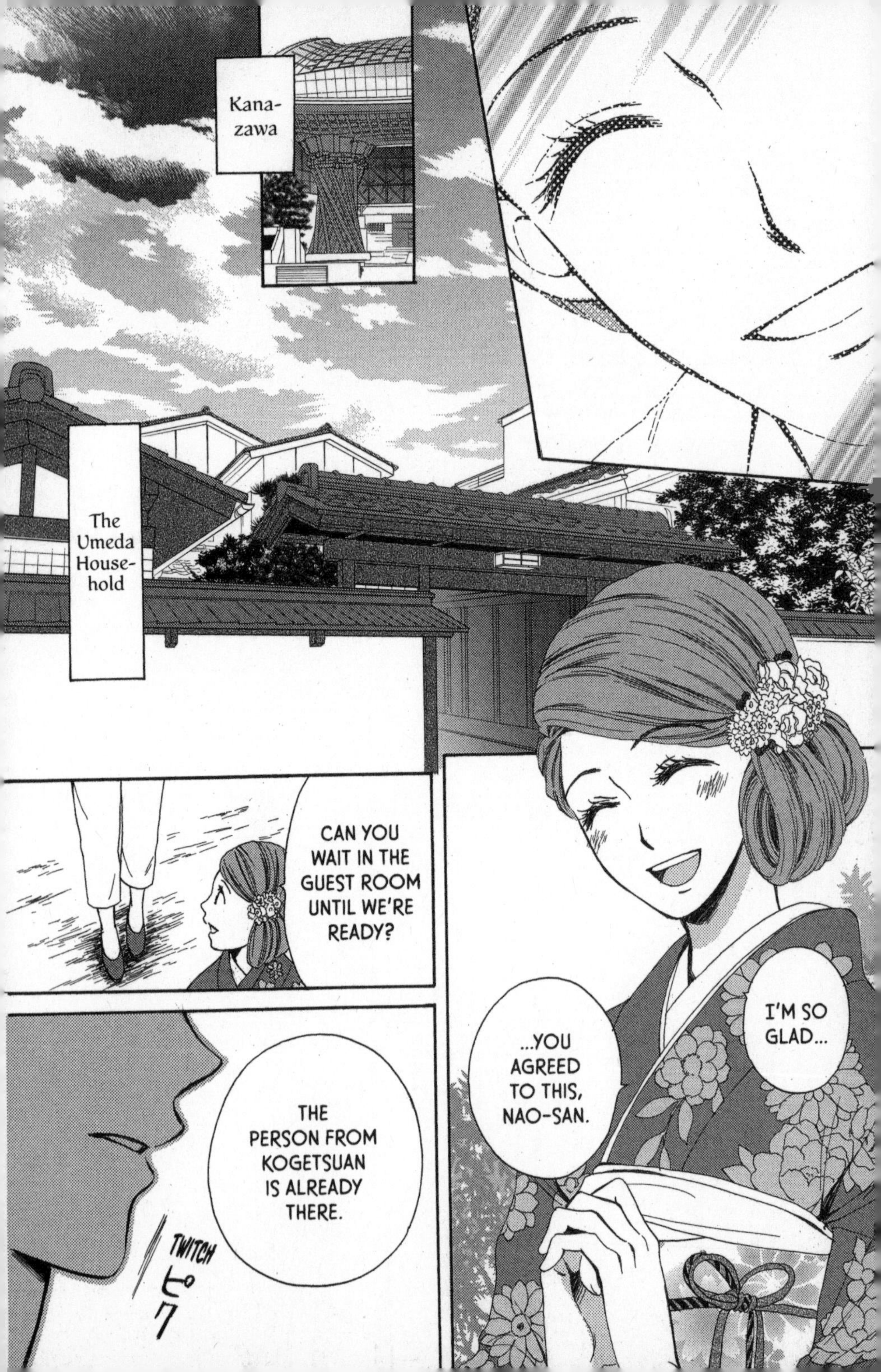
Kana-zawa
The Umeda House-hold
I'M SO GLAD...
...YOU AGREED TO THIS, NAO-SAN.
CAN YOU WAIT IN THE GUEST ROOM UNTIL WE'RE READY?
THE PERSON FROM KOGETSUAN IS ALREADY THERE.
TWITCH
ピク

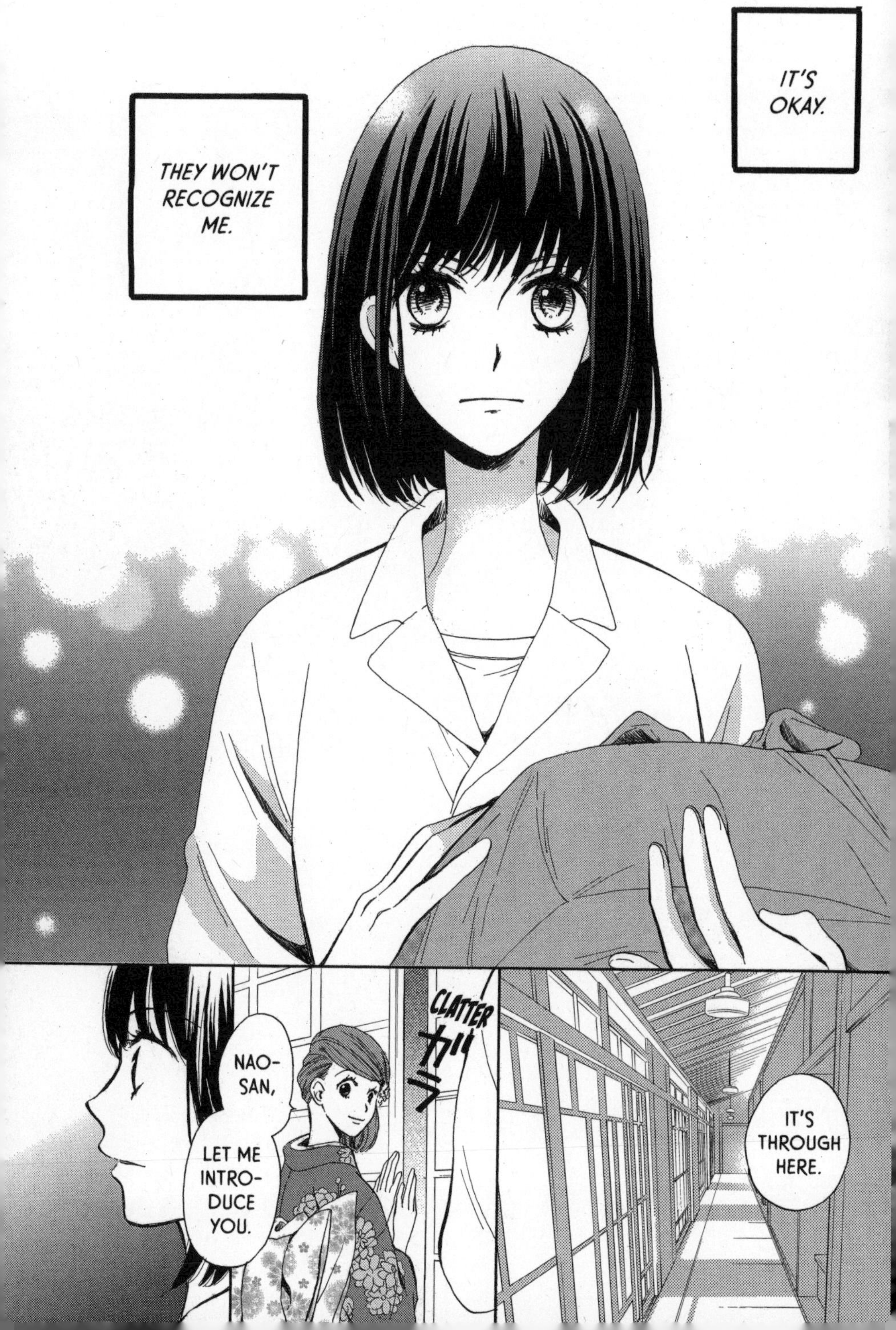
IT'S OKAY.
THEY WON'T RECOGNIZE ME.
IT'S THROUGH HERE.
CLATTER
ガラ
NAO-SAN,
LET ME INTRO-DUCE YOU.

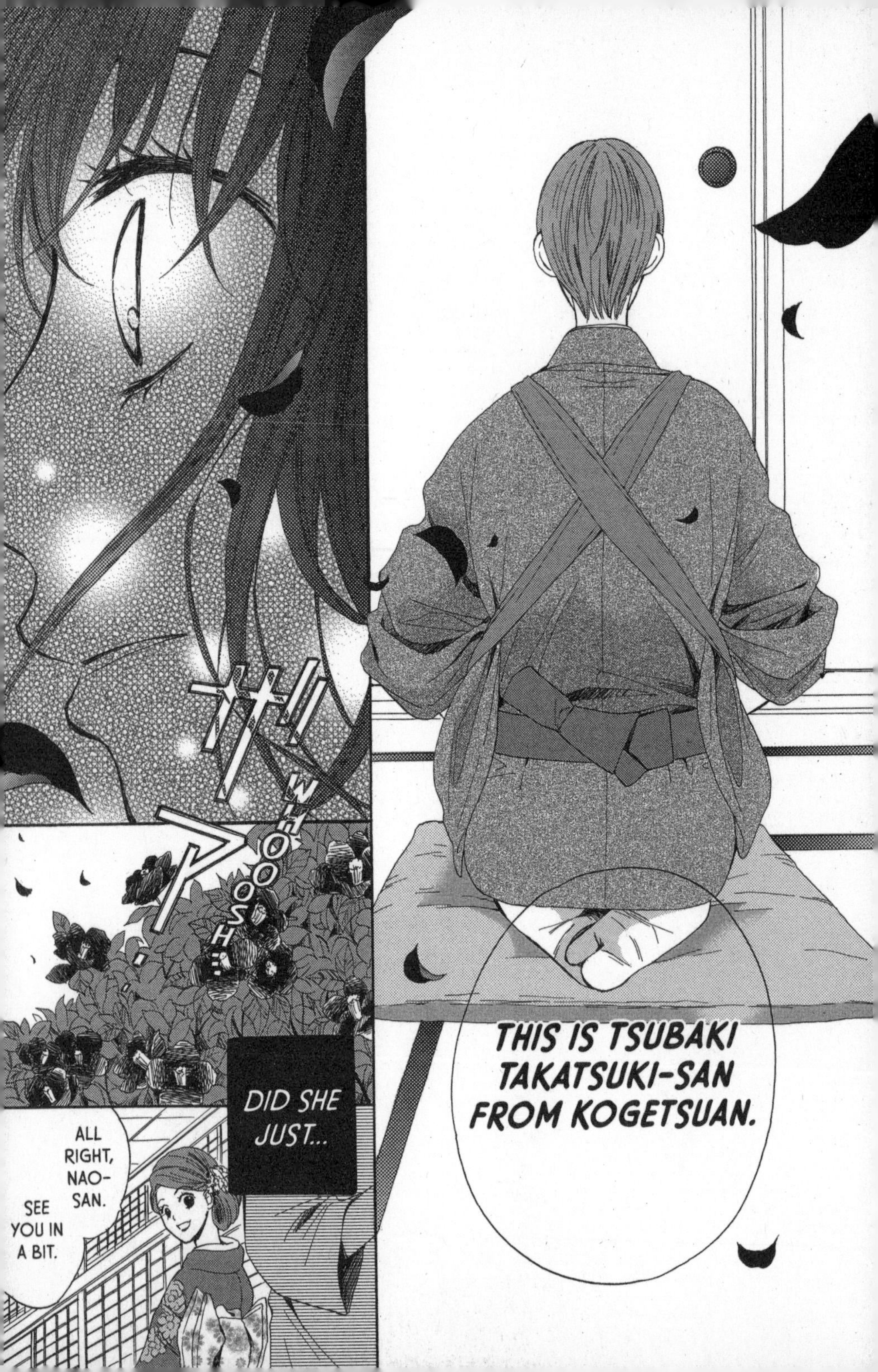
THIS IS TSUBAKI TAKATSUKI-SAN FROM KOGETSUAN.
WHOOOSH!!
DID SHE JUST...
ALL RIGHT, NAO-SAN.
SEE YOU IN A BIT.

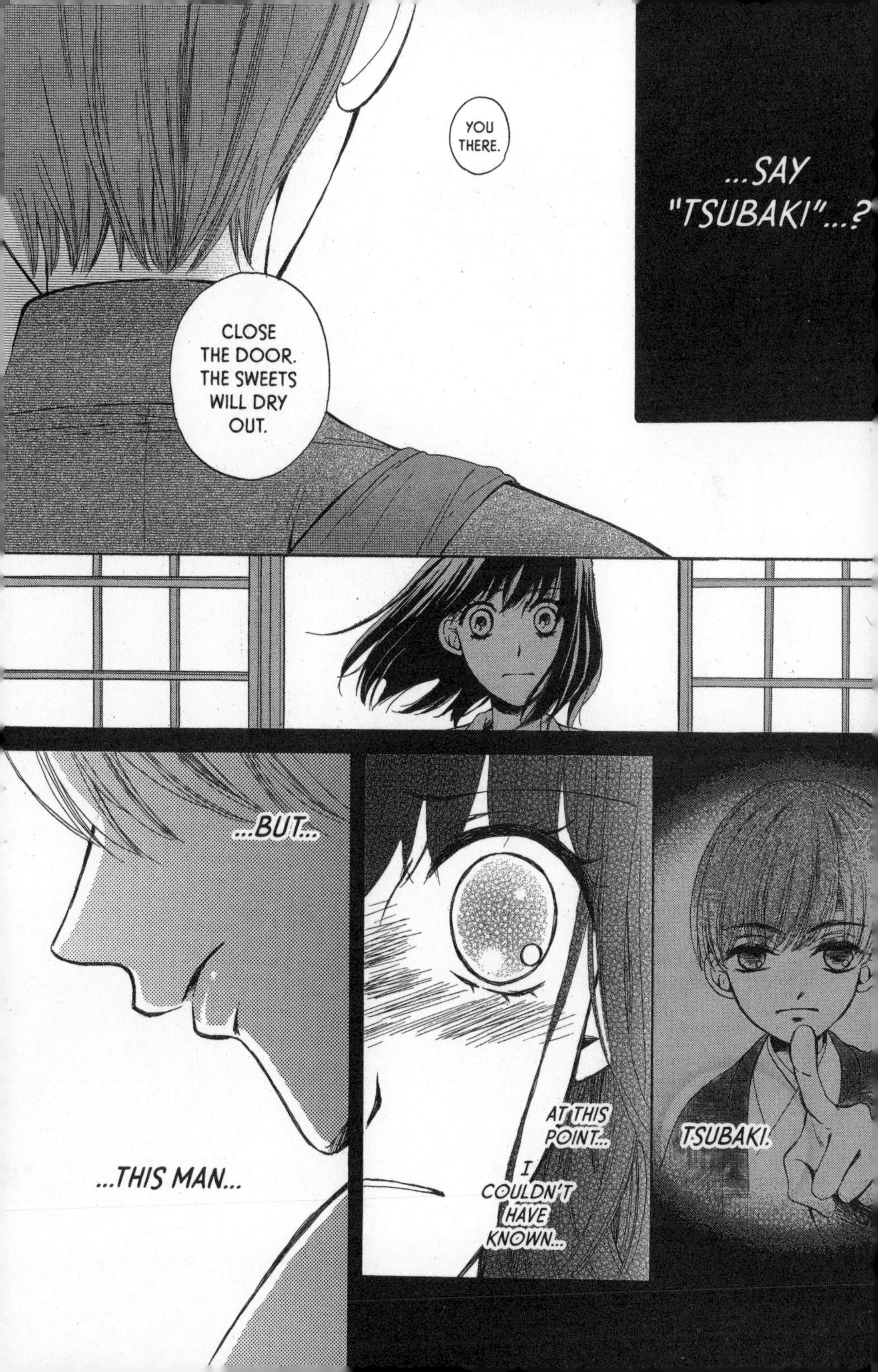
...SAY "TSUBAKI"...?
YOU THERE.
CLOSE THE DOOR. THE SWEETS WILL DRY OUT.
TSUBAKI.
AT THIS POINT...
I COULDN'T HAVE KNOWN...
...BUT...
...THIS MAN...

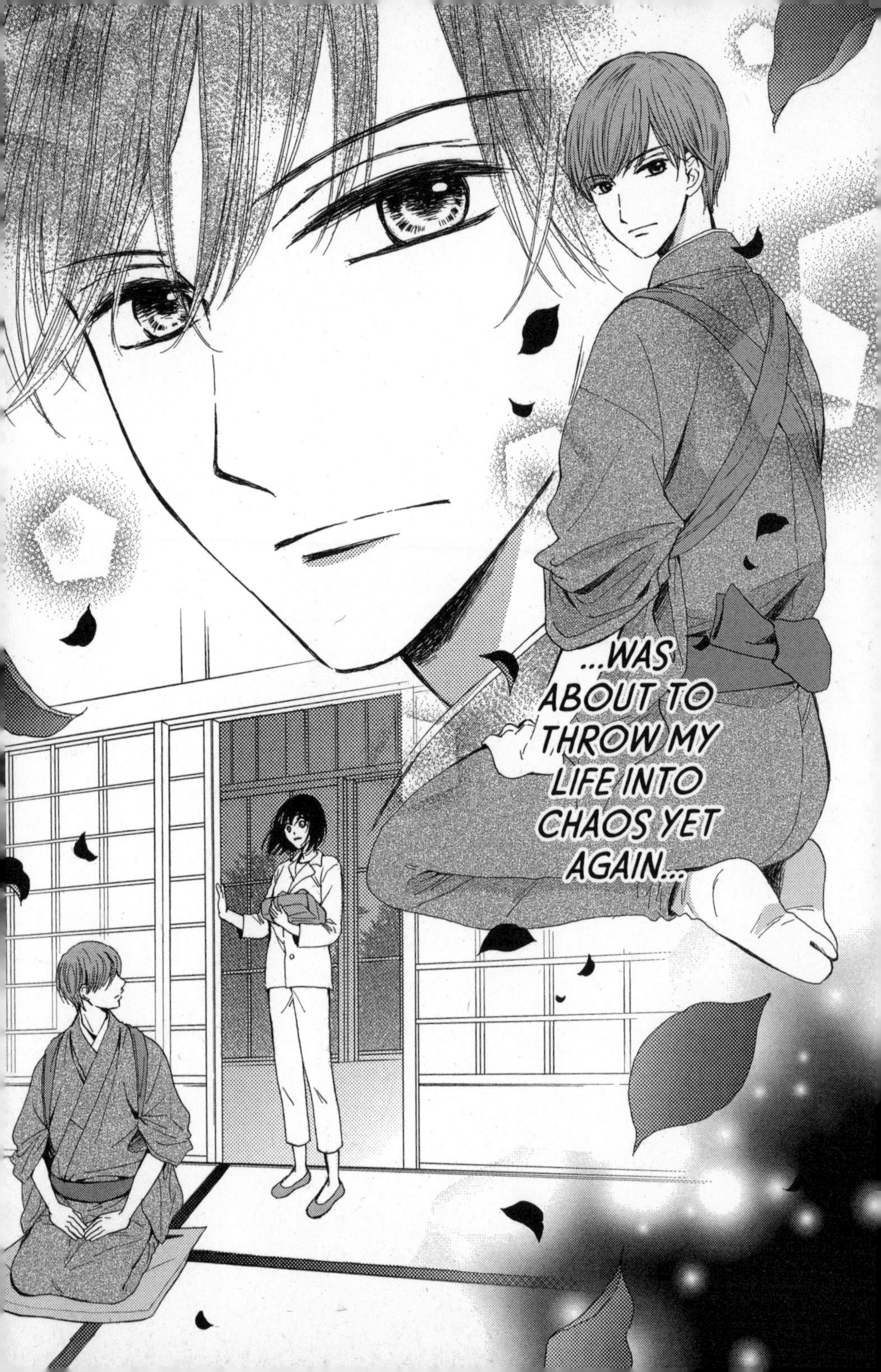
...WAS ABOUT TO THROW MY LIFE INTO CHAOS YET AGAIN...

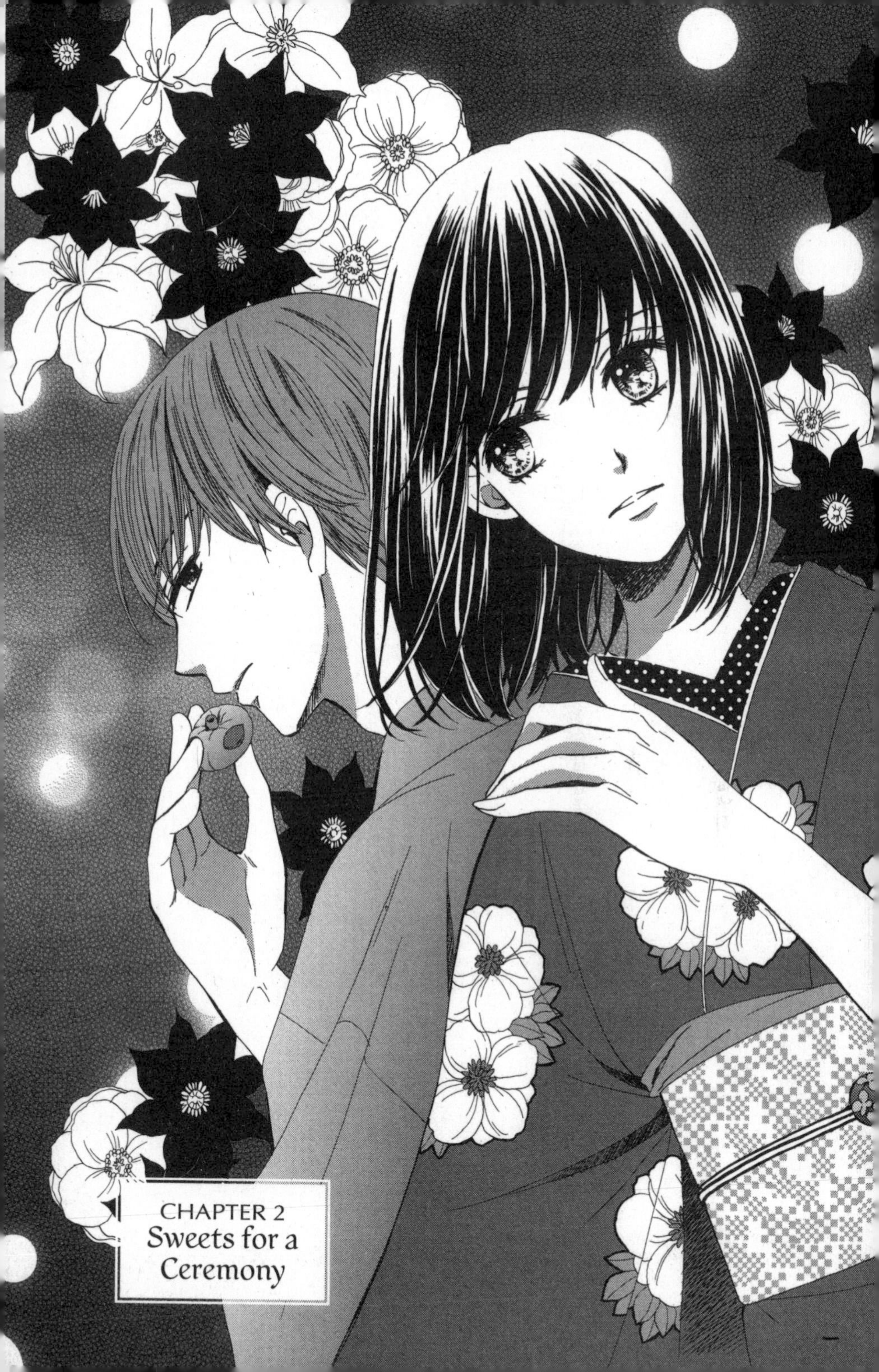
CHAPTER 2
Sweets for a Ceremony

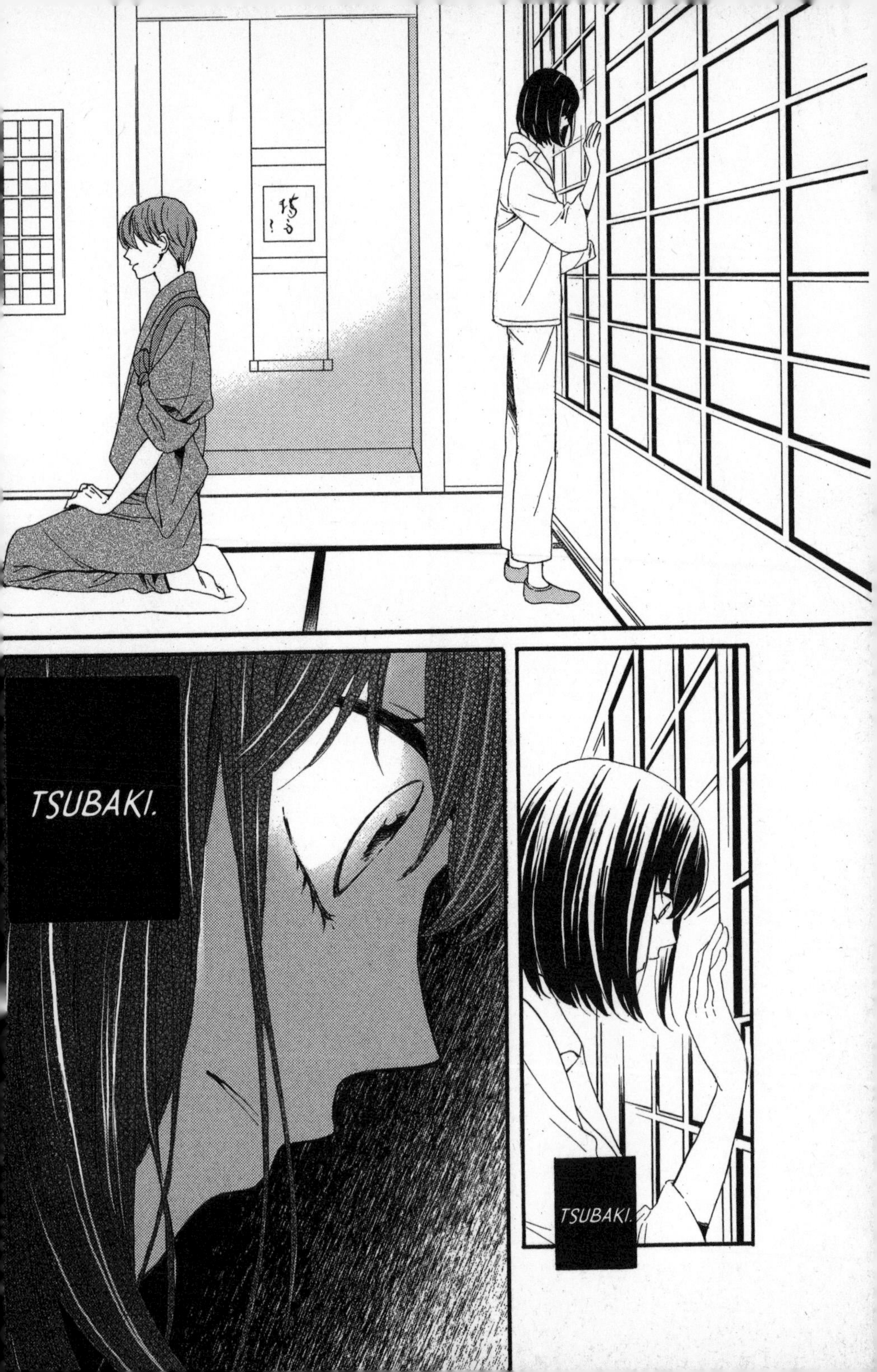
TSUBAKI.
TSUBAKI.

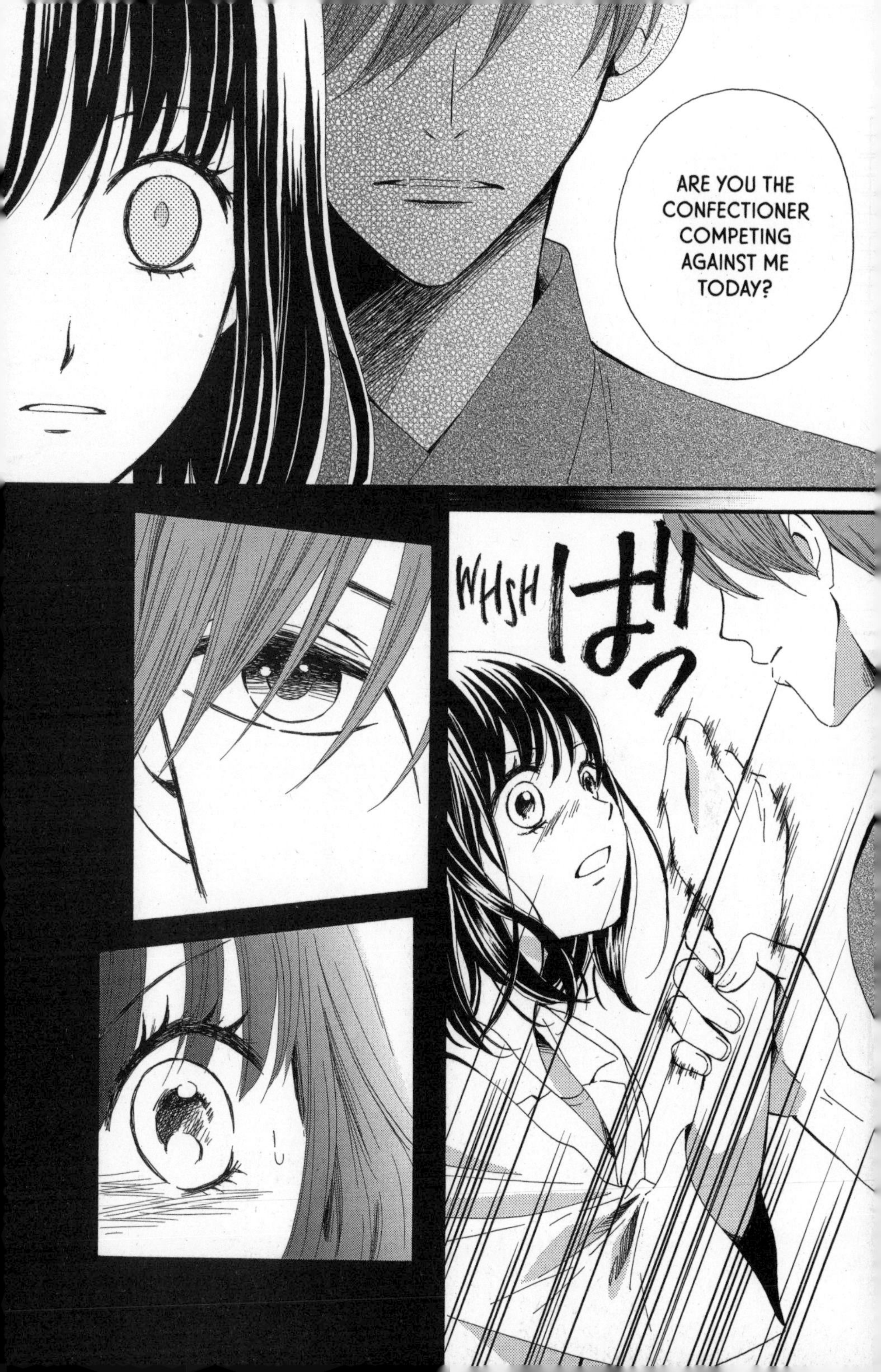
ARE YOU THE CONFECTIONER COMPETING AGAINST ME TODAY?
WHSH
はっ

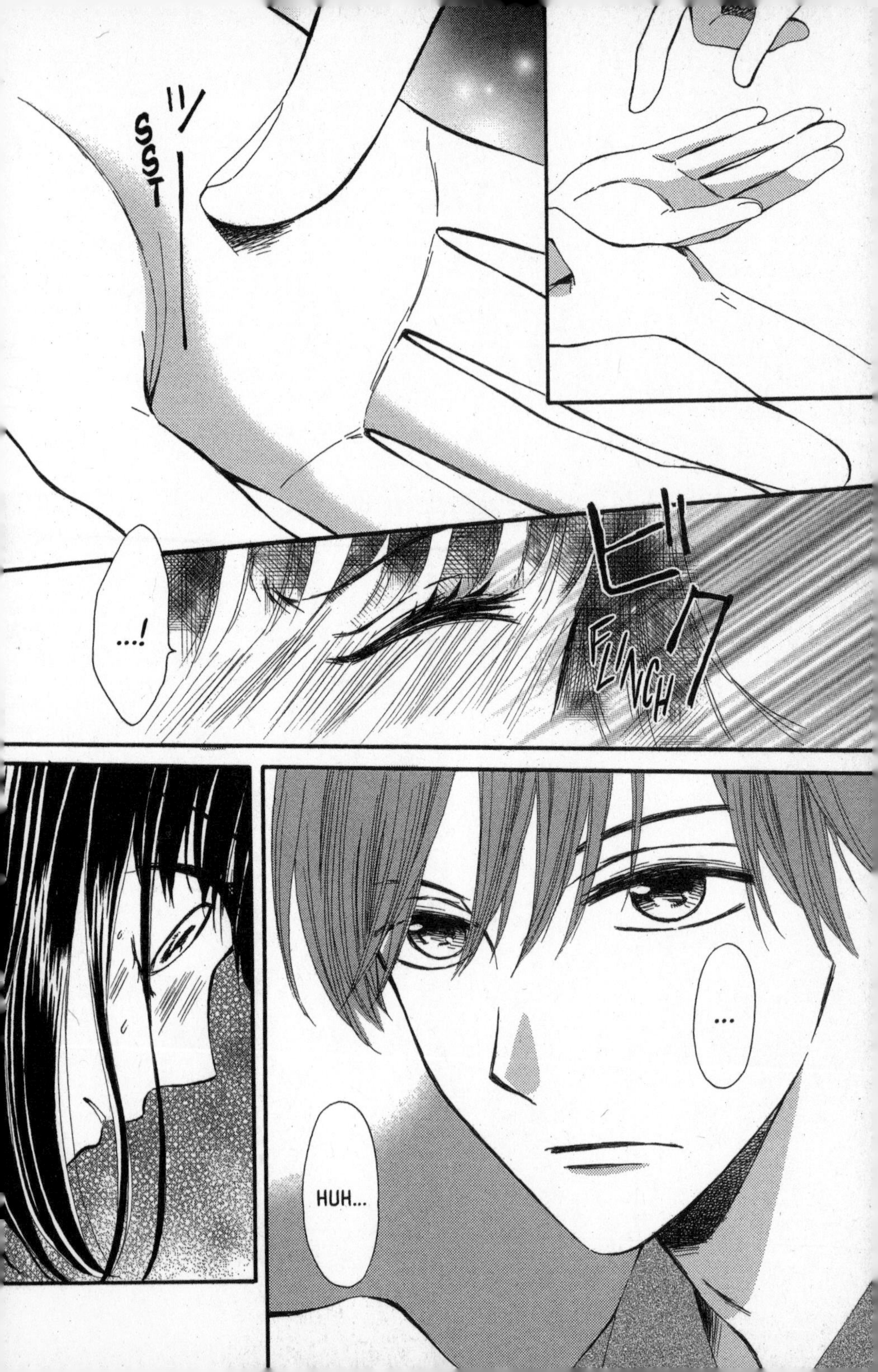
SSST
ビク
FLINCH
...!
...
HUH...

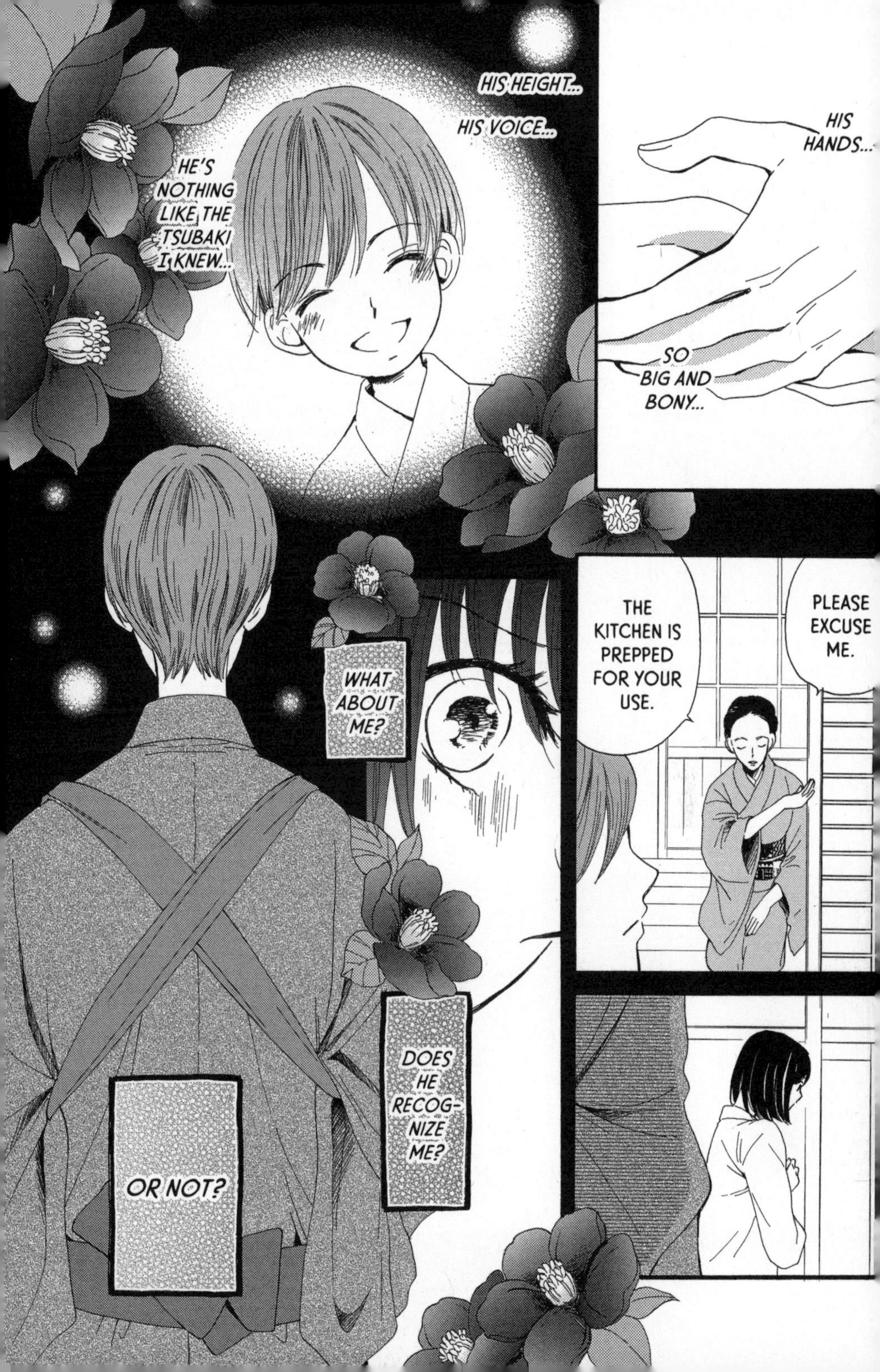
HIS HANDS...
SO BIG AND BONY...
PLEASE EXCUSE ME.
THE KITCHEN IS PREPPED FOR YOUR USE.
HIS HEIGHT...
HIS VOICE...
HE'S NOTHING LIKE THE TSUBAKI I KNEW...
WHAT ABOUT ME?
DOES HE RECOG-NIZE ME?
OR NOT?

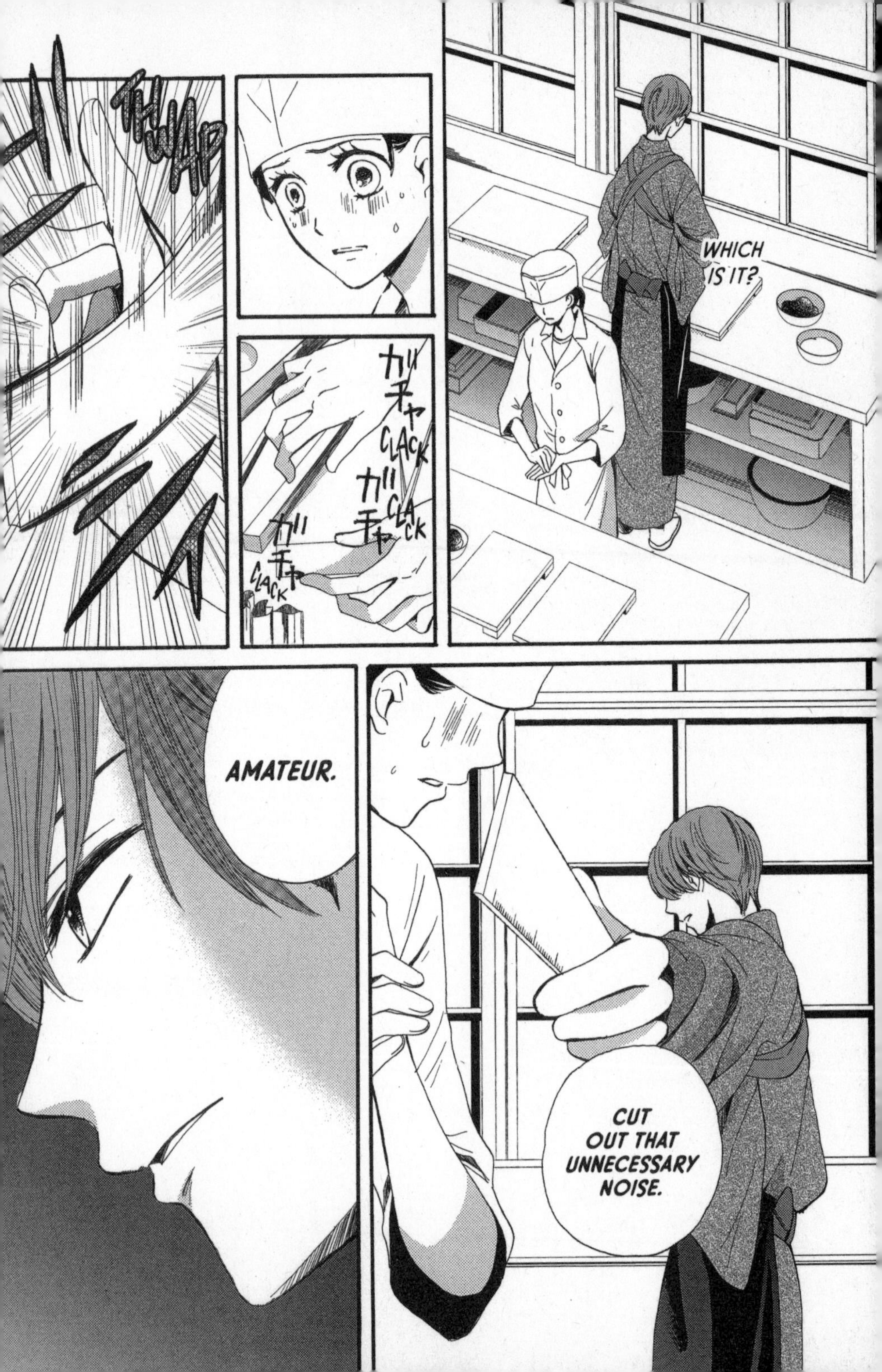
WHICH IS IT?
カチャ
CLACK
カチャ
CLACK
カチャ
CLACK
THWAP
CUT OUT THAT UNNECESSARY NOISE.
AMATEUR.

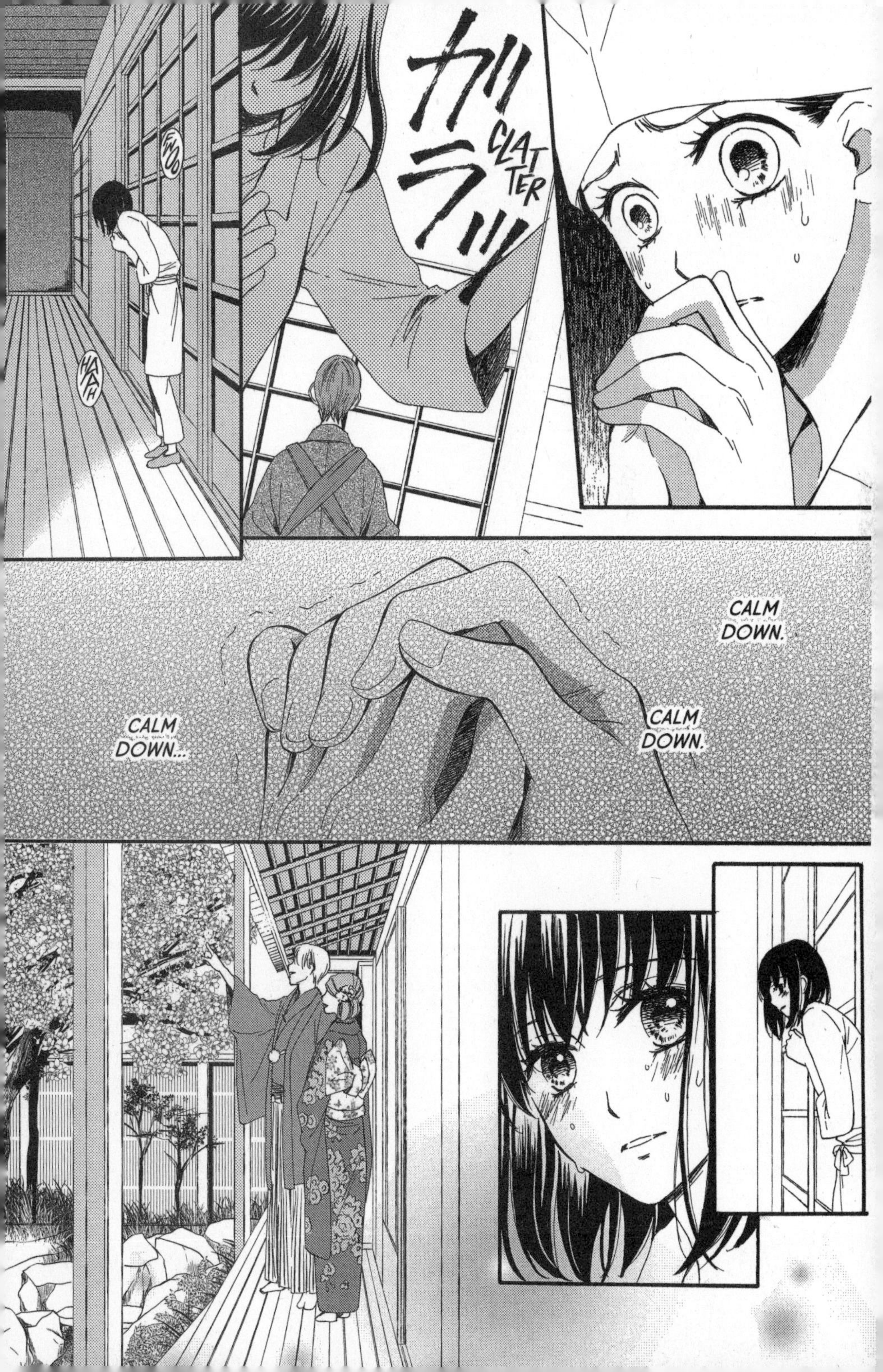
カラッ
CLATTER
FWOO
HAAH
CALM DOWN.
CALM DOWN.
CALM DOWN...

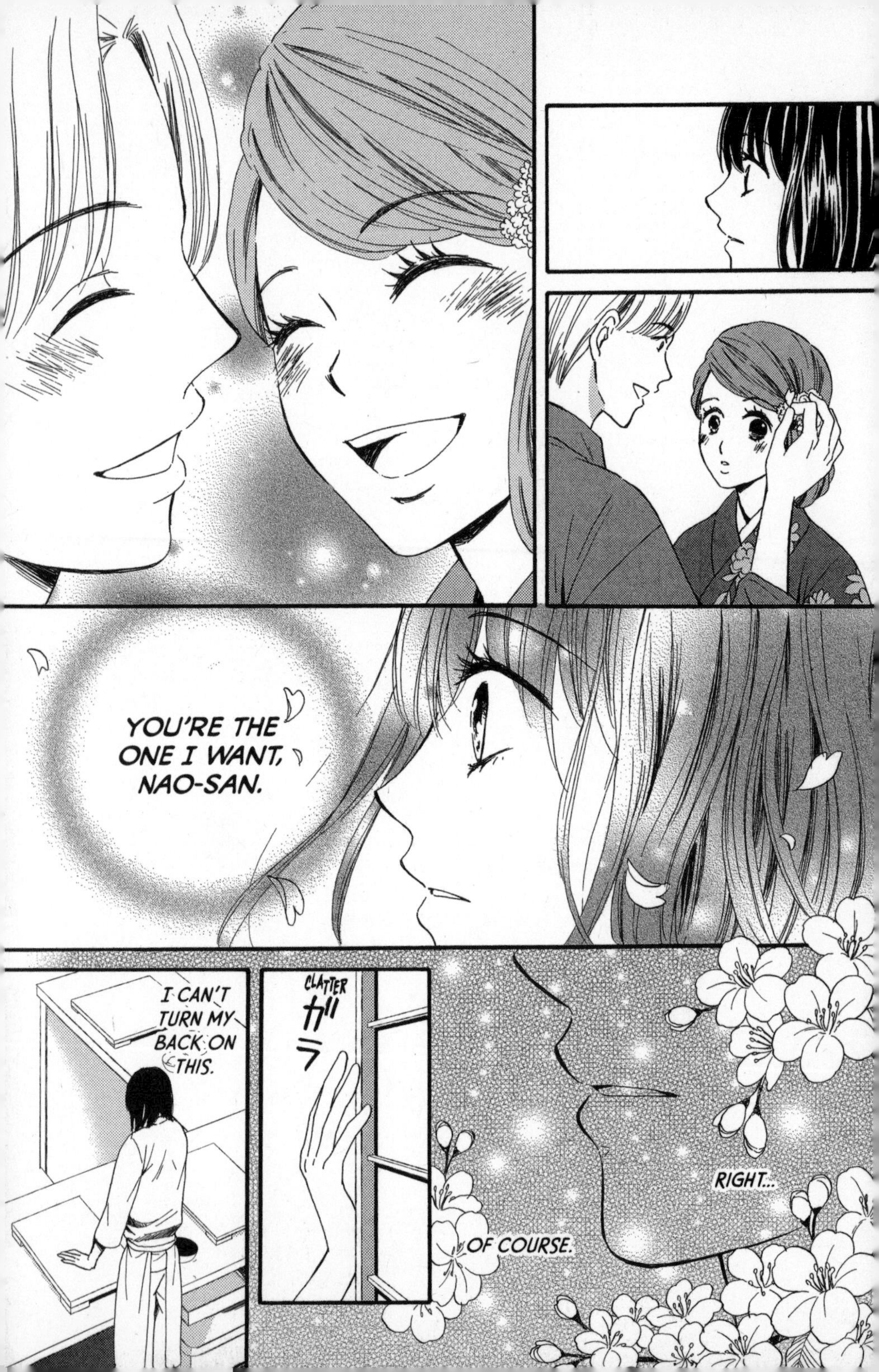
YOU'RE THE ONE I WANT, NAO-SAN.
RIGHT...
OF COURSE.
CLATTER
ガラ
I CAN'T TURN MY BACK ON THIS.

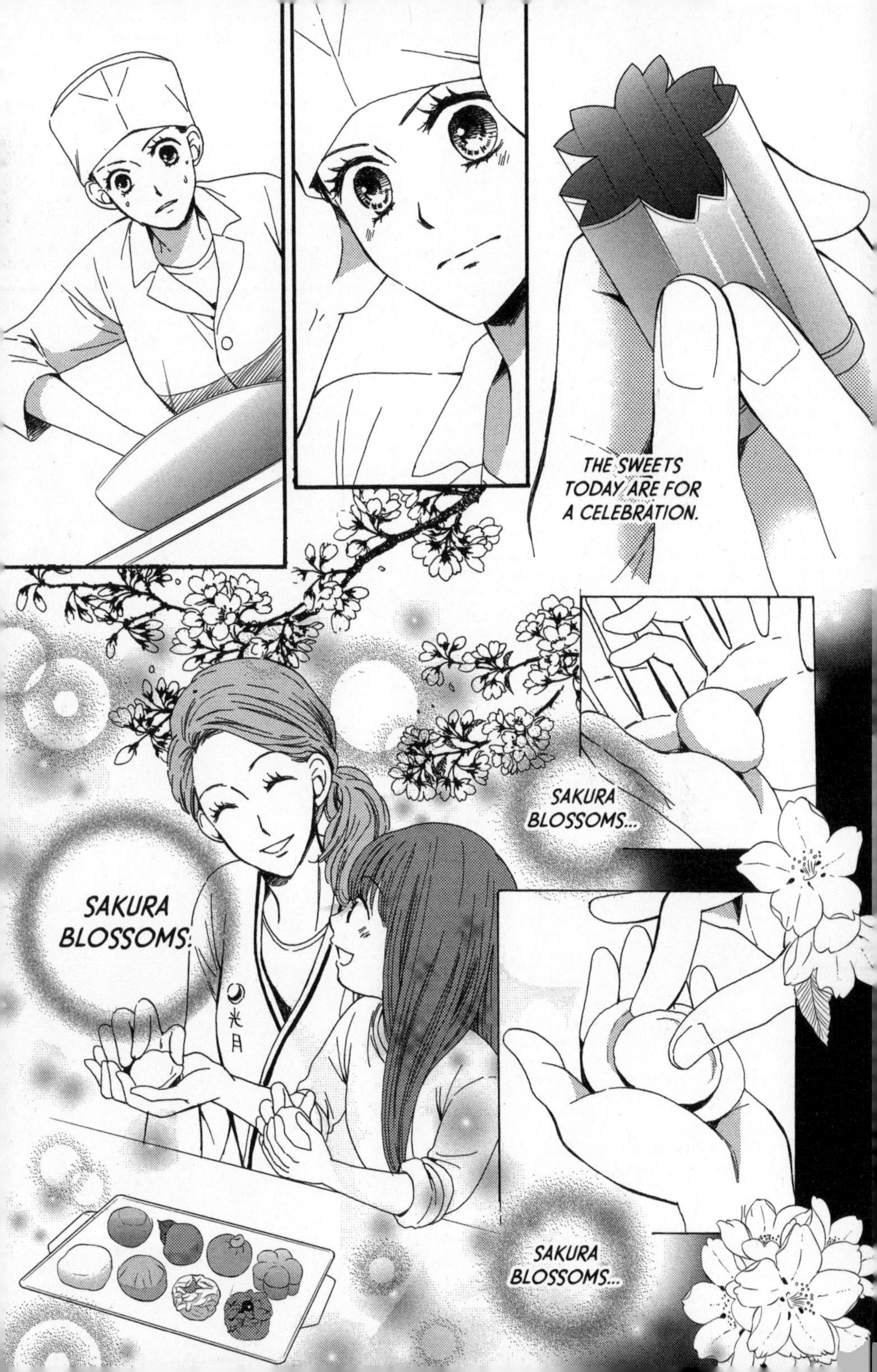
THE SWEETS TODAY ARE FOR A CELEBRATION.
SAKURA BLOSSOMS...
SAKURA BLOSSOMS!
SAKURA BLOSSOMS...

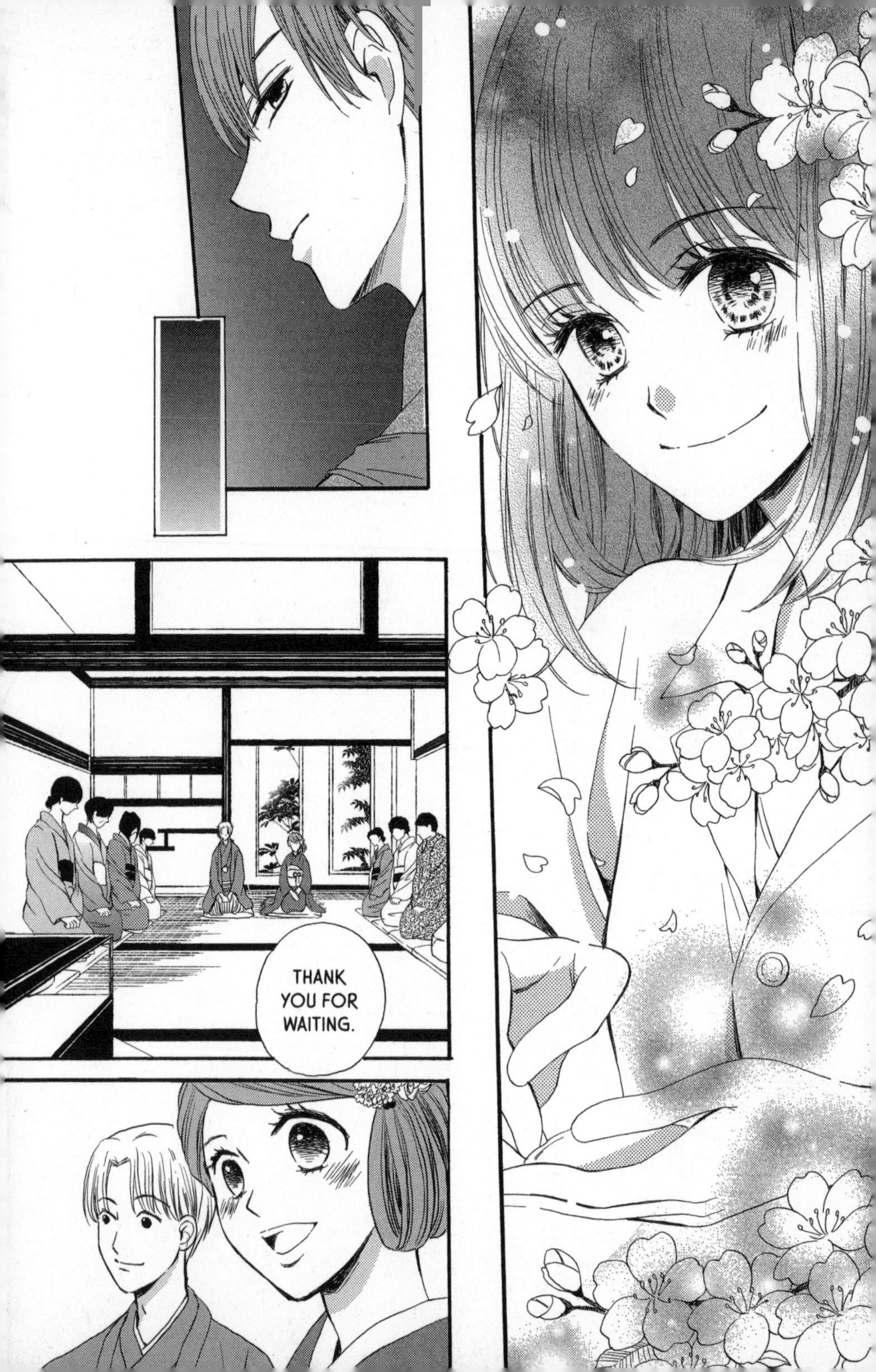
THANK YOU FOR WAITING.

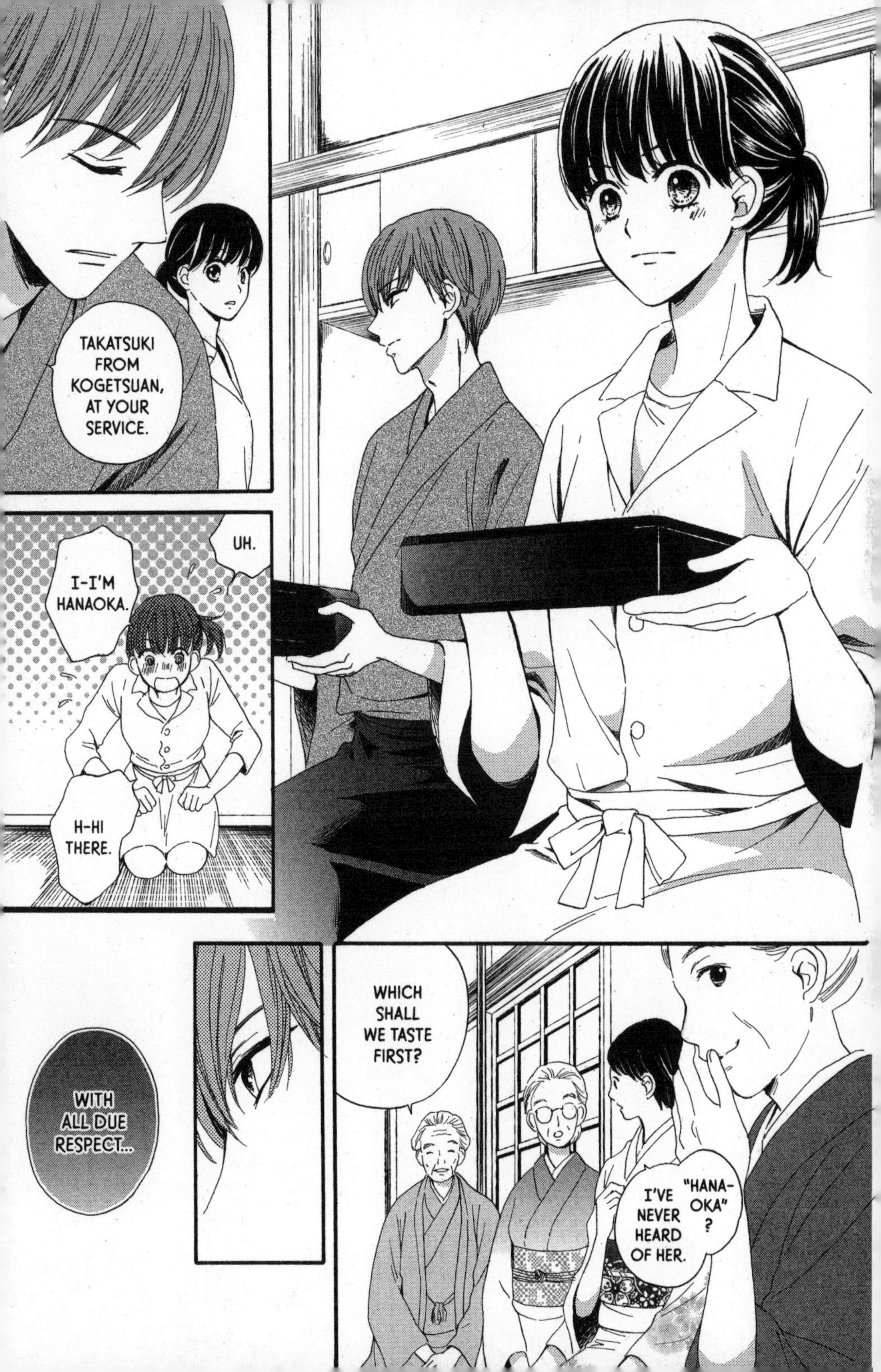
TAKATSUKI FROM KOGETSUAN, AT YOUR SERVICE.
UH.
I-I'M HANAOKA.
H-HI THERE.
WHICH SHALL WE TASTE FIRST?
"HANA-OKA"?
I'VE NEVER HEARD OF HER.
WITH ALL DUE RESPECT...

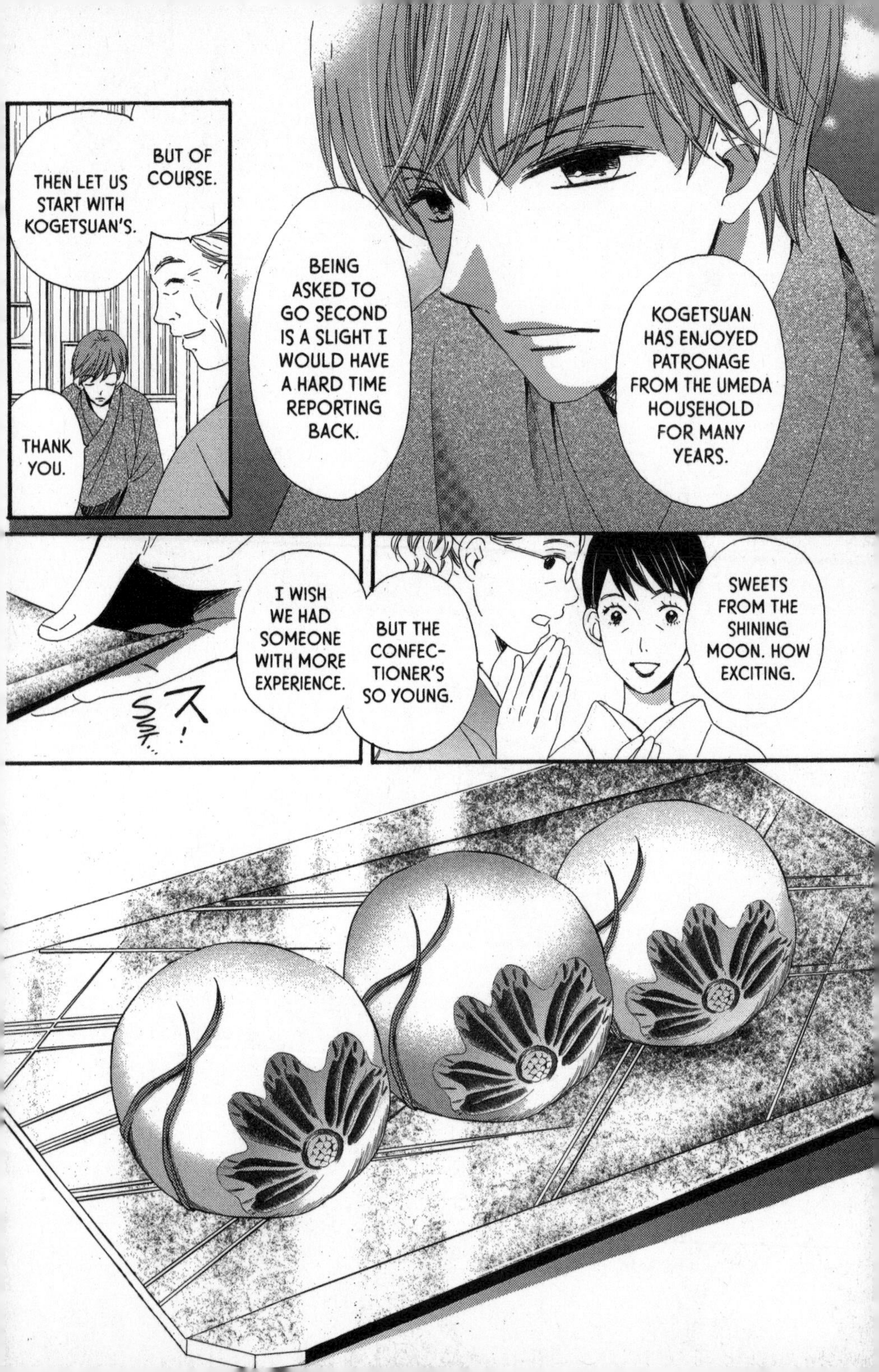
KOGETSUAN HAS ENJOYED PATRONAGE FROM THE UMEDA HOUSEHOLD FOR MANY YEARS.
BEING ASKED TO GO SECOND IS A SLIGHT I WOULD HAVE A HARD TIME REPORTING BACK.
BUT OF COURSE.
THEN LET US START WITH KOGETSUAN'S.
THANK YOU.
SWEETS FROM THE SHINING MOON. HOW EXCITING.
BUT THE CONFEC-TIONER'S SO YOUNG.
I WISH WE HAD SOMEONE WITH MORE EXPERIENCE.
ス!
SSSK...

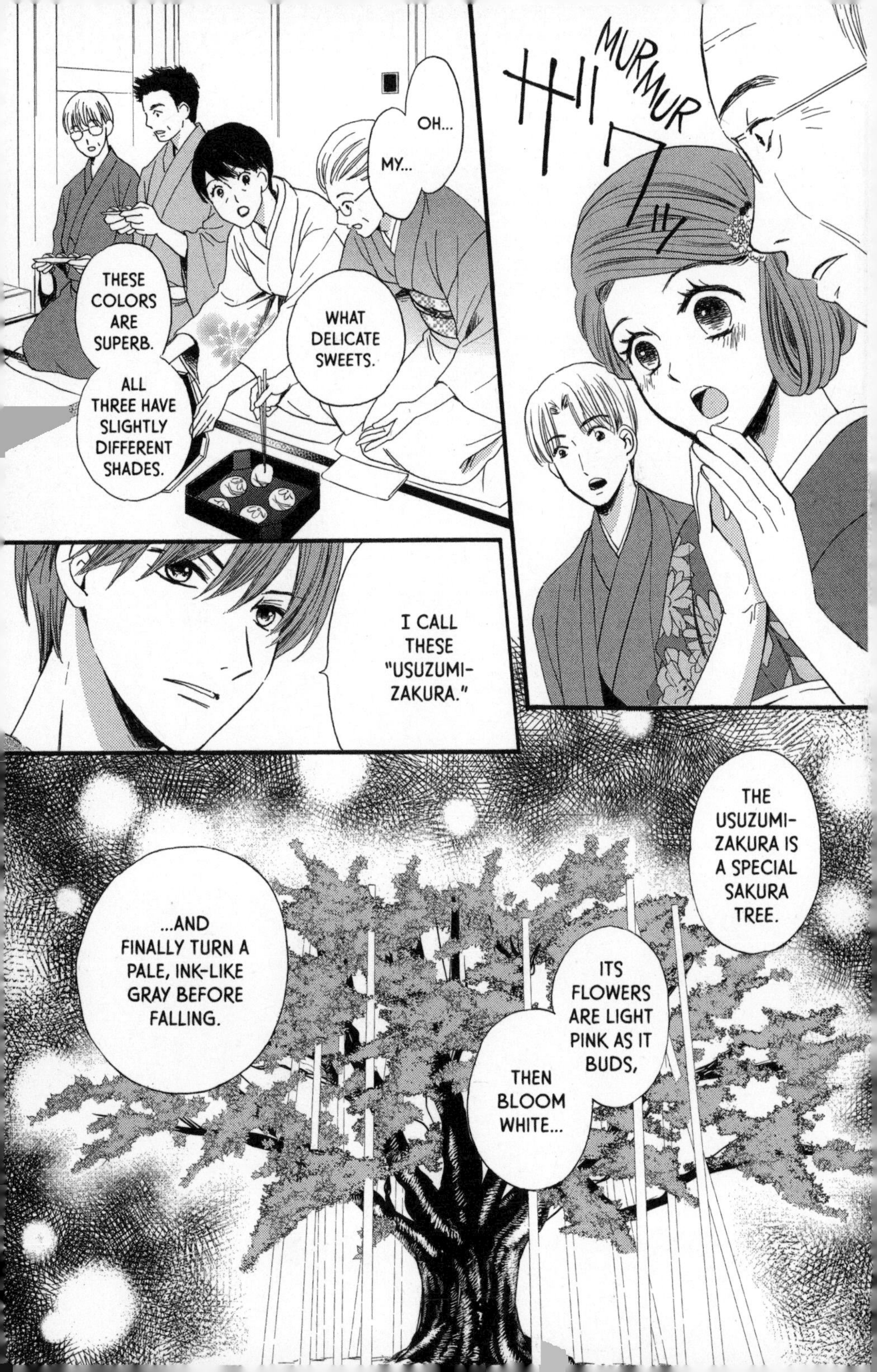
MURMUR
OH... MY...
WHAT DELICATE SWEETS.
THESE COLORS ARE SUPERB.
ALL THREE HAVE SLIGHTLY DIFFERENT SHADES.
I CALL THESE "USUZUMI-ZAKURA."
THE USUZUMI-ZAKURA IS A SPECIAL SAKURA TREE.
ITS FLOWERS ARE LIGHT PINK AS IT BUDS,
THEN BLOOM WHITE...
...AND FINALLY TURN A PALE, INK-LIKE GRAY BEFORE FALLING.

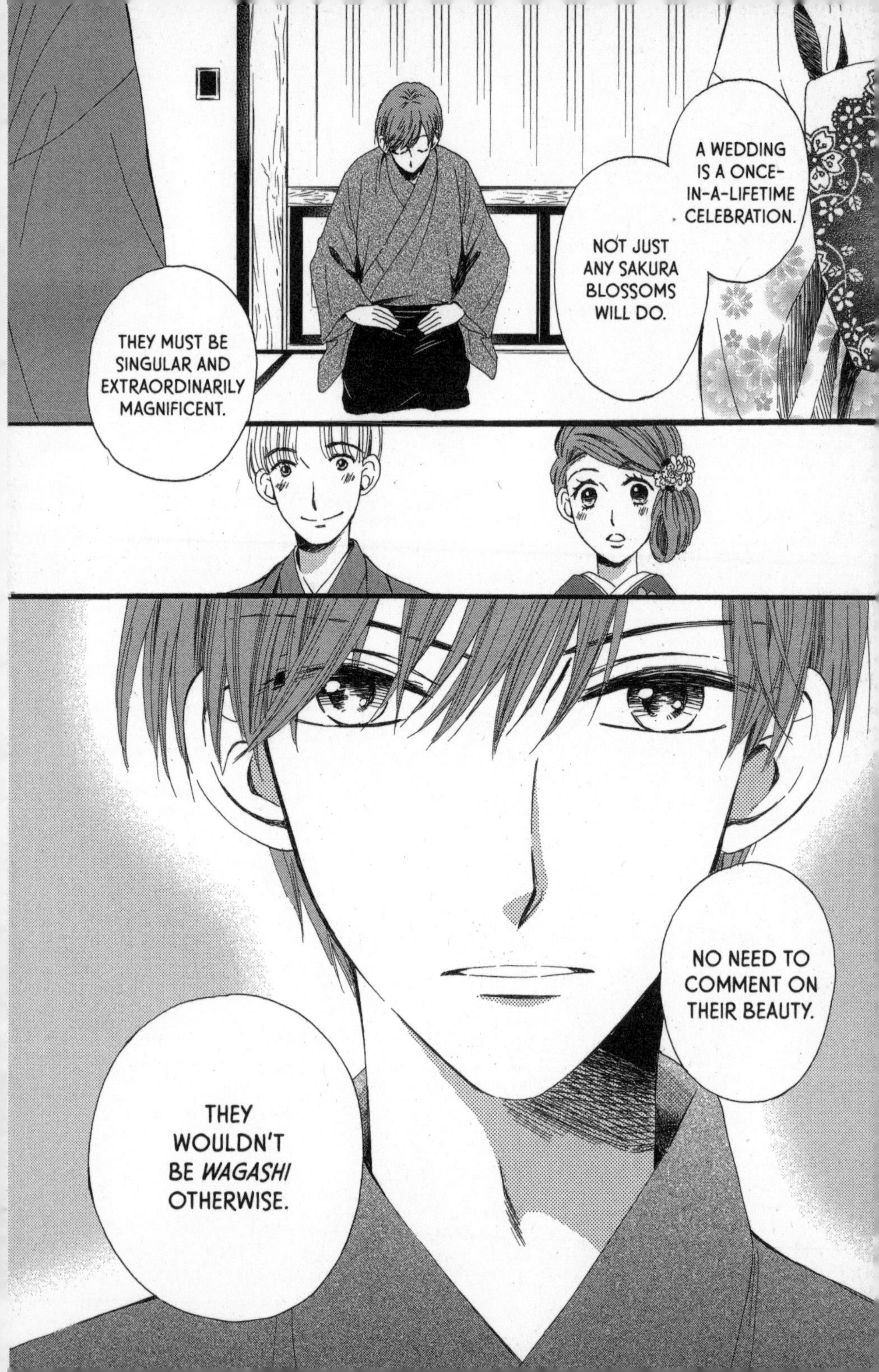
A WEDDING IS A ONCE-IN-A-LIFETIME CELEBRATION.
NOT JUST ANY SAKURA BLOSSOMS WILL DO.
THEY MUST BE SINGULAR AND EXTRAORDINARILY MAGNIFICENT.
NO NEED TO COMMENT ON THEIR BEAUTY.
THEY WOULDN'T BE *WAGASHI* OTHERWISE.

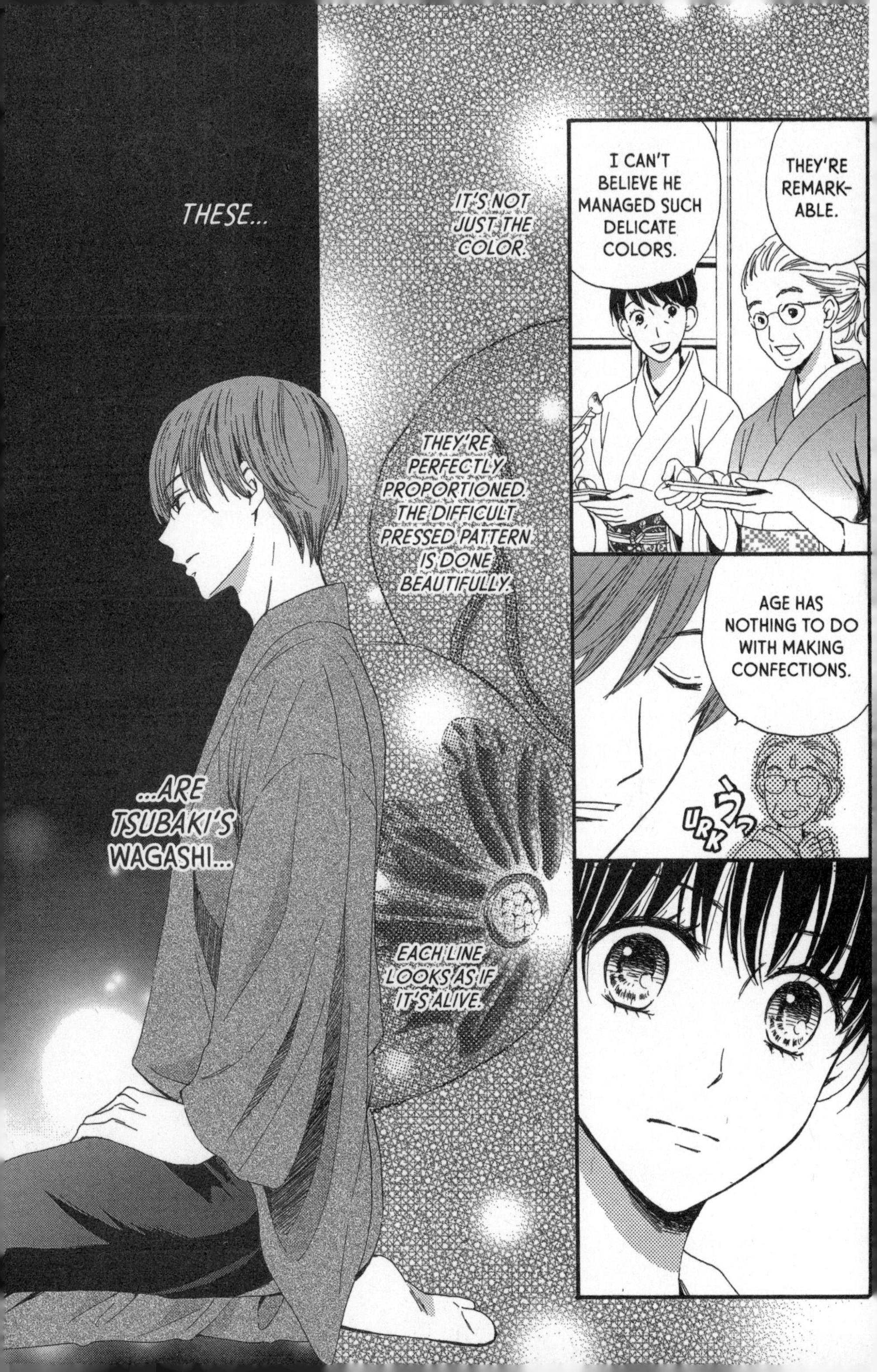
THEY'RE REMARKABLE.
I CAN'T BELIEVE HE MANAGED SUCH DELICATE COLORS.
AGE HAS NOTHING TO DO WITH MAKING CONFECTIONS.
うっ
URK
IT'S NOT JUST THE COLOR.
THESE...
THEY'RE PERFECTLY PROPORTIONED. THE DIFFICULT PRESSED PATTERN IS DONE BEAUTIFULLY.
...ARE TSUBAKI'S WAGASHI...
EACH LINE LOOKS AS IF IT'S ALIVE.

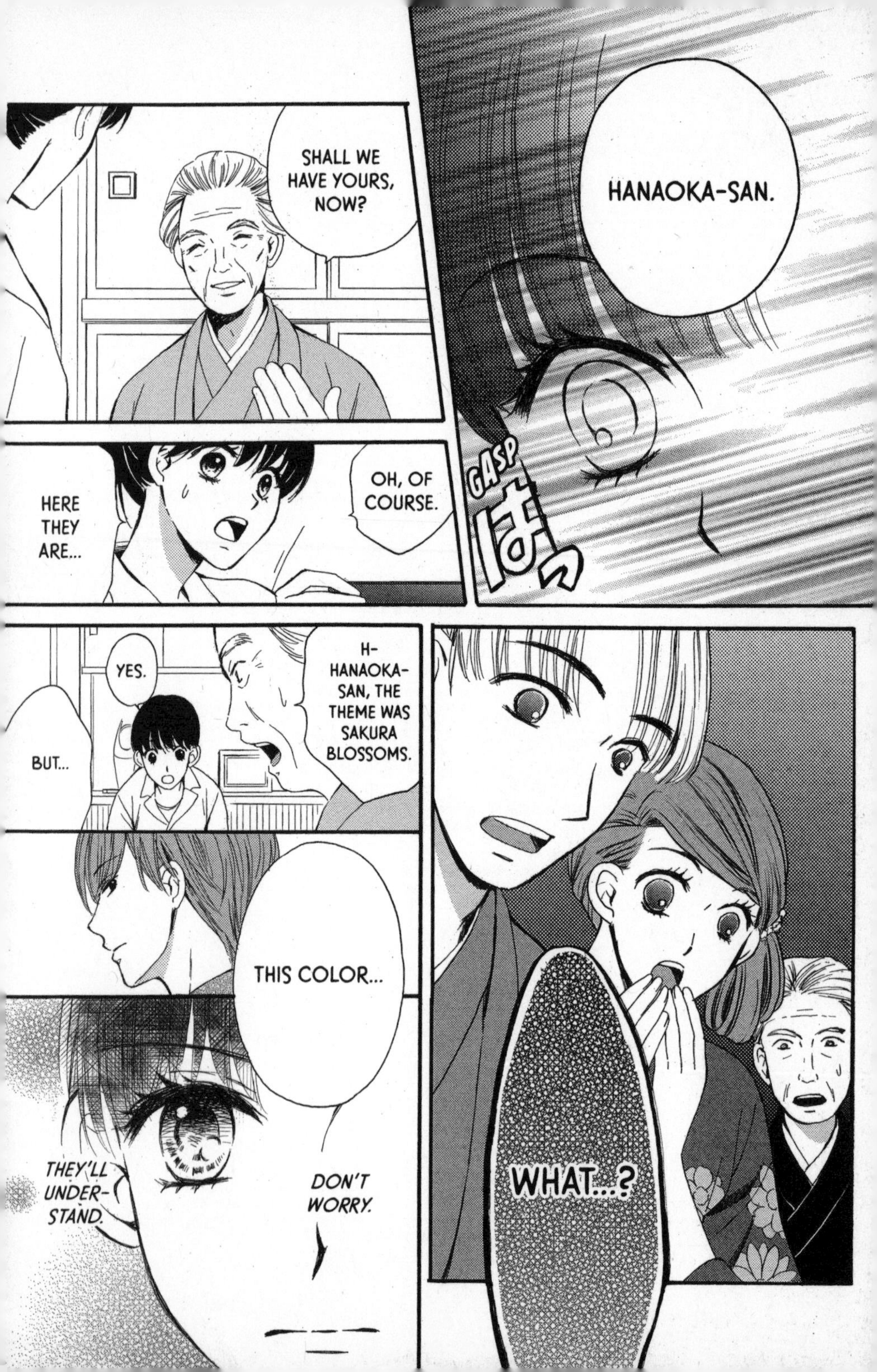
HANAOKA-SAN.
GASP
はっ
SHALL WE HAVE YOURS, NOW?
OH, OF COURSE.
HERE THEY ARE...
WHAT...?
H-HANAOKA-SAN, THE THEME WAS SAKURA BLOSSOMS.
YES.
BUT...
THIS COLOR...
DON'T WORRY.
THEY'LL UNDER-STAND.

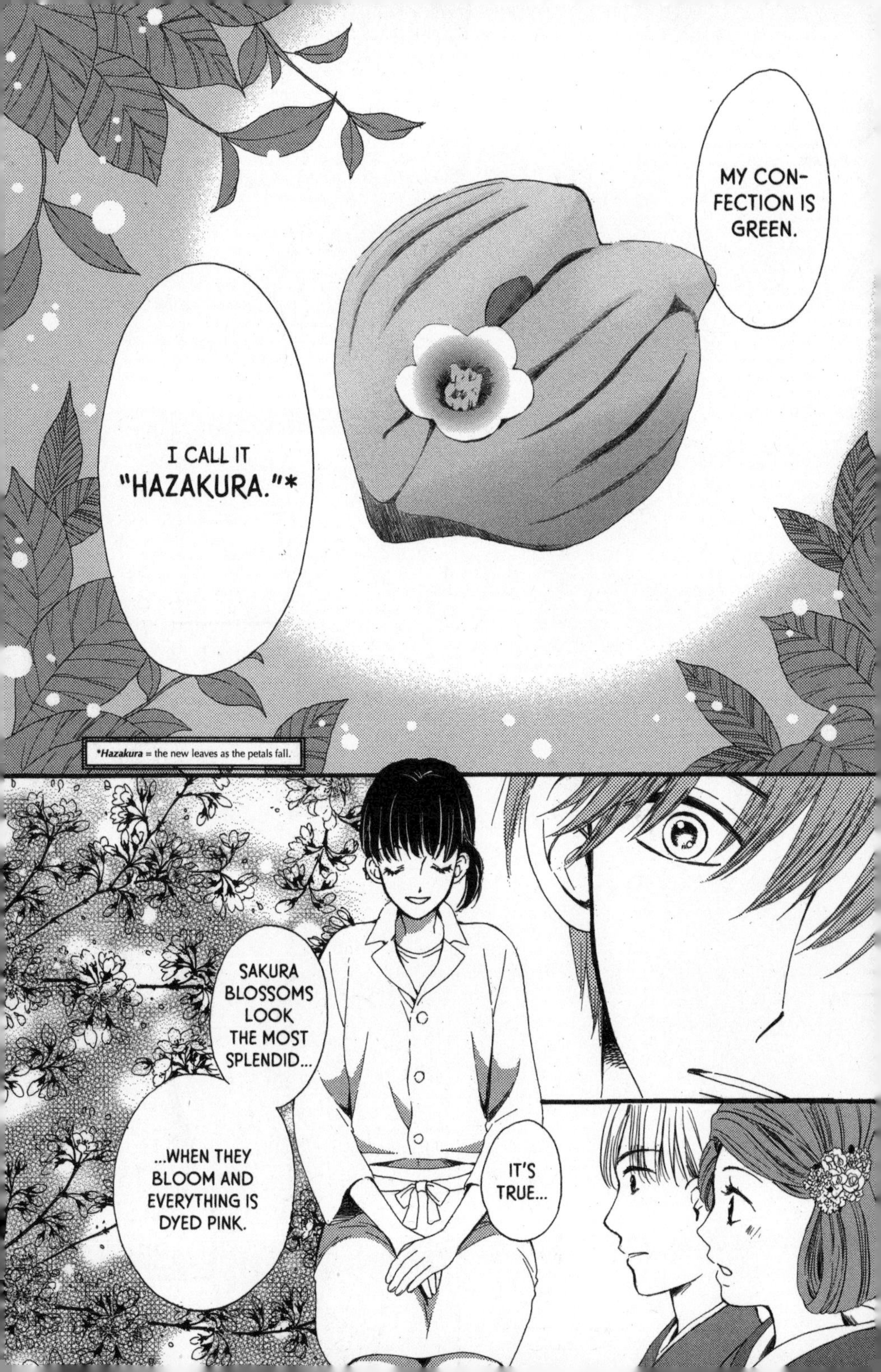
MY CON-FECTION IS GREEN.
I CALL IT "HAZAKURA."*
*Hazakura = the new leaves as the petals fall.
SAKURA BLOSSOMS LOOK THE MOST SPLENDID...
...WHEN THEY BLOOM AND EVERYTHING IS DYED PINK.
IT'S TRUE...

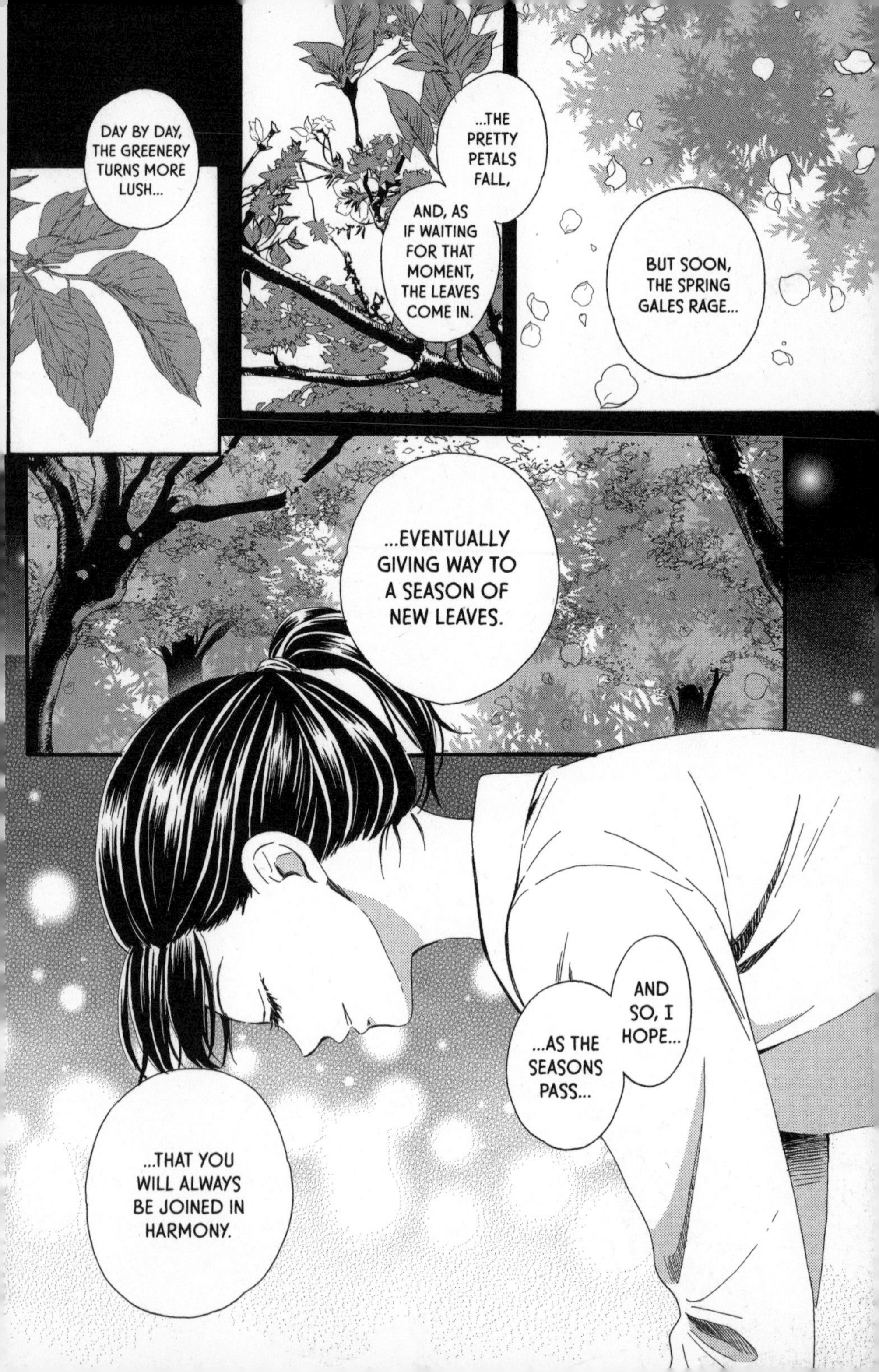
BUT SOON, THE SPRING GALES RAGE...
...THE PRETTY PETALS FALL,
AND, AS IF WAITING FOR THAT MOMENT, THE LEAVES COME IN.
DAY BY DAY, THE GREENERY TURNS MORE LUSH...
...EVENTUALLY GIVING WAY TO A SEASON OF NEW LEAVES.
AND SO, I HOPE...
...AS THE SEASONS PASS...
...THAT YOU WILL ALWAYS BE JOINED IN HARMONY.

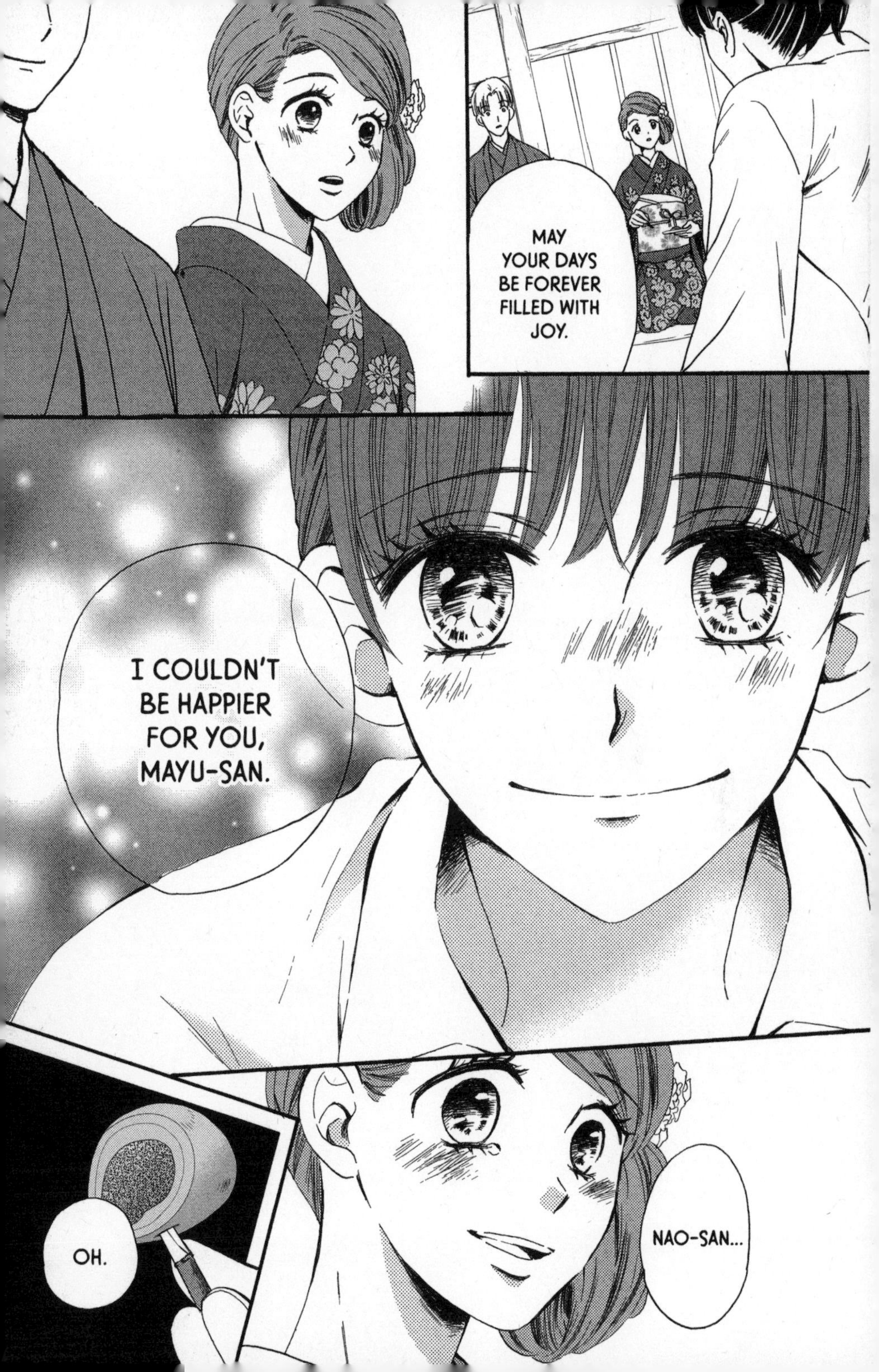
MAY YOUR DAYS BE FOREVER FILLED WITH JOY.
I COULDN'T BE HAPPIER FOR YOU, MAYU-SAN.
NAO-SAN...
OH.

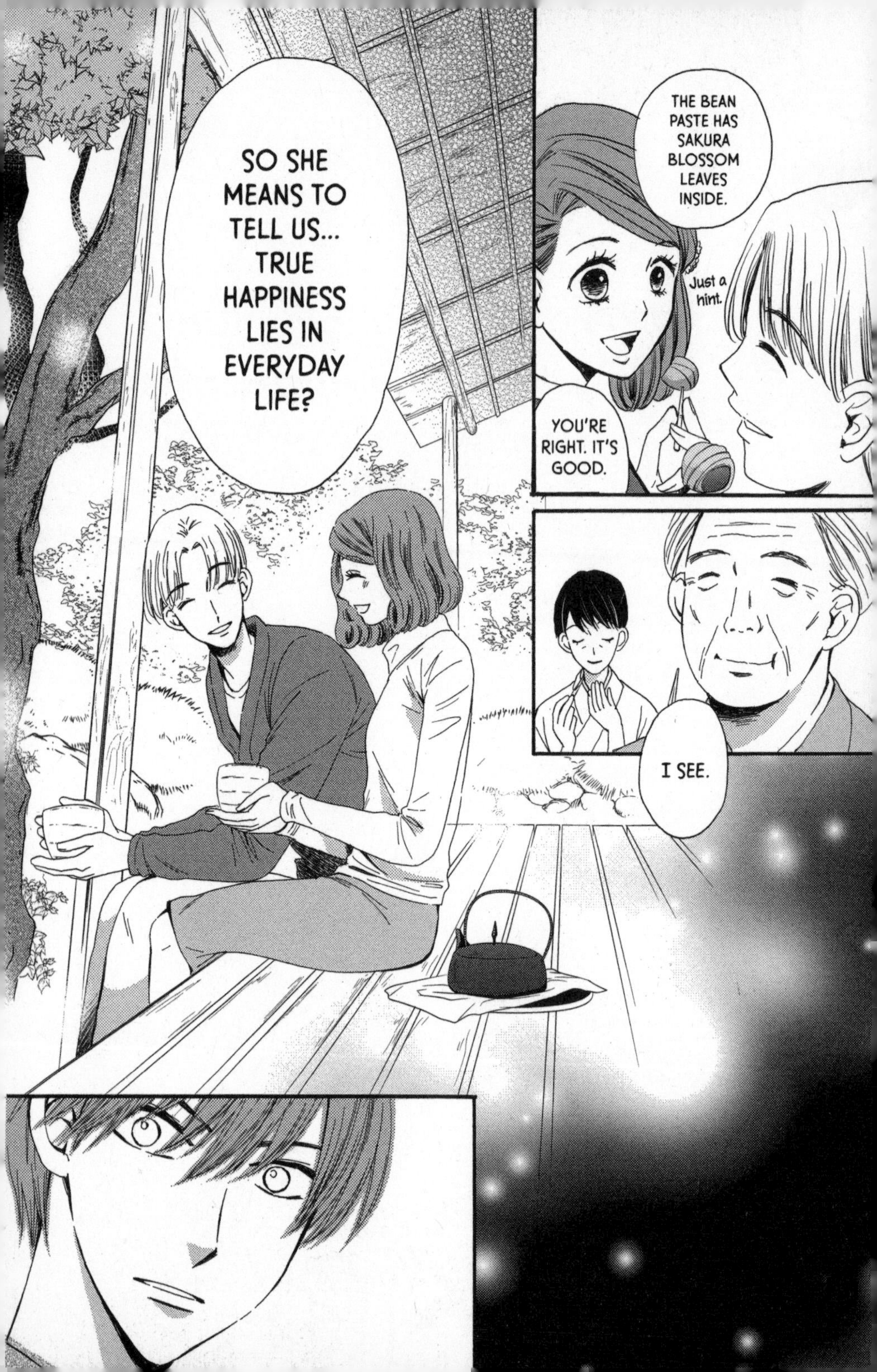
THE BEAN PASTE HAS SAKURA BLOSSOM LEAVES INSIDE.
Just a hint.
YOU'RE RIGHT. IT'S GOOD.
I SEE.
SO SHE MEANS TO TELL US... TRUE HAPPINESS LIES IN EVERYDAY LIFE?

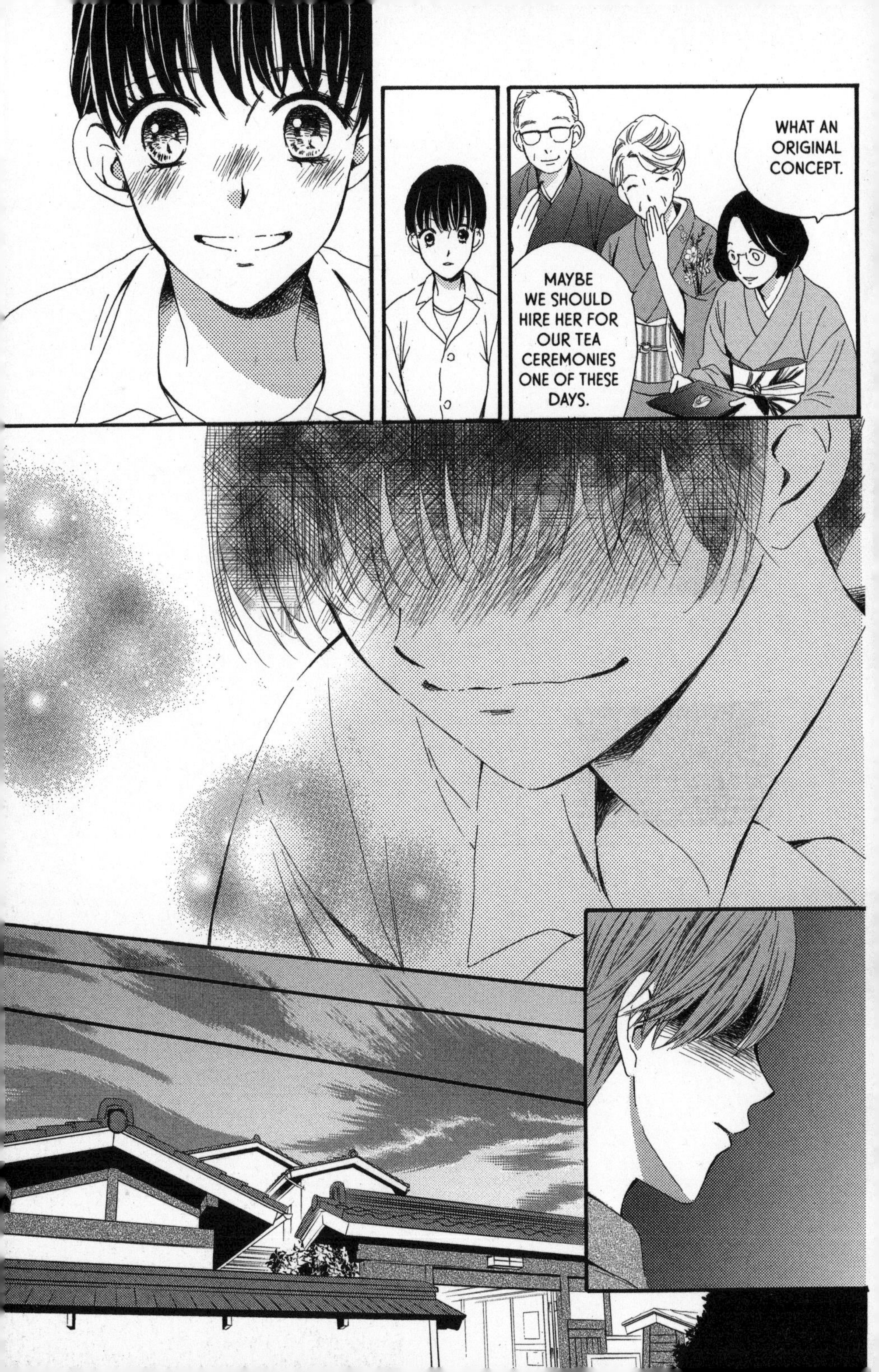
WHAT AN ORIGINAL CONCEPT.
MAYBE WE SHOULD HIRE HER FOR OUR TEA CEREMONIES ONE OF THESE DAYS.

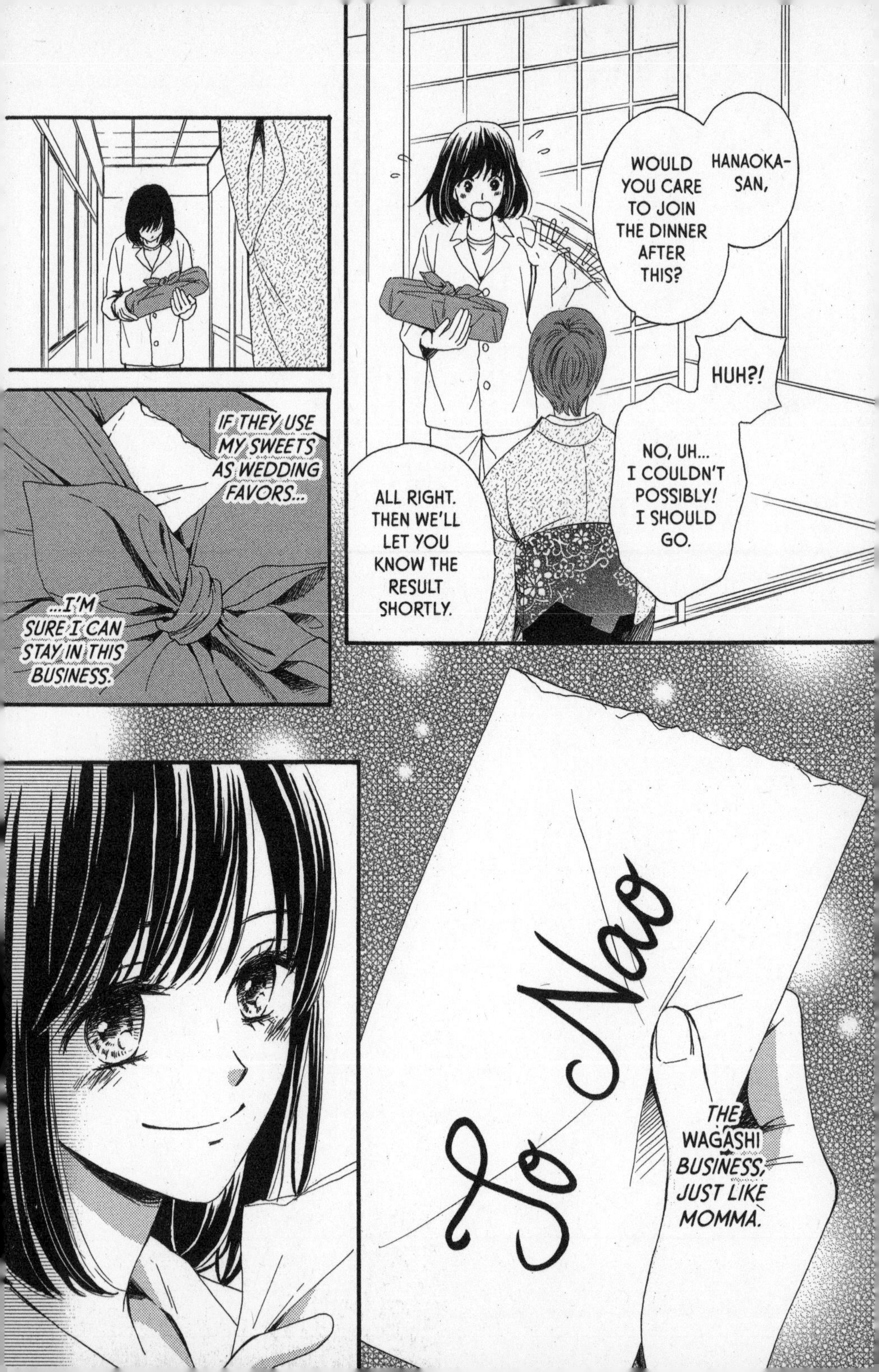
HANAOKA-SAN, WOULD YOU CARE TO JOIN THE DINNER AFTER THIS?
HUH?!
NO, UH... I COULDN'T POSSIBLY! I SHOULD GO.
ALL RIGHT. THEN WE'LL LET YOU KNOW THE RESULT SHORTLY.
IF THEY USE MY SWEETS AS WEDDING FAVORS...
...I'M SURE I CAN STAY IN THIS BUSINESS.
To Nao
THE WAGASHI BUSINESS, JUST LIKE MOMMA.

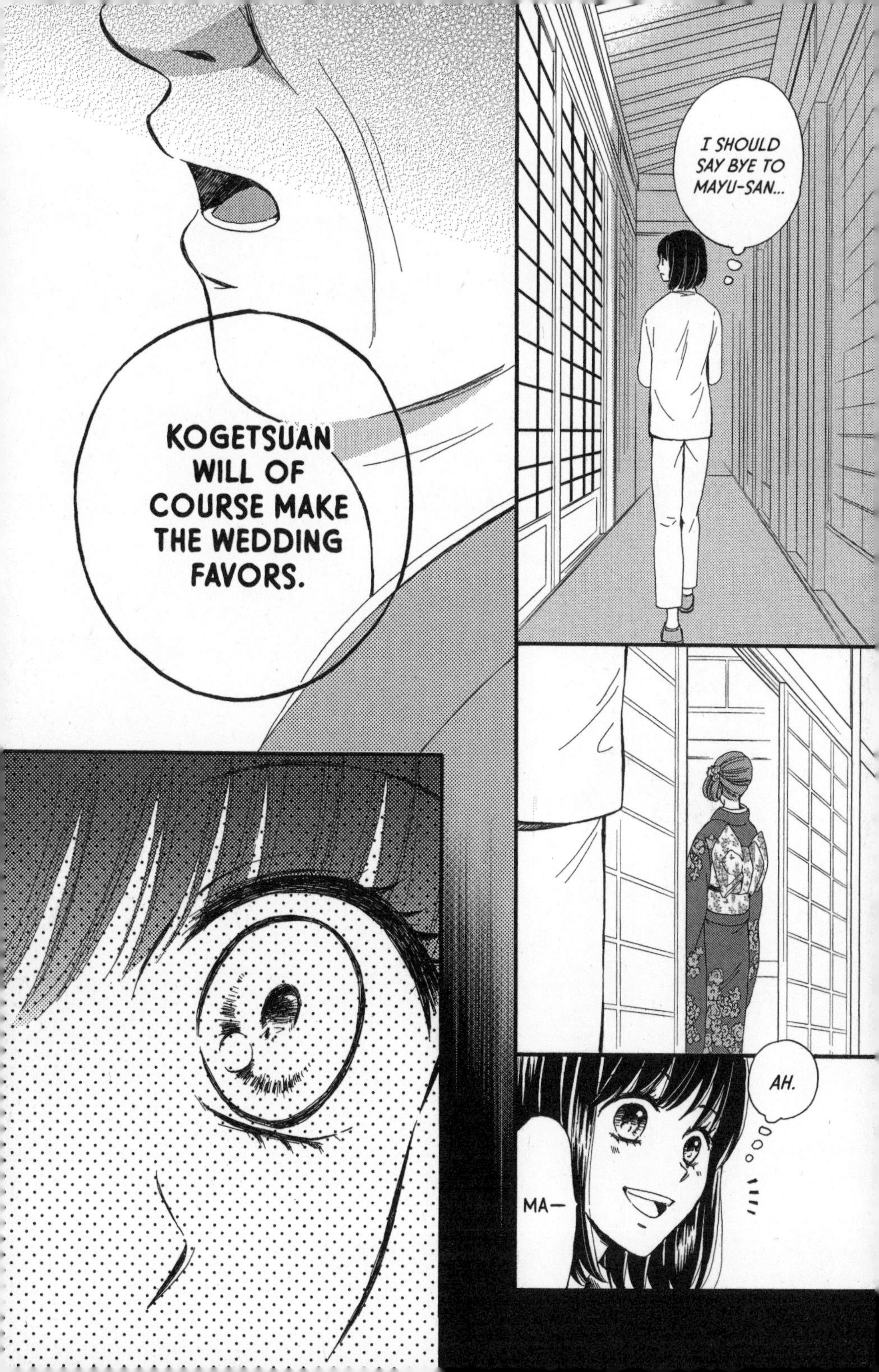
I SHOULD SAY BYE TO MAYU-SAN...
AH.
MA—
KOGETSUAN WILL OF COURSE MAKE THE WEDDING FAVORS.

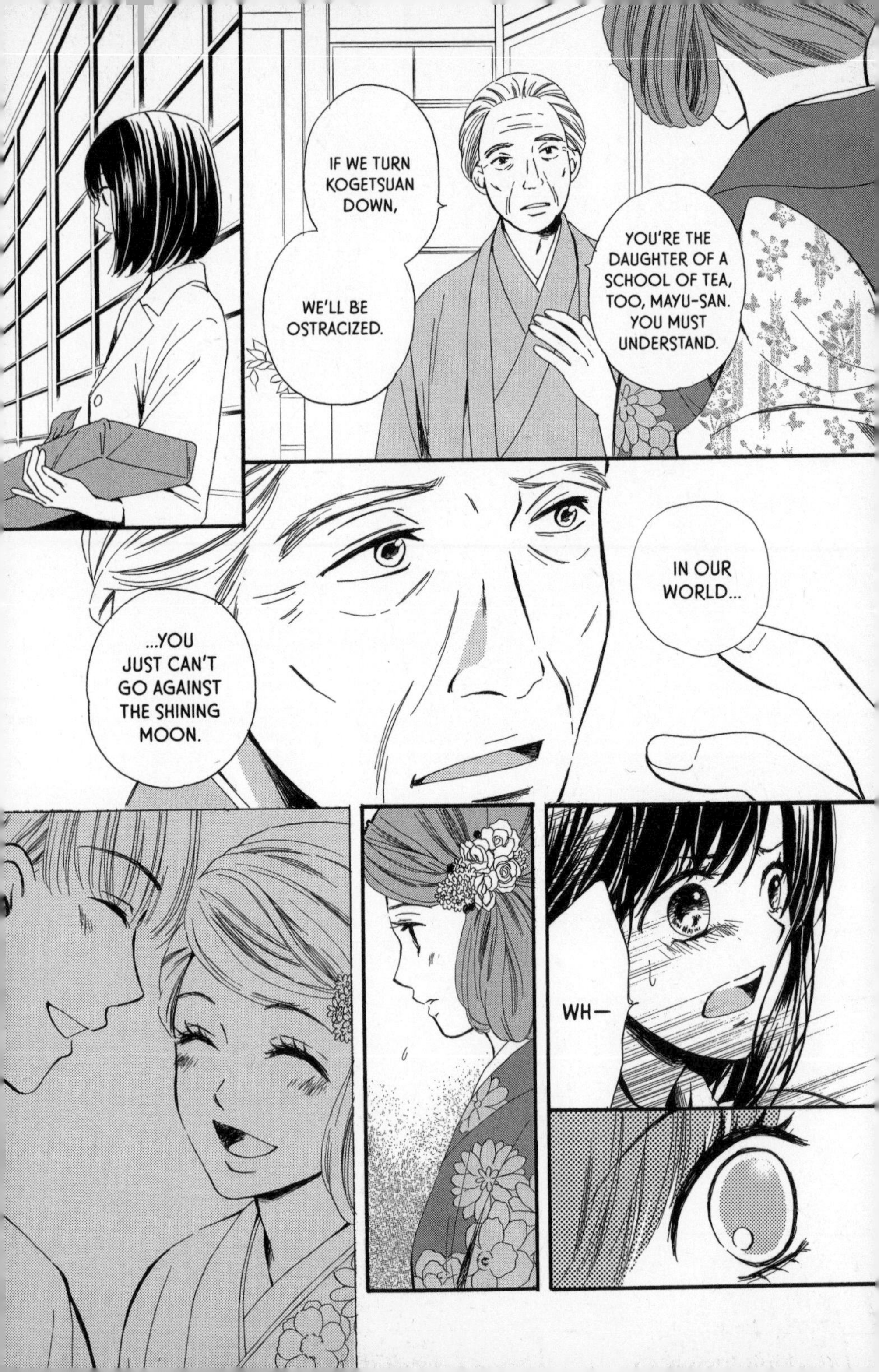
YOU'RE THE DAUGHTER OF A SCHOOL OF TEA, TOO, MAYU-SAN. YOU MUST UNDERSTAND.
IF WE TURN KOGETSUAN DOWN,
WE'LL BE OSTRACIZED.
IN OUR WORLD...
...YOU JUST CAN'T GO AGAINST THE SHINING MOON.
WH—

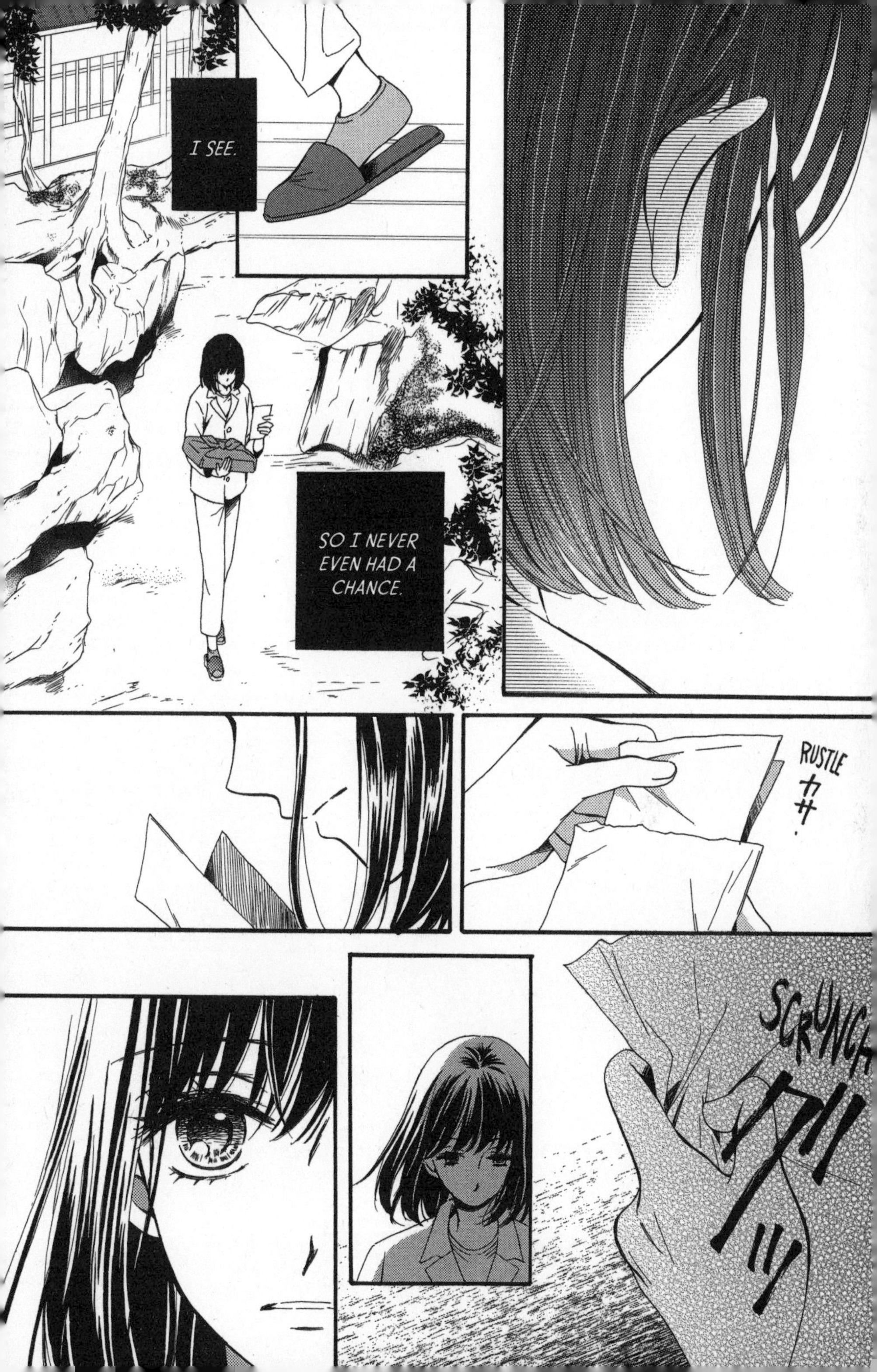
I SEE.
SO I NEVER EVEN HAD A CHANCE.
RUSTLE
SCRUNCH

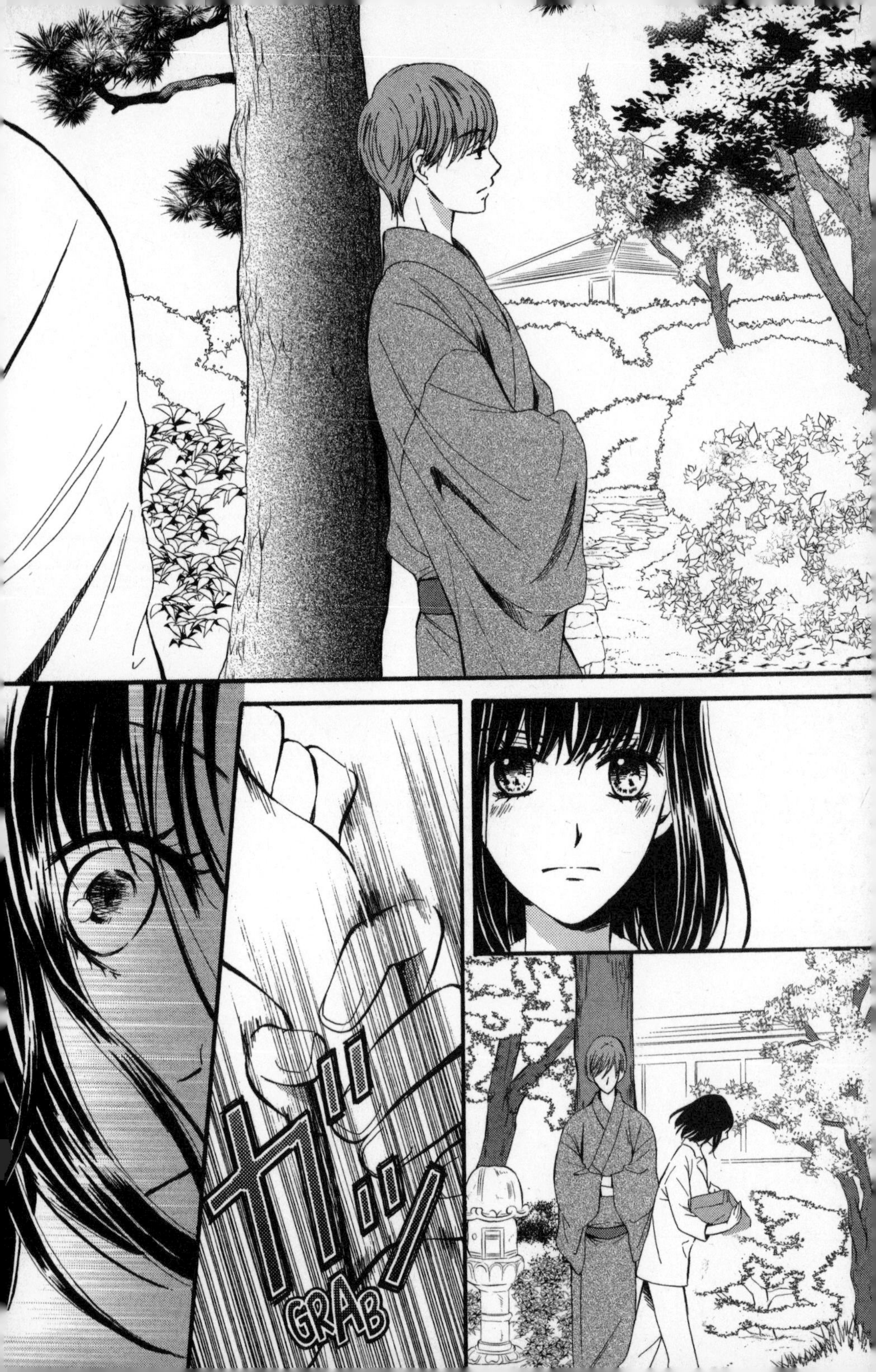
GRAB

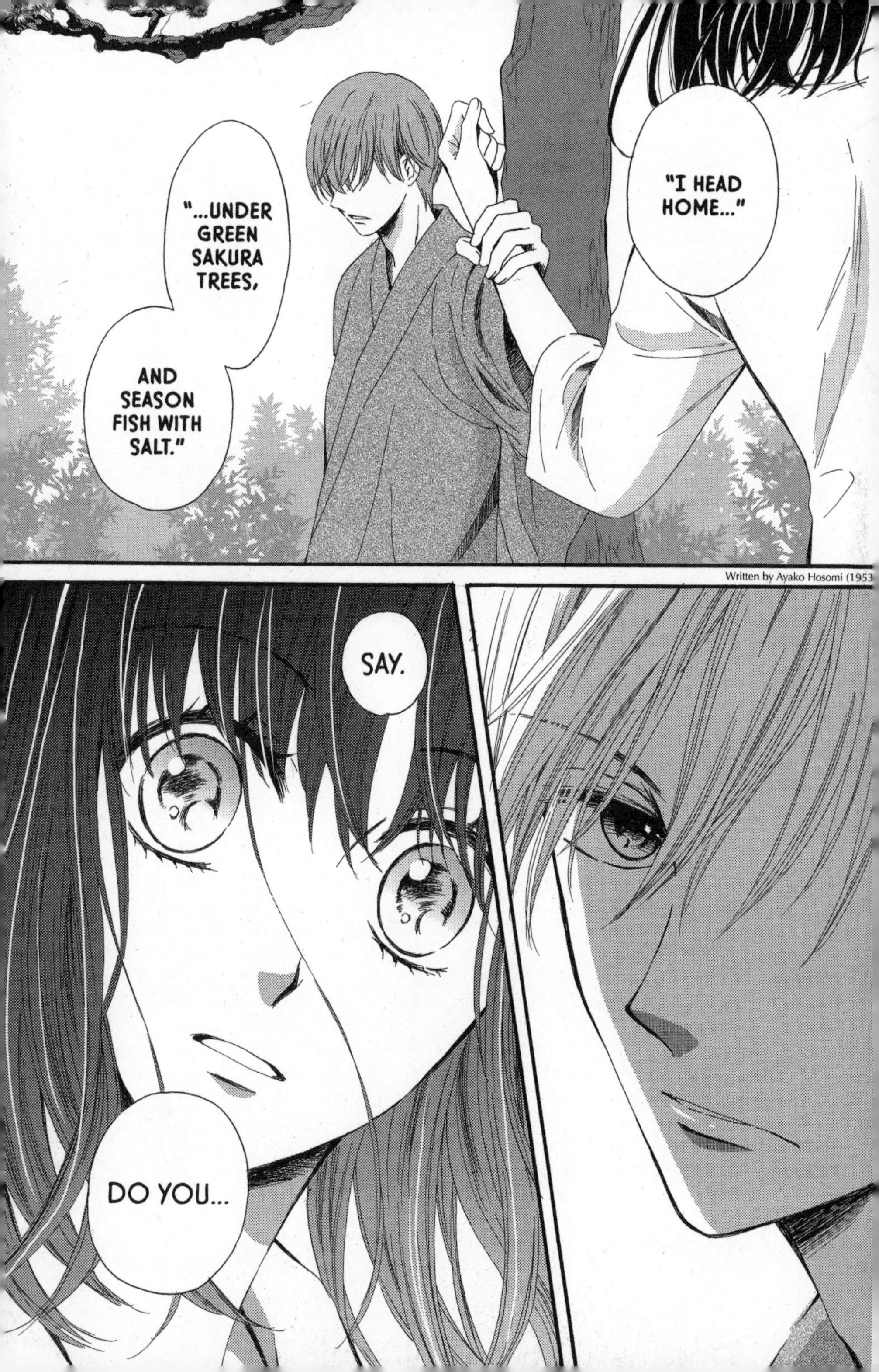
"I HEAD HOME..."
"...UNDER GREEN SAKURA TREES,
AND SEASON FISH WITH SALT."
Written by Ayako Hosomi (1953
SAY.
DO YOU...

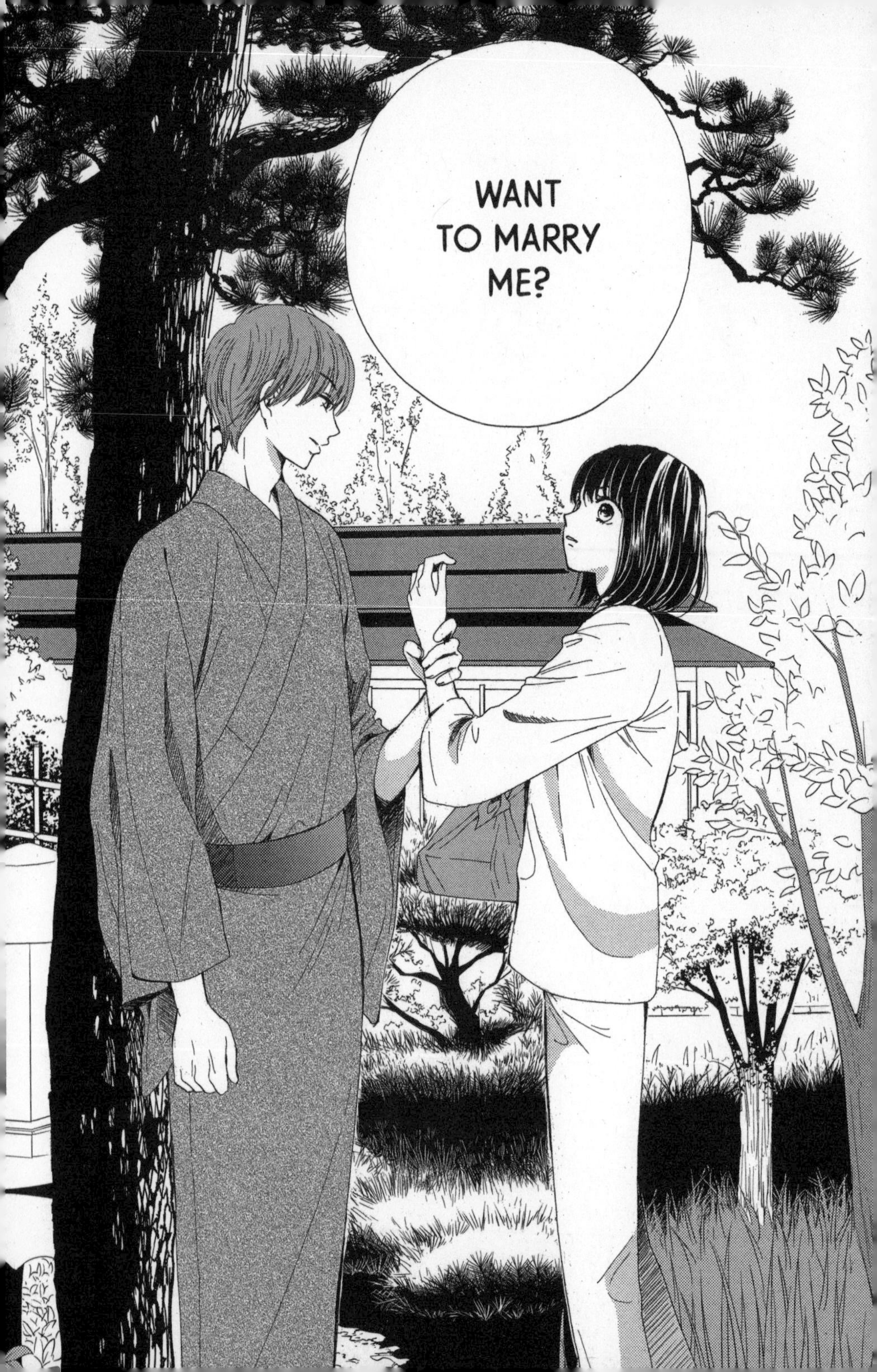
WANT TO MARRY ME?

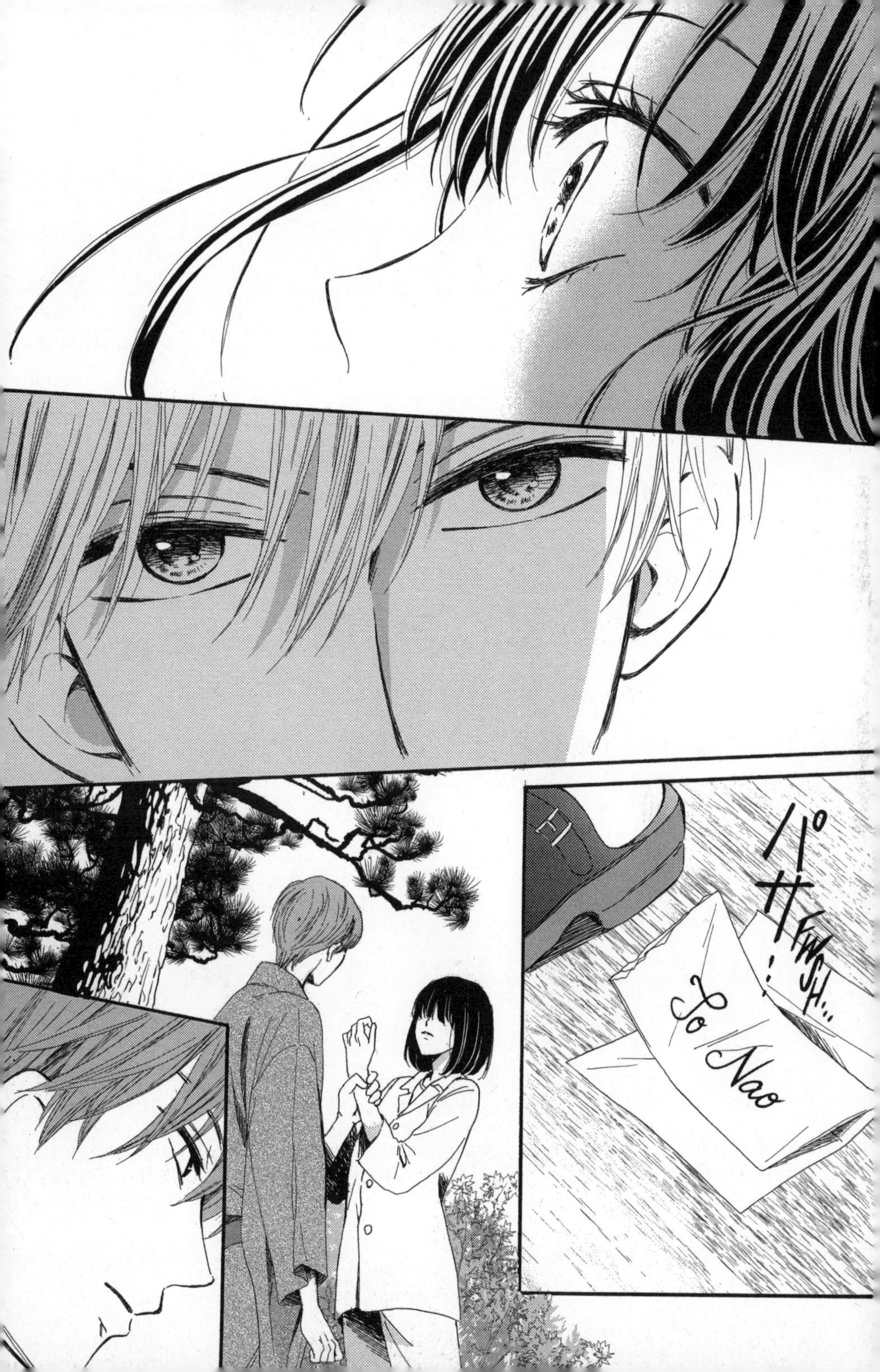
パサ
FWSH...
To Nao

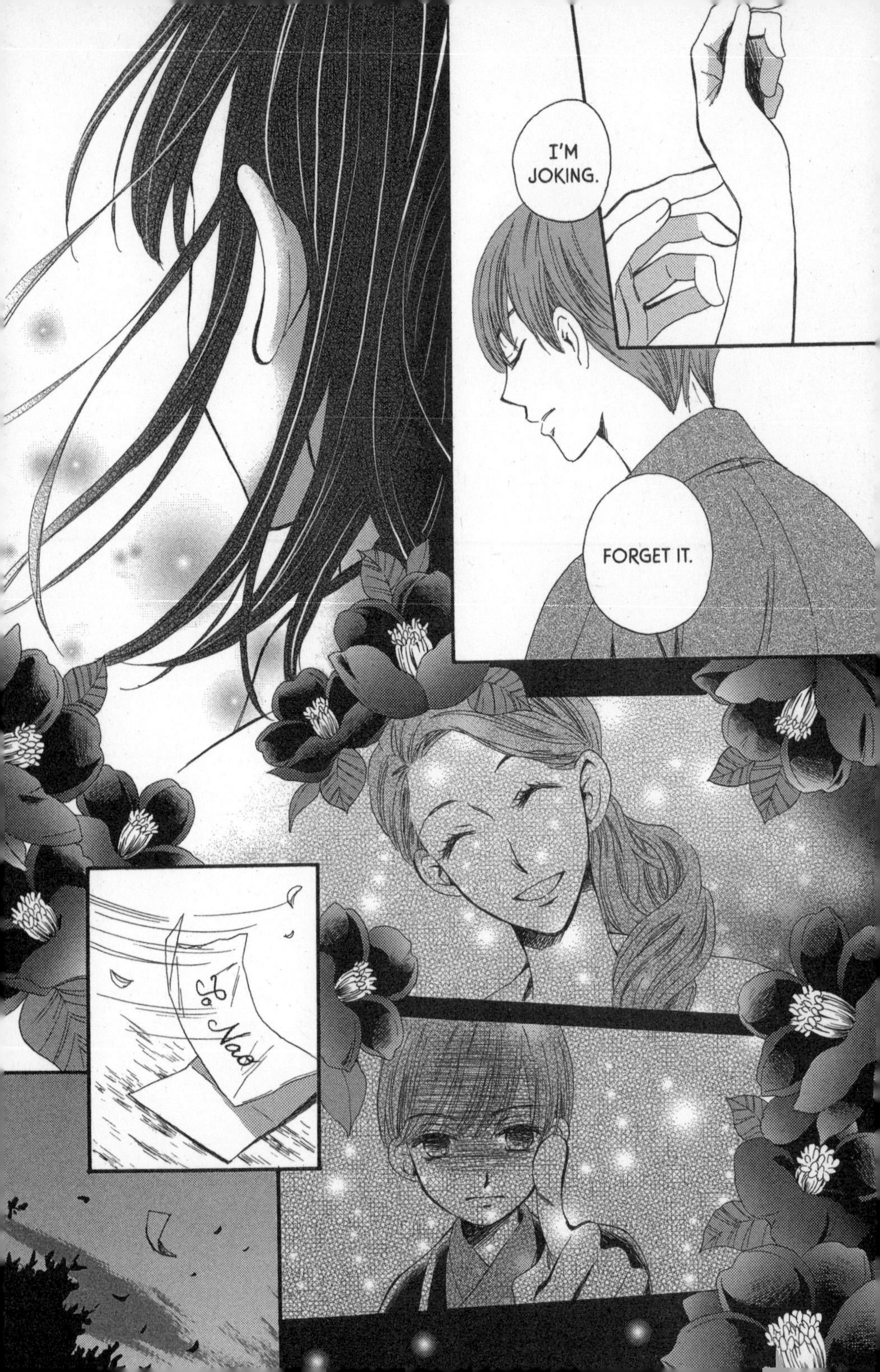
I'M JOKING.
FORGET IT.
To Nao

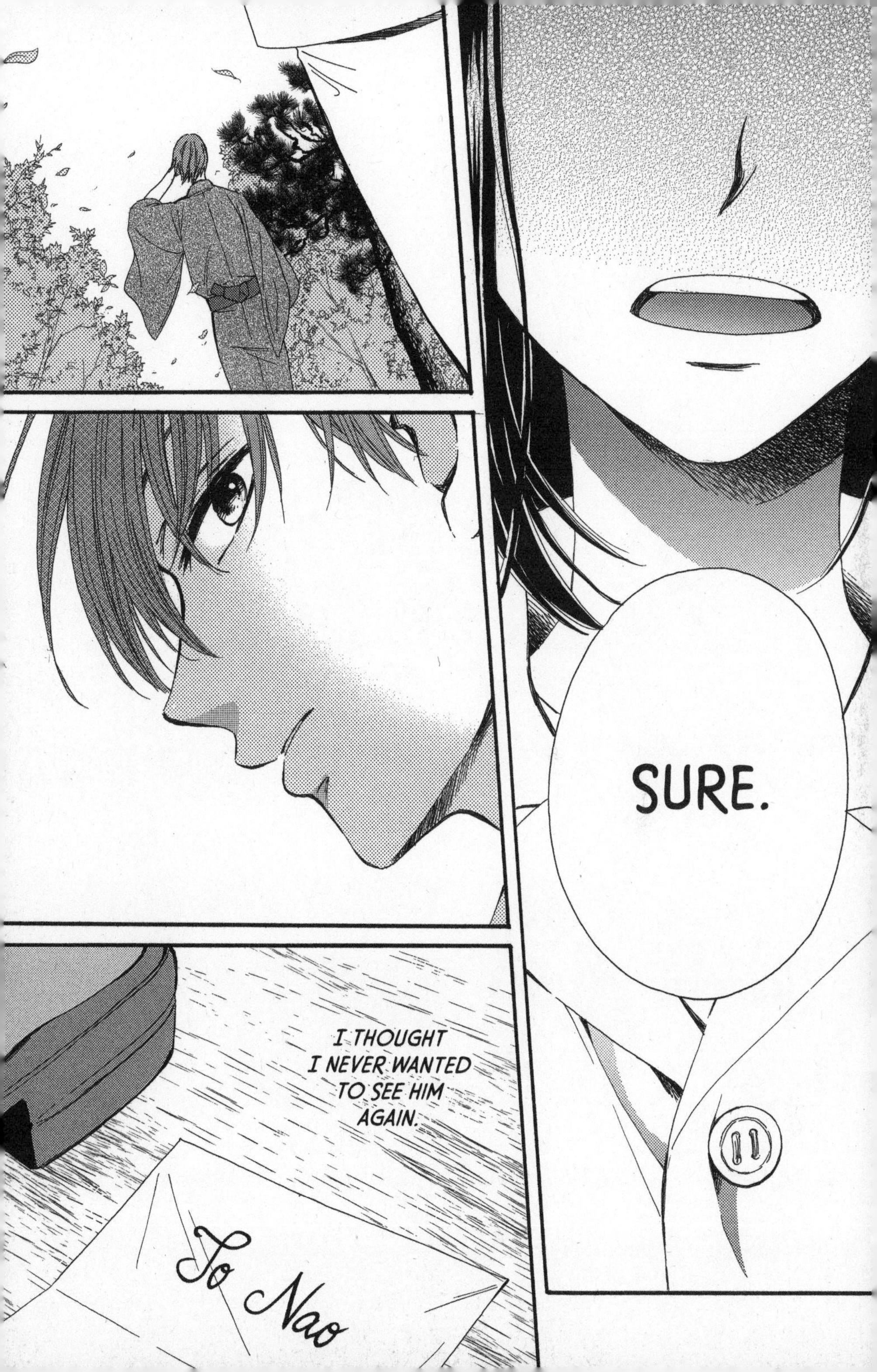
SURE.
I THOUGHT I NEVER WANTED TO SEE HIM AGAIN.
To Nao

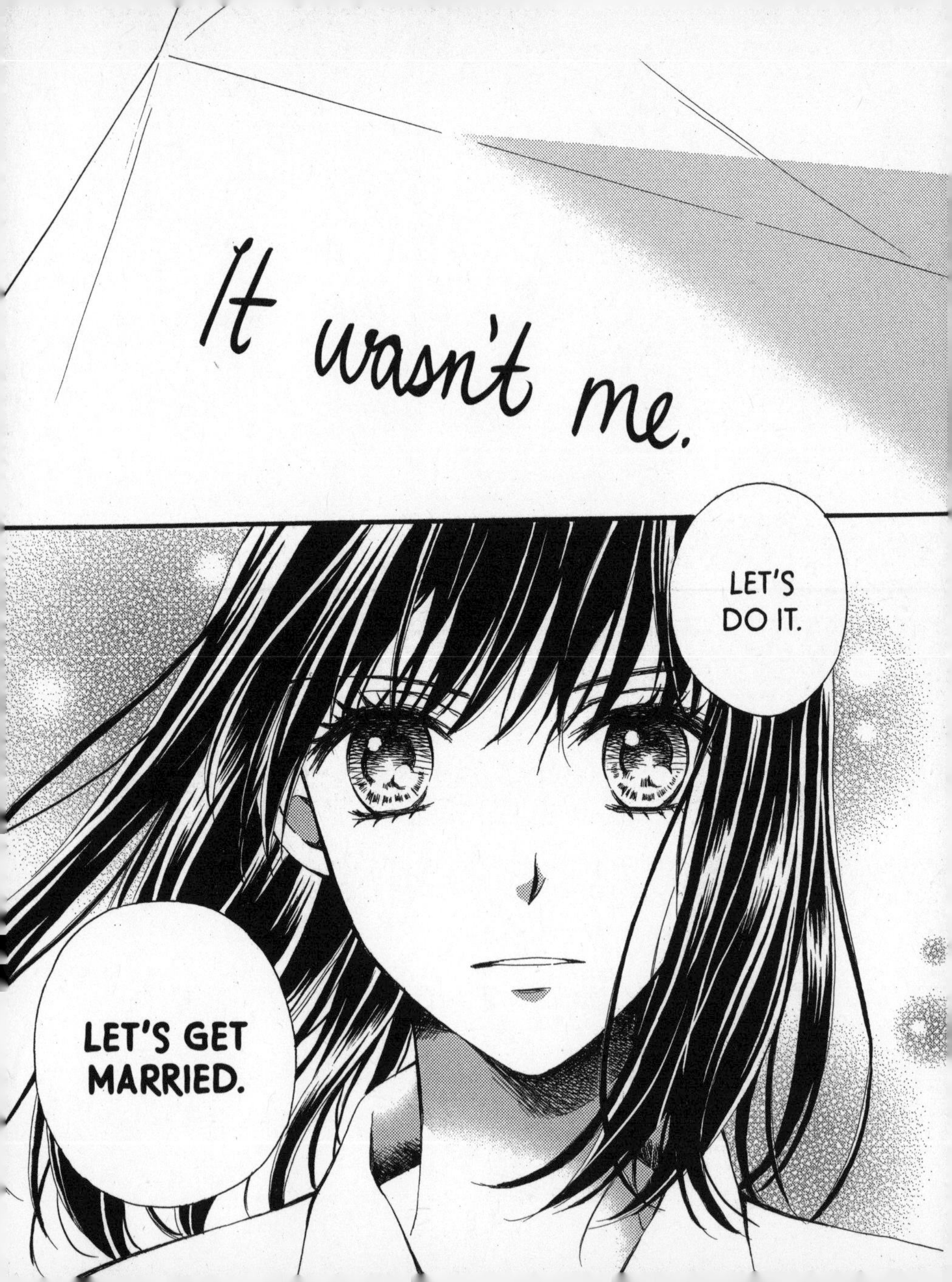
It wasn't me.
LET'S DO IT.
LET'S GET MARRIED.

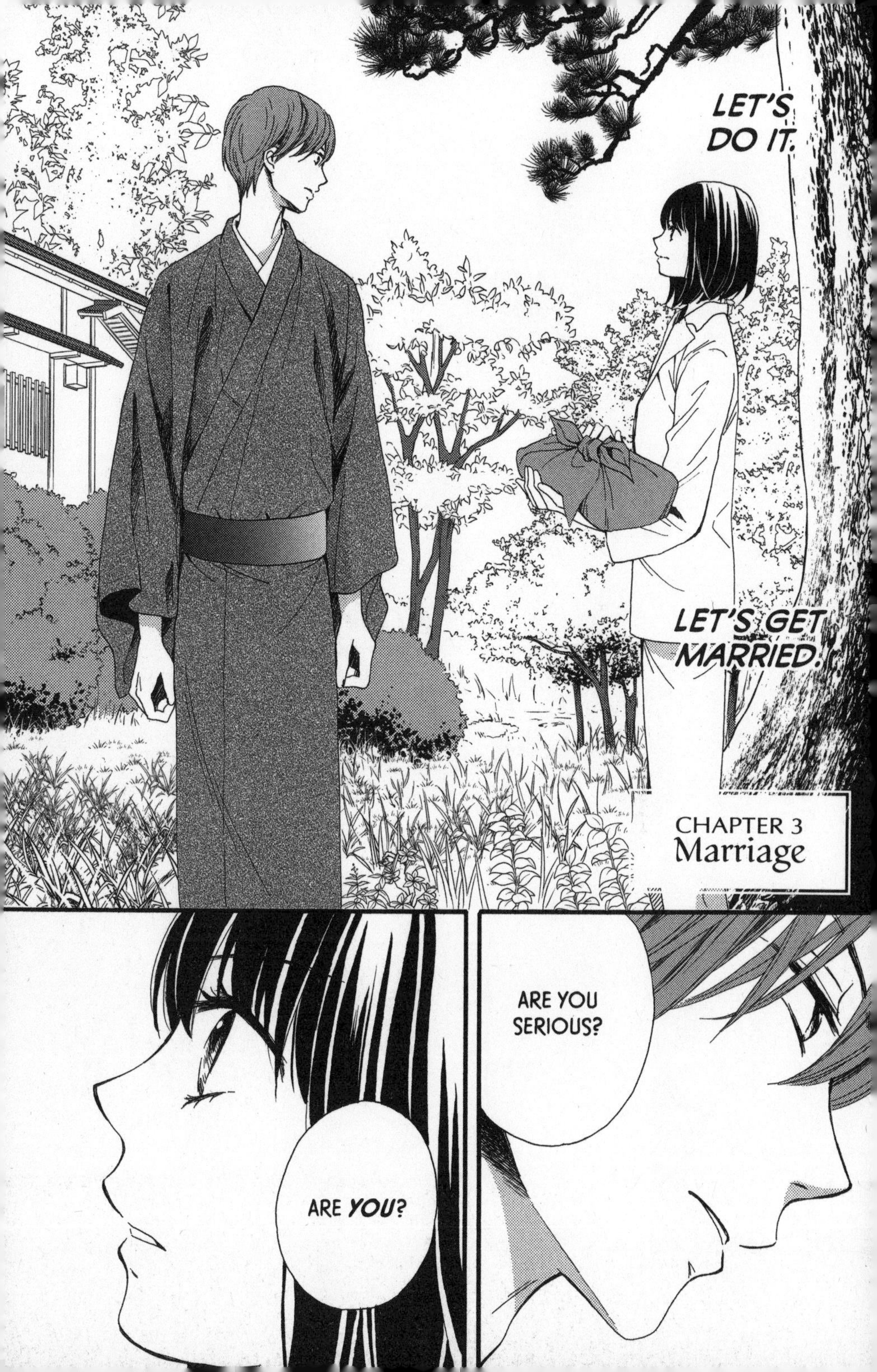
LET'S DO IT.
LET'S GET MARRIED.
CHAPTER 3
Marriage
ARE YOU SERIOUS?
ARE *YOU*?

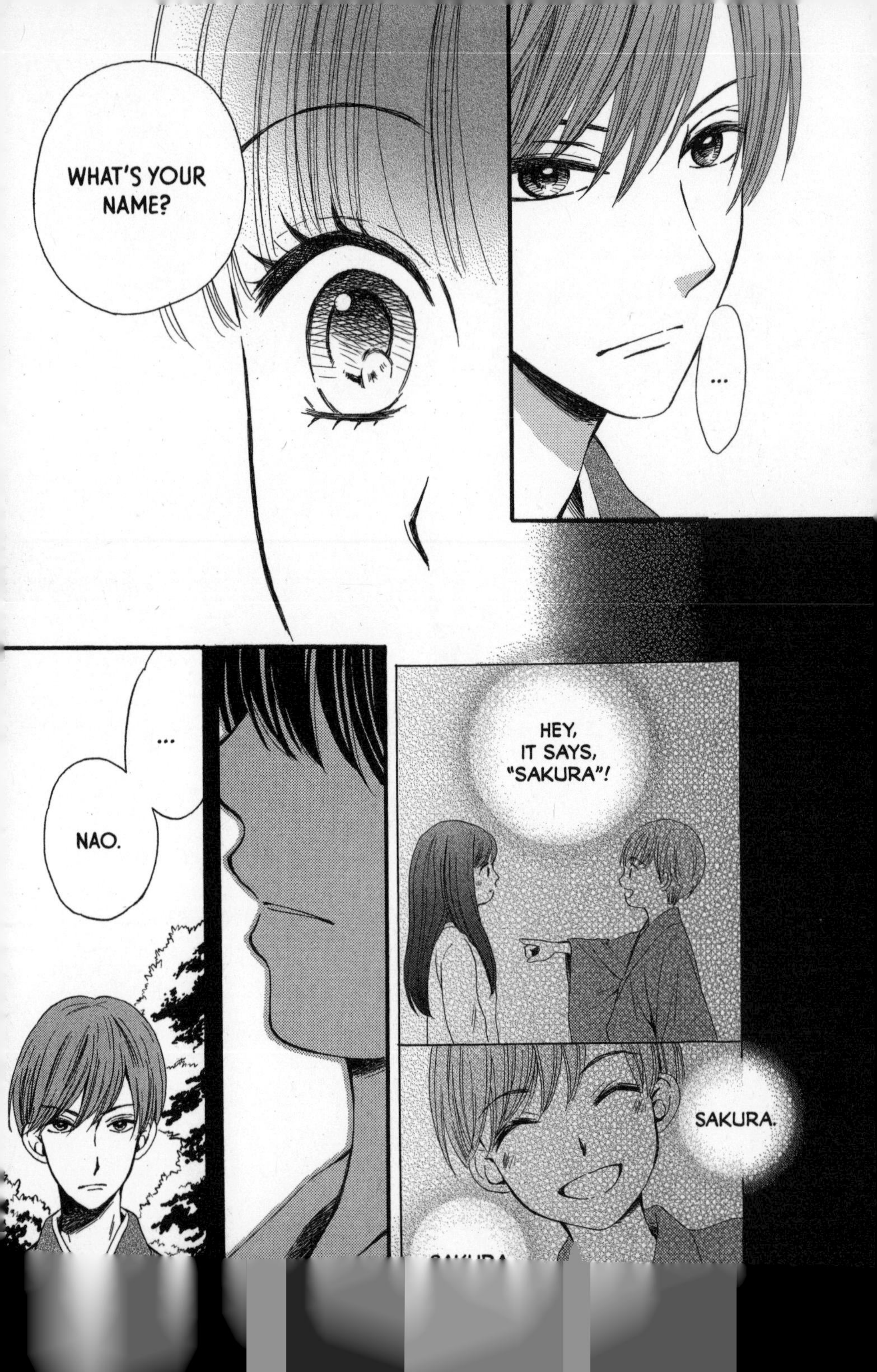
...
WHAT'S YOUR NAME?
HEY, IT SAYS, "SAKURA"!
SAKURA.
...
NAO.

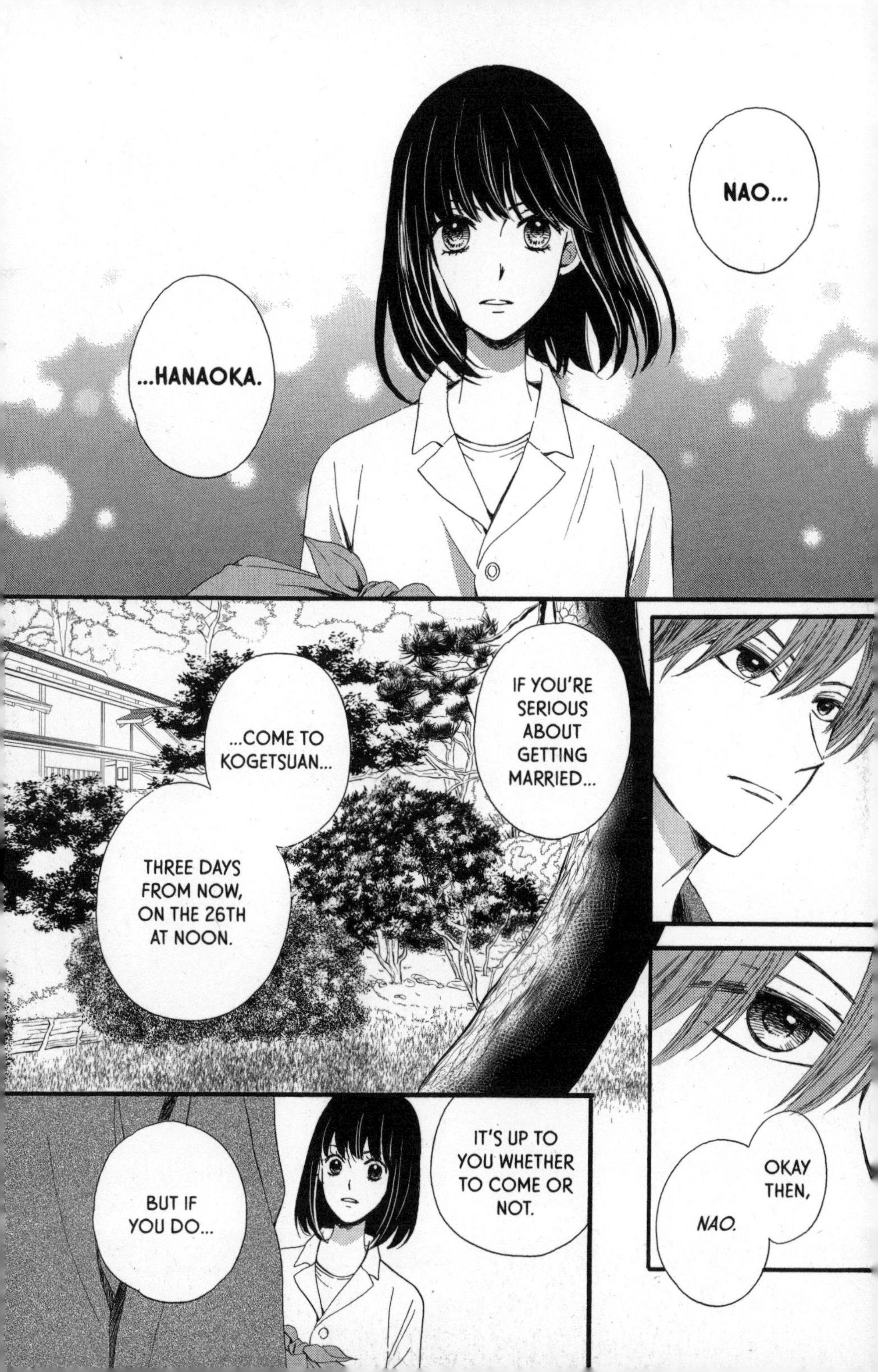
NAO...
...HANAOKA.
IF YOU'RE SERIOUS ABOUT GETTING MARRIED...
...COME TO KOGETSUAN...
THREE DAYS FROM NOW, ON THE 26TH AT NOON.
IT'S UP TO YOU WHETHER TO COME OR NOT.
BUT IF YOU DO...
OKAY THEN, NAO.

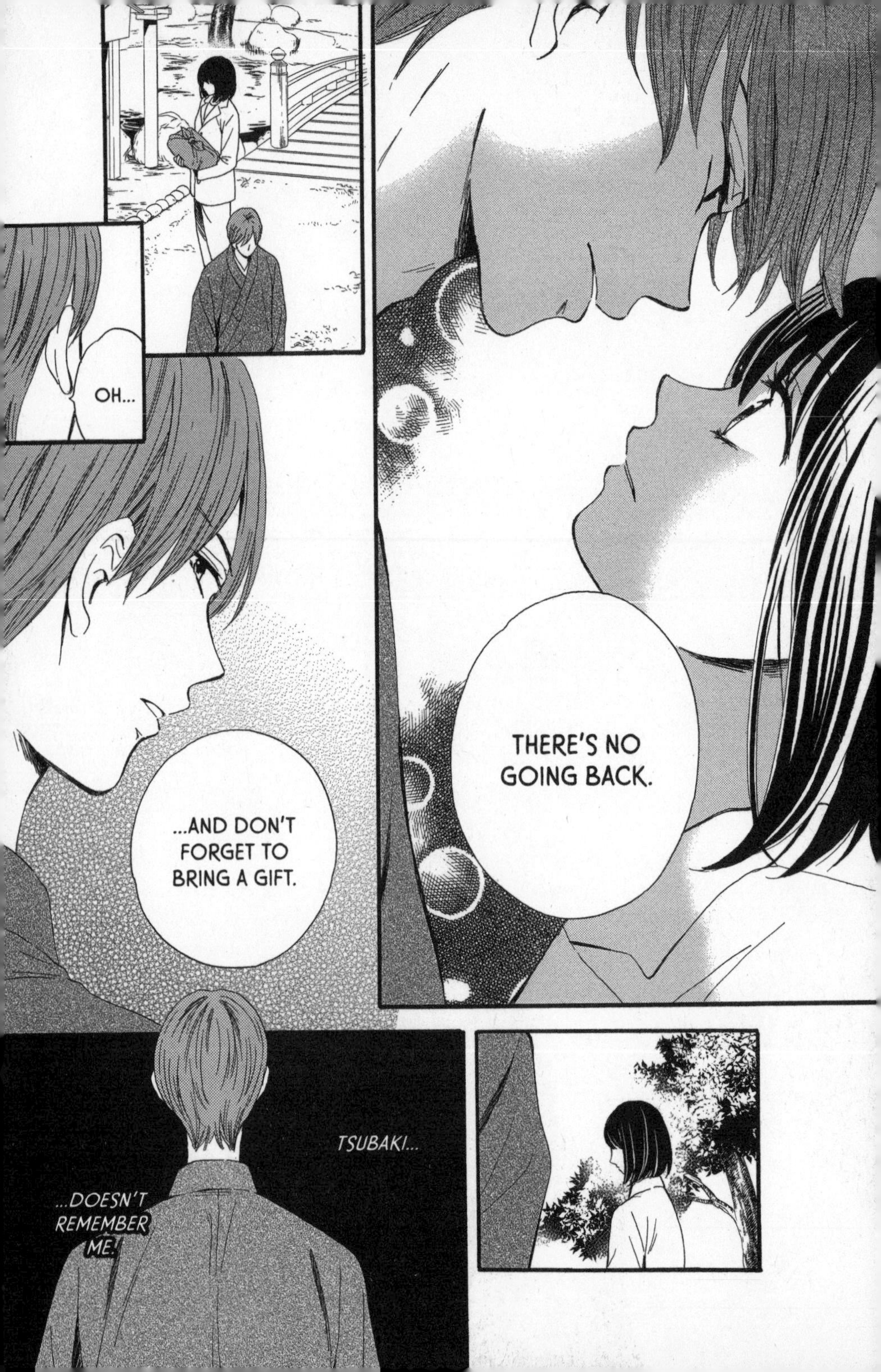
THERE'S NO GOING BACK.
OH...
...AND DON'T FORGET TO BRING A GIFT.
TSUBAKI...
...DOESN'T REMEMBER ME.

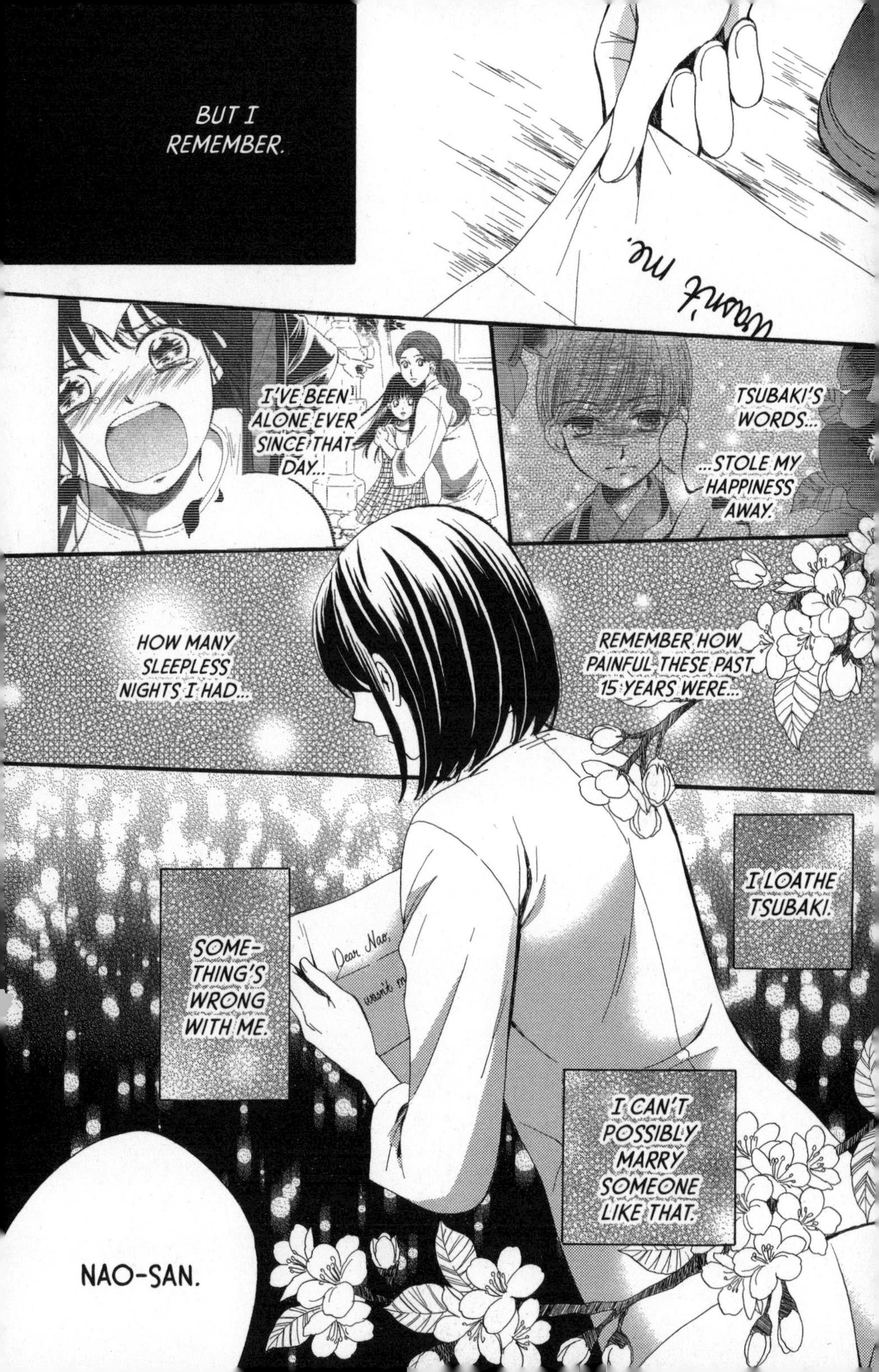

wasn't me.
BUT I REMEMBER.
TSUBAKI'S WORDS...
...STOLE MY HAPPINESS AWAY.
I'VE BEEN ALONE EVER SINCE THAT DAY...
REMEMBER HOW PAINFUL THESE PAST 15 YEARS WERE...
HOW MANY SLEEPLESS NIGHTS I HAD...
I LOATHE TSUBAKI.
SOME-THING'S WRONG WITH ME.
Dear Nao,
I CAN'T POSSIBLY MARRY SOMEONE LIKE THAT.
NAO-SAN.

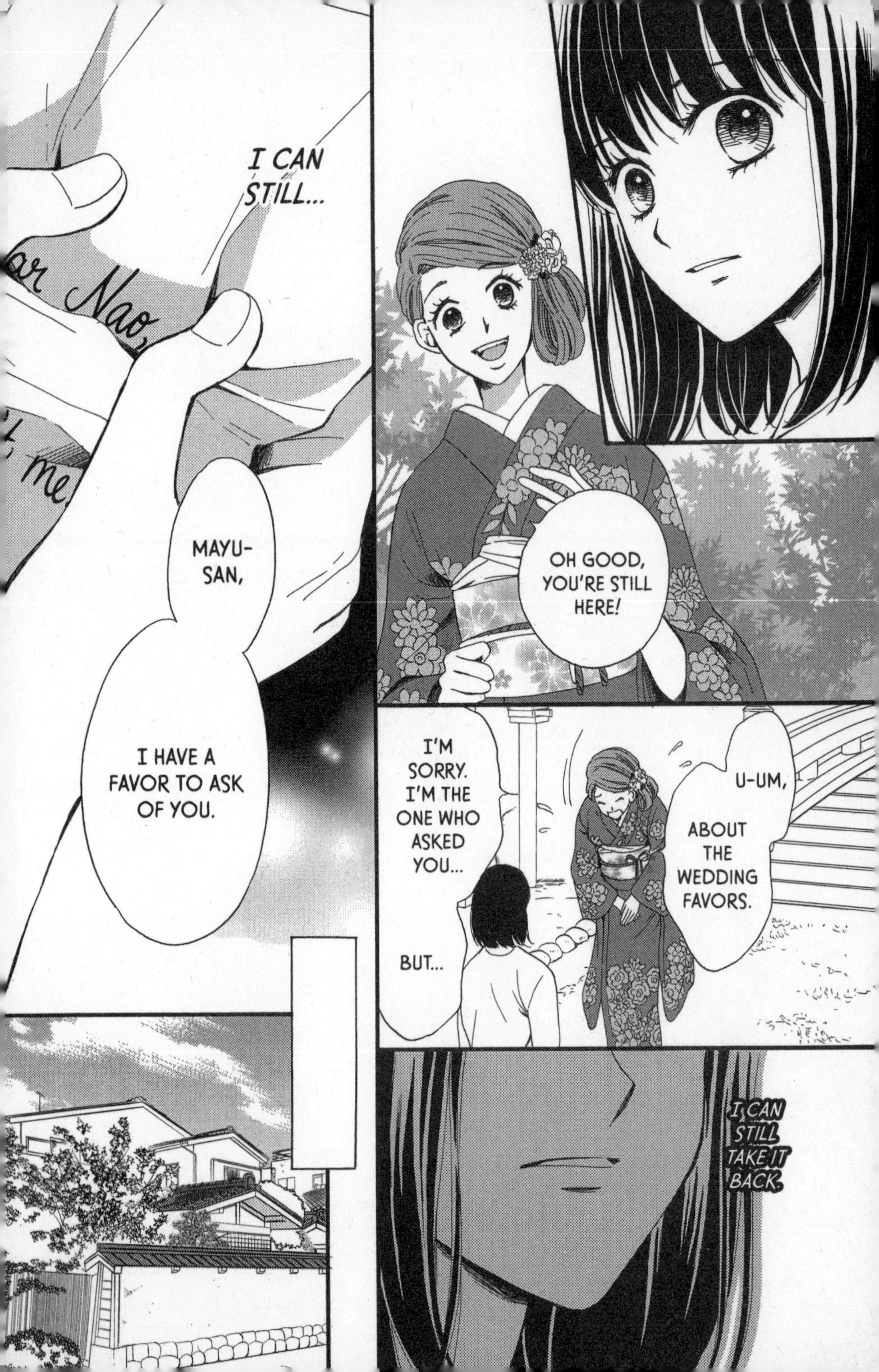
OH GOOD, YOU'RE STILL HERE!
I CAN STILL...
MAYU-SAN,
I HAVE A FAVOR TO ASK OF YOU.
U-UM,
ABOUT THE WEDDING FAVORS.
I'M SORRY. I'M THE ONE WHO ASKED YOU...
BUT...
I CAN STILL TAKE IT BACK.

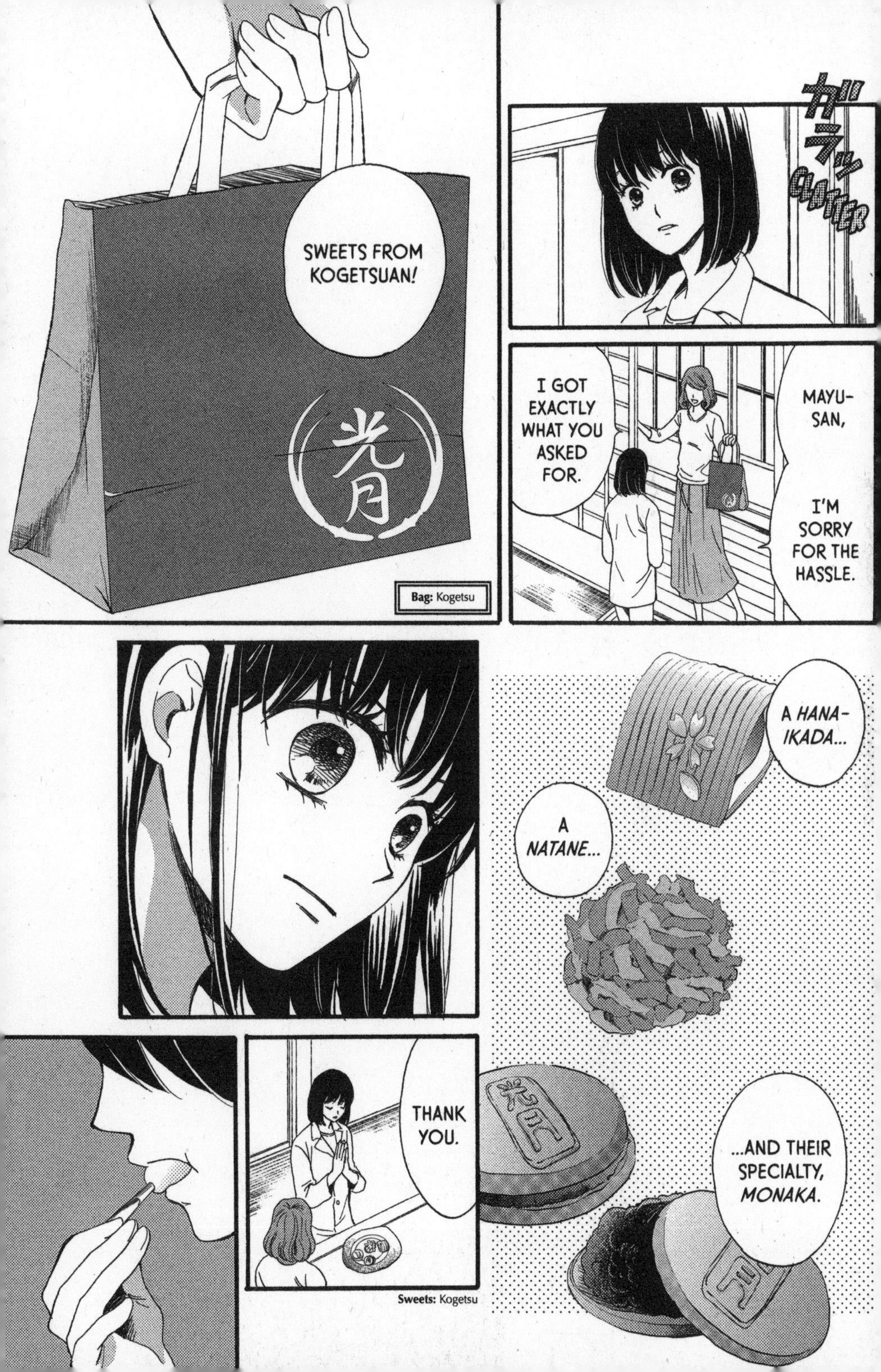
ガラッ
CLATTER
MAYU-SAN,
I'M SORRY FOR THE HASSLE.
I GOT EXACTLY WHAT YOU ASKED FOR.
SWEETS FROM KOGETSUAN!
Bag: Kogetsu
A HANA-IKADA...
A NATANE...
...AND THEIR SPECIALTY, MONAKA.
THANK YOU.
Sweets: Kogetsu

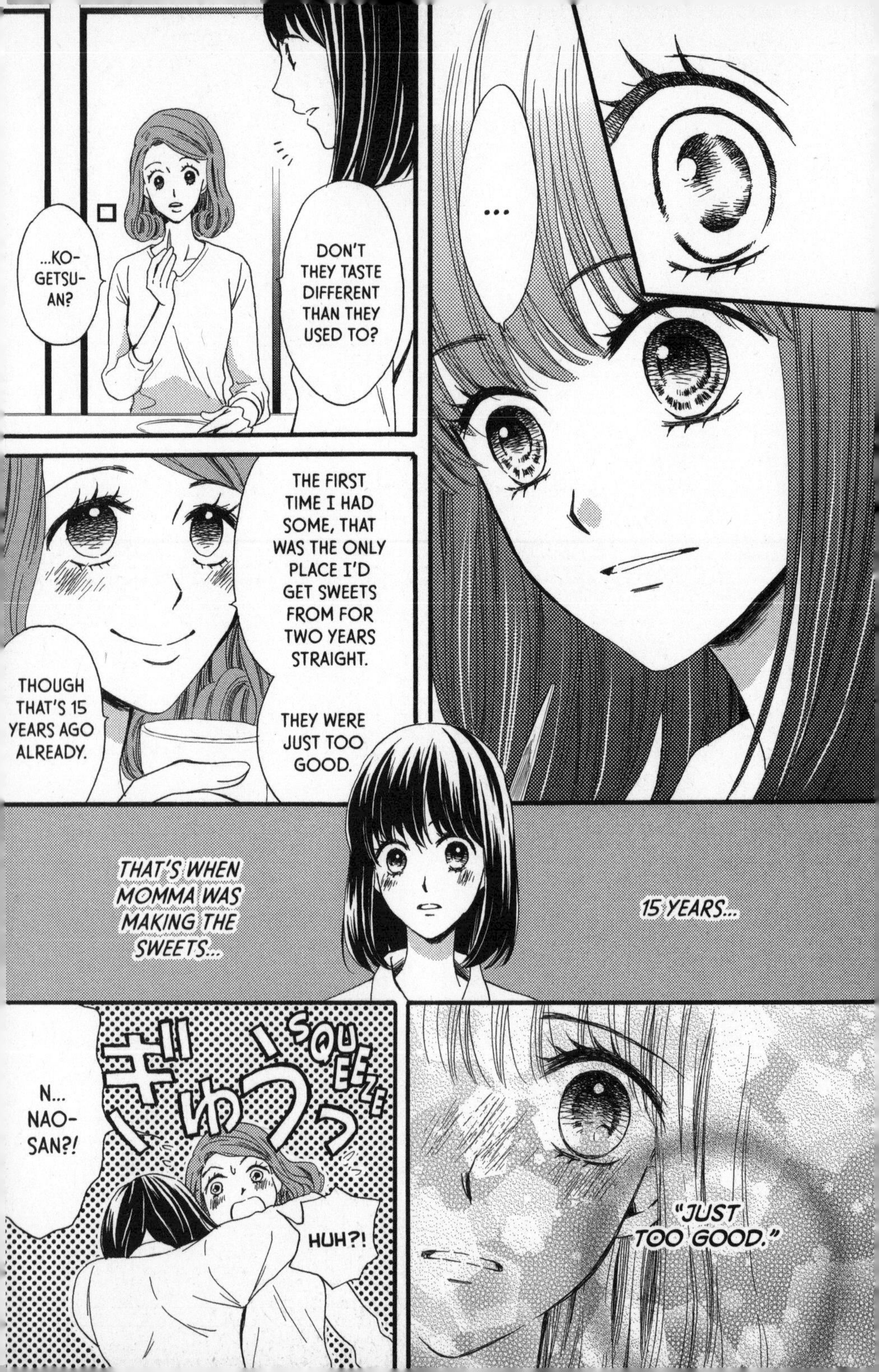
...
DON'T THEY TASTE DIFFERENT THAN THEY USED TO?
...KO-GETSU-AN?
THE FIRST TIME I HAD SOME, THAT WAS THE ONLY PLACE I'D GET SWEETS FROM FOR TWO YEARS STRAIGHT.
THEY WERE JUST TOO GOOD.
THOUGH THAT'S 15 YEARS AGO ALREADY.
15 YEARS...
THAT'S WHEN MOMMA WAS MAKING THE SWEETS...
"JUST TOO GOOD."
SQUEEZE
ぎゅうっ
N... NAO-SAN?!
HUH?!

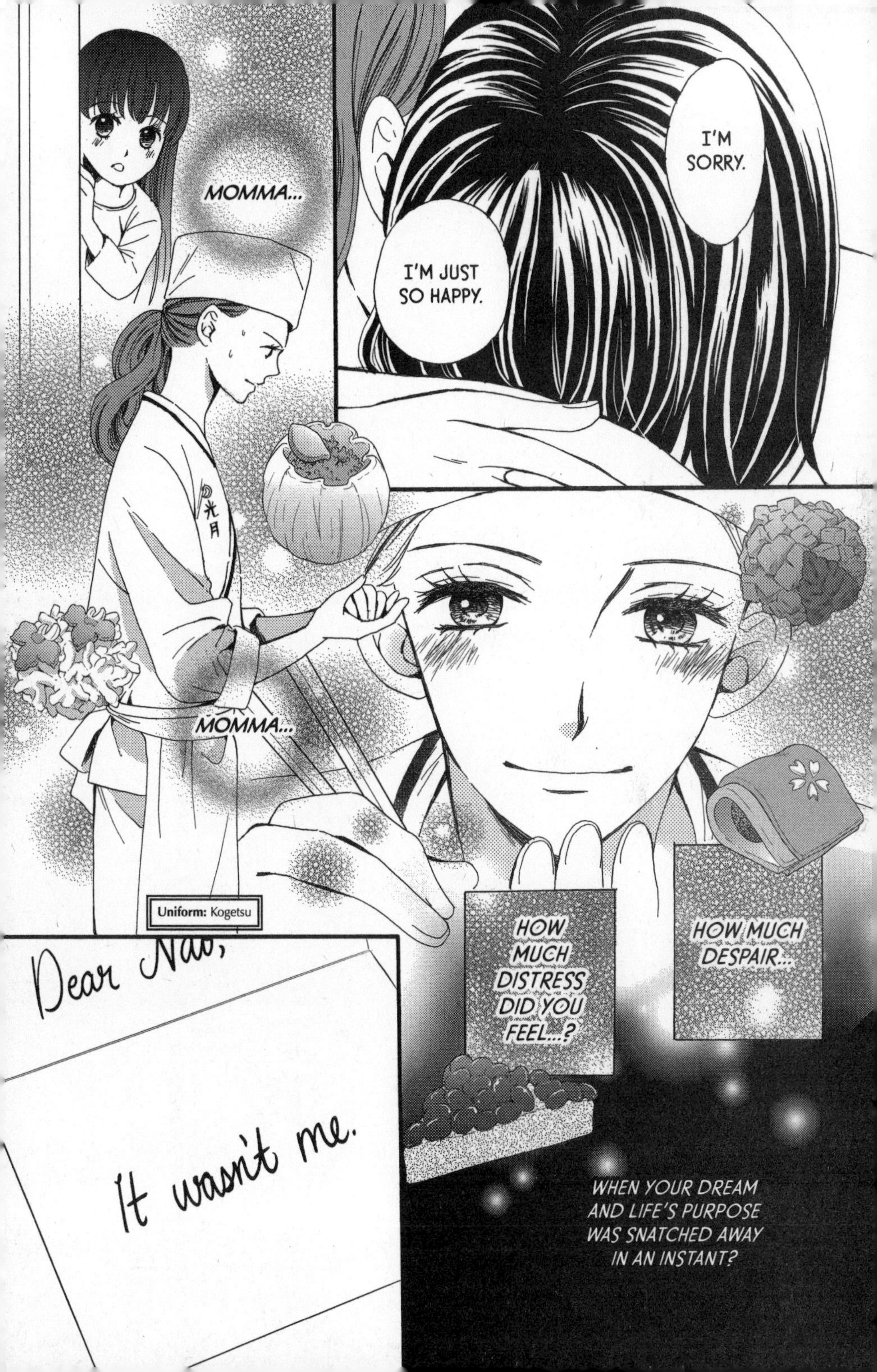
I'M SORRY.
I'M JUST SO HAPPY.
HOW MUCH DESPAIR...
HOW MUCH DISTRESS DID YOU FEEL...?
WHEN YOUR DREAM AND LIFE'S PURPOSE WAS SNATCHED AWAY IN AN INSTANT?
MOMMA...
MOMMA...
Uniform: Kogetsu
Dear Nao,
It wasn't me.

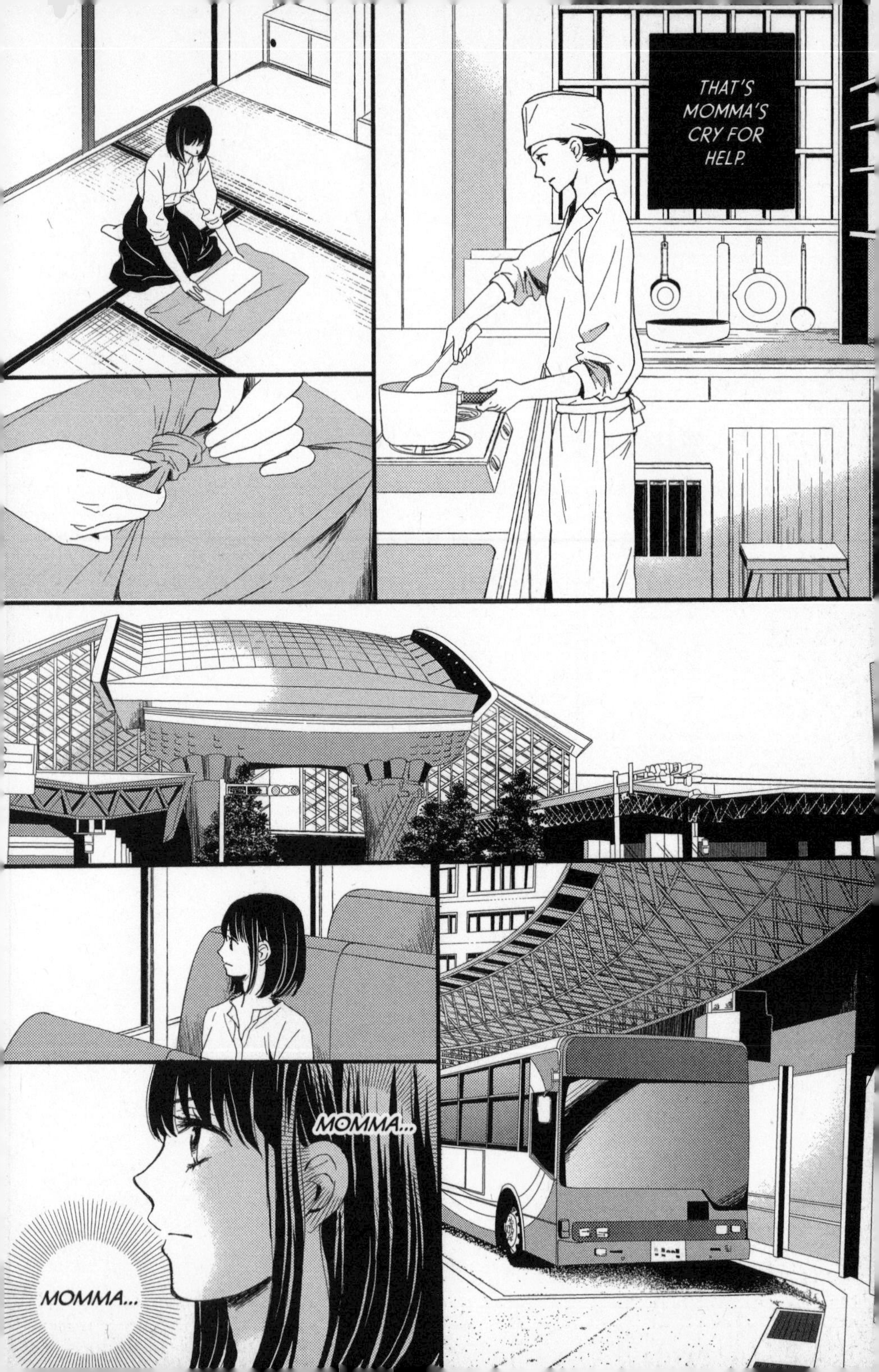
THAT'S MOMMA'S CRY FOR HELP.
MOMMA...
MOMMA...

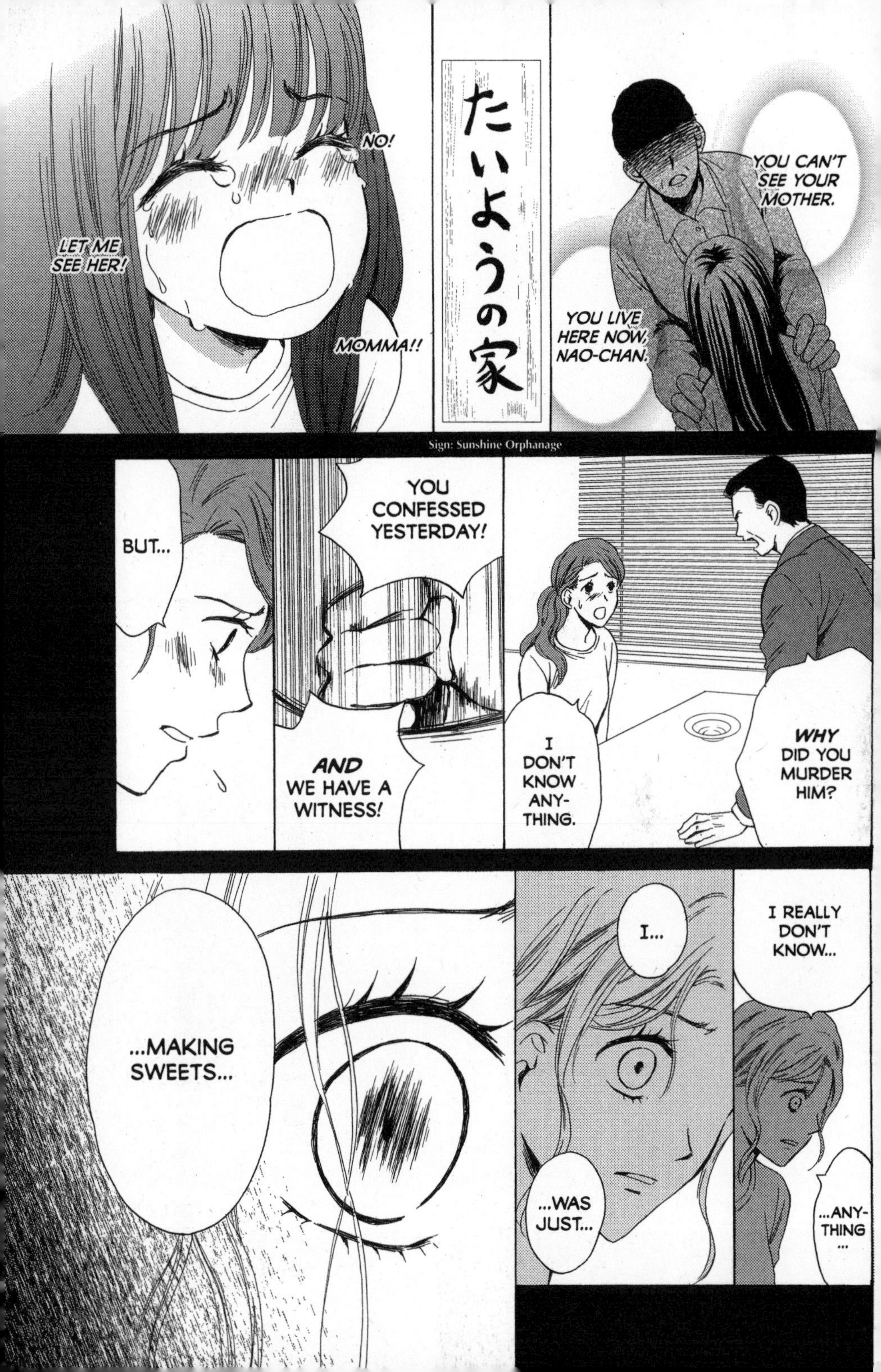
YOU CAN'T SEE YOUR MOTHER.
YOU LIVE HERE NOW, NAO-CHAN.
たいようの家
Sign: Sunshine Orphanage
NO!
LET ME SEE HER!
MOMMA!!
WHY DID YOU MURDER HIM?
I DON'T KNOW ANY-THING.
YOU CONFESSED YESTERDAY!
AND WE HAVE A WITNESS!
BUT...
I REALLY DON'T KNOW...
...ANY-THING...
I...
...WAS JUST...
...MAKING SWEETS...

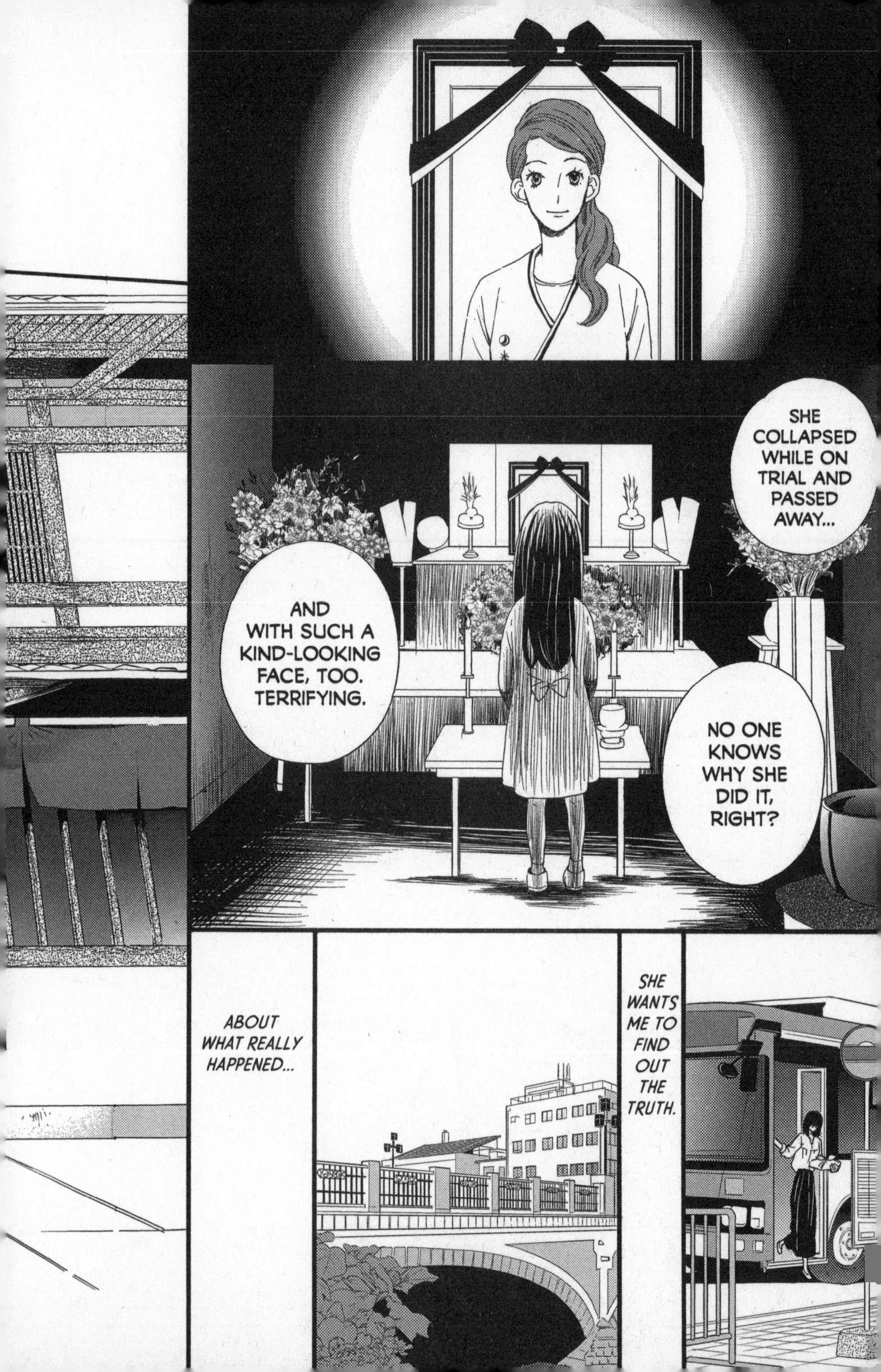
SHE COLLAPSED WHILE ON TRIAL AND PASSED AWAY...
AND WITH SUCH A KIND-LOOKING FACE, TOO. TERRIFYING.
NO ONE KNOWS WHY SHE DID IT, RIGHT?
SHE WANTS ME TO FIND OUT THE TRUTH.
ABOUT WHAT REALLY HAPPENED...

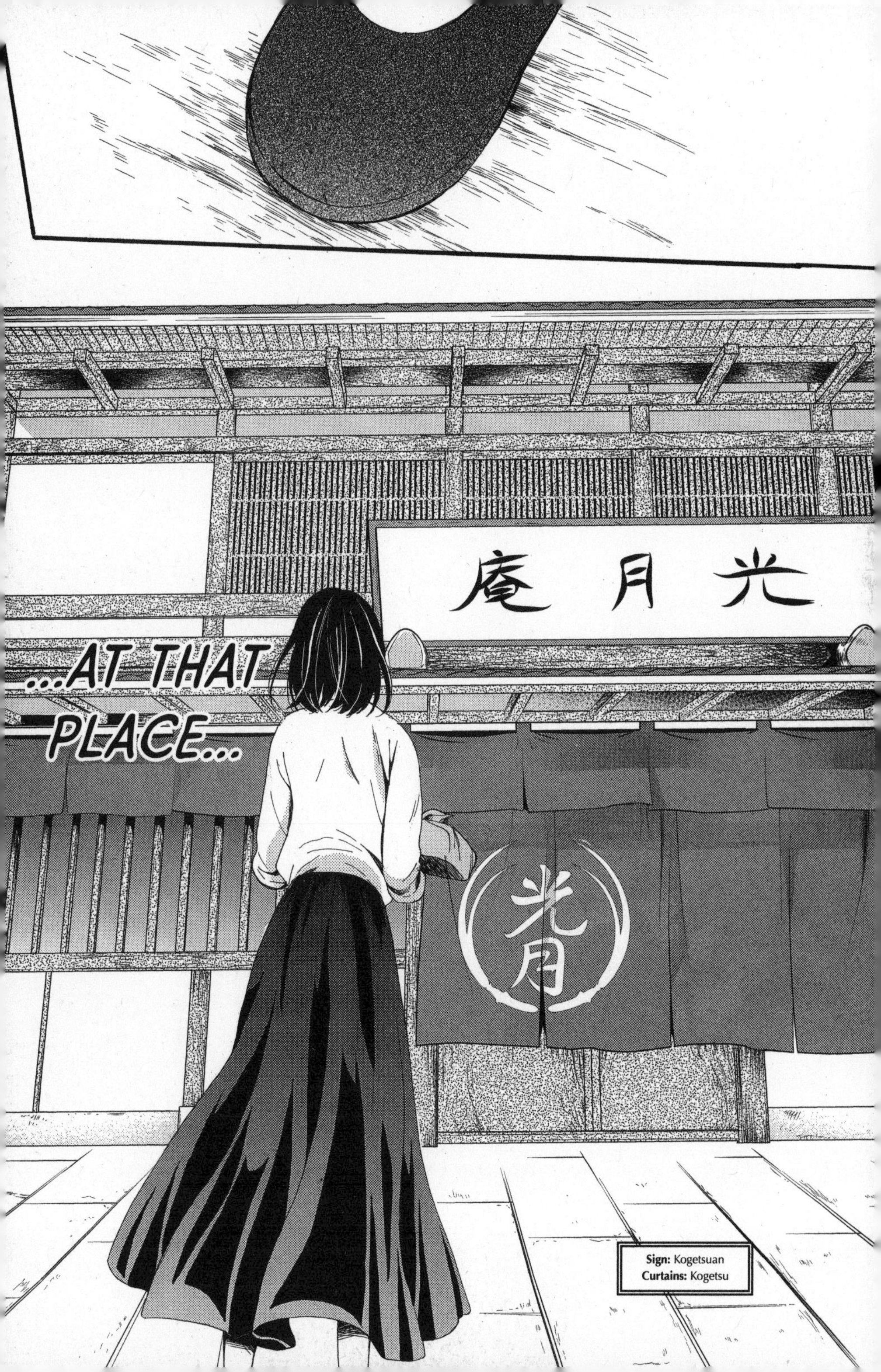
...AT THAT PLACE...
光月庵
光月
Sign: Kogetsuan
Curtains: Kogetsu

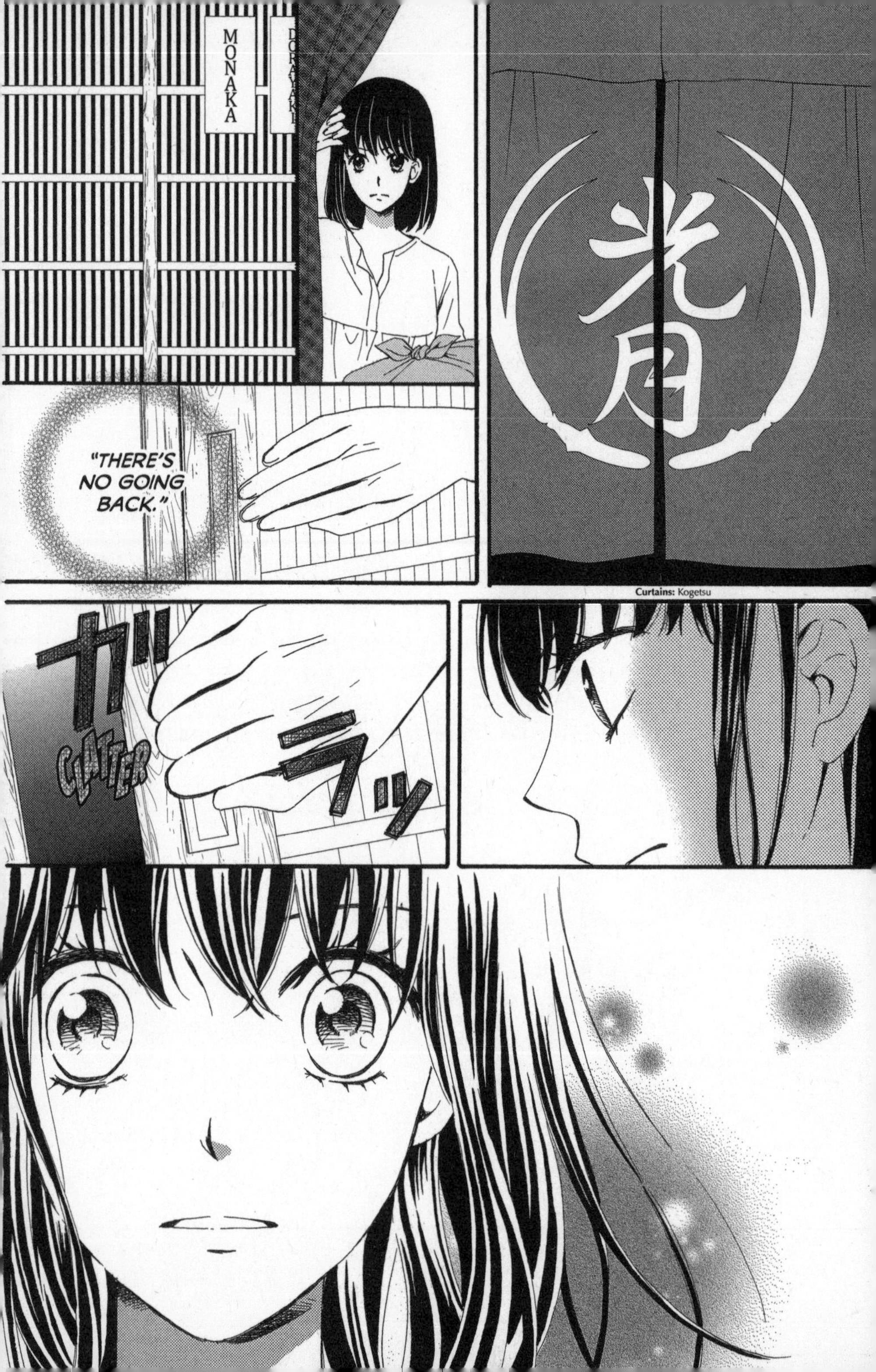
光月
Curtains: Kogetsu
MONAKA
DORAYAKI
"THERE'S NO GOING BACK."
CLATTER

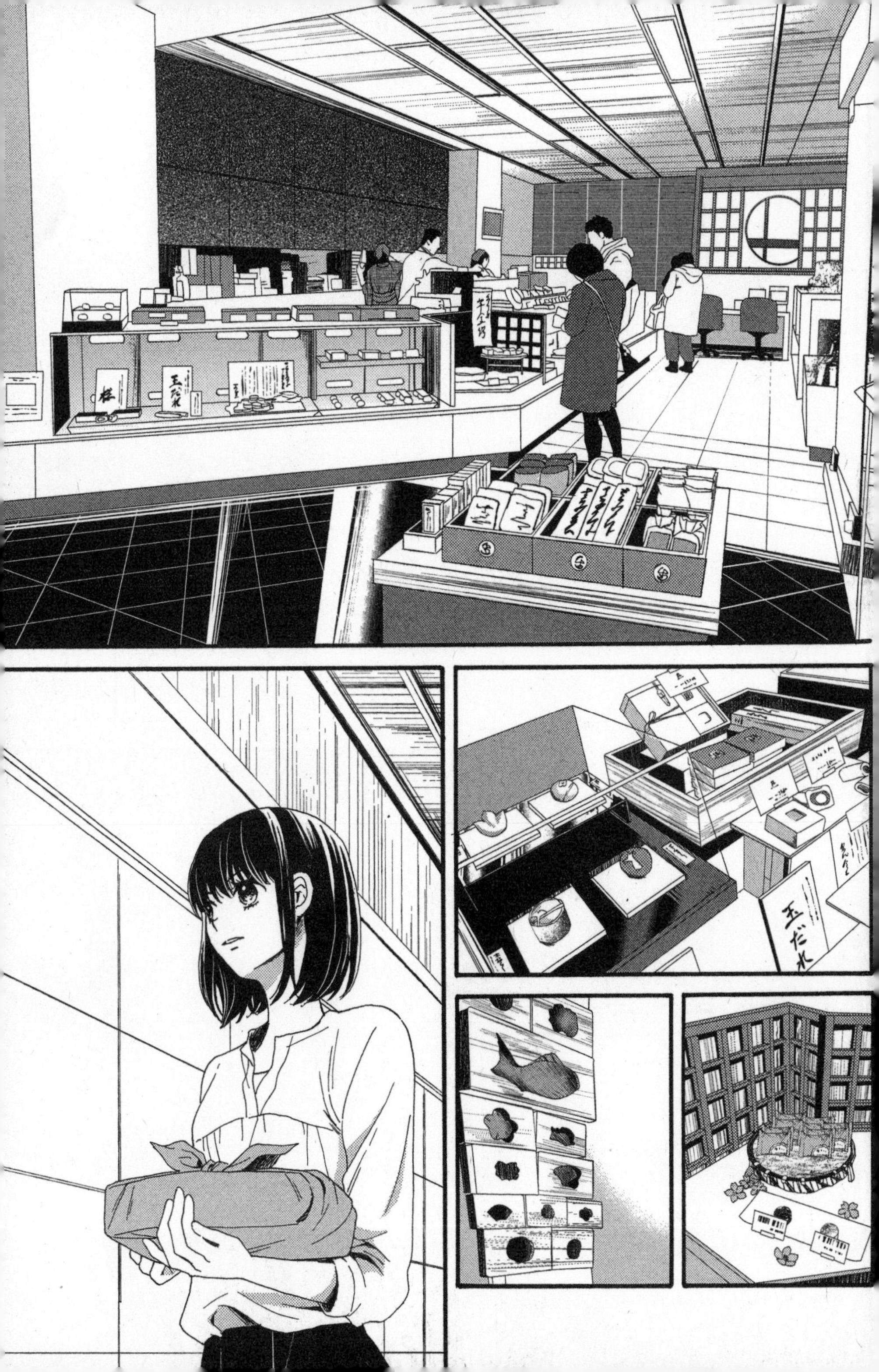
玉だれ

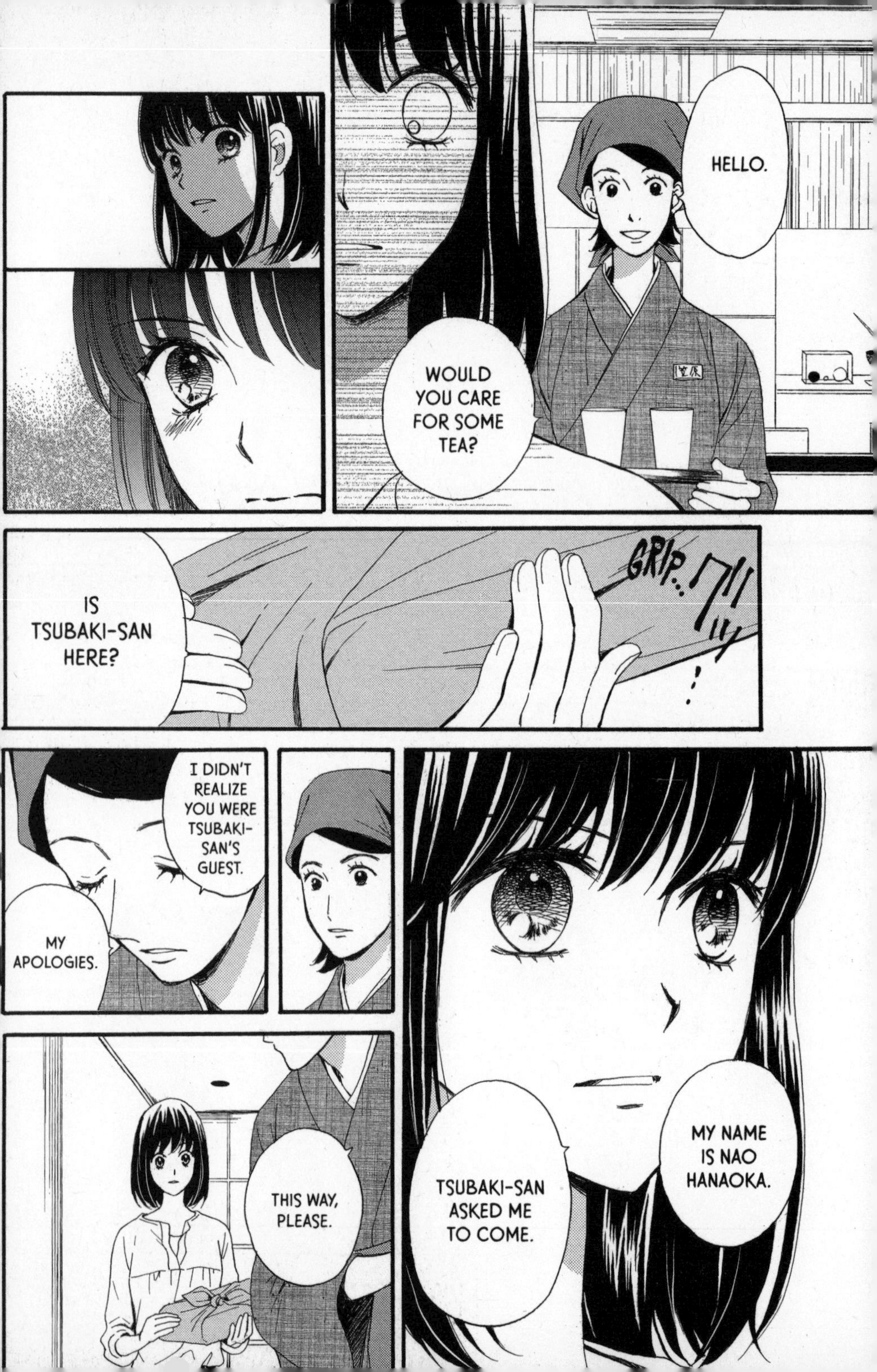
HELLO.
WOULD YOU CARE FOR SOME TEA?
GRIP...
IS TSUBAKI-SAN HERE?
MY NAME IS NAO HANAOKA.
TSUBAKI-SAN ASKED ME TO COME.
I DIDN'T REALIZE YOU WERE TSUBAKI-SAN'S GUEST.
MY APOLOGIES.
THIS WAY, PLEASE.

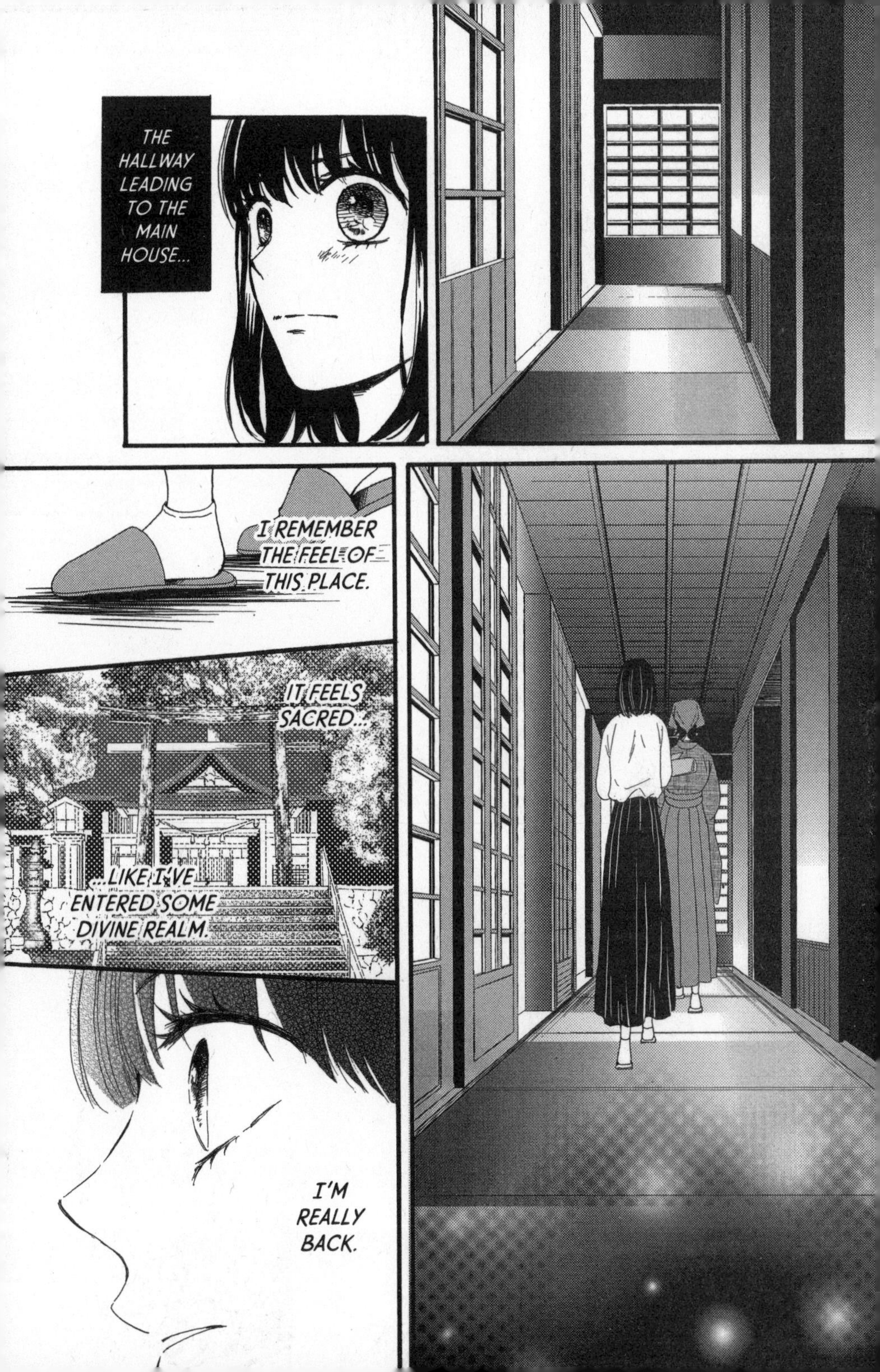
THE HALLWAY LEADING TO THE MAIN HOUSE...
I REMEMBER THE FEEL OF THIS PLACE.
IT FEELS SACRED...
...LIKE I'VE ENTERED SOME DIVINE REALM.
I'M REALLY BACK.

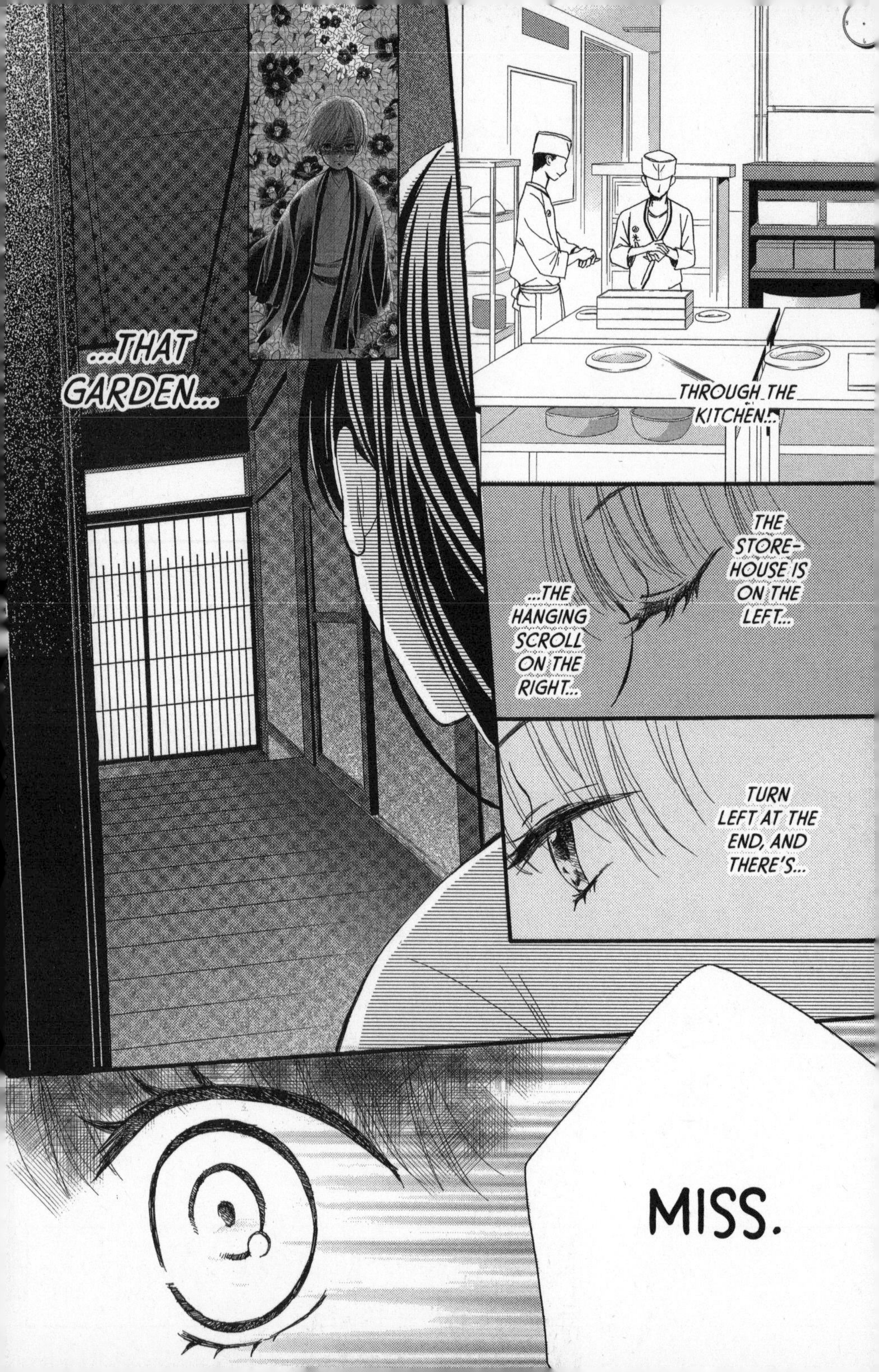
THROUGH THE KITCHEN...
THE STORE-HOUSE IS ON THE LEFT...
...THE HANGING SCROLL ON THE RIGHT...
TURN LEFT AT THE END, AND THERE'S...
...THAT GARDEN...
MISS.

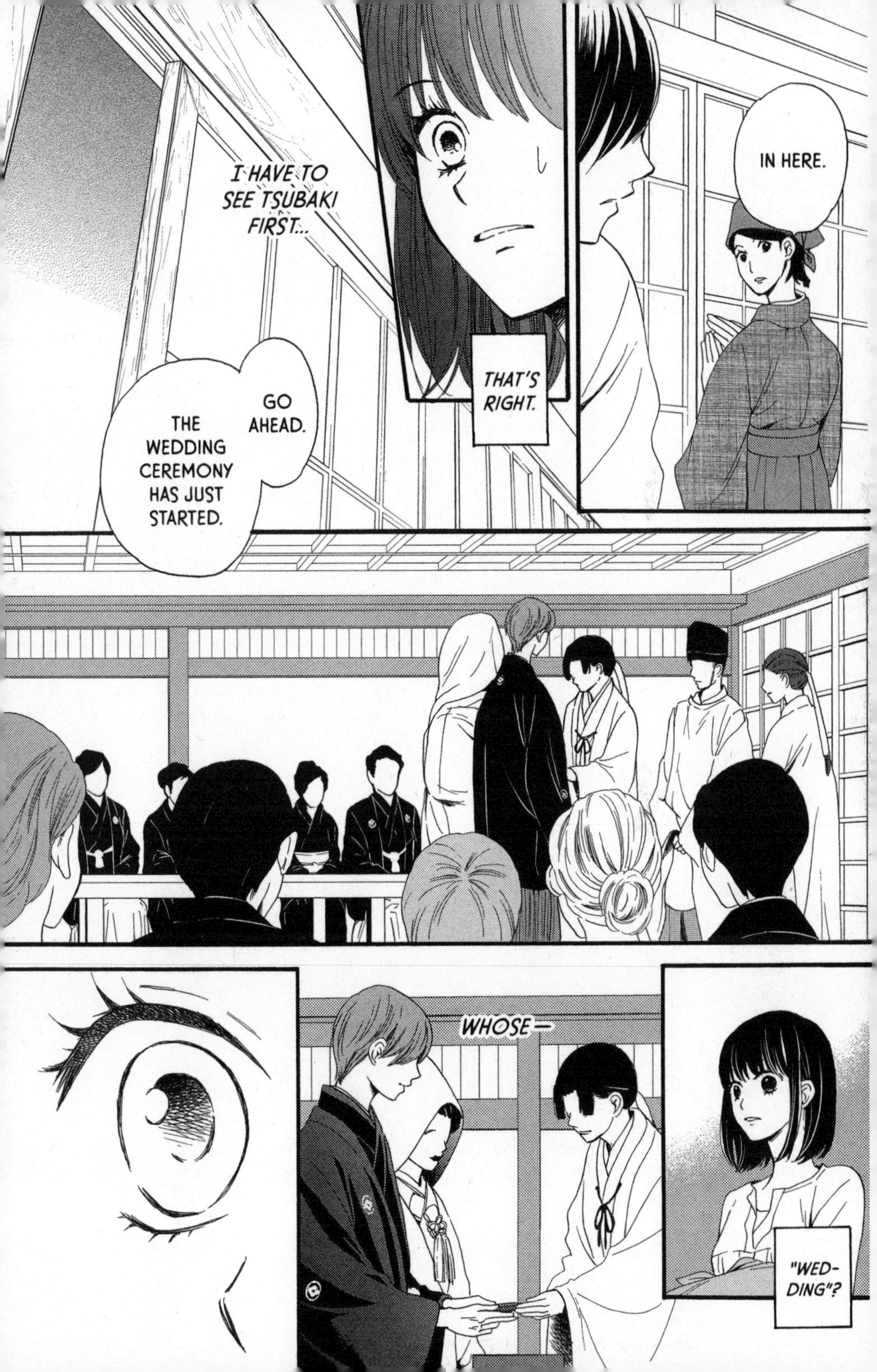
IN HERE.
THAT'S RIGHT.
I HAVE TO SEE TSUBAKI FIRST...
GO AHEAD. THE WEDDING CEREMONY HAS JUST STARTED.
"WED-DING"?
WHOSE—

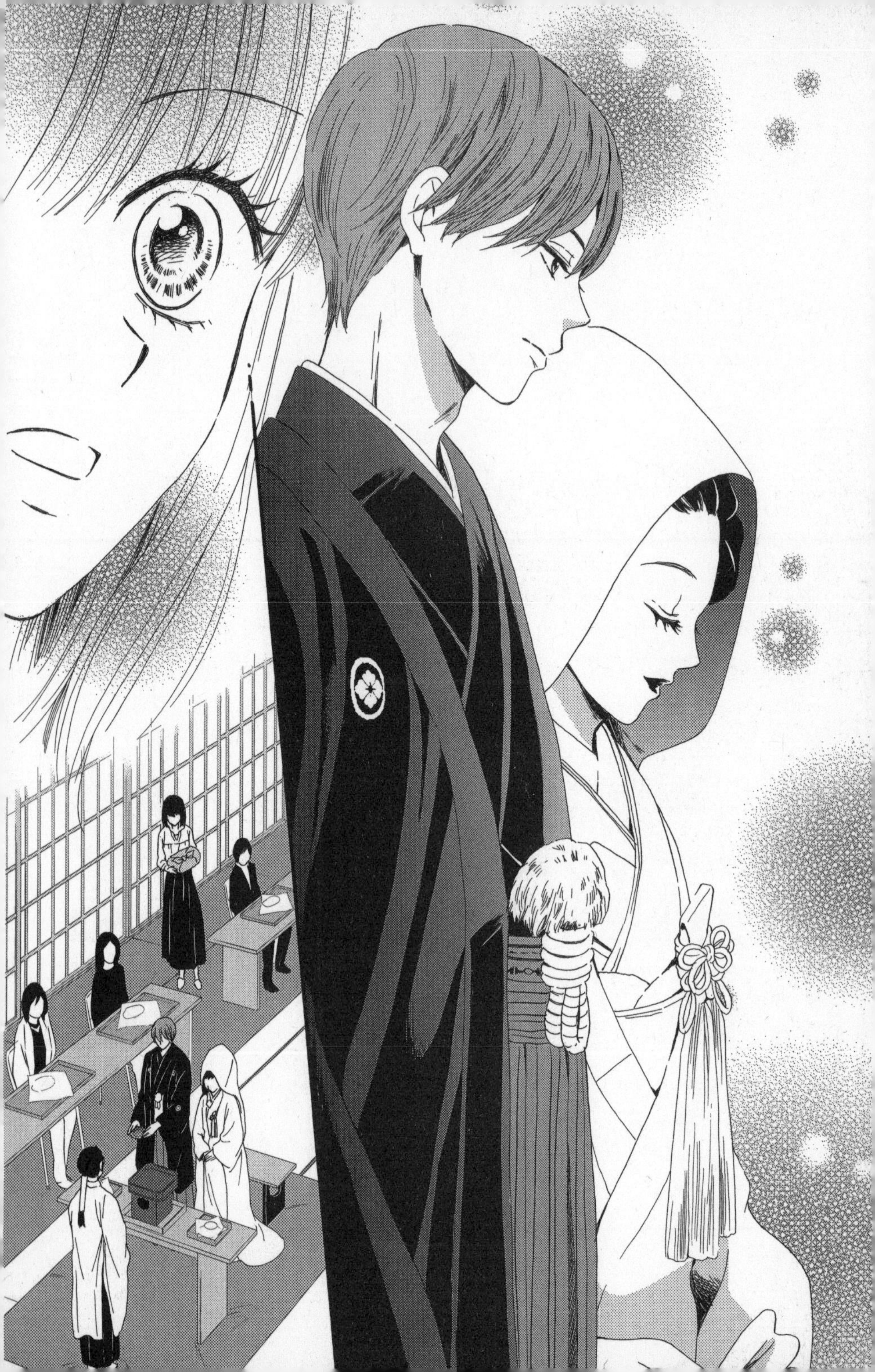

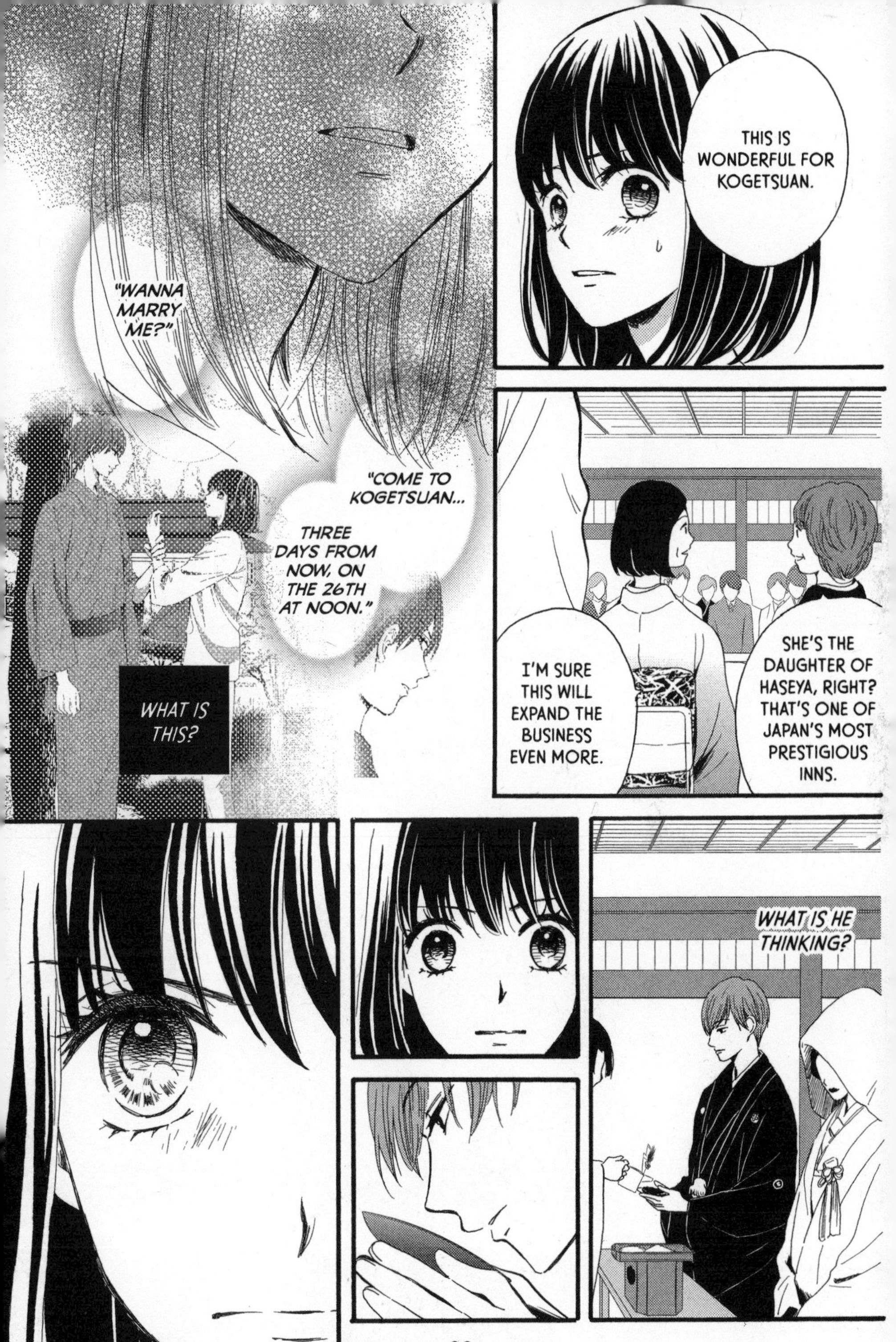
THIS IS WONDERFUL FOR KOGETSUAN.
SHE'S THE DAUGHTER OF HASEYA, RIGHT? THAT'S ONE OF JAPAN'S MOST PRESTIGIOUS INNS.
I'M SURE THIS WILL EXPAND THE BUSINESS EVEN MORE.
"WANNA MARRY ME?"
"COME TO KOGETSUAN...
THREE DAYS FROM NOW, ON THE 26TH AT NOON."
WHAT IS THIS?
WHAT IS HE THINKING?

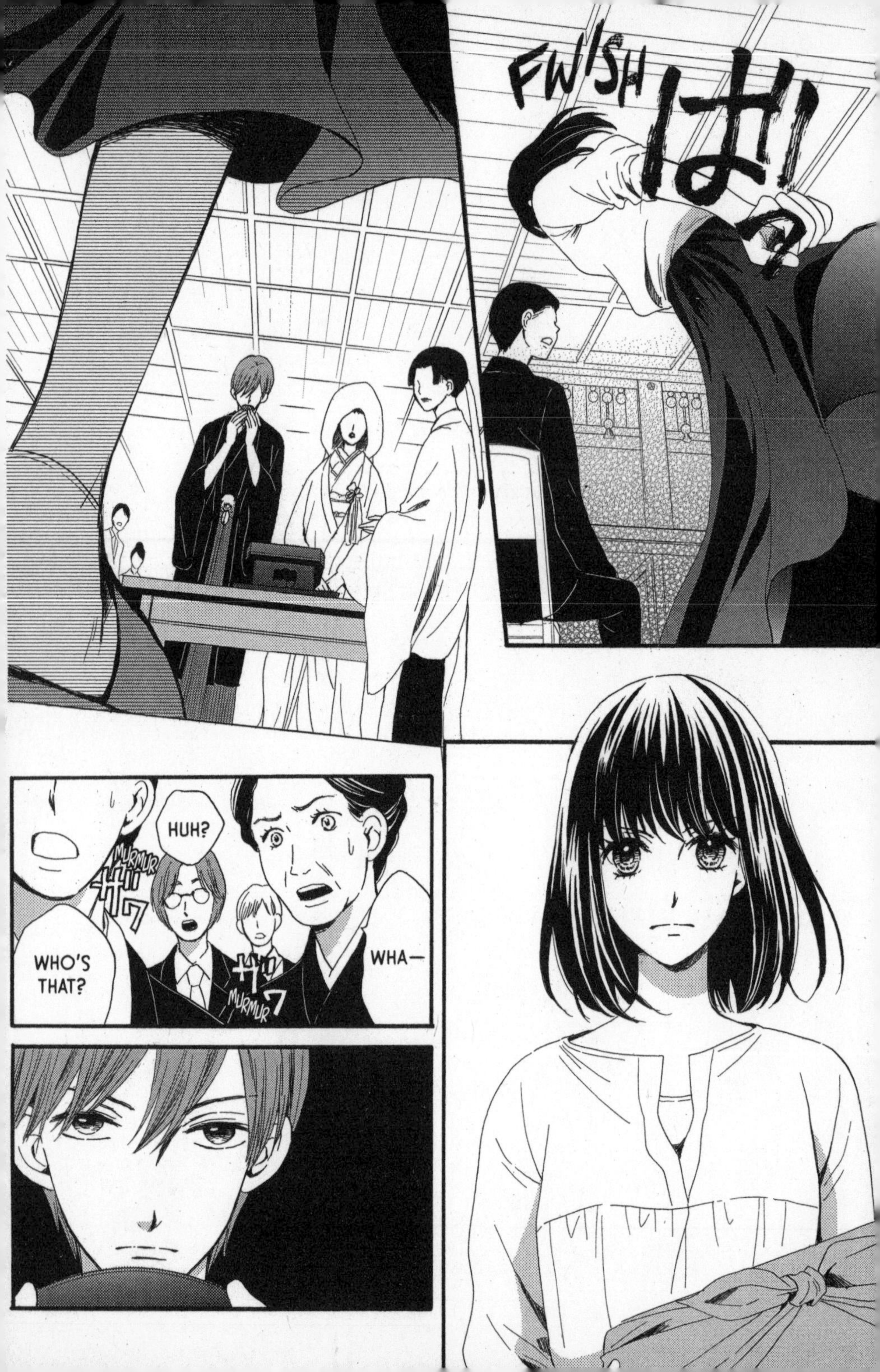
FWISH
WHA—
HUH?
MURMUR
WHO'S THAT?
MURMUR

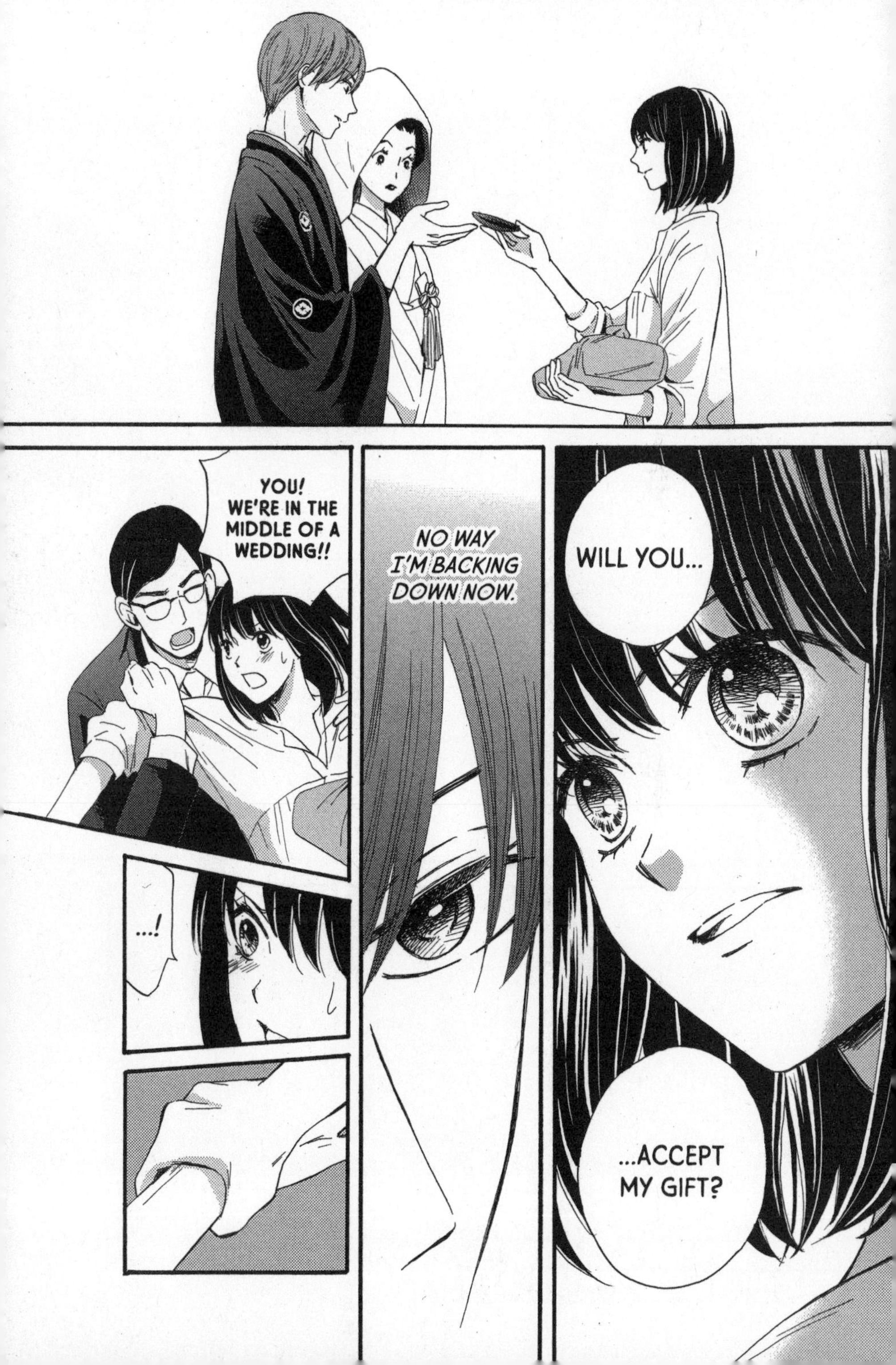
WILL YOU...
...ACCEPT MY GIFT?
NO WAY I'M BACKING DOWN NOW.
YOU! WE'RE IN THE MIDDLE OF A WEDDING!!
...!

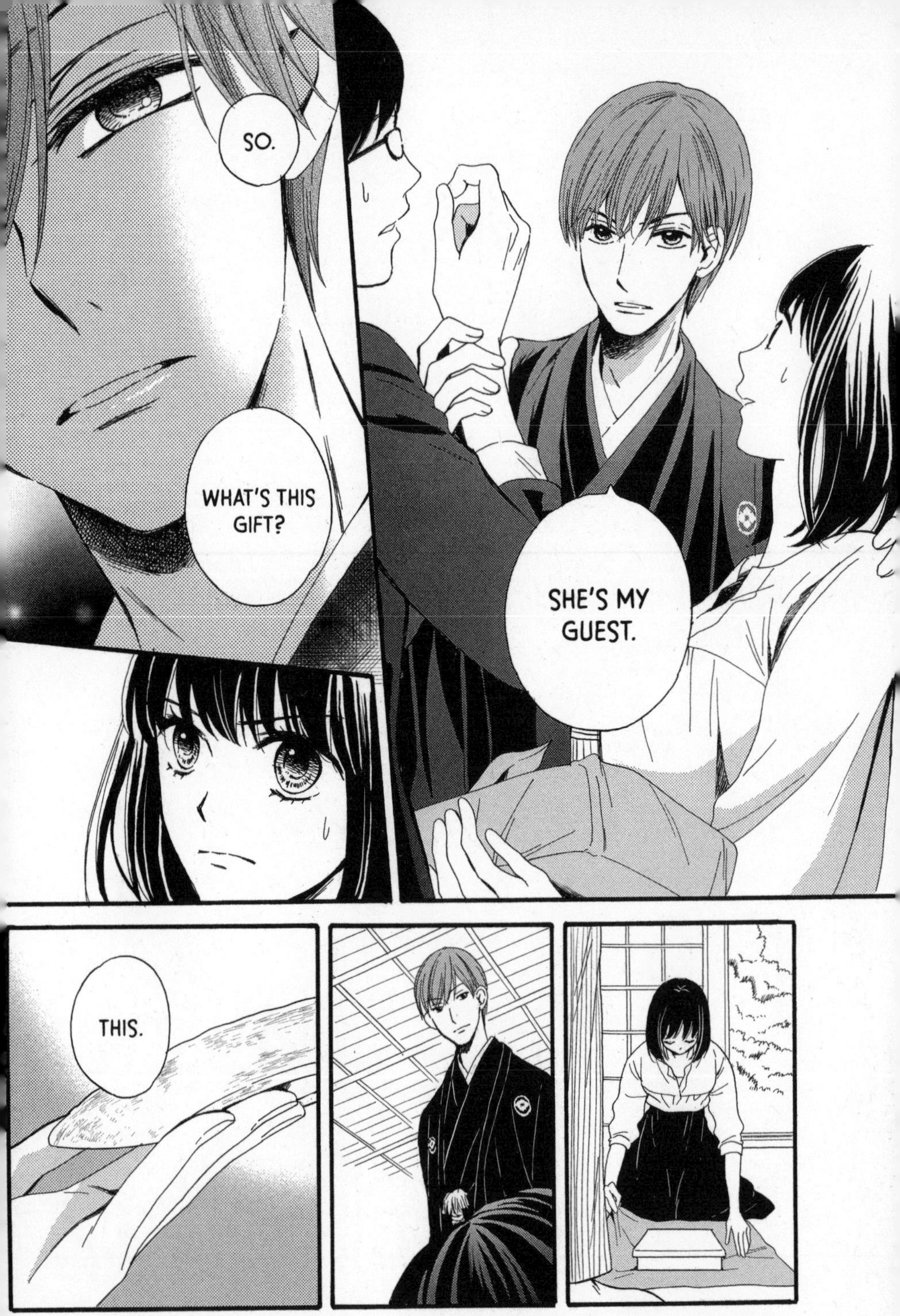
SHE'S MY GUEST.
SO.
WHAT'S THIS GIFT?
THIS.

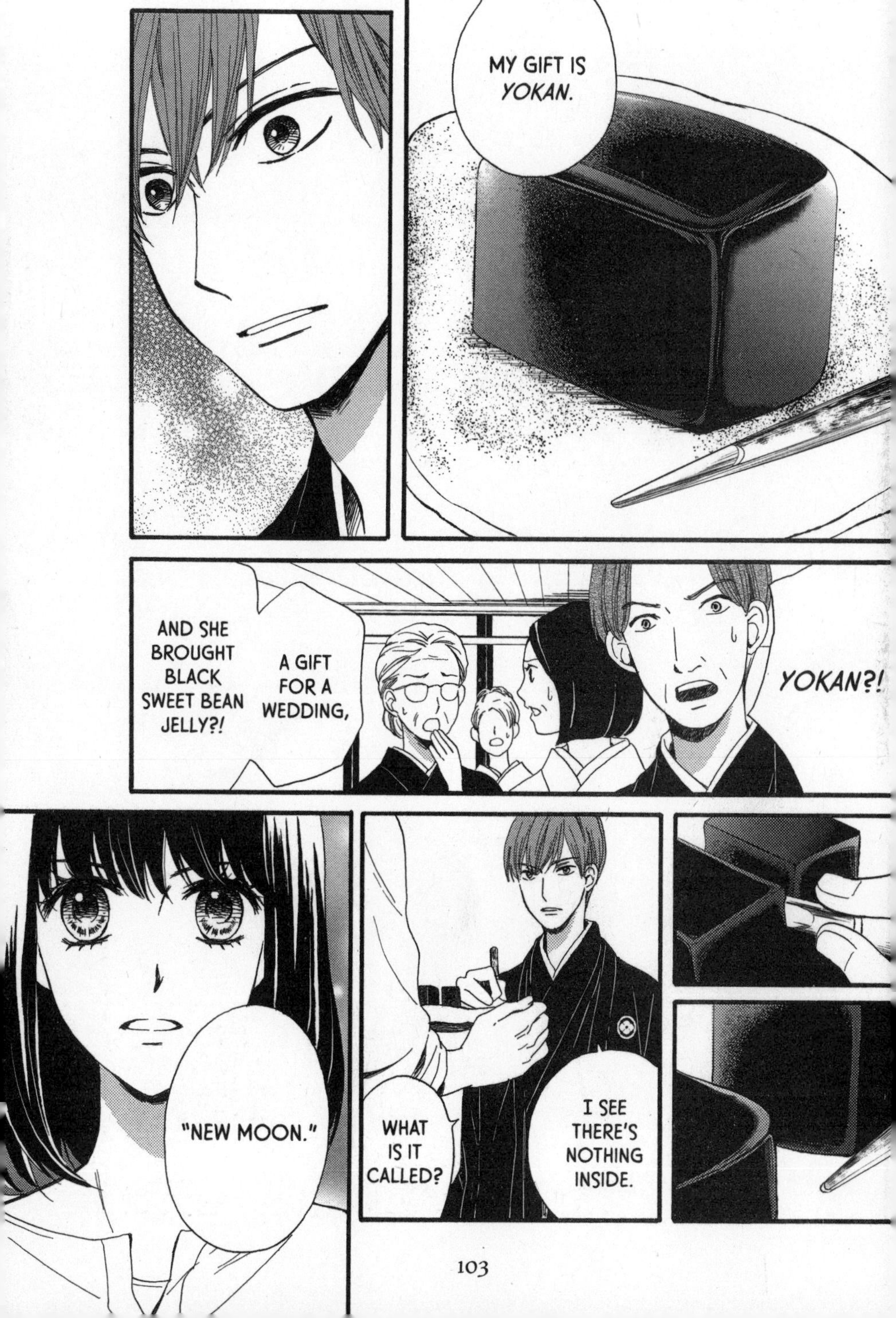
MY GIFT IS *YOKAN.*
YOKAN?!
A GIFT FOR A WEDDING,
AND SHE BROUGHT BLACK SWEET BEAN JELLY?!
I SEE THERE'S NOTHING INSIDE.
WHAT IS IT CALLED?
"NEW MOON."

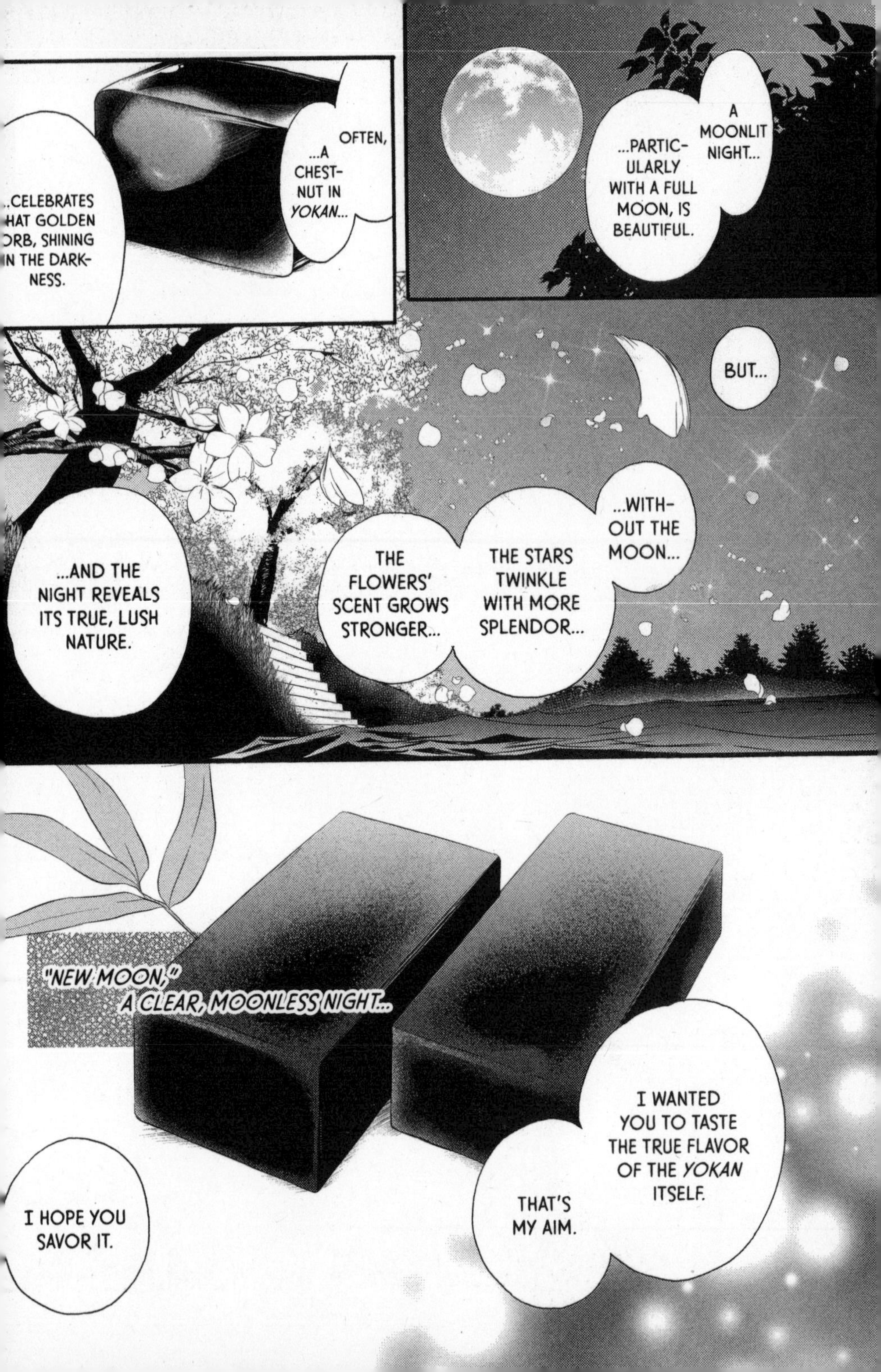
A MOONLIT NIGHT...
...PARTICULARLY WITH A FULL MOON, IS BEAUTIFUL.
OFTEN, ...A CHESTNUT IN *YOKAN*...
..CELEBRATES HAT GOLDEN RB, SHINING N THE DARKNESS.
BUT...
...WITHOUT THE MOON...
THE STARS TWINKLE WITH MORE SPLENDOR...
THE FLOWERS' SCENT GROWS STRONGER...
...AND THE NIGHT REVEALS ITS TRUE, LUSH NATURE.
"NEW MOON," A CLEAR, MOONLESS NIGHT...
I WANTED YOU TO TASTE THE TRUE FLAVOR OF THE *YOKAN* ITSELF.
THAT'S MY AIM.
I HOPE YOU SAVOR IT.

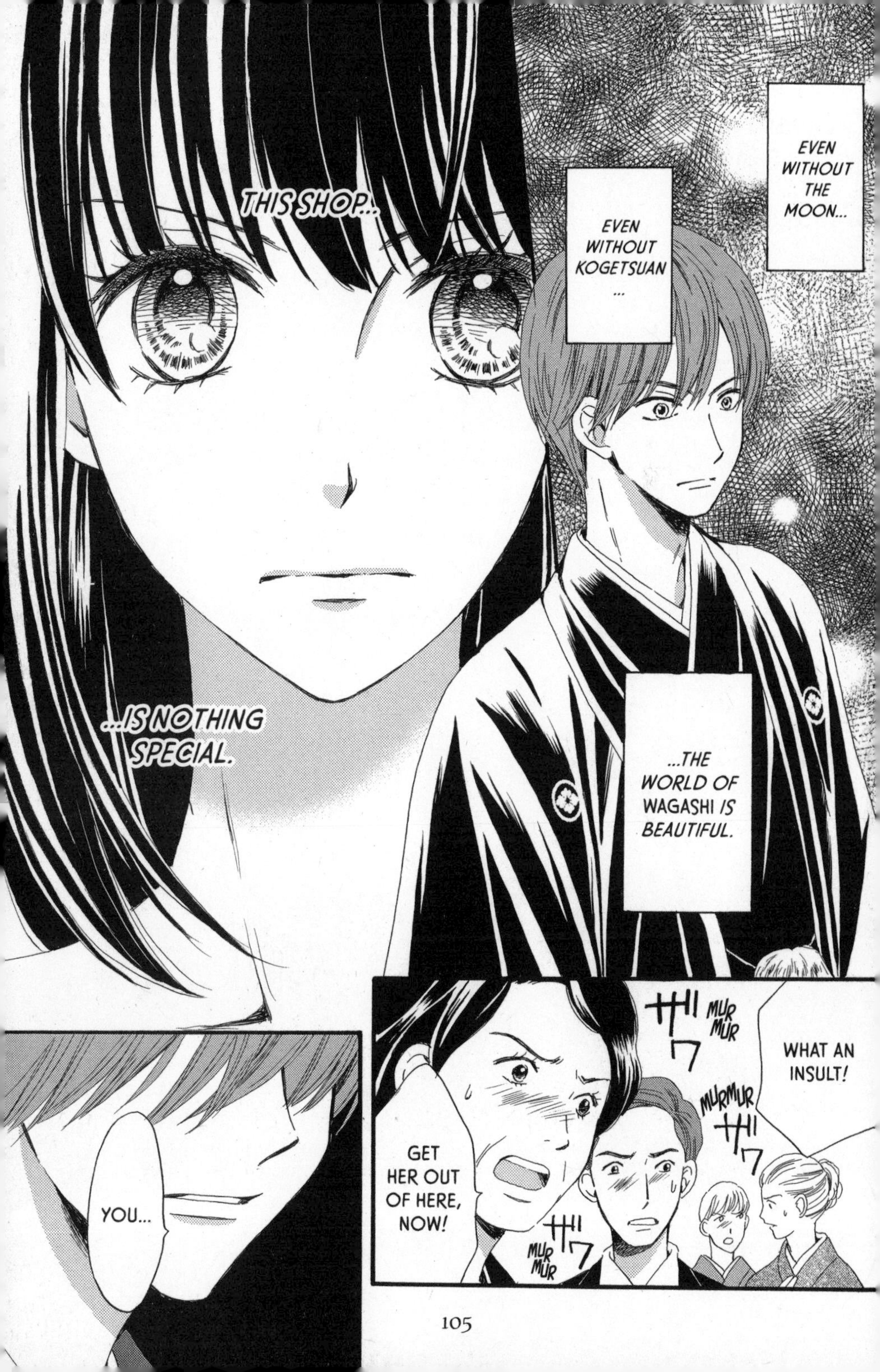
EVEN WITHOUT THE MOON...
EVEN WITHOUT KOGETSUAN ...
THIS SHOP...
...IS NOTHING SPECIAL.
...THE WORLD OF WAGASHI IS BEAUTIFUL.
ザワ
MURMUR
WHAT AN INSULT!
MURMUR
ザワ
GET HER OUT OF HERE, NOW!
ザワ
MURMUR
YOU...

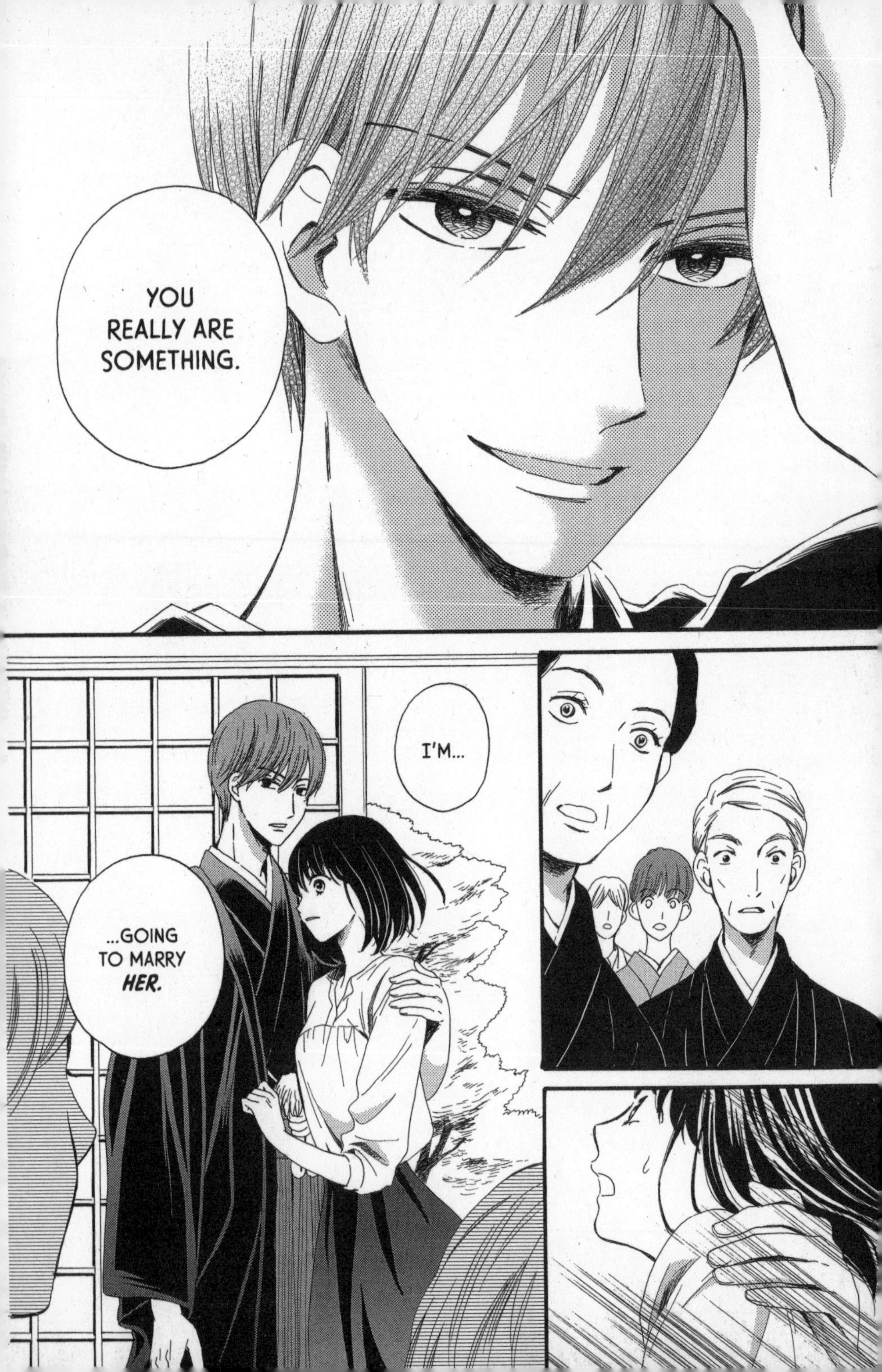
YOU REALLY ARE SOMETHING.
I'M...
...GOING TO MARRY *HER.*

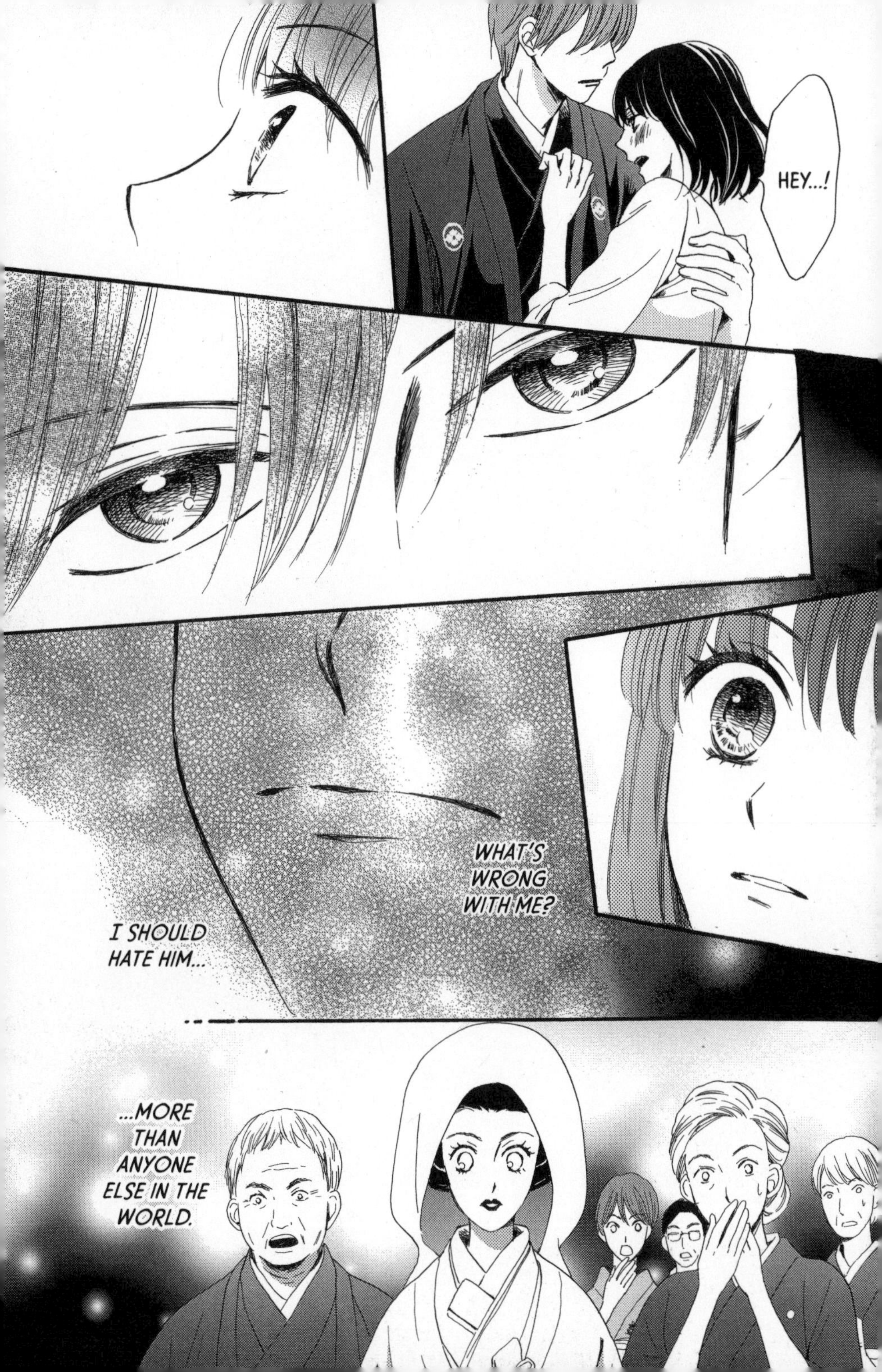
HEY...!
WHAT'S WRONG WITH ME?
I SHOULD HATE HIM...
...MORE THAN ANYONE ELSE IN THE WORLD.

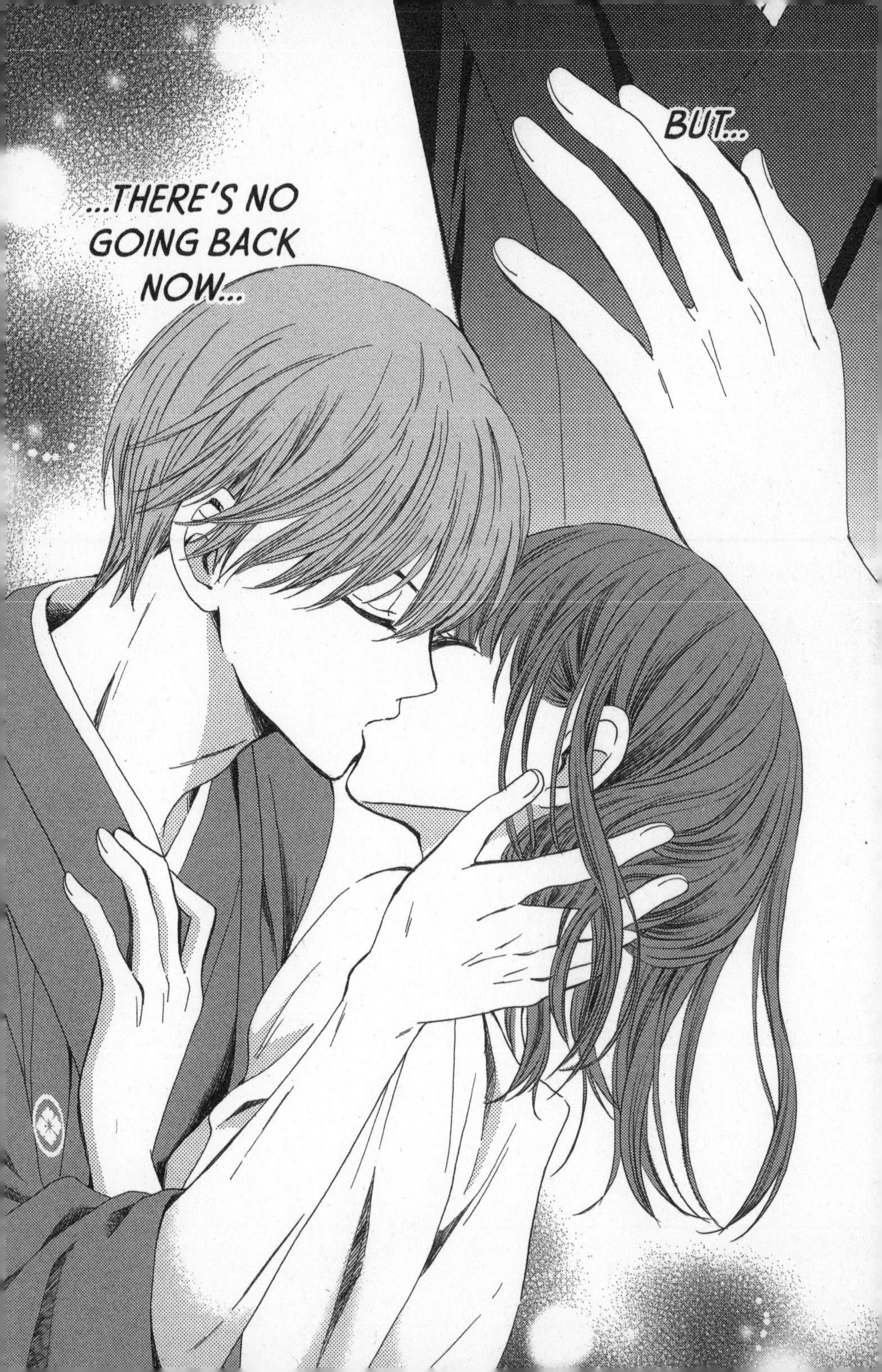
BUT...
...THERE'S NO GOING BACK NOW...

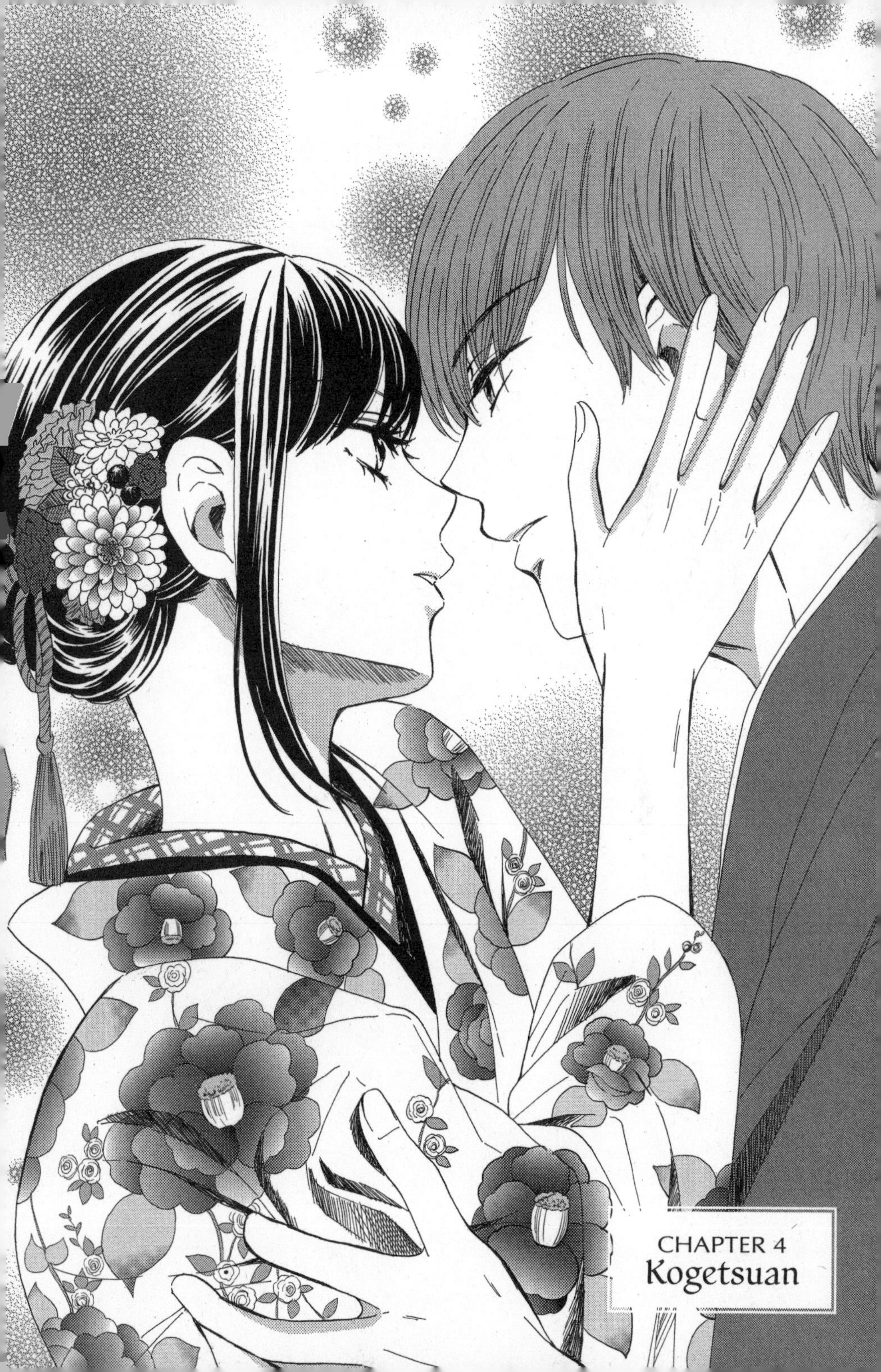
CHAPTER 4
Kogetsuan

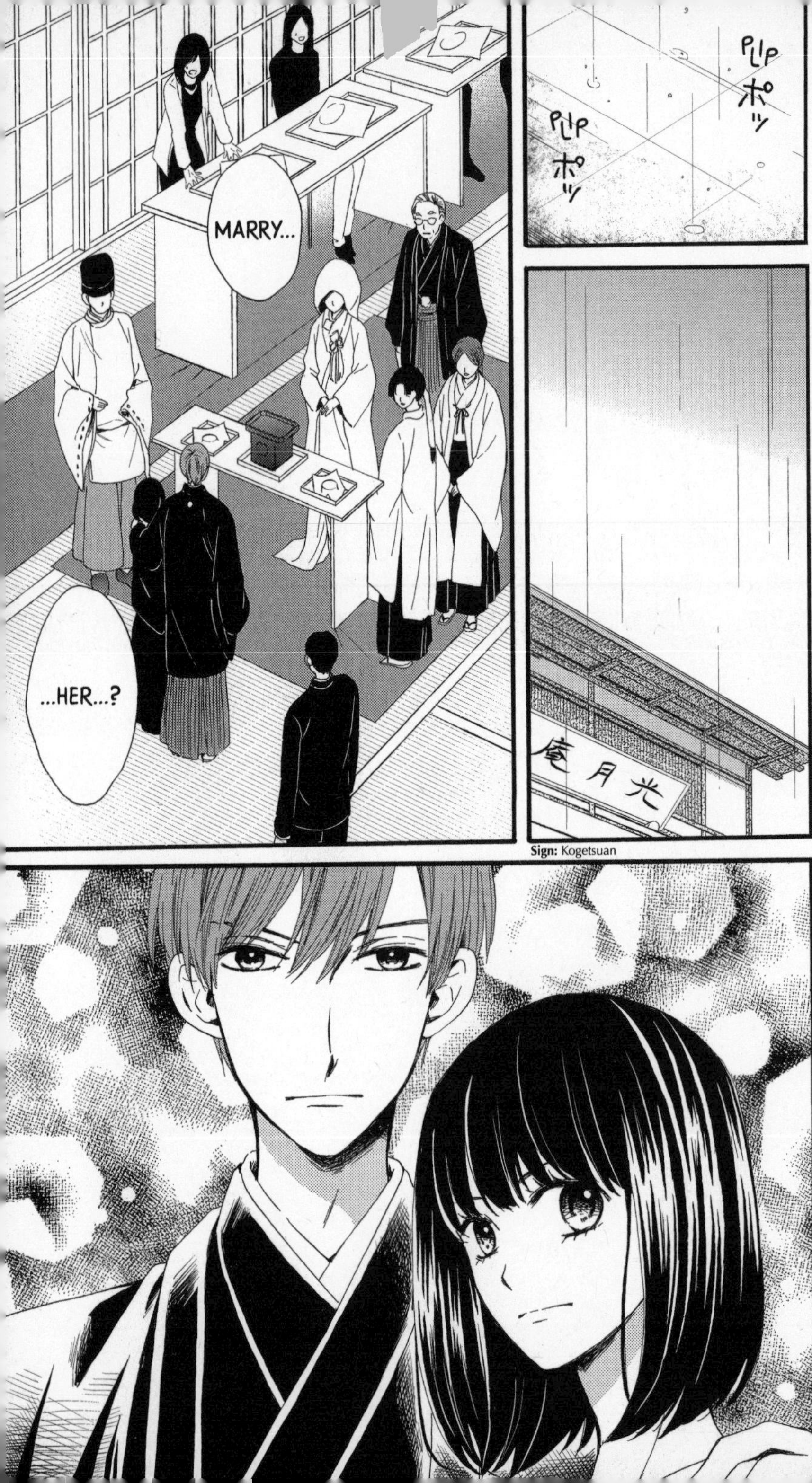
PLIP
ポツ
PLIP
ポツ
光月庵
Sign: Kogetsuan
MARRY...
...HER...?

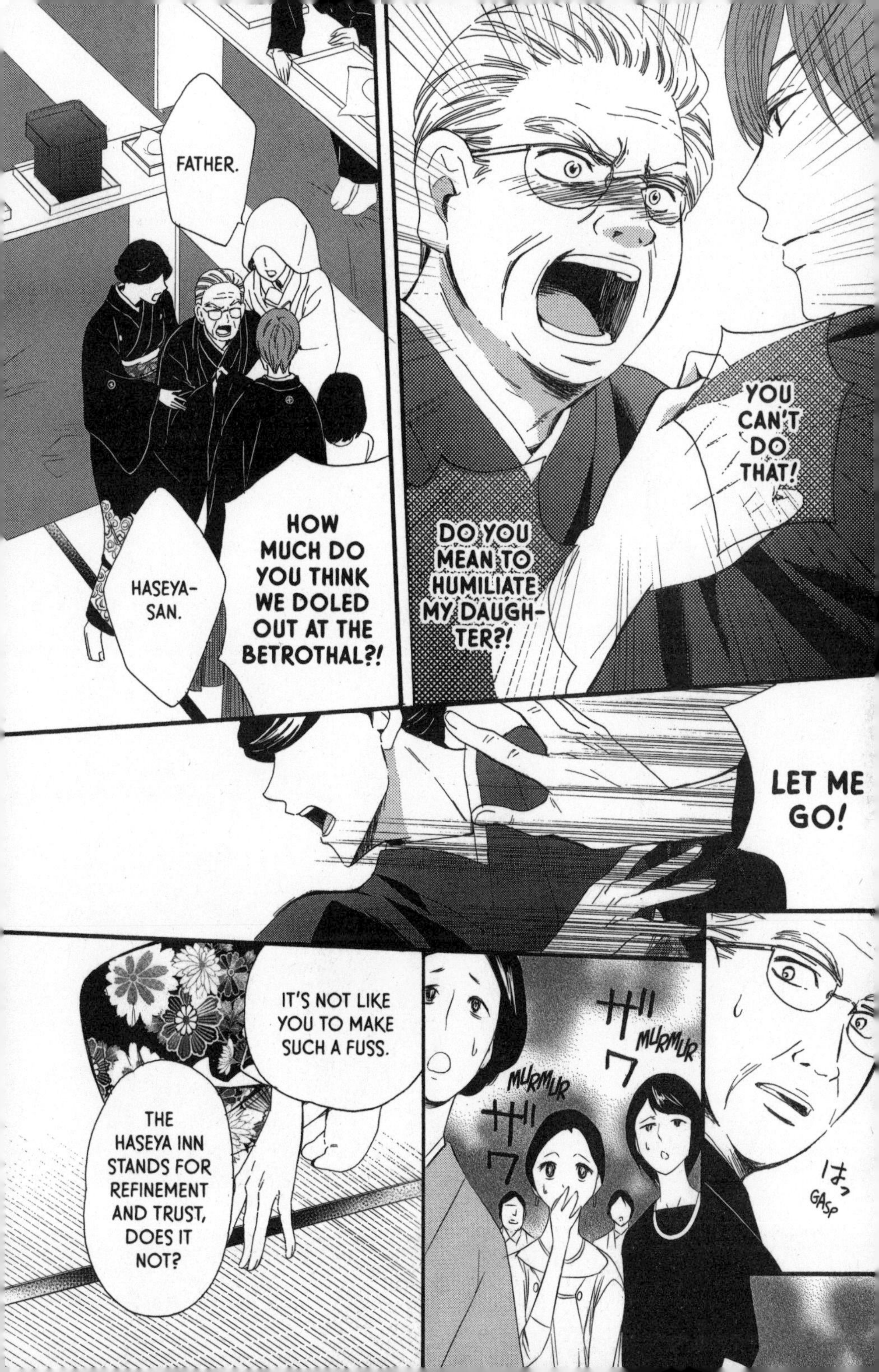
YOU CAN'T DO THAT!
DO YOU MEAN TO HUMILIATE MY DAUGH-TER?!
FATHER.
HOW MUCH DO YOU THINK WE DOLED OUT AT THE BETROTHAL?!
HASEYA-SAN.
LET ME GO!
はっ GASP
ザワ MURMUR
ザワ MURMUR
IT'S NOT LIKE YOU TO MAKE SUCH A FUSS.
THE HASEYA INN STANDS FOR REFINEMENT AND TRUST, DOES IT NOT?

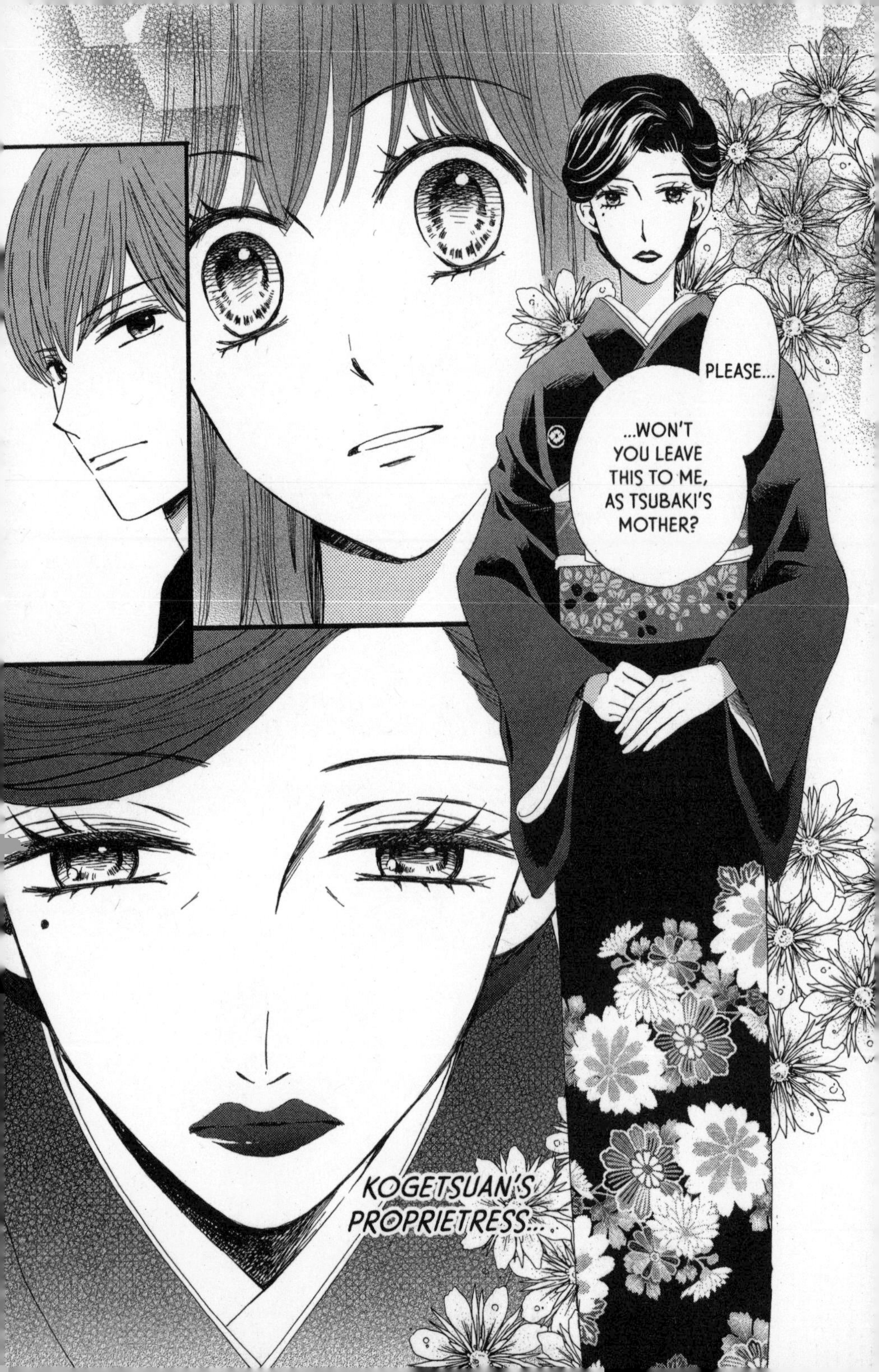
PLEASE...
...WON'T YOU LEAVE THIS TO ME, AS TSUBAKI'S MOTHER?
KOGETSUAN'S PROPRIETRESS...

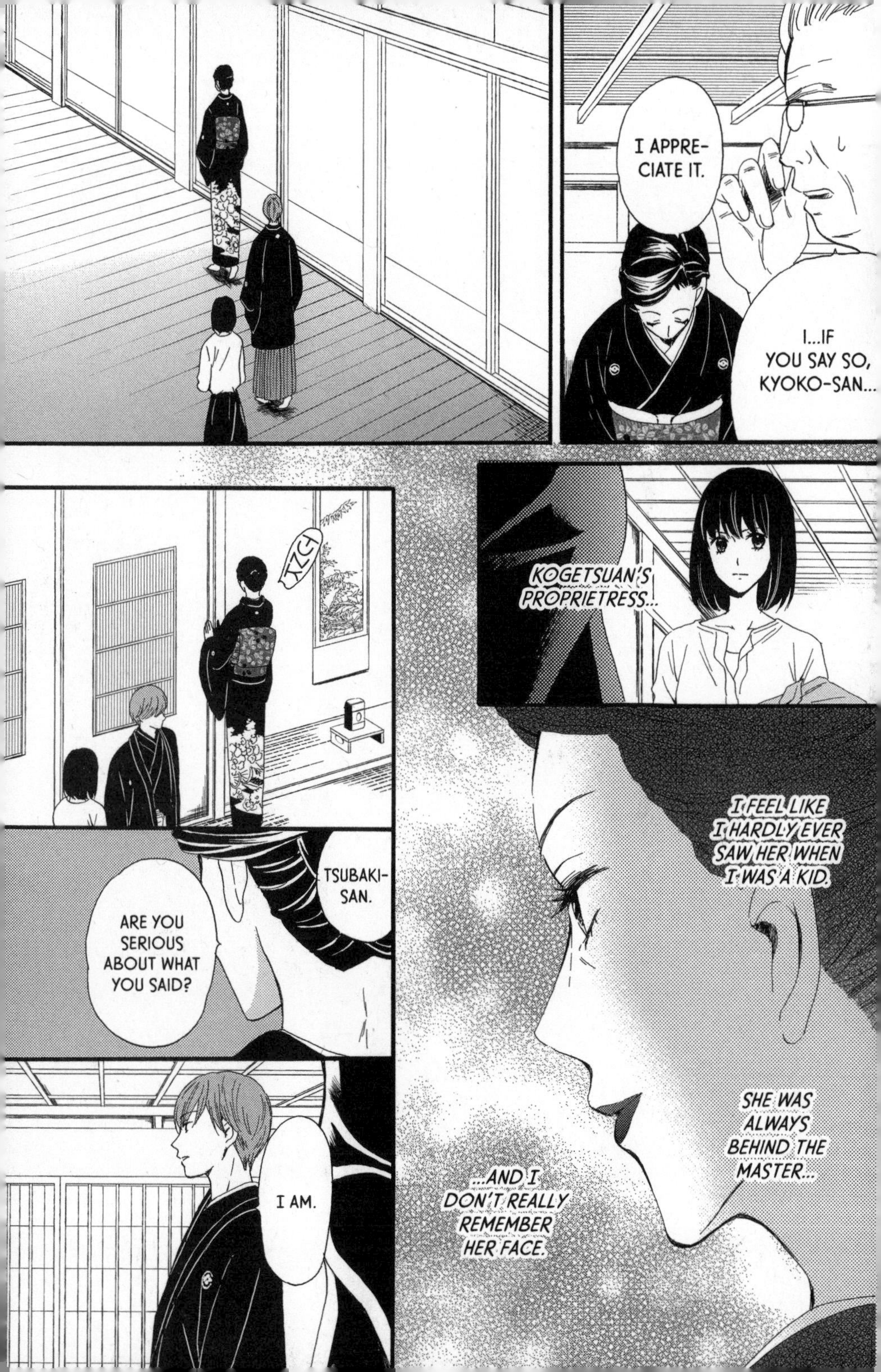
I...IF YOU SAY SO, KYOKO-SAN...
I APPRE-CIATE IT.
KOGETSUAN'S PROPRIETRESS...
I FEEL LIKE I HARDLY EVER SAW HER WHEN I WAS A KID.
SHE WAS ALWAYS BEHIND THE MASTER...
...AND I DON'T REALLY REMEMBER HER FACE.
TSUBAKI-SAN.
ARE YOU SERIOUS ABOUT WHAT YOU SAID?
I AM.

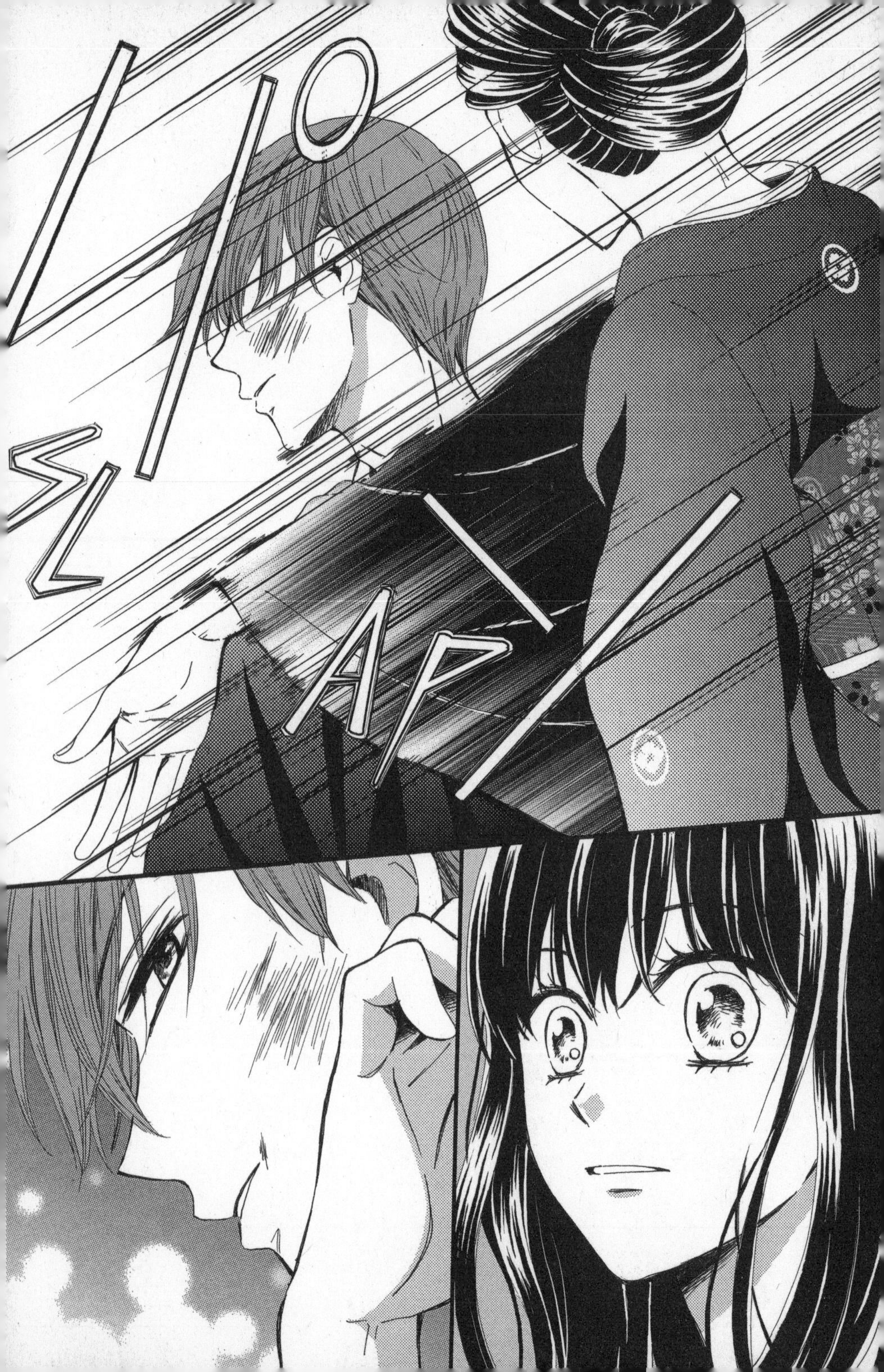
SLAP!!

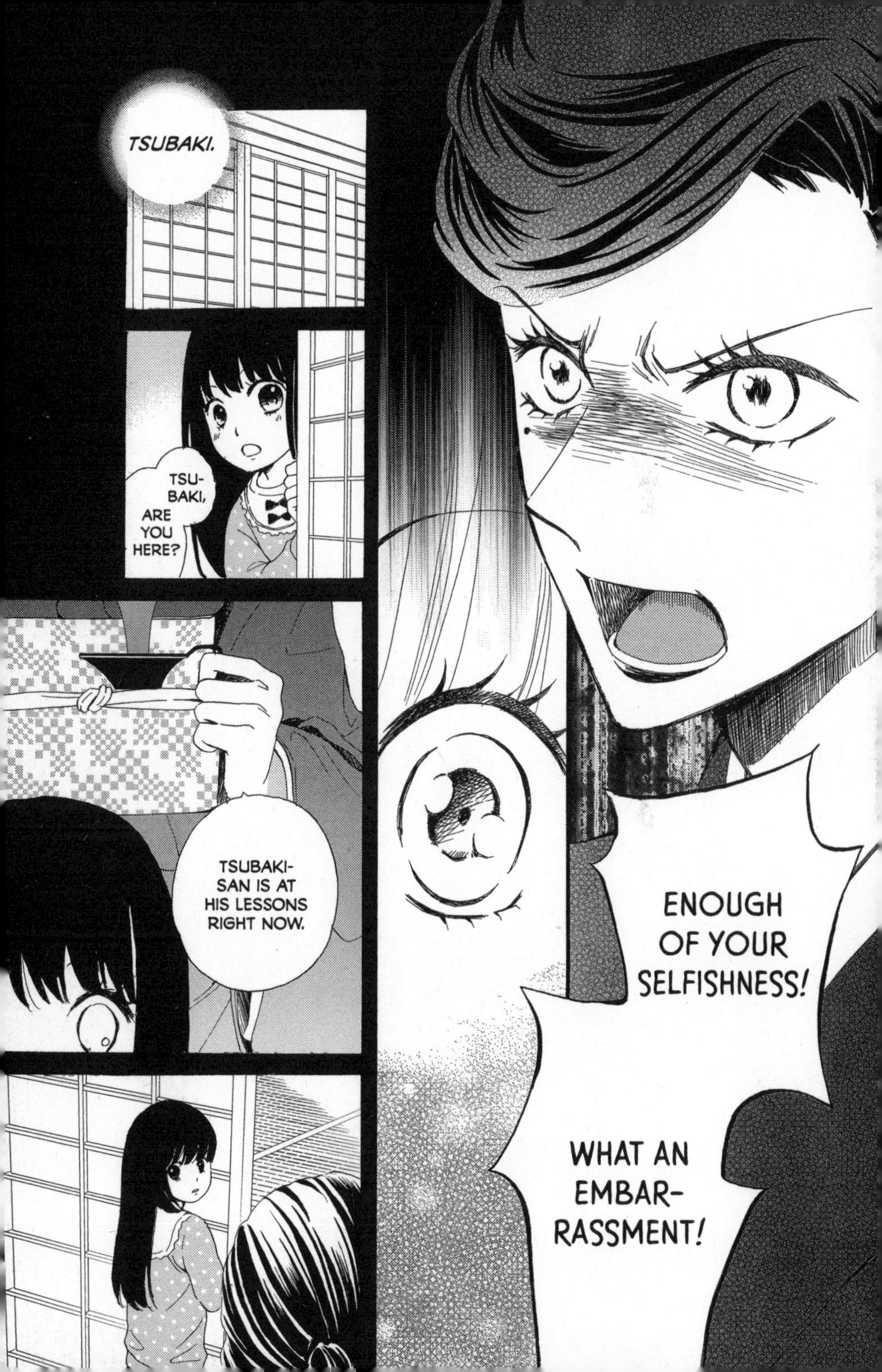
ENOUGH OF YOUR SELFISHNESS!
WHAT AN EMBARRASSMENT!
TSUBAKI.
TSUBAKI, ARE YOU HERE?
TSUBAKI-SAN IS AT HIS LESSONS RIGHT NOW.

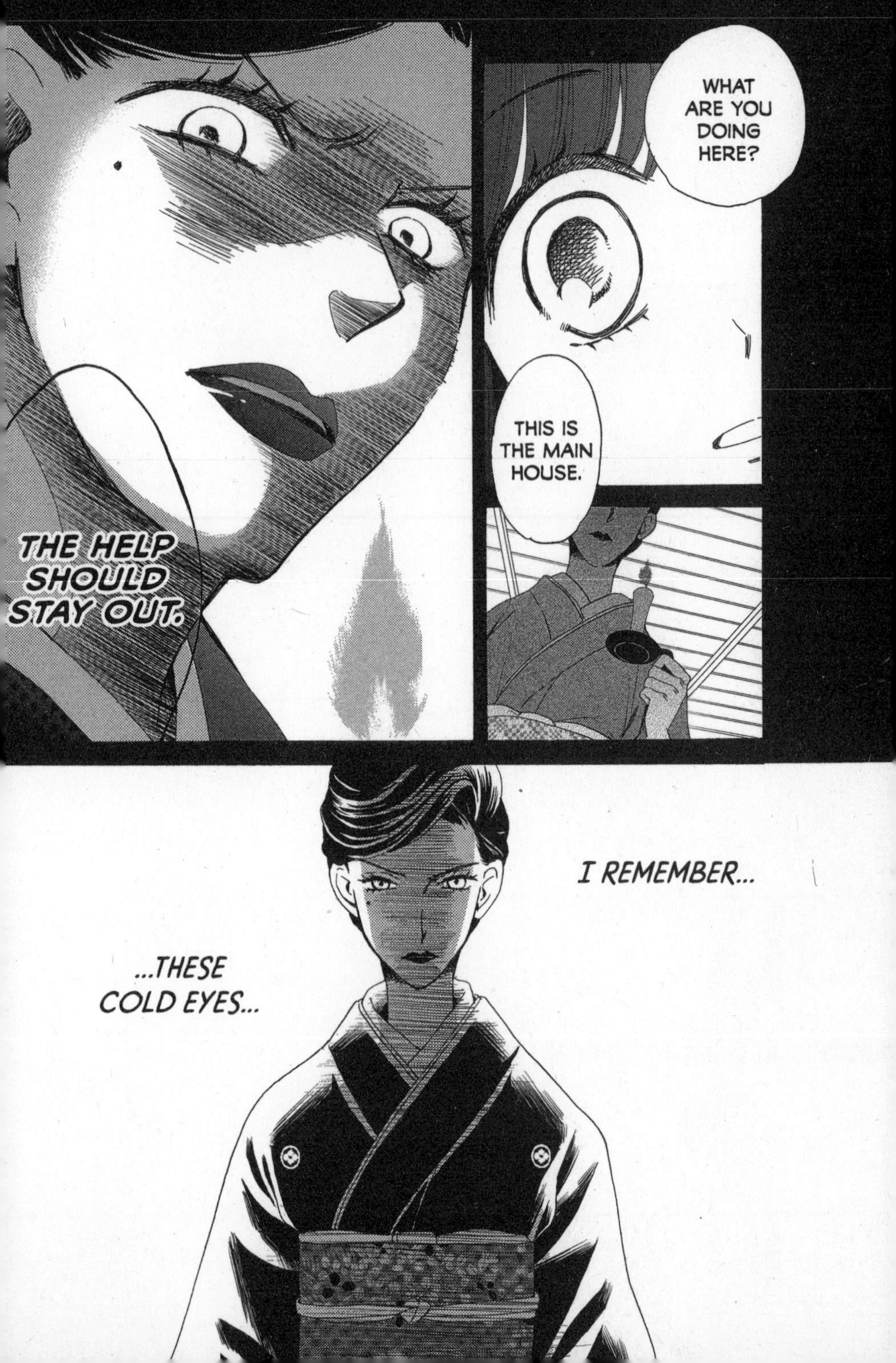
WHAT ARE YOU DOING HERE?
THIS IS THE MAIN HOUSE.
THE HELP SHOULD STAY OUT.
I REMEMBER...
...THESE COLD EYES...

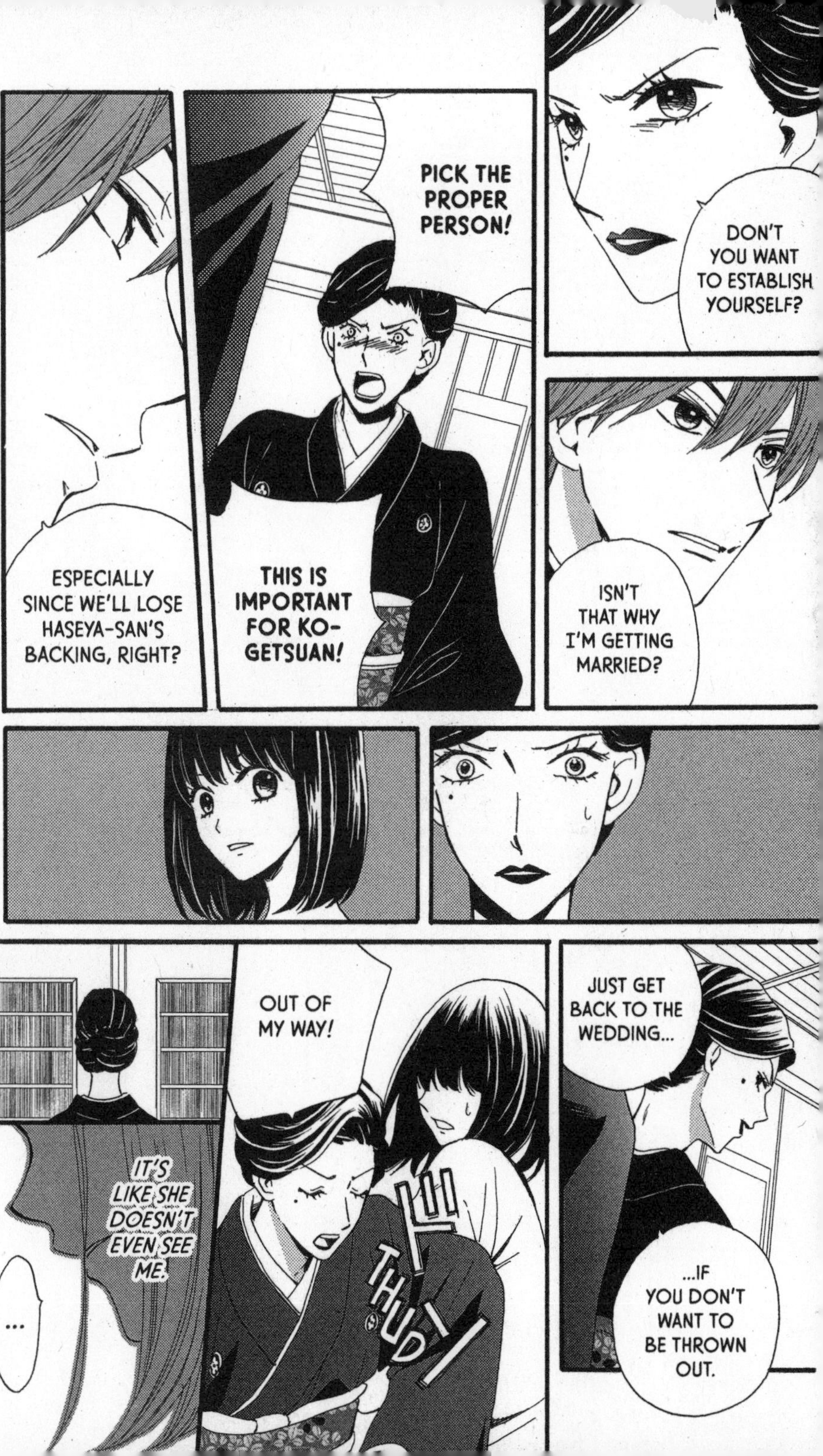
DON'T YOU WANT TO ESTABLISH YOURSELF?
ISN'T THAT WHY I'M GETTING MARRIED?
PICK THE PROPER PERSON!
THIS IS IMPORTANT FOR KO-GETSUAN!
ESPECIALLY SINCE WE'LL LOSE HASEYA-SAN'S BACKING, RIGHT?
JUST GET BACK TO THE WEDDING...
...IF YOU DON'T WANT TO BE THROWN OUT.
OUT OF MY WAY!
THUD!
IT'S LIKE SHE DOESN'T EVEN SEE ME.
...

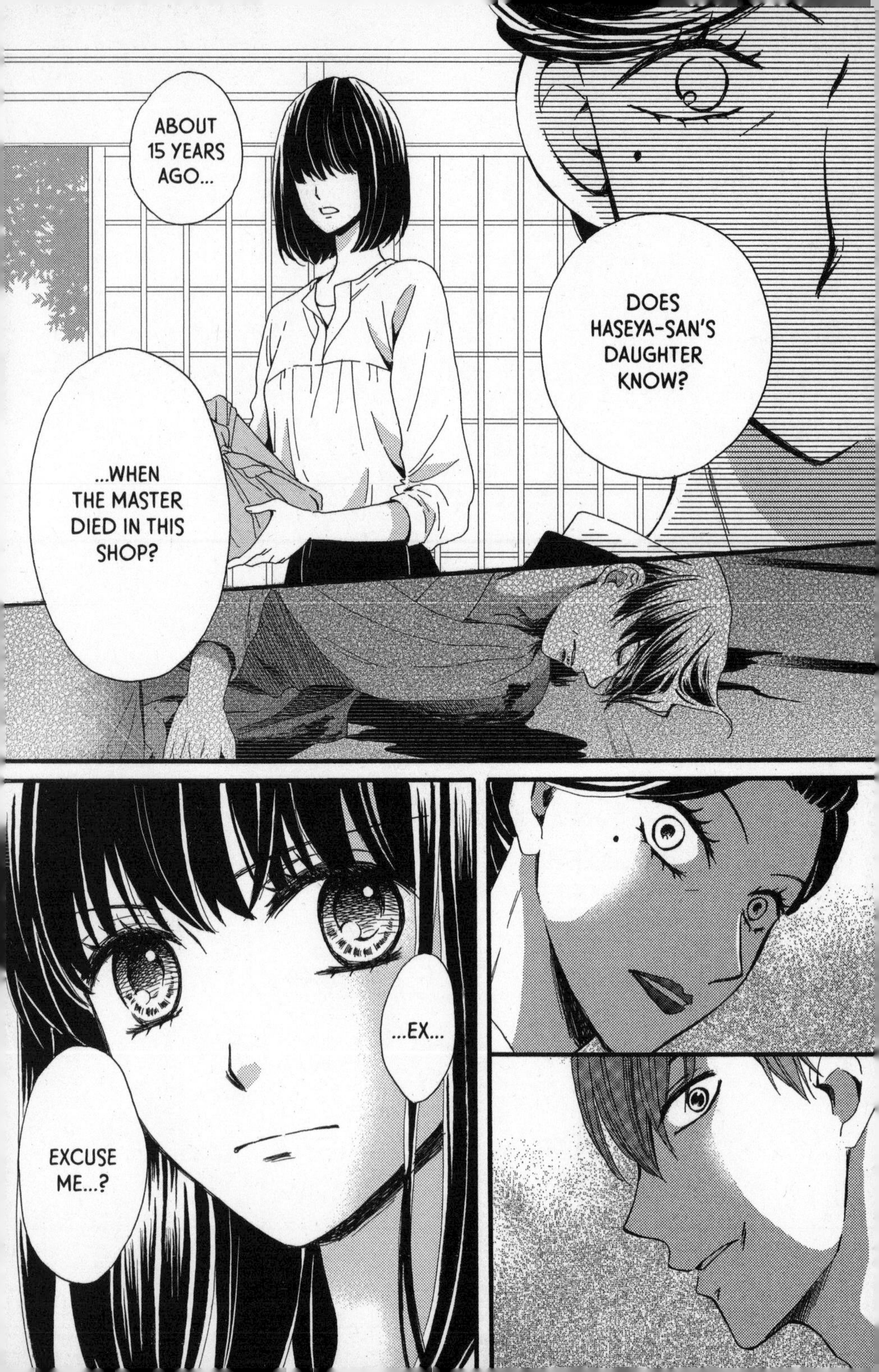
DOES HASEYA-SAN'S DAUGHTER KNOW?
ABOUT 15 YEARS AGO...
...WHEN THE MASTER DIED IN THIS SHOP?
...EX...
EXCUSE ME...?

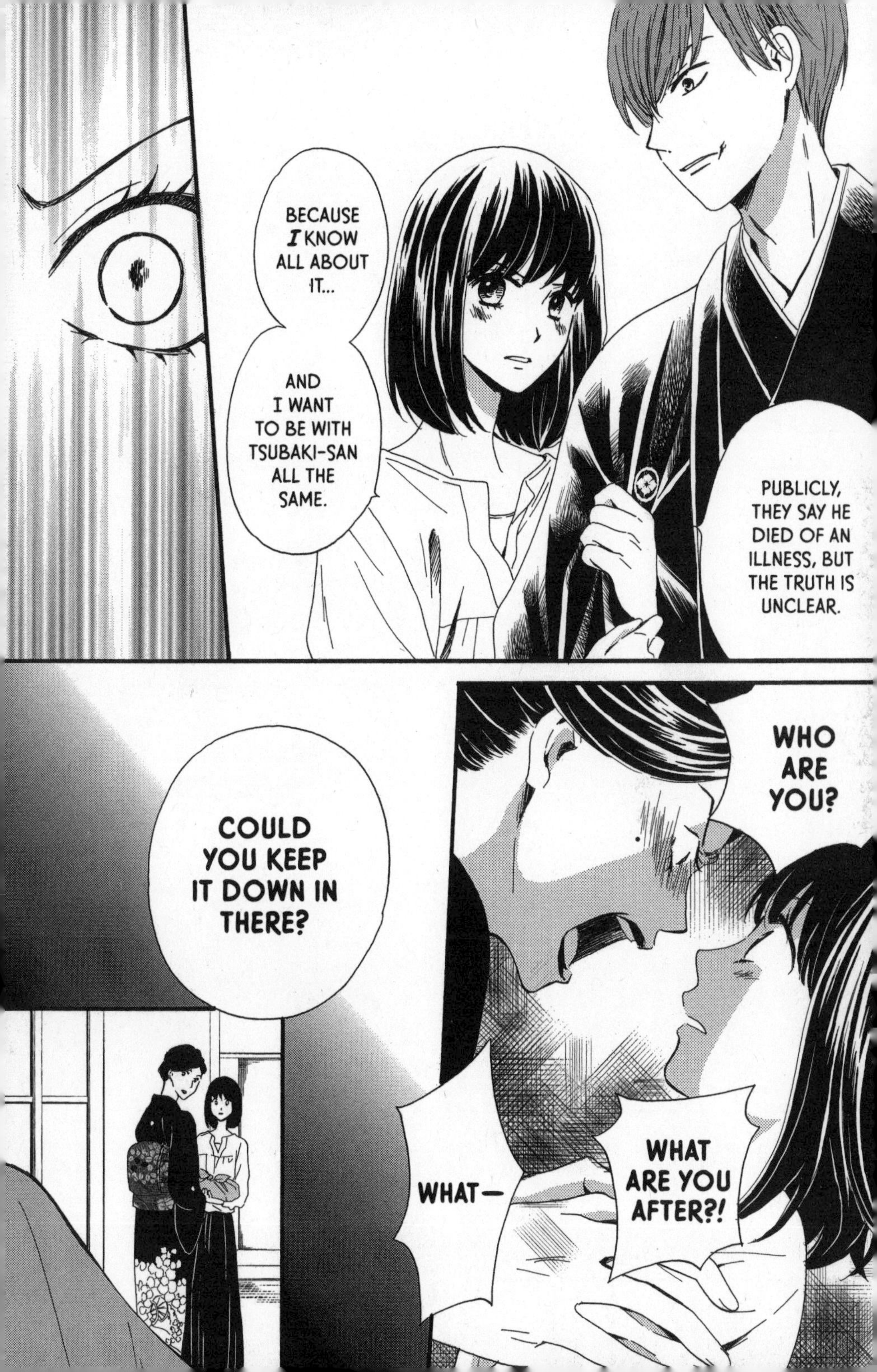
PUBLICLY, THEY SAY HE DIED OF AN ILLNESS, BUT THE TRUTH IS UNCLEAR.
BECAUSE *I* KNOW ALL ABOUT IT...
AND I WANT TO BE WITH TSUBAKI-SAN ALL THE SAME.
WHO ARE YOU?
WHAT ARE YOU AFTER?!
WHAT—
COULD YOU KEEP IT DOWN IN THERE?

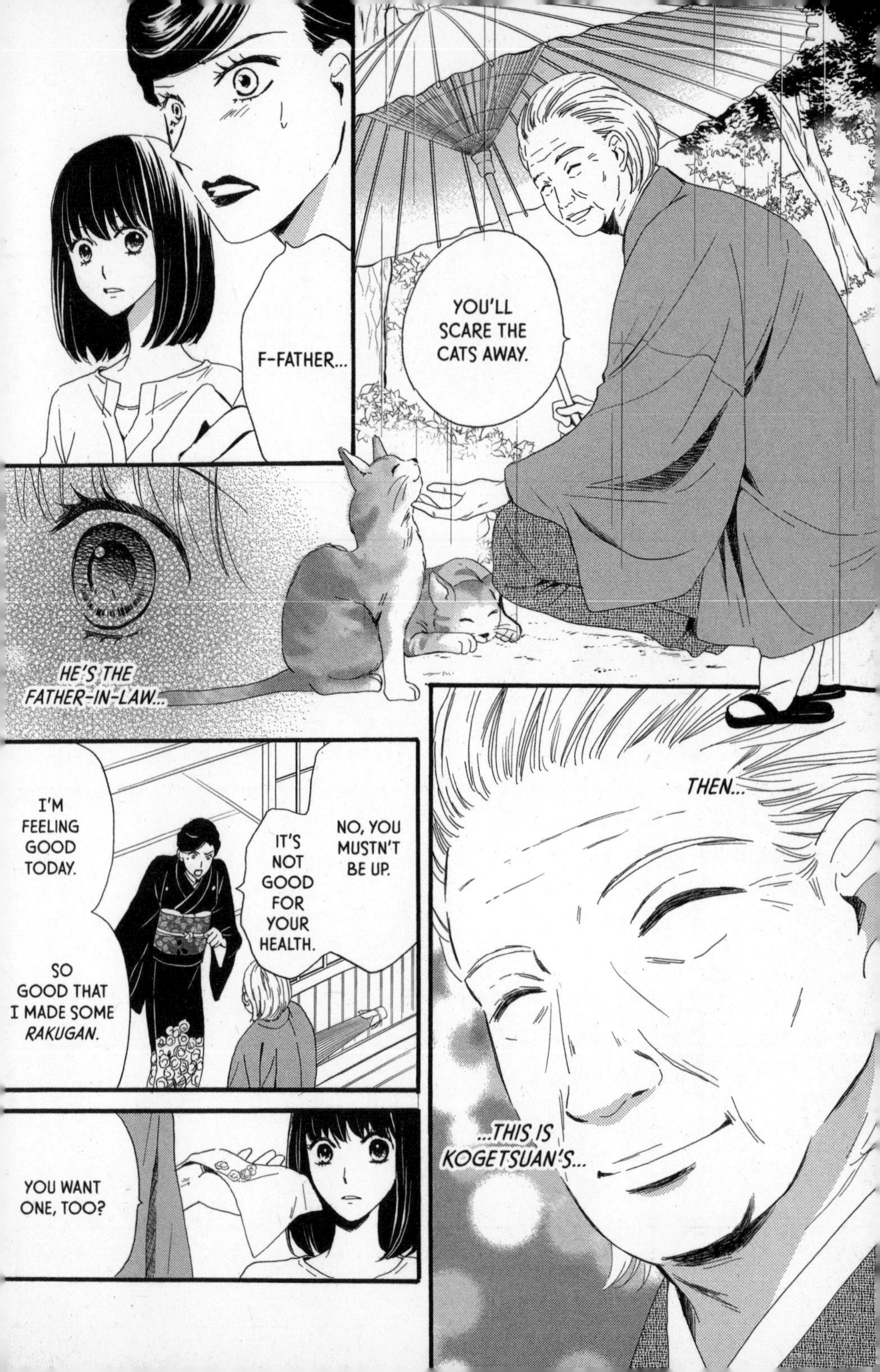
YOU'LL SCARE THE CATS AWAY.
F-FATHER...
HE'S THE FATHER-IN-LAW...
THEN...
...THIS IS KOGETSUAN'S...
NO, YOU MUSTN'T BE UP.
IT'S NOT GOOD FOR YOUR HEALTH.
I'M FEELING GOOD TODAY.
SO GOOD THAT I MADE SOME *RAKUGAN*.
YOU WANT ONE, TOO?

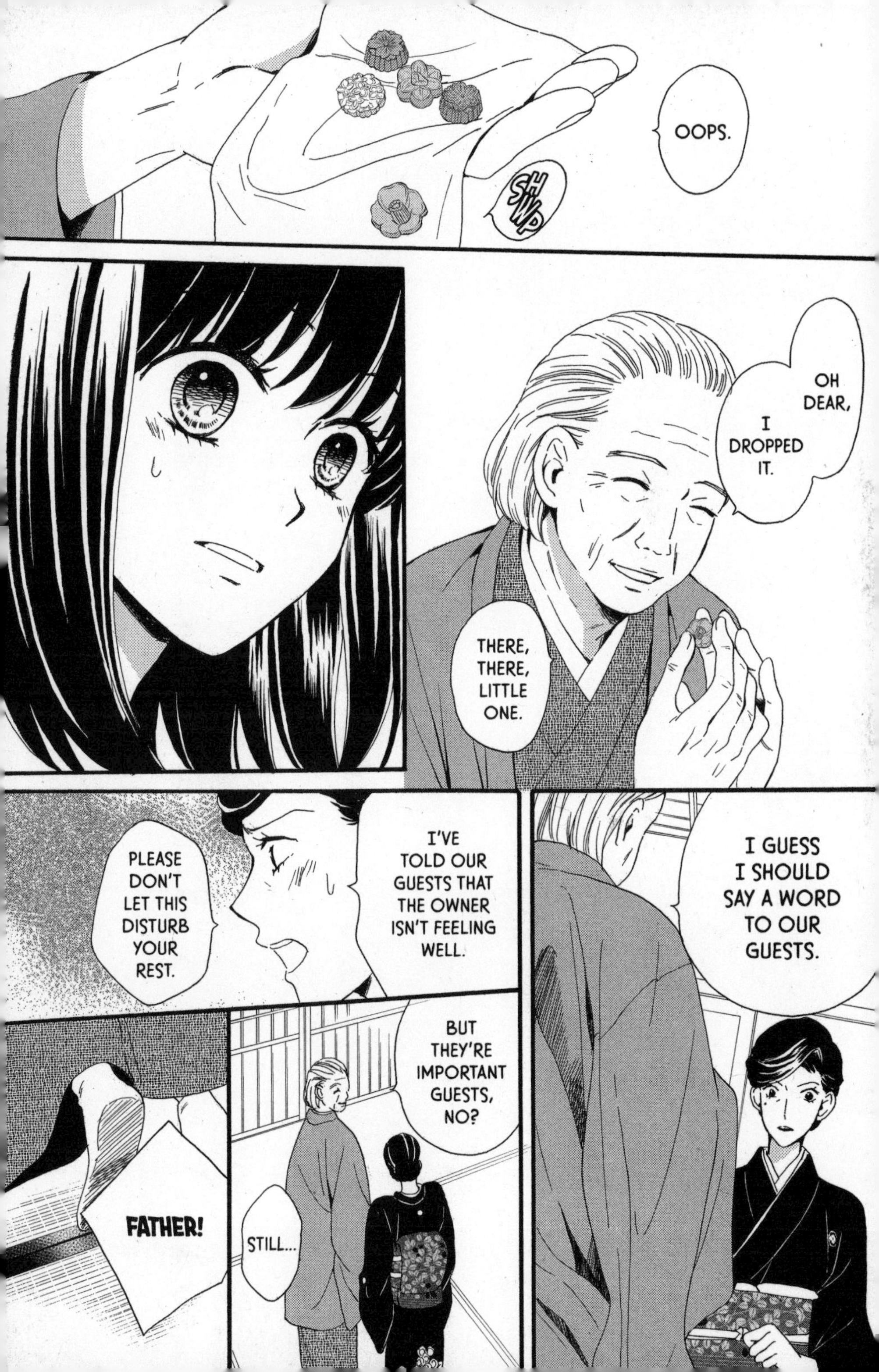
OOPS.
SHWP
OH DEAR, I DROPPED IT.
THERE, THERE, LITTLE ONE.
I GUESS I SHOULD SAY A WORD TO OUR GUESTS.
I'VE TOLD OUR GUESTS THAT THE OWNER ISN'T FEELING WELL.
PLEASE DON'T LET THIS DISTURB YOUR REST.
BUT THEY'RE IMPORTANT GUESTS, NO?
STILL...
FATHER!

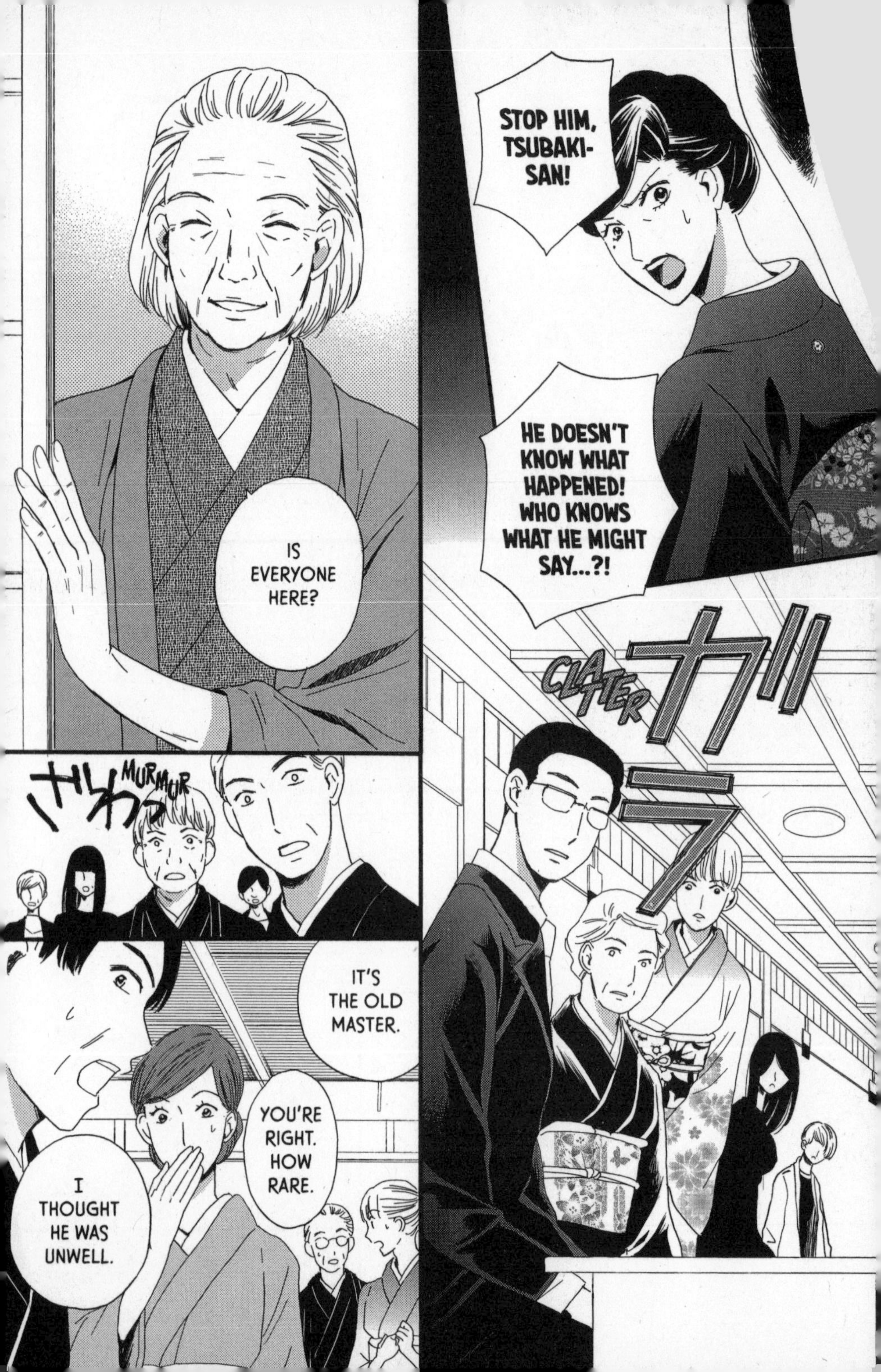
STOP HIM, TSUBAKI-SAN!
HE DOESN'T KNOW WHAT HAPPENED! WHO KNOWS WHAT HE MIGHT SAY...?!
ガラ
CLATTER
IS EVERYONE HERE?
ざわっ
MURMUR
IT'S THE OLD MASTER.
YOU'RE RIGHT. HOW RARE.
I THOUGHT HE WAS UNWELL.

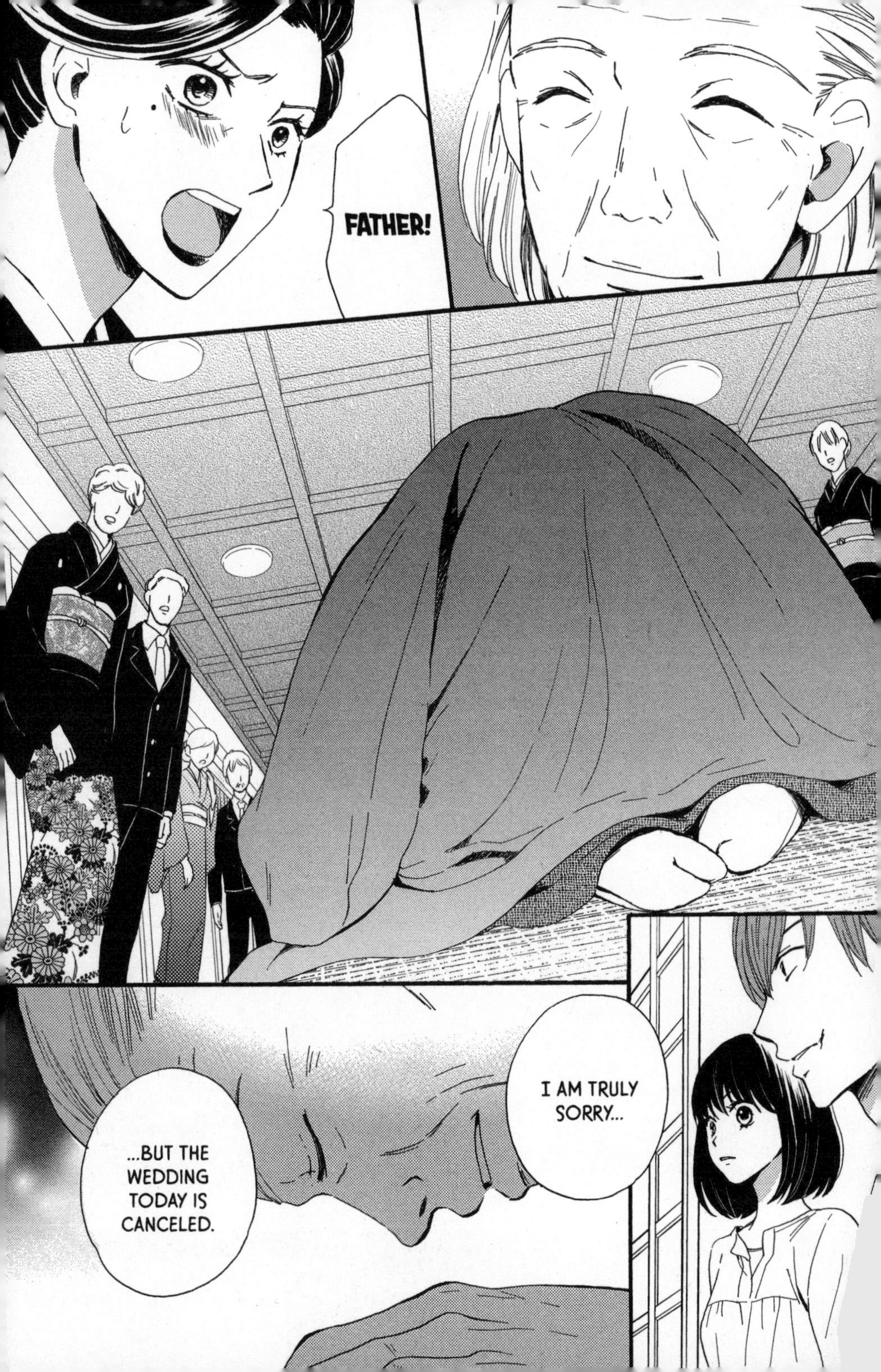
FATHER!
I AM TRULY SORRY...
...BUT THE WEDDING TODAY IS CANCELED.

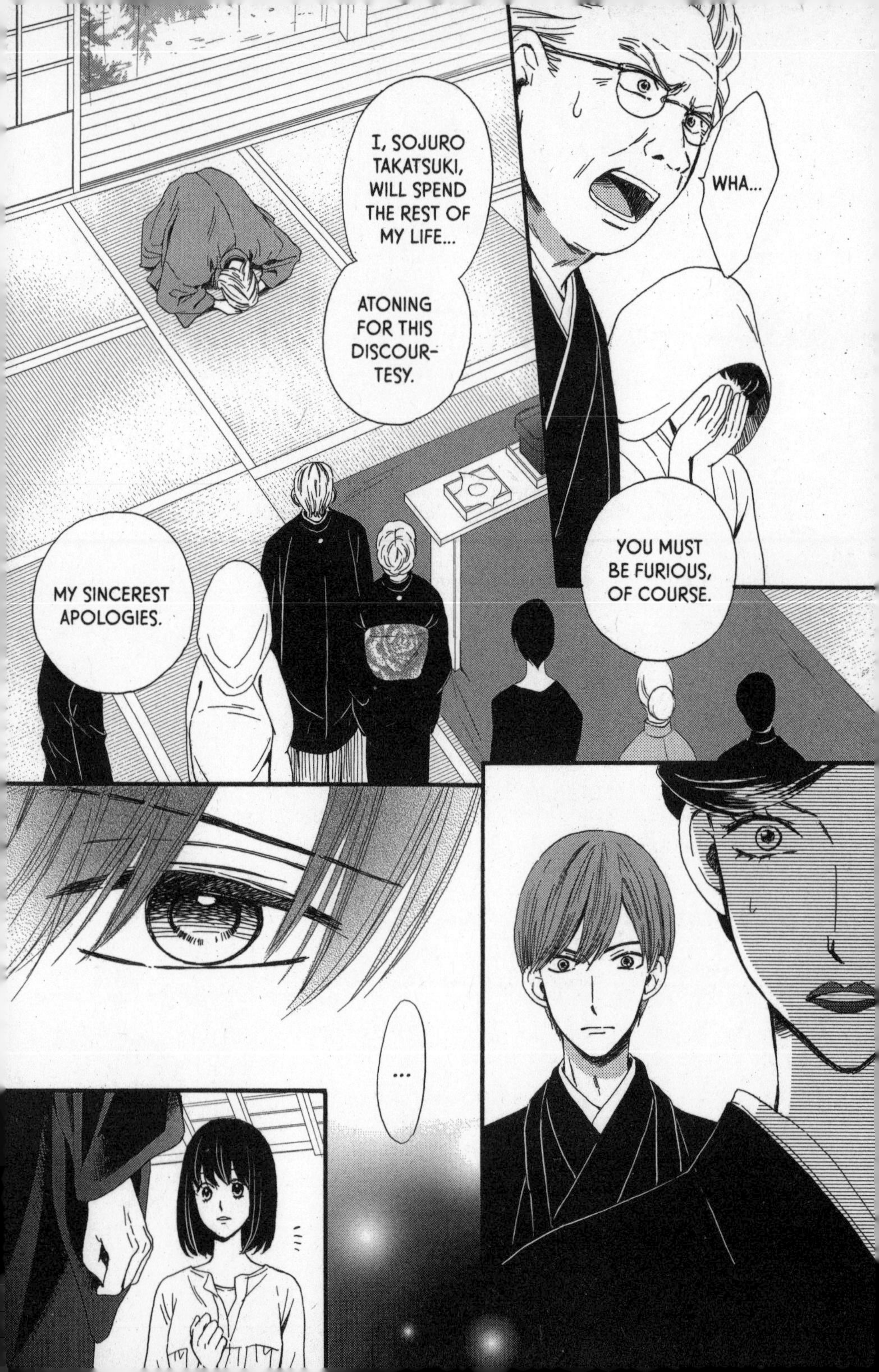
WHA...
YOU MUST BE FURIOUS, OF COURSE.
I, SOJURO TAKATSUKI, WILL SPEND THE REST OF MY LIFE...
ATONING FOR THIS DISCOURTESY.
MY SINCEREST APOLOGIES.
...

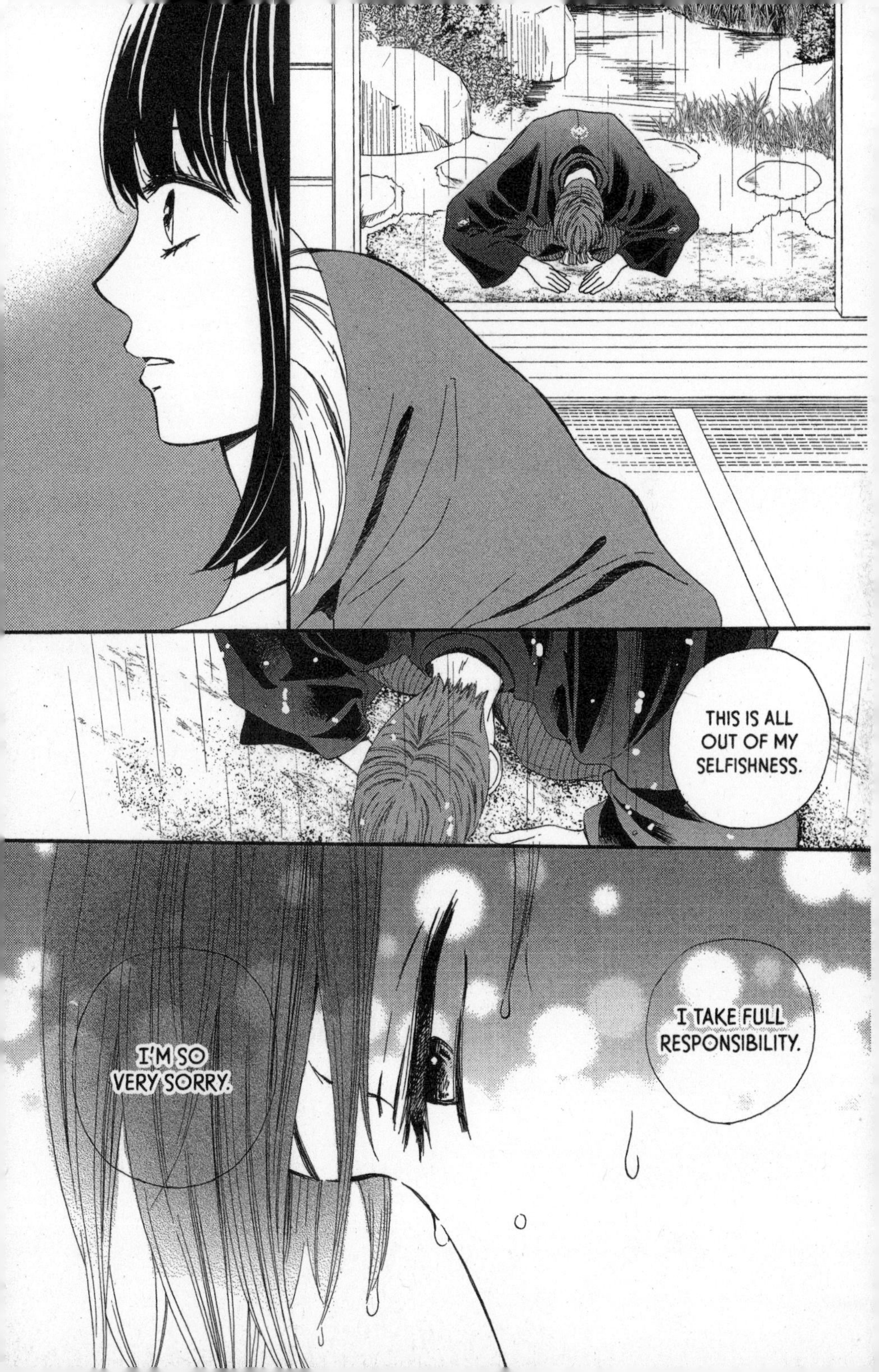
THIS IS ALL OUT OF MY SELFISHNESS.
I TAKE FULL RESPONSIBILITY.
I'M SO VERY SORRY.

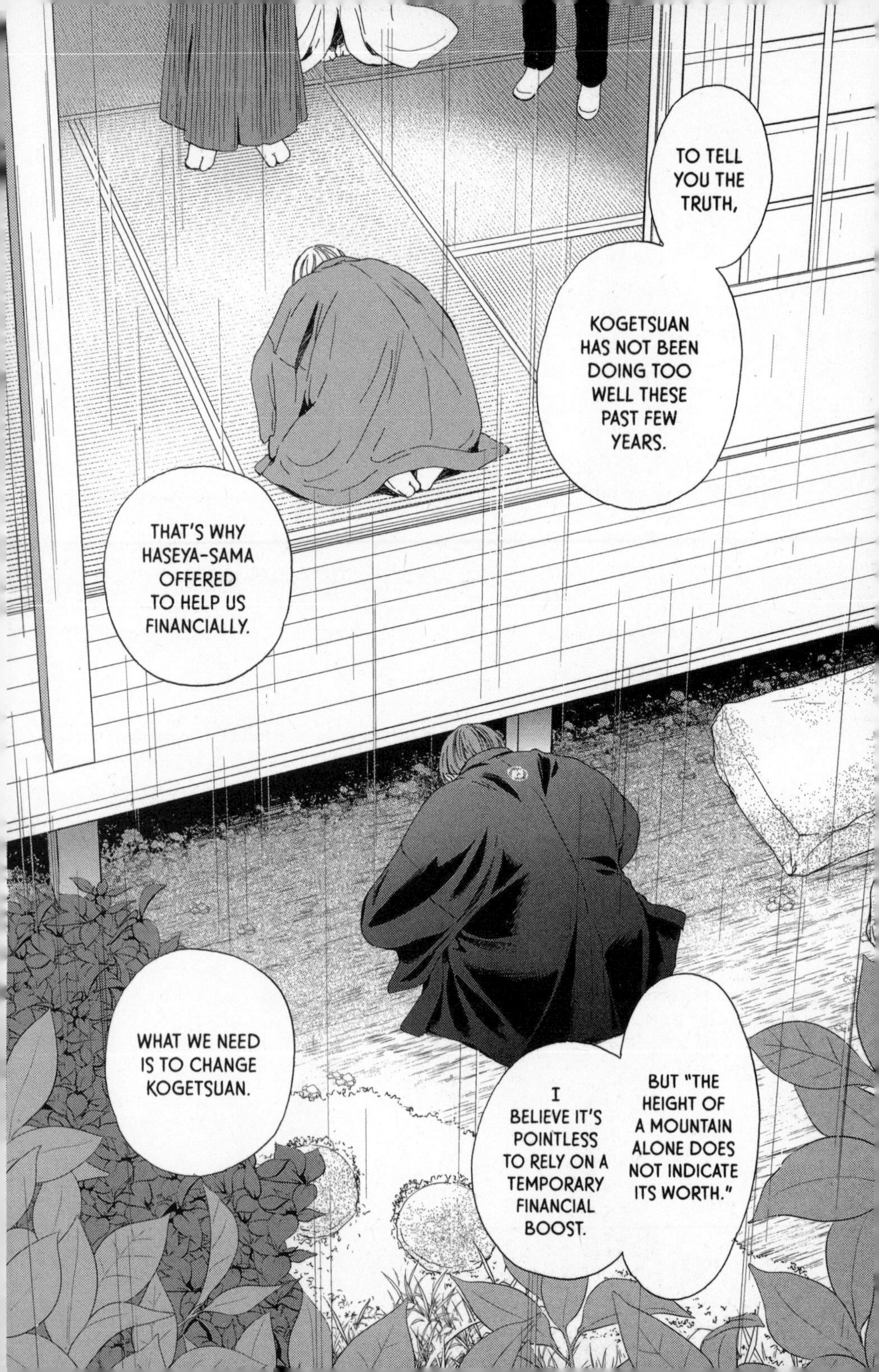
TO TELL YOU THE TRUTH,
KOGETSUAN HAS NOT BEEN DOING TOO WELL THESE PAST FEW YEARS.
THAT'S WHY HASEYA-SAMA OFFERED TO HELP US FINANCIALLY.
BUT "THE HEIGHT OF A MOUNTAIN ALONE DOES NOT INDICATE ITS WORTH."
I BELIEVE IT'S POINTLESS TO RELY ON A TEMPORARY FINANCIAL BOOST.
WHAT WE NEED IS TO CHANGE KOGETSUAN.

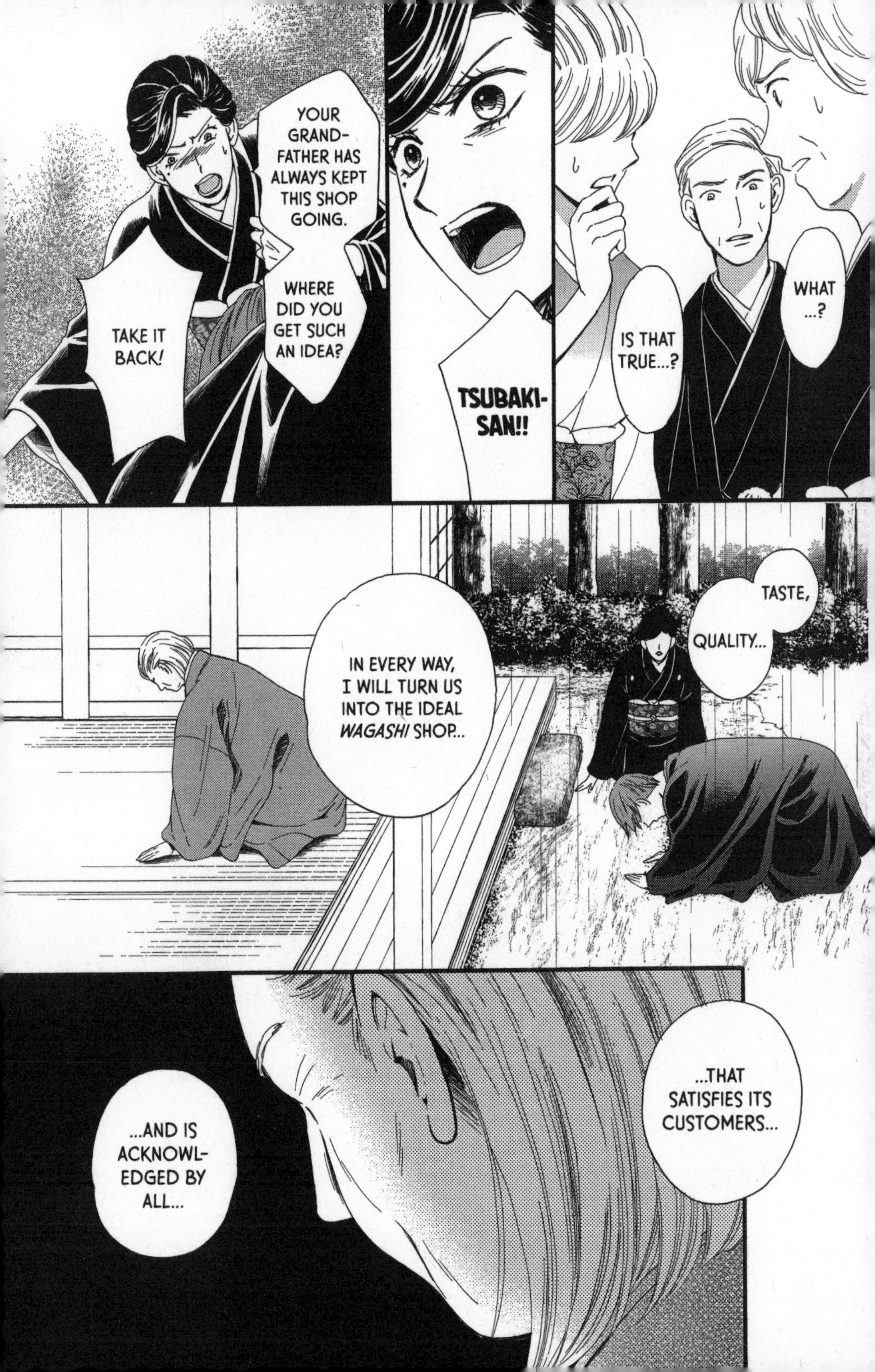
WHAT ...?
IS THAT TRUE...?
TSUBAKI-SAN!!
YOUR GRAND-FATHER HAS ALWAYS KEPT THIS SHOP GOING.
WHERE DID YOU GET SUCH AN IDEA?
TAKE IT BACK!
TASTE,
QUALITY...
IN EVERY WAY, I WILL TURN US INTO THE IDEAL *WAGASHI* SHOP...
...THAT SATISFIES ITS CUSTOMERS...
...AND IS ACKNOWL-EDGED BY ALL...

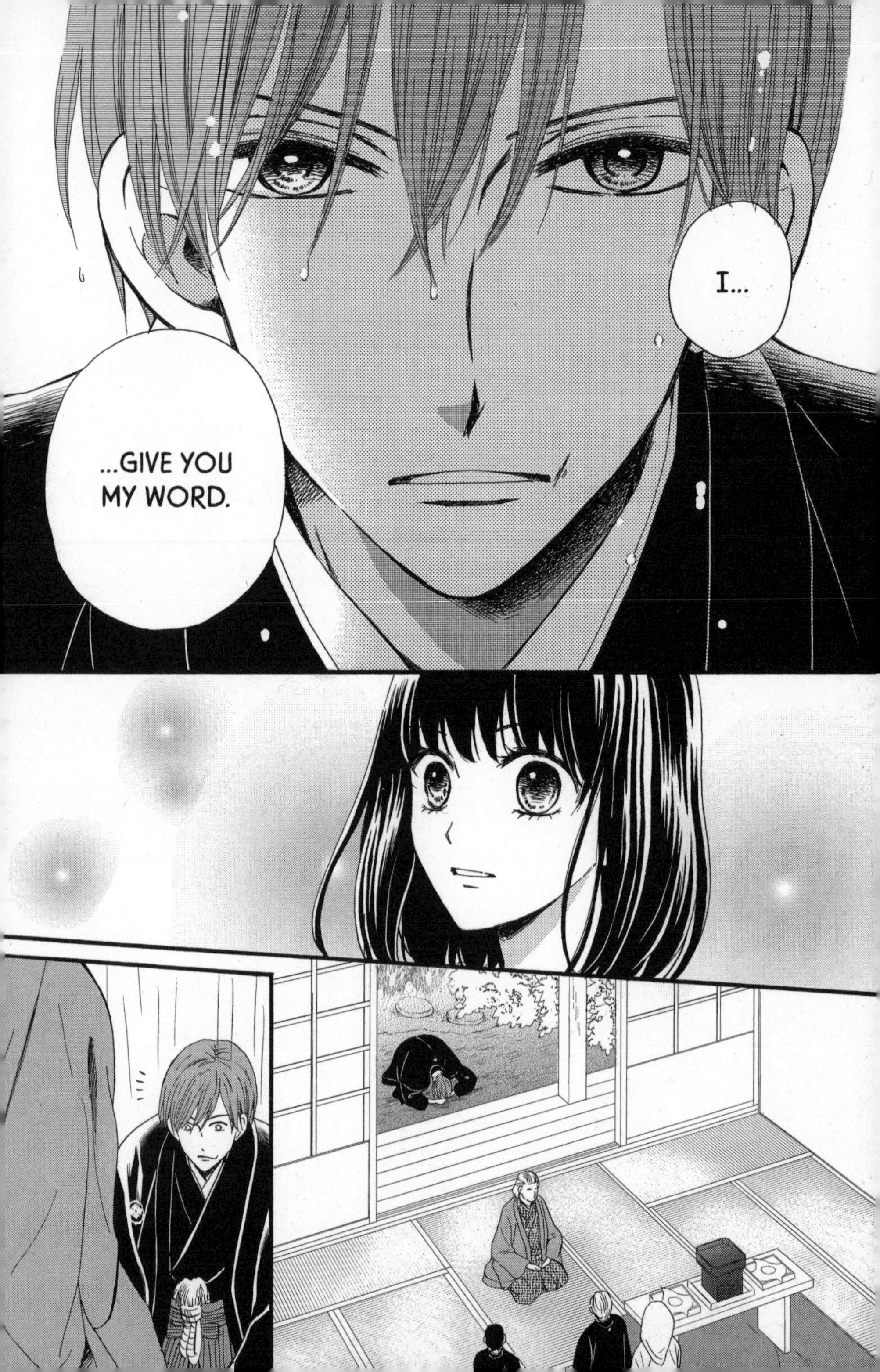
I...
...GIVE YOU MY WORD.

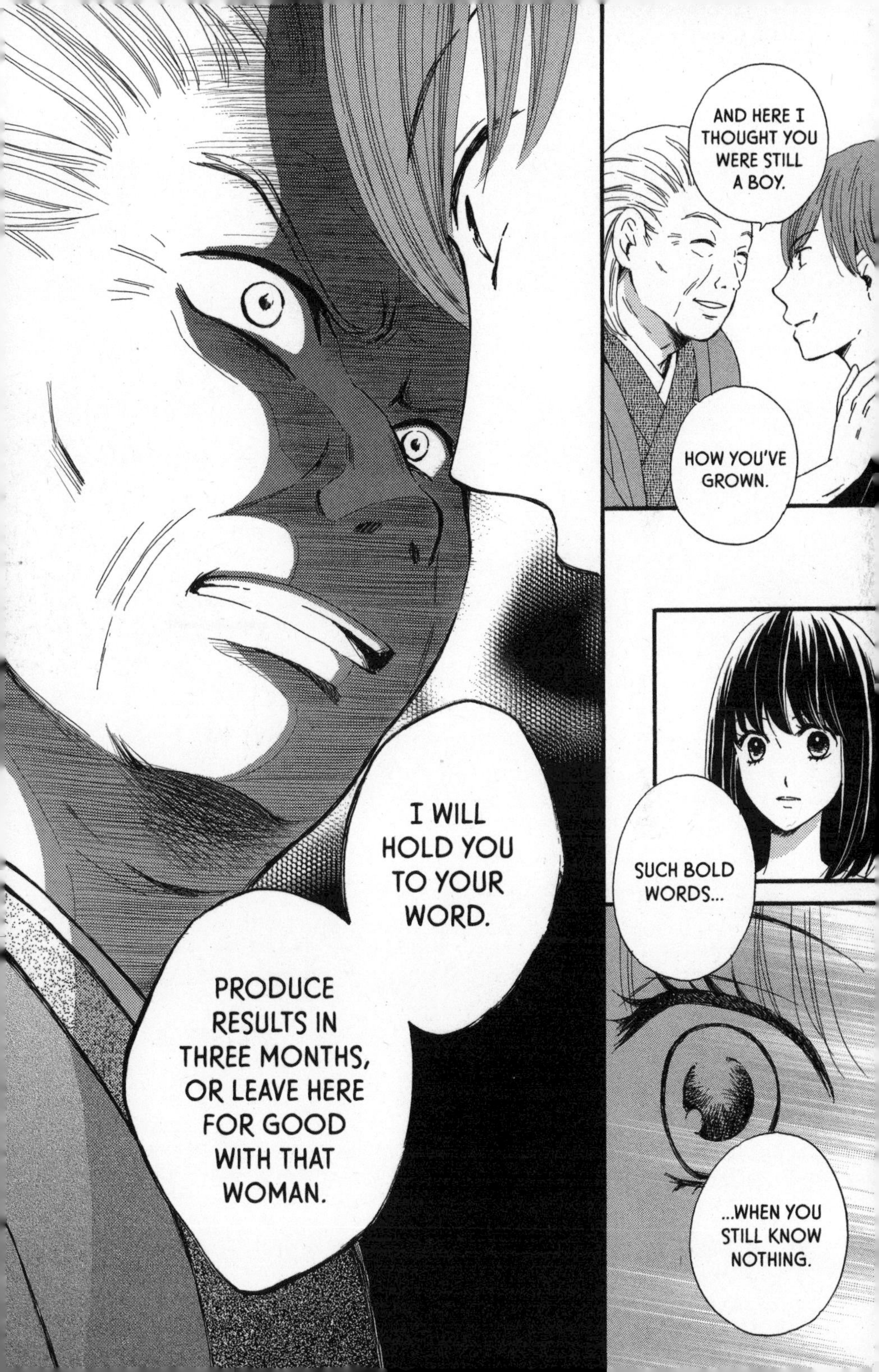
AND HERE I THOUGHT YOU WERE STILL A BOY.
HOW YOU'VE GROWN.
SUCH BOLD WORDS...
...WHEN YOU STILL KNOW NOTHING.
I WILL HOLD YOU TO YOUR WORD.
PRODUCE RESULTS IN THREE MONTHS, OR LEAVE HERE FOR GOOD WITH THAT WOMAN.

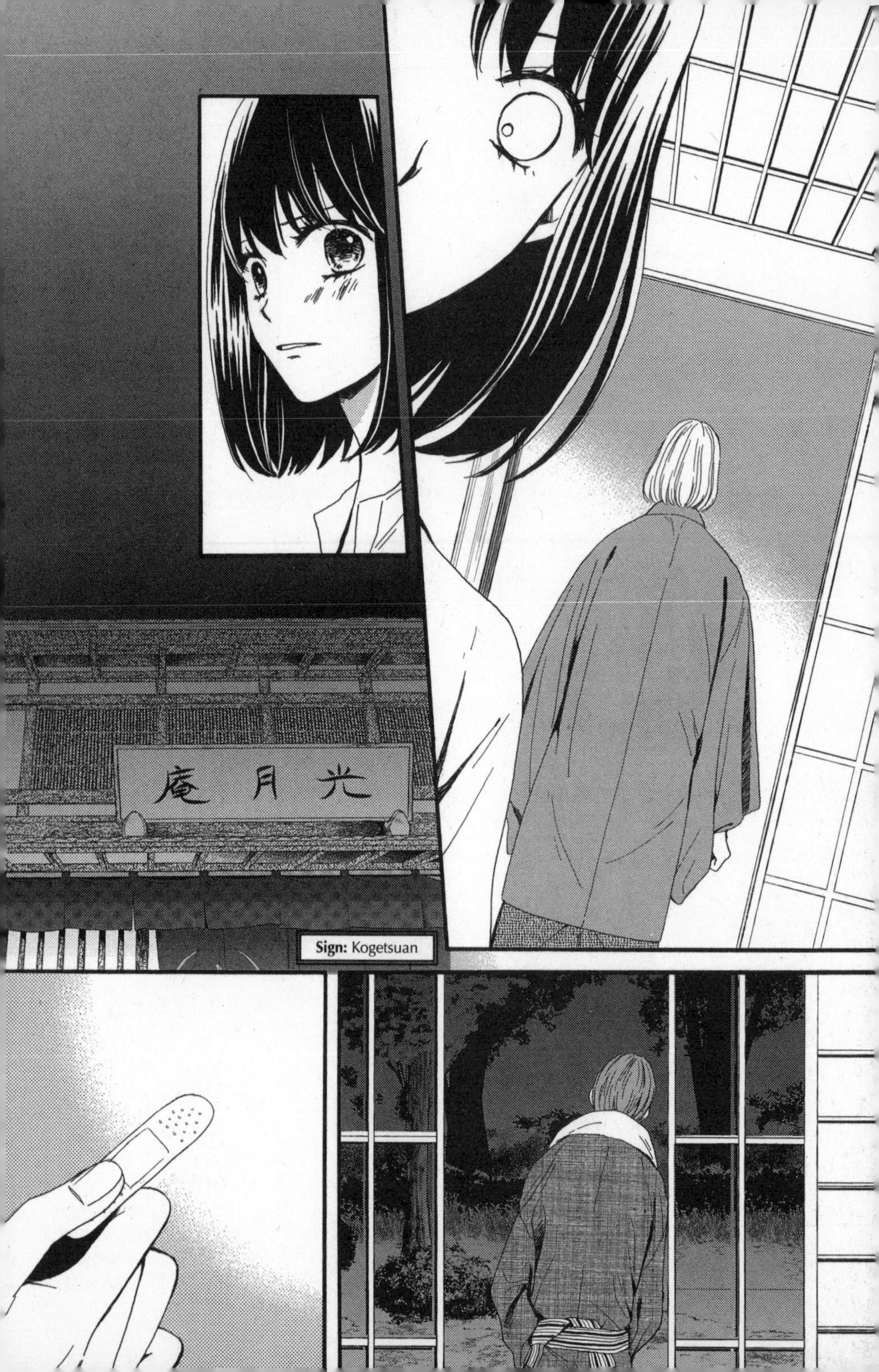
光月庵
Sign: Kogetsuan

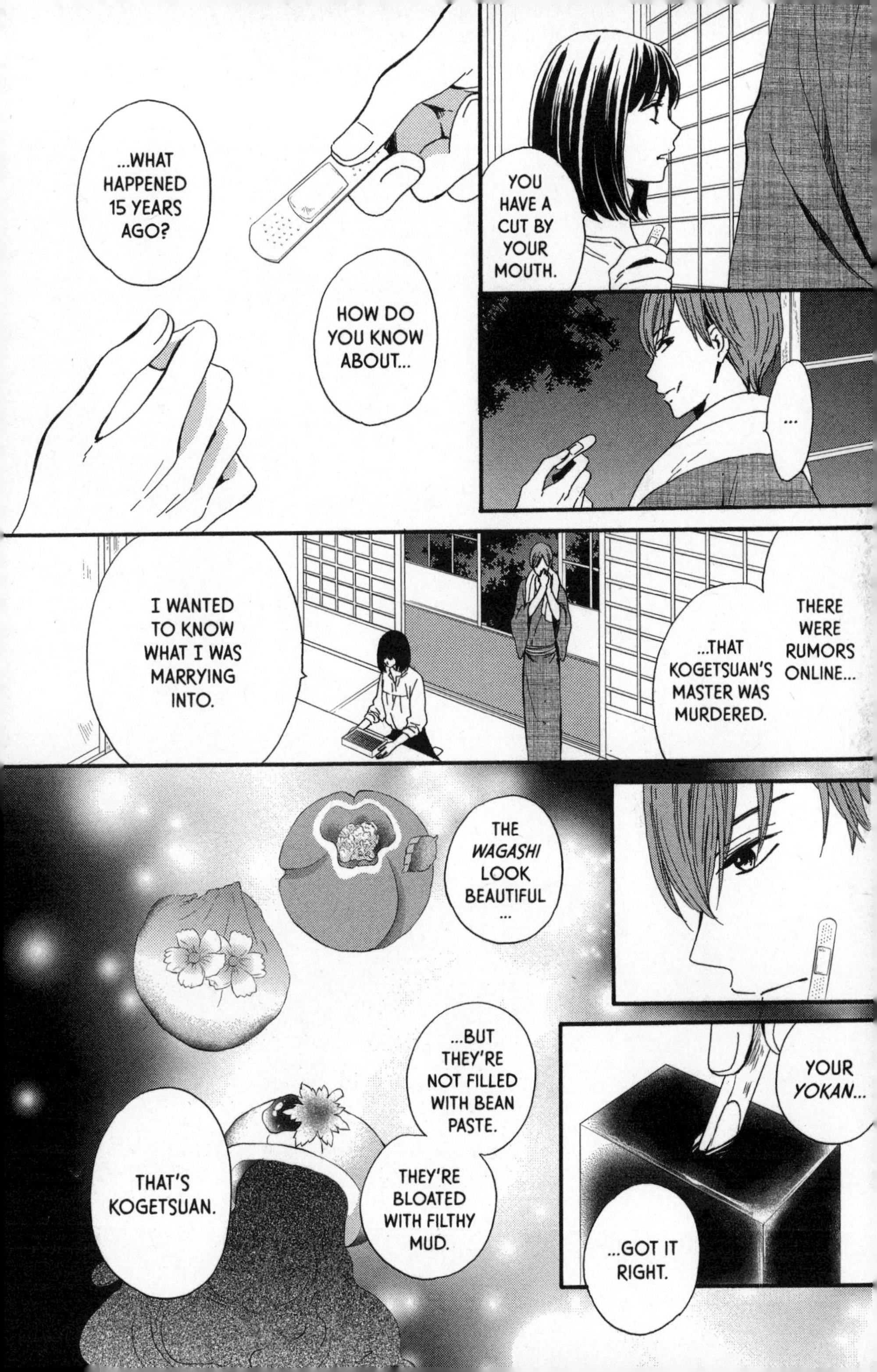
YOU HAVE A CUT BY YOUR MOUTH.
...
HOW DO YOU KNOW ABOUT...
...WHAT HAPPENED 15 YEARS AGO?
THERE WERE RUMORS ONLINE...
...THAT KOGETSUAN'S MASTER WAS MURDERED.
I WANTED TO KNOW WHAT I WAS MARRYING INTO.
YOUR *YOKAN*...
...GOT IT RIGHT.
THE *WAGASHI* LOOK BEAUTIFUL ...
...BUT THEY'RE NOT FILLED WITH BEAN PASTE.
THEY'RE BLOATED WITH FILTHY MUD.
THAT'S KOGETSUAN.

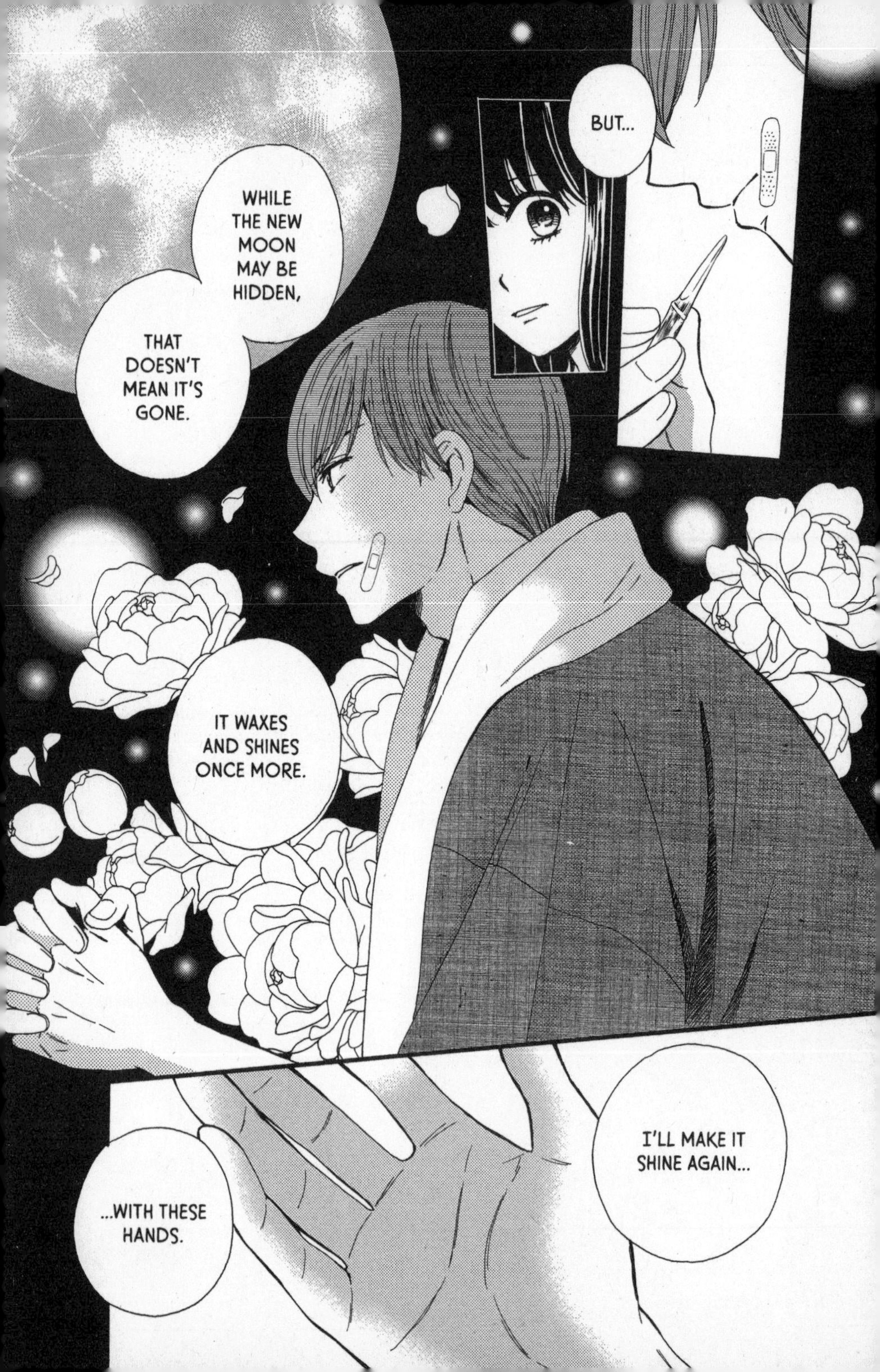
BUT...
WHILE THE NEW MOON MAY BE HIDDEN,
THAT DOESN'T MEAN IT'S GONE.
IT WAXES AND SHINES ONCE MORE.
I'LL MAKE IT SHINE AGAIN...
...WITH THESE HANDS.

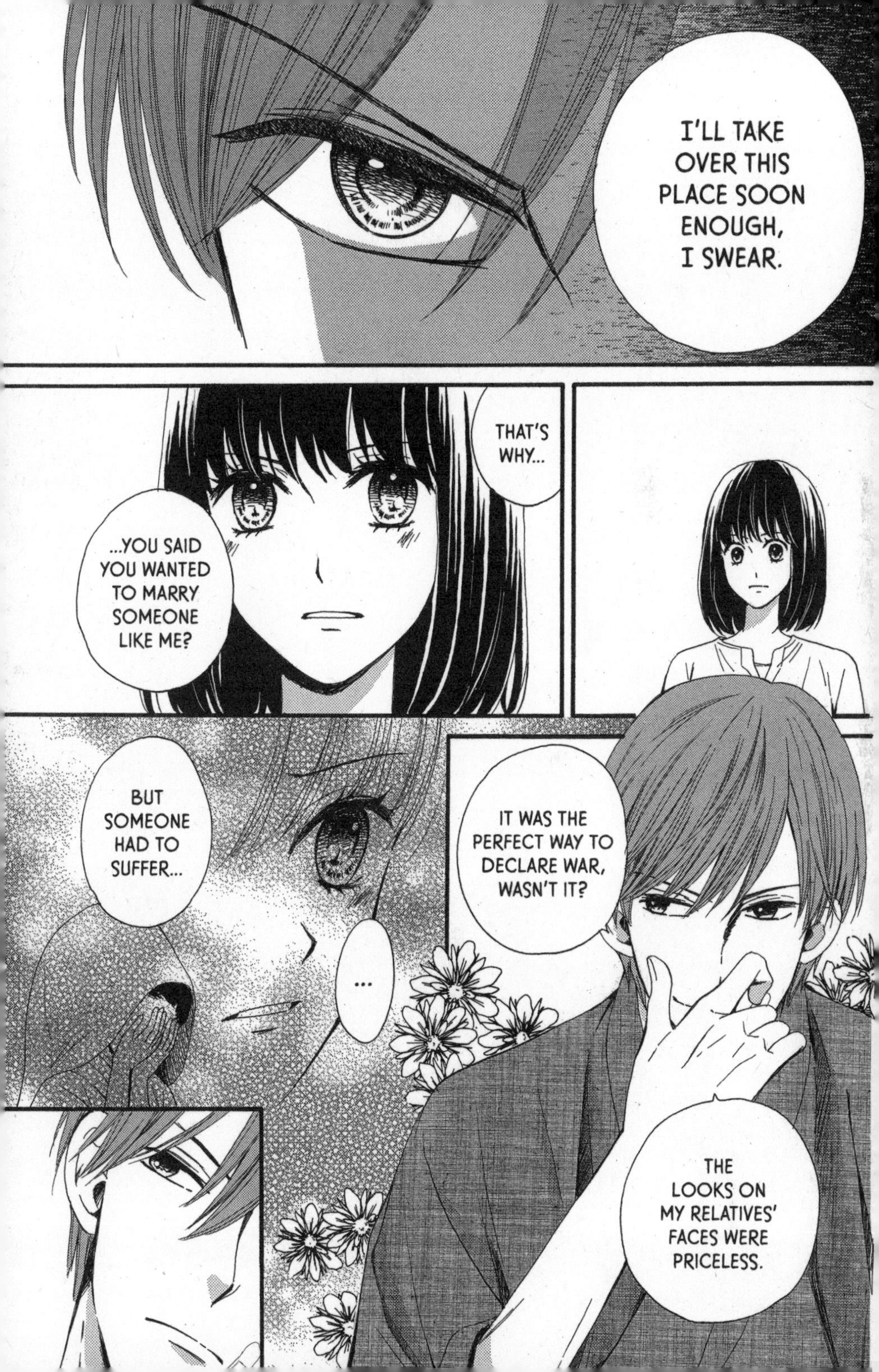
I'LL TAKE OVER THIS PLACE SOON ENOUGH, I SWEAR.
THAT'S WHY...
...YOU SAID YOU WANTED TO MARRY SOMEONE LIKE ME?
IT WAS THE PERFECT WAY TO DECLARE WAR, WASN'T IT?
THE LOOKS ON MY RELATIVES' FACES WERE PRICELESS.
BUT SOMEONE HAD TO SUFFER...
...

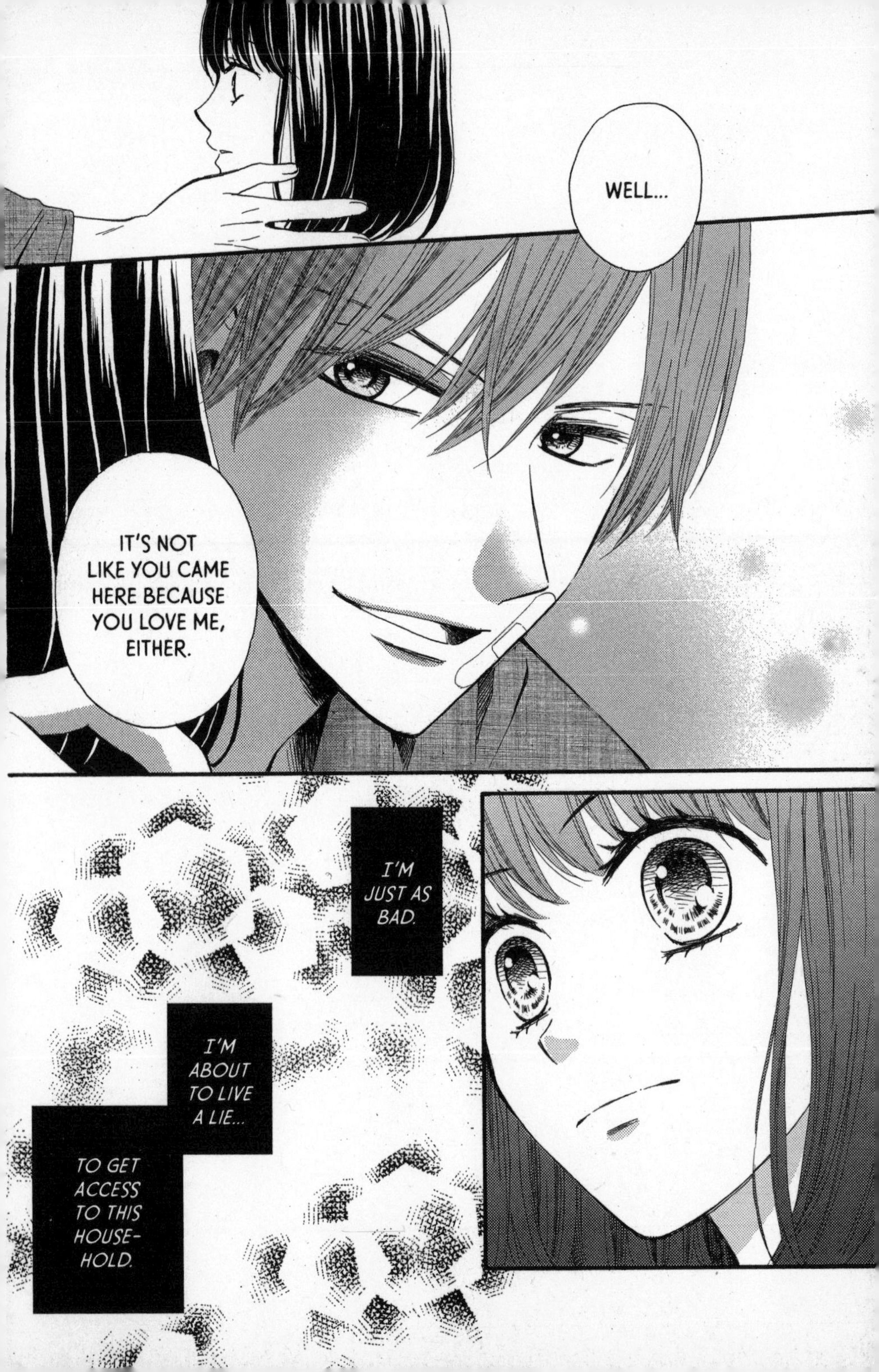
WELL...
IT'S NOT LIKE YOU CAME HERE BECAUSE YOU LOVE ME, EITHER.
I'M JUST AS BAD.
I'M ABOUT TO LIVE A LIE...
TO GET ACCESS TO THIS HOUSE-HOLD.

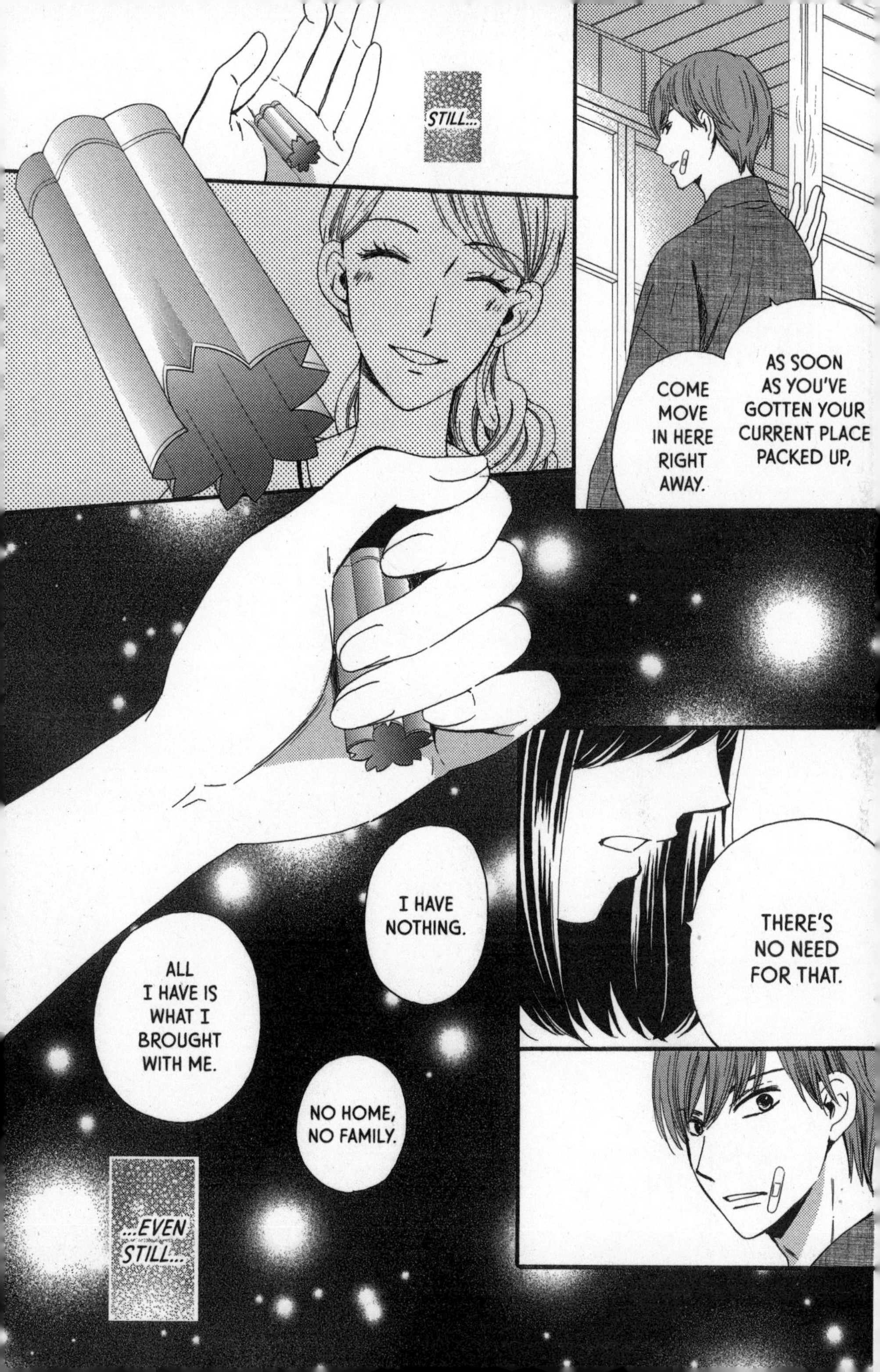
AS SOON AS YOU'VE GOTTEN YOUR CURRENT PLACE PACKED UP,
COME MOVE IN HERE RIGHT AWAY.
STILL...
THERE'S NO NEED FOR THAT.
I HAVE NOTHING.
ALL I HAVE IS WHAT I BROUGHT WITH ME.
NO HOME, NO FAMILY.
...EVEN STILL...

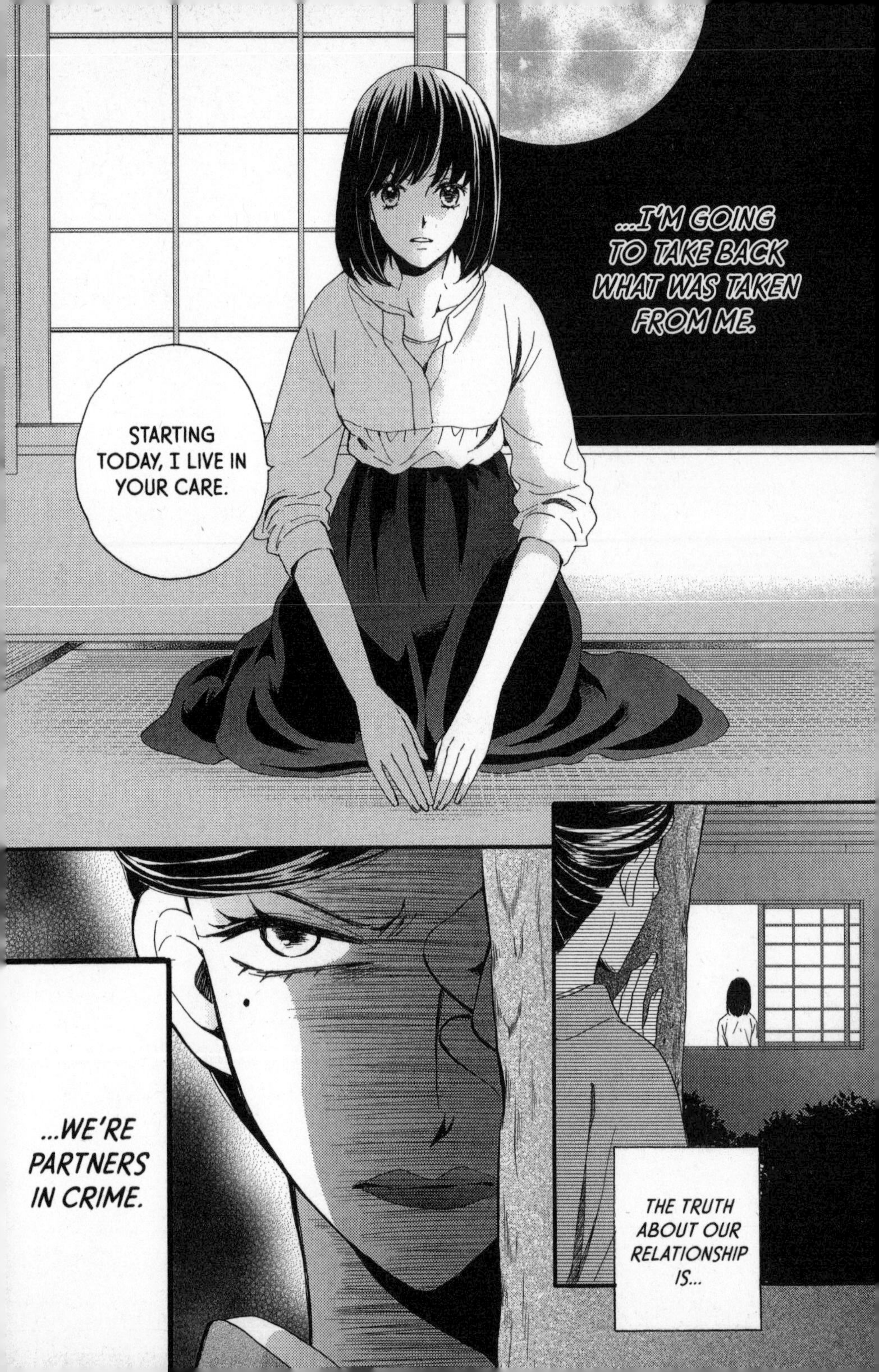
...I'M GOING TO TAKE BACK WHAT WAS TAKEN FROM ME.
STARTING TODAY, I LIVE IN YOUR CARE.
THE TRUTH ABOUT OUR RELATIONSHIP IS...
...WE'RE PARTNERS IN CRIME.

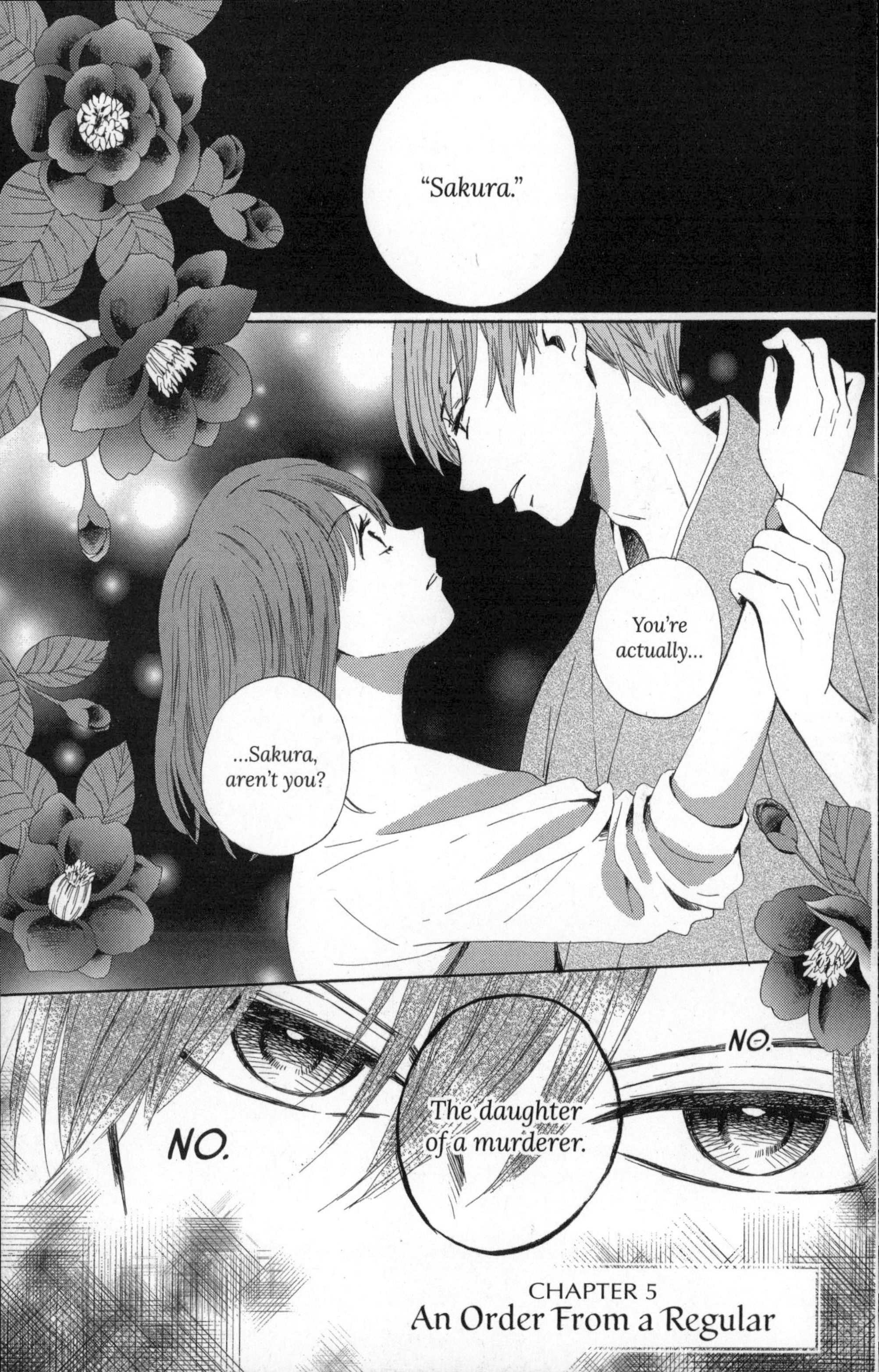
"Sakura."
You're actually...
...Sakura, aren't you?
NO.
The daughter of a murderer.
NO.

CHAPTER 5
An Order From a Regular

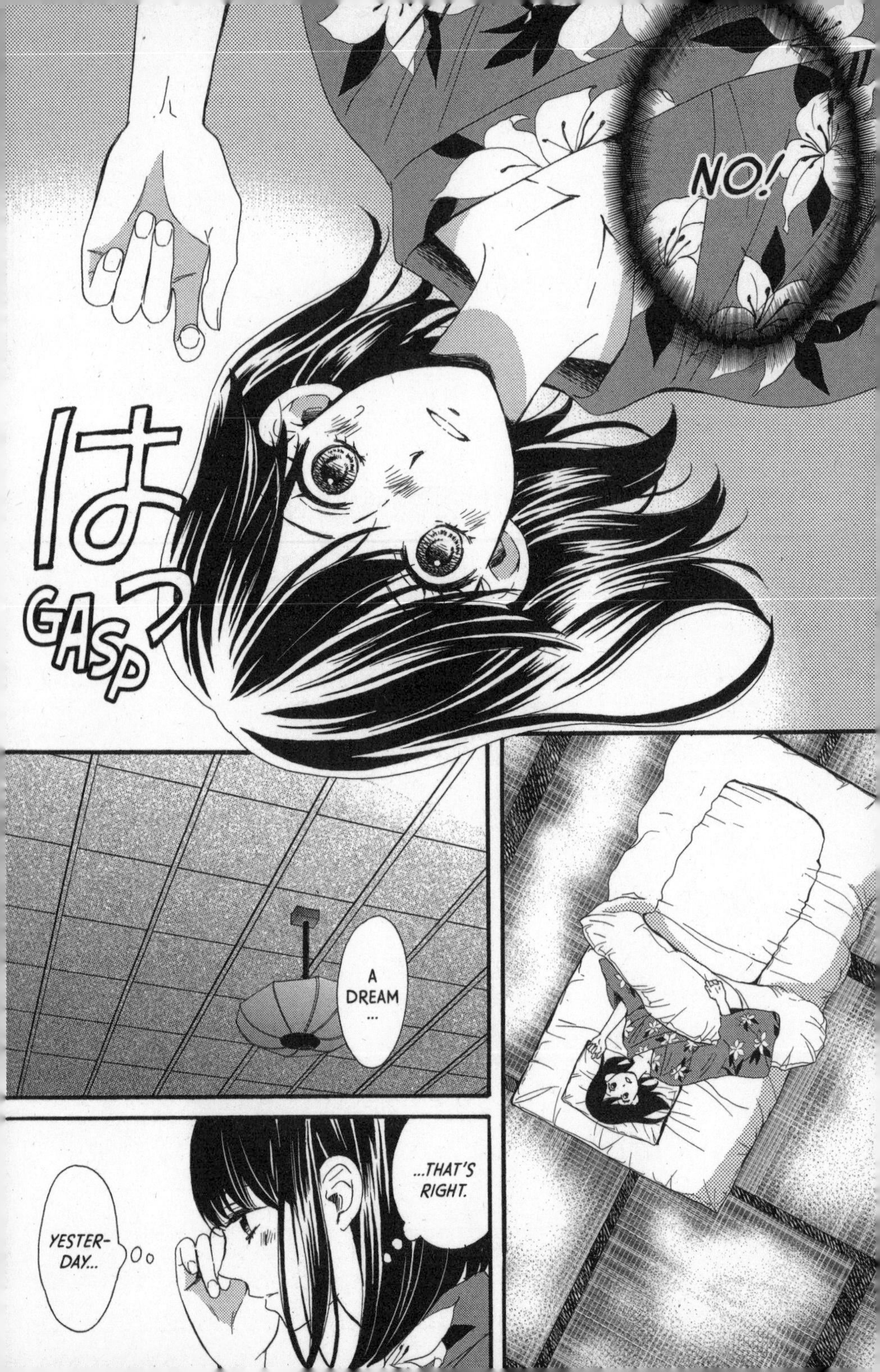
NO!
はっ
GASP
A DREAM ...
...THAT'S RIGHT.
YESTER-DAY...

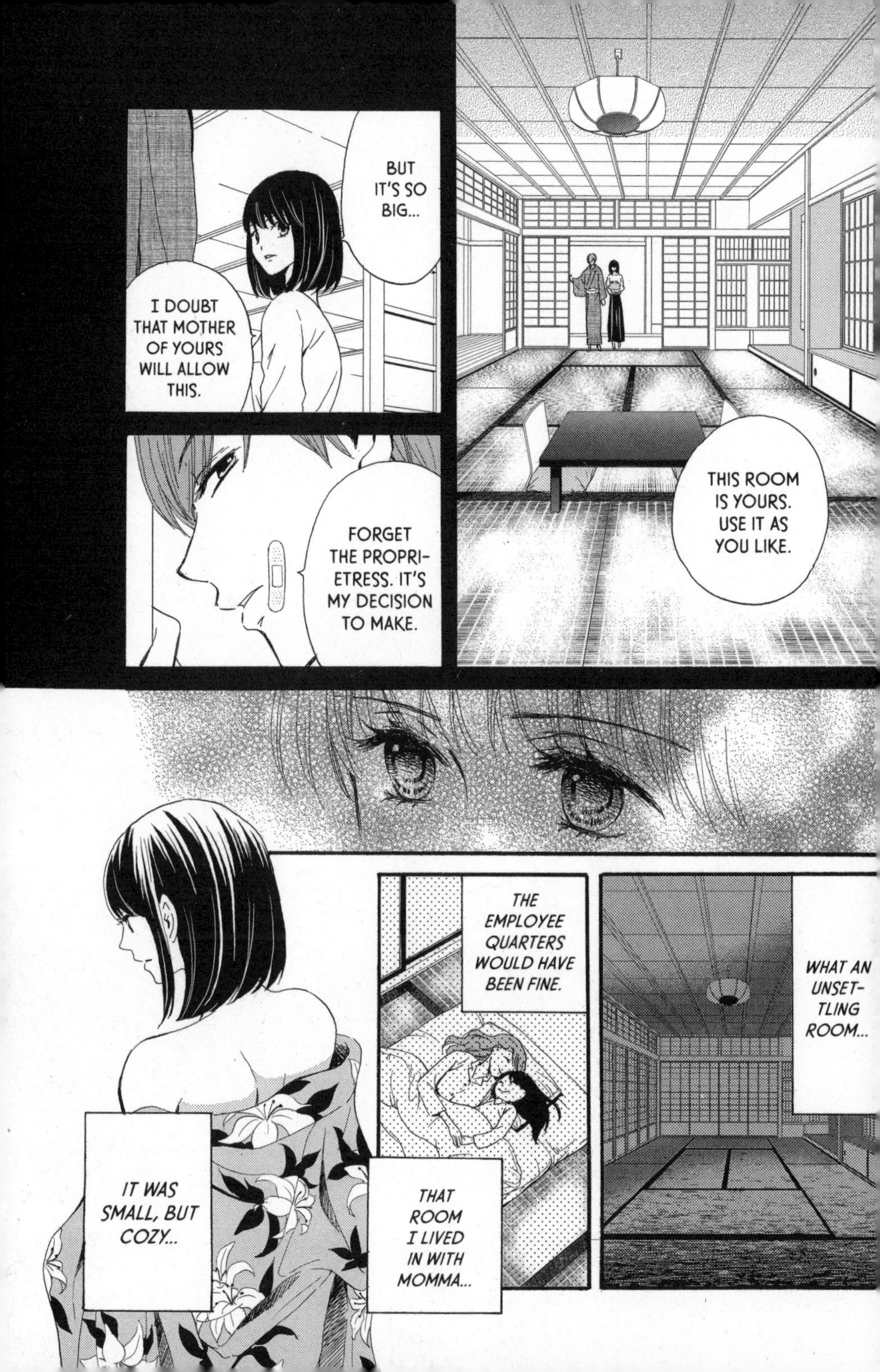
THIS ROOM IS YOURS. USE IT AS YOU LIKE.
BUT IT'S SO BIG...
I DOUBT THAT MOTHER OF YOURS WILL ALLOW THIS.
FORGET THE PROPRI-ETRESS. IT'S MY DECISION TO MAKE.
WHAT AN UNSET-TLING ROOM...
THE EMPLOYEE QUARTERS WOULD HAVE BEEN FINE.
THAT ROOM I LIVED IN WITH MOMMA...
IT WAS SMALL, BUT COZY...

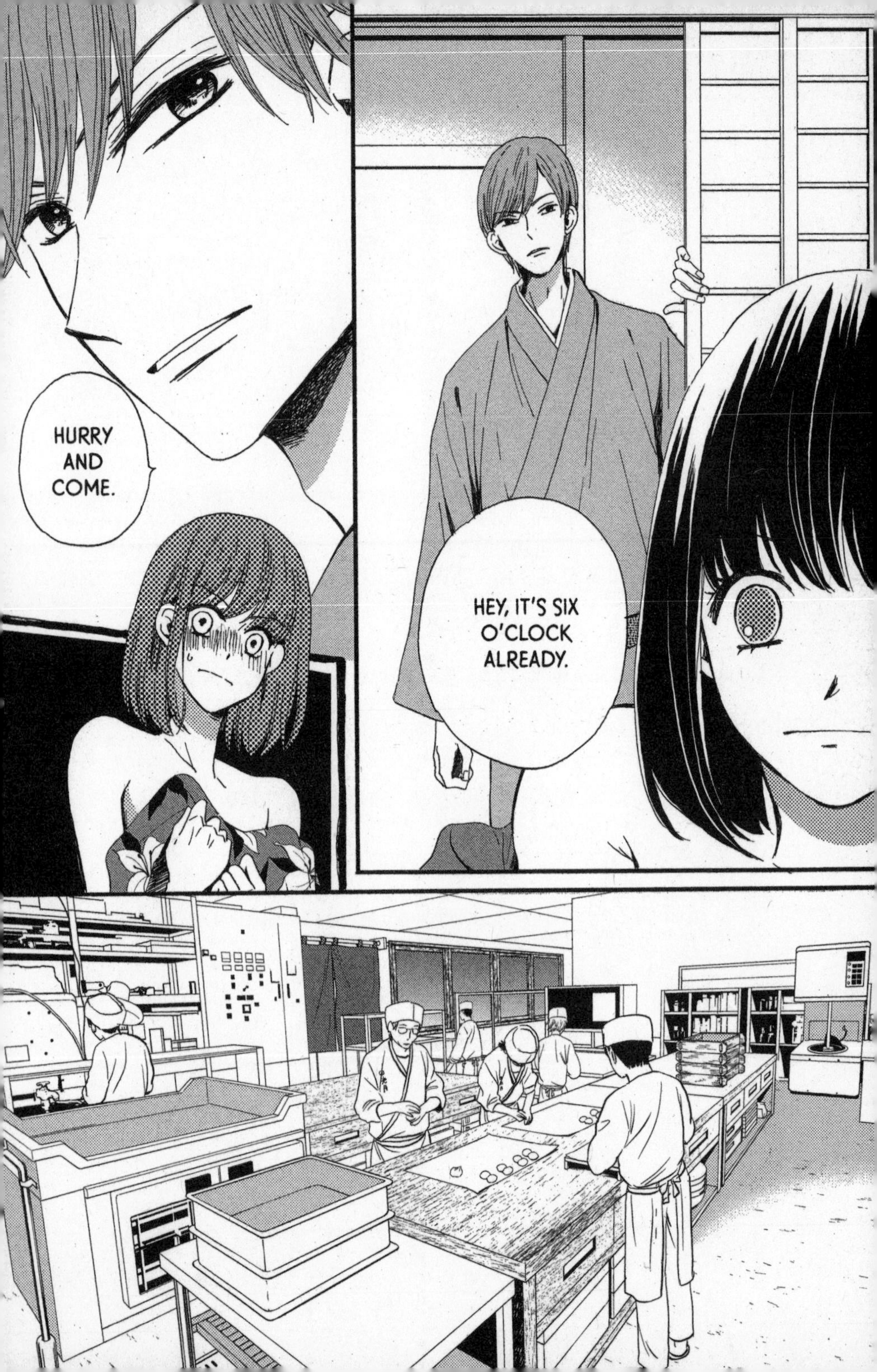
HEY, IT'S SIX O'CLOCK ALREADY.
HURRY AND COME.

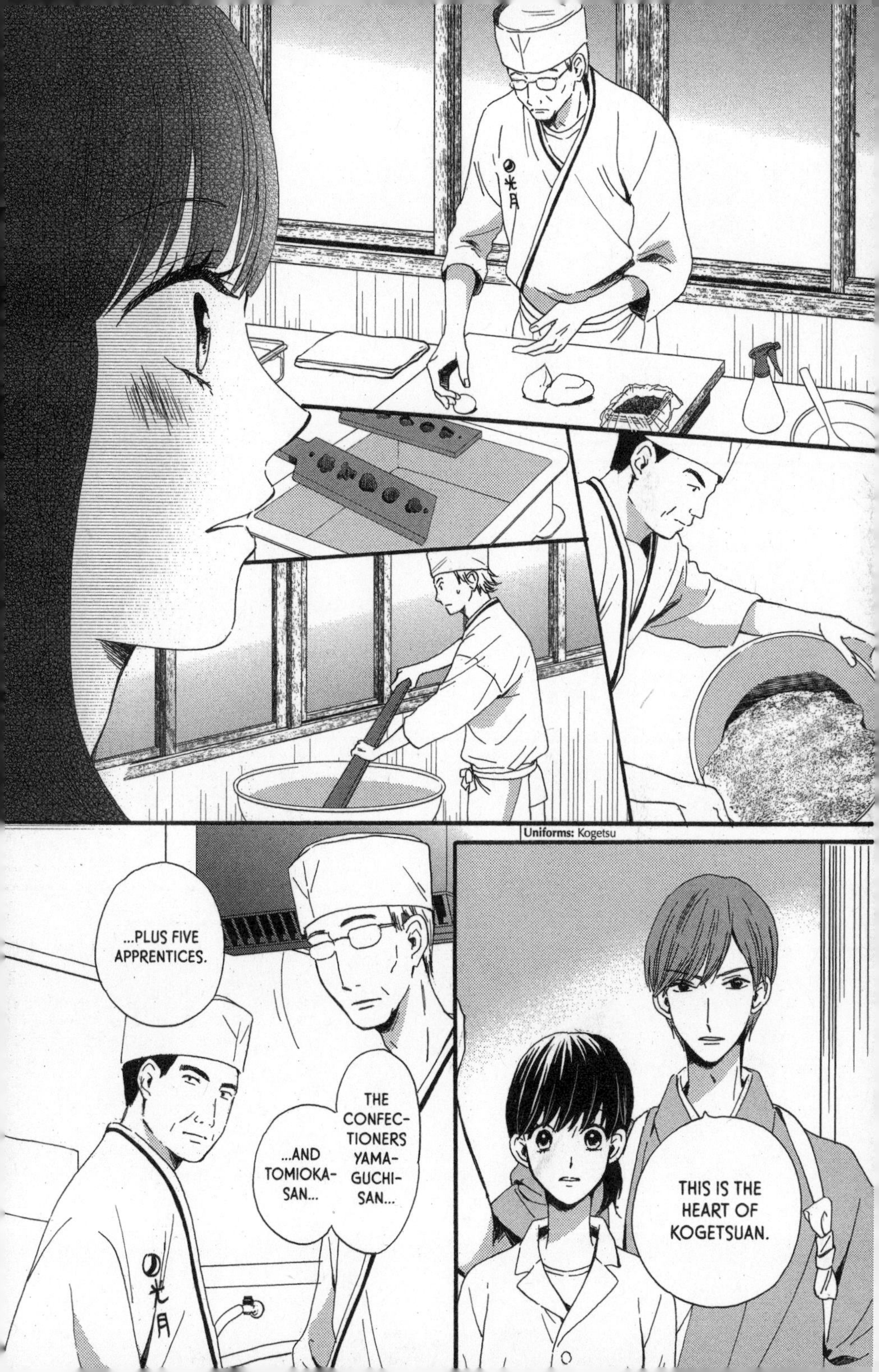
Uniforms: Kogetsu
THIS IS THE HEART OF KOGETSUAN.
THE CONFECTIONERS YAMAGUCHI-SAN...
...AND TOMIOKA-SAN...
...PLUS FIVE APPRENTICES.

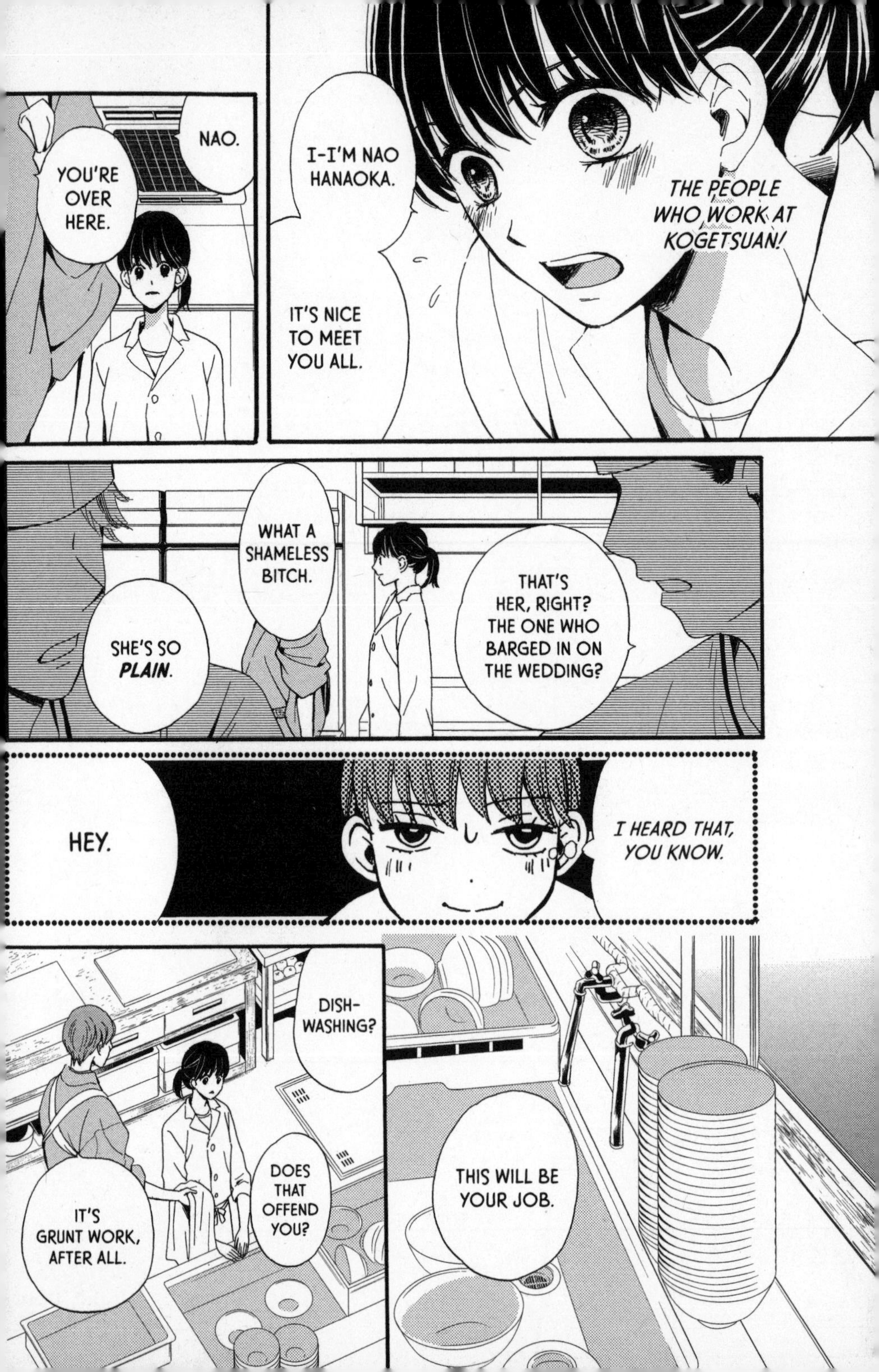
THE PEOPLE WHO WORK AT KOGETSUAN!
I-I'M NAO HANAOKA.
IT'S NICE TO MEET YOU ALL.
NAO.
YOU'RE OVER HERE.
THAT'S HER, RIGHT? THE ONE WHO BARGED IN ON THE WEDDING?
WHAT A SHAMELESS BITCH.
SHE'S SO *PLAIN*.
I HEARD THAT, YOU KNOW.
HEY.
THIS WILL BE YOUR JOB.
DISH-WASHING?
DOES THAT OFFEND YOU?
IT'S GRUNT WORK, AFTER ALL.

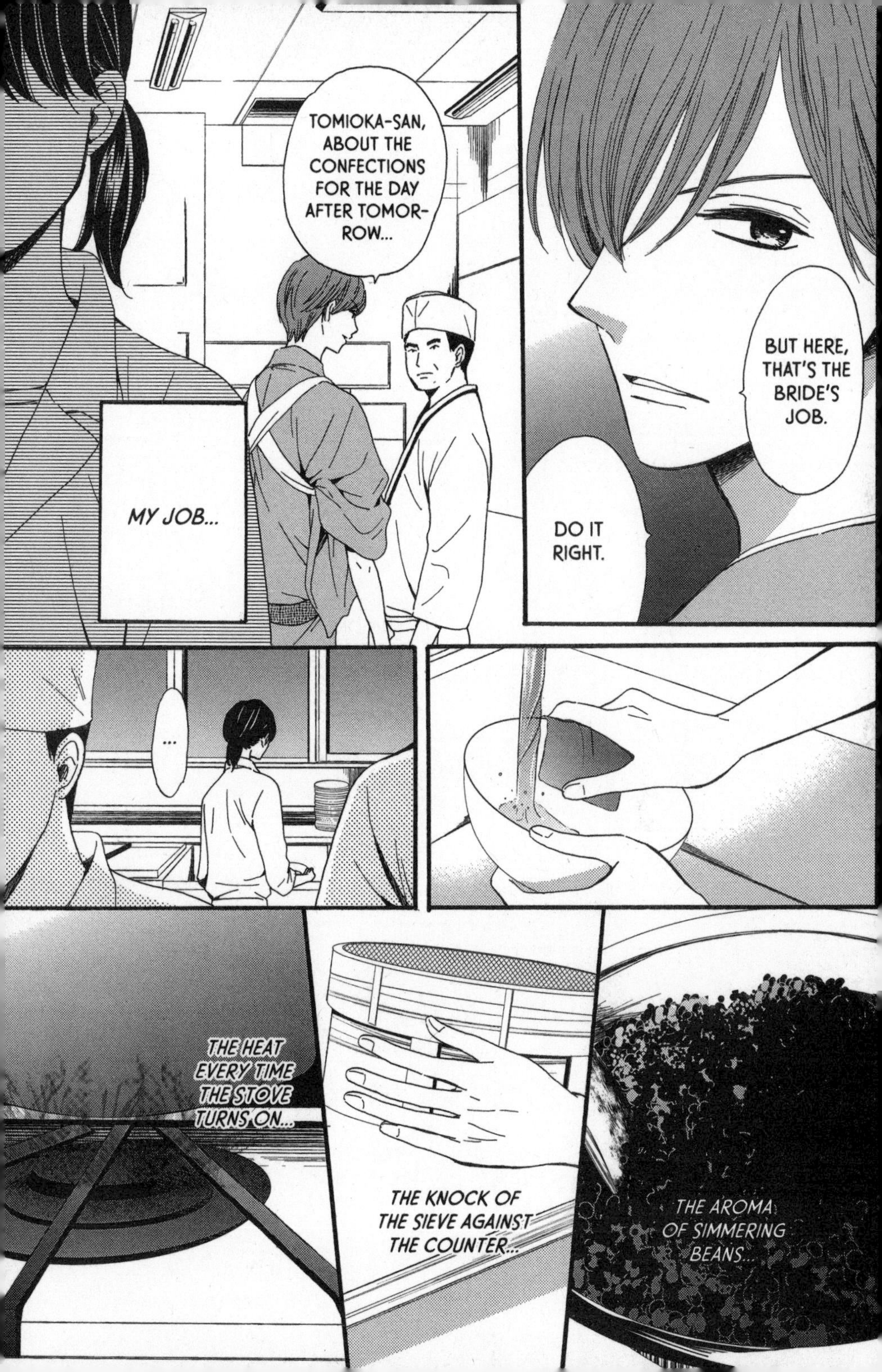
BUT HERE, THAT'S THE BRIDE'S JOB.
DO IT RIGHT.
TOMIOKA-SAN, ABOUT THE CONFECTIONS FOR THE DAY AFTER TOMOR-ROW...
MY JOB...
...
THE AROMA OF SIMMERING BEANS...
THE KNOCK OF THE SIEVE AGAINST THE COUNTER...
THE HEAT EVERY TIME THE STOVE TURNS ON...

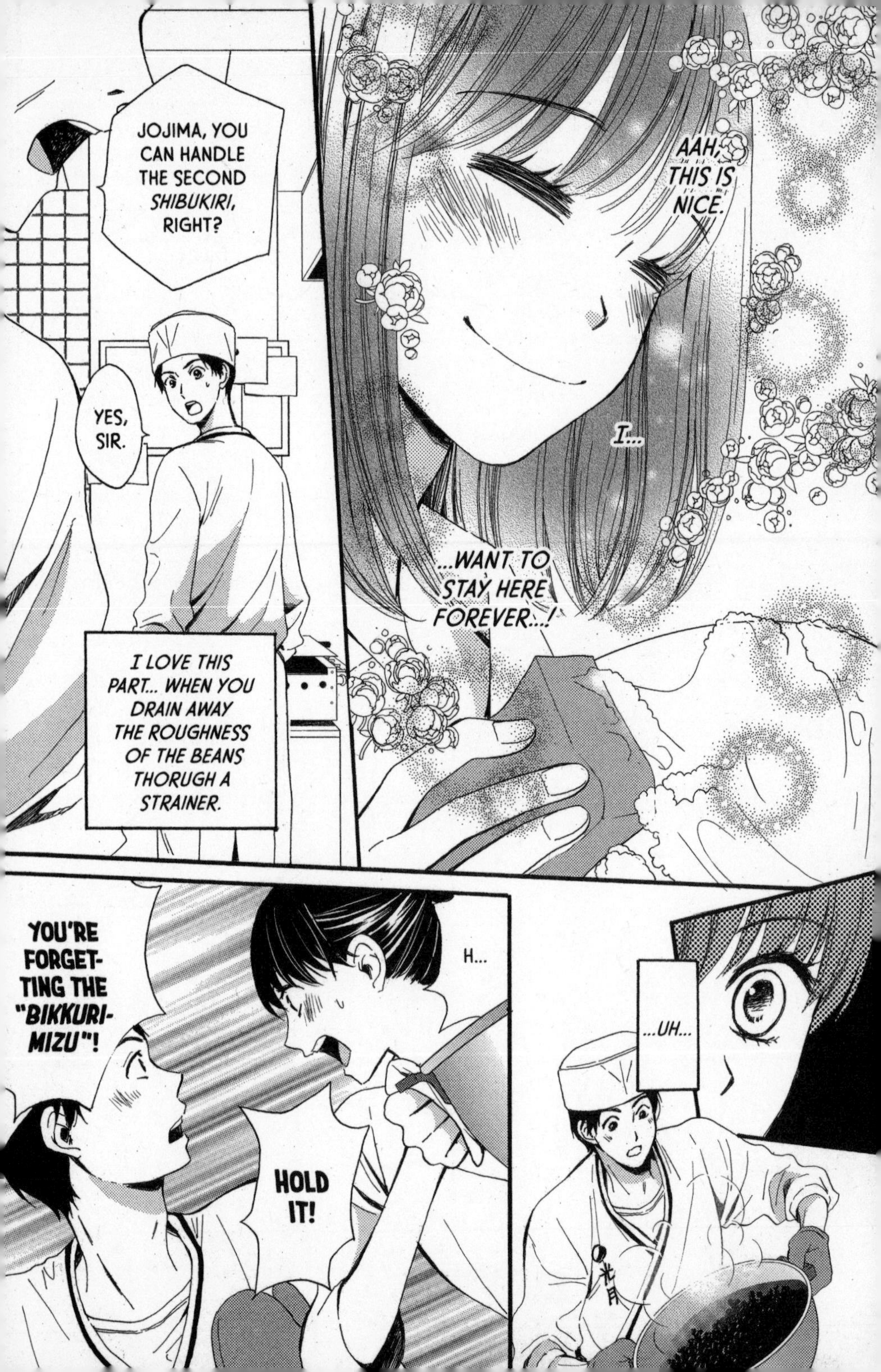
AAH, THIS IS NICE.
I...
...WANT TO STAY HERE FOREVER...!
JOJIMA, YOU CAN HANDLE THE SECOND *SHIBUKIRI*, RIGHT?
YES, SIR.
I LOVE THIS PART... WHEN YOU DRAIN AWAY THE ROUGHNESS OF THE BEANS THORUGH A STRAINER.
...UH...
H...
HOLD IT!
YOU'RE FORGETTING THE "*BIKKURI-MIZU*"!

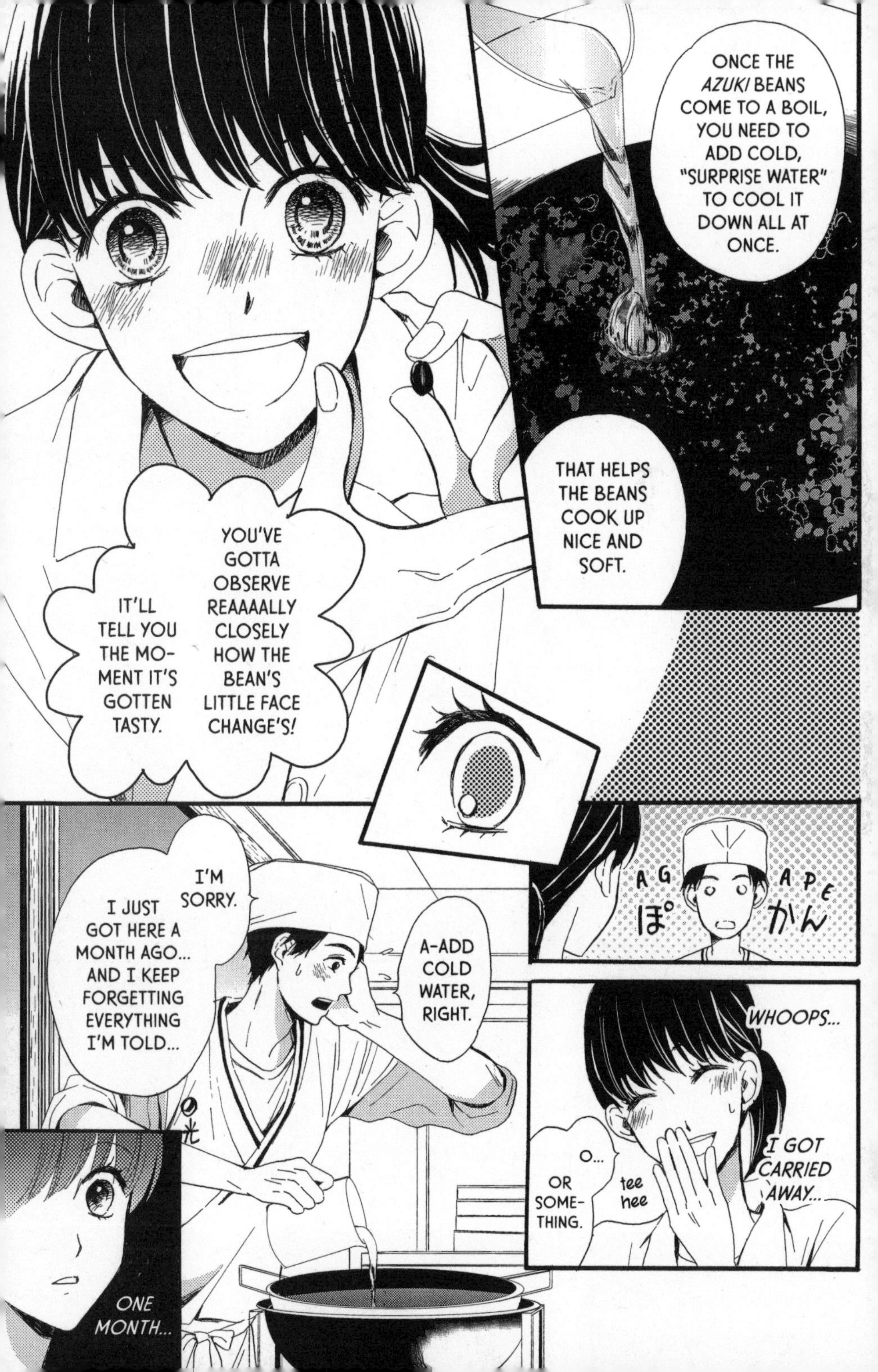
ONCE THE *AZUKI* BEANS COME TO A BOIL, YOU NEED TO ADD COLD, "SURPRISE WATER" TO COOL IT DOWN ALL AT ONCE.
THAT HELPS THE BEANS COOK UP NICE AND SOFT.
YOU'VE GOTTA OBSERVE REAAAALLY CLOSELY HOW THE BEAN'S LITTLE FACE CHANGE'S!
IT'LL TELL YOU THE MO- MENT IT'S GOTTEN TASTY.
APE かん
AG ぽ
WHOOPS...
I GOT CARRIED AWAY...
tee hee
O... OR SOME- THING.
A-ADD COLD WATER, RIGHT.
I'M SORRY.
I JUST GOT HERE A MONTH AGO... AND I KEEP FORGETTING EVERYTHING I'M TOLD...
ONE MONTH...

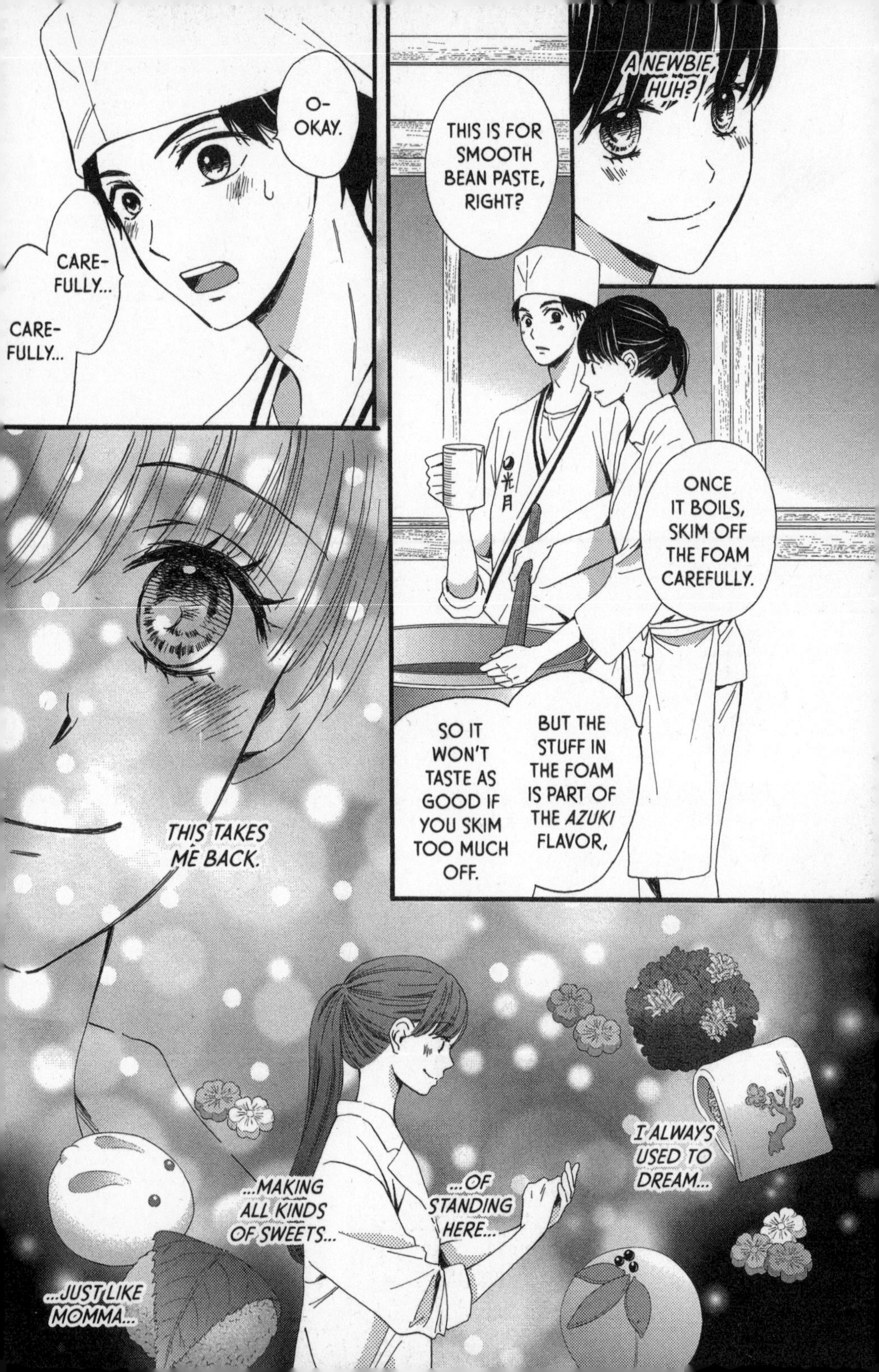
THIS IS FOR SMOOTH BEAN PASTE, RIGHT?
A NEWBIE, HUH?
ONCE IT BOILS, SKIM OFF THE FOAM CAREFULLY.
BUT THE STUFF IN THE FOAM IS PART OF THE AZUKI FLAVOR,
SO IT WON'T TASTE AS GOOD IF YOU SKIM TOO MUCH OFF.
O-OKAY.
CARE-FULLY...
CARE-FULLY...
THIS TAKES ME BACK.
I ALWAYS USED TO DREAM...
...OF STANDING HERE...
...MAKING ALL KINDS OF SWEETS...
...JUST LIKE MOMMA...

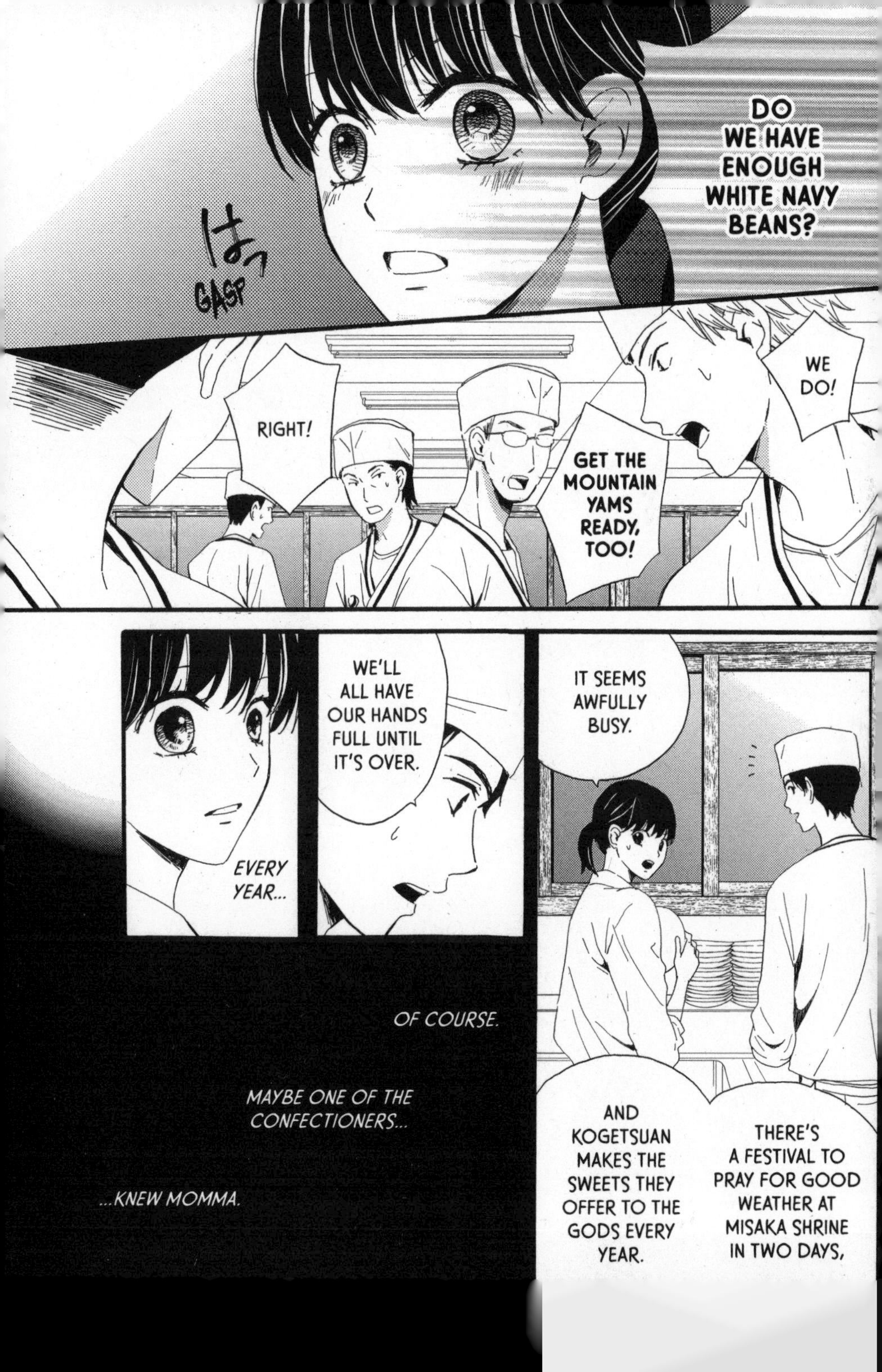
DO WE HAVE ENOUGH WHITE NAVY BEANS?
はっ GASP
WE DO!
GET THE MOUNTAIN YAMS READY, TOO!
RIGHT!
IT SEEMS AWFULLY BUSY.
THERE'S A FESTIVAL TO PRAY FOR GOOD WEATHER AT MISAKA SHRINE IN TWO DAYS,
AND KOGETSUAN MAKES THE SWEETS THEY OFFER TO THE GODS EVERY YEAR.
WE'LL ALL HAVE OUR HANDS FULL UNTIL IT'S OVER.
EVERY YEAR...
OF COURSE.
MAYBE ONE OF THE CONFECTIONERS...
...KNEW MOMMA.

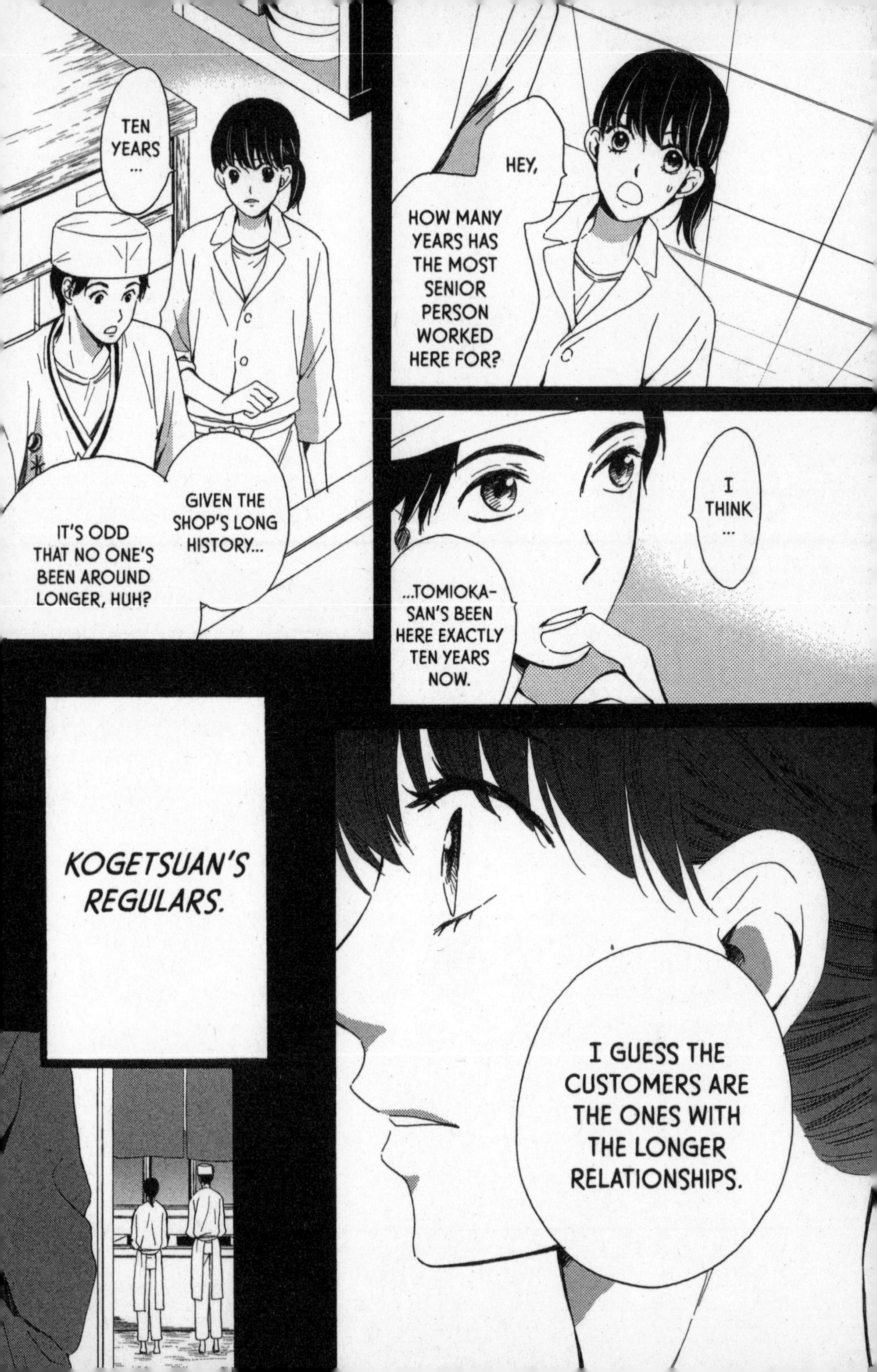
HEY,
HOW MANY YEARS HAS THE MOST SENIOR PERSON WORKED HERE FOR?
I THINK...
...TOMIOKA-SAN'S BEEN HERE EXACTLY TEN YEARS NOW.
TEN YEARS...
GIVEN THE SHOP'S LONG HISTORY...
IT'S ODD THAT NO ONE'S BEEN AROUND LONGER, HUH?
I GUESS THE CUSTOMERS ARE THE ONES WITH THE LONGER RELATIONSHIPS.
KOGETSUAN'S REGULARS.

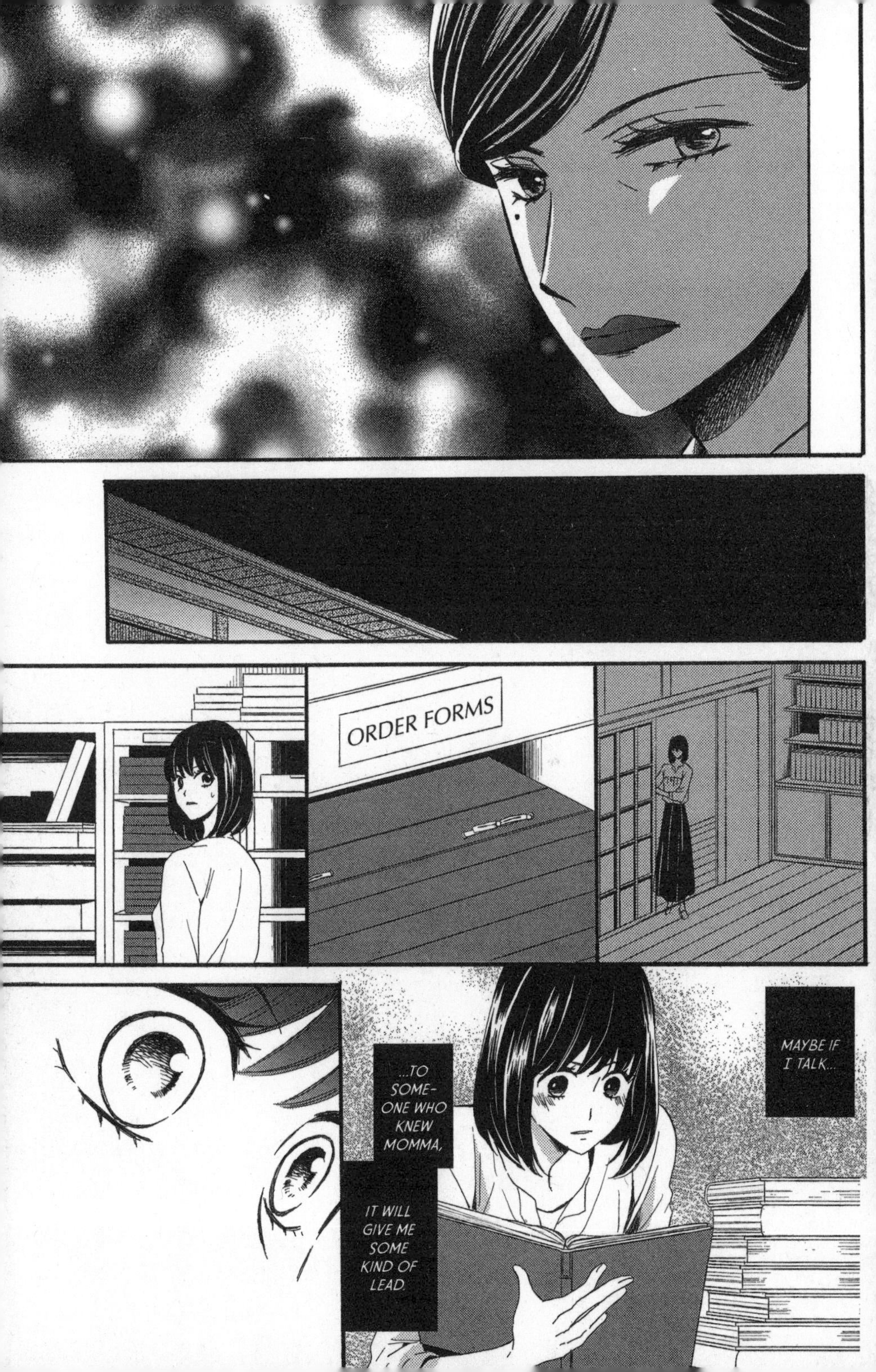
ORDER FORMS
MAYBE IF I TALK...
...TO SOME-ONE WHO KNEW MOMMA,
IT WILL GIVE ME SOME KIND OF LEAD.

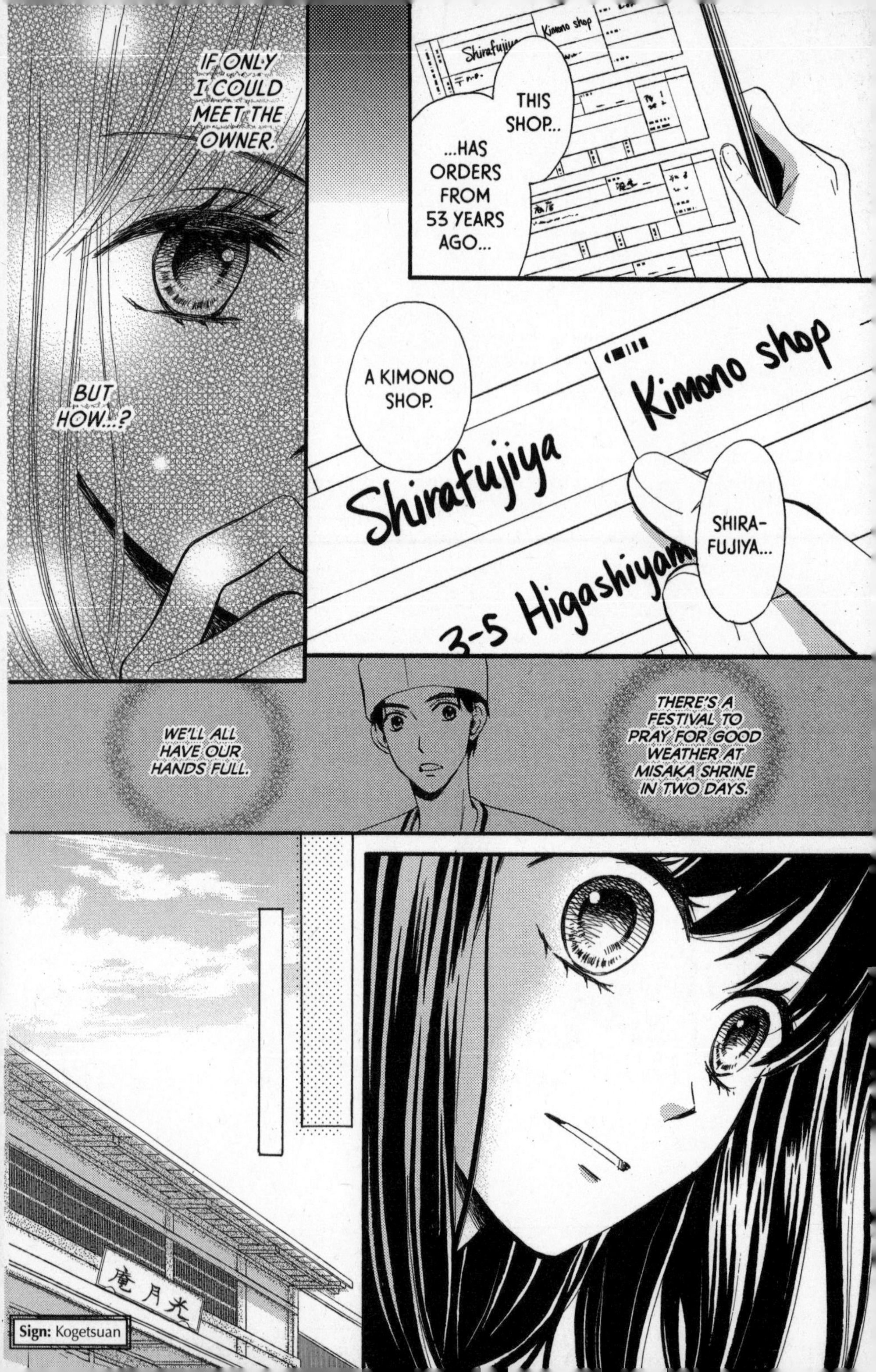
Kimono shop
Shirafujiya
THIS SHOP...
...HAS ORDERS FROM 53 YEARS AGO...
Kimono shop
A KIMONO SHOP.
SHIRA-FUJIYA...
Shirafujiya
3-5 Higashiyam
IF ONLY I COULD MEET THE OWNER.
BUT HOW...?
THERE'S A FESTIVAL TO PRAY FOR GOOD WEATHER AT MISAKA SHRINE IN TWO DAYS.
WE'LL ALL HAVE OUR HANDS FULL.
庵月光
Sign: Kogetsuan

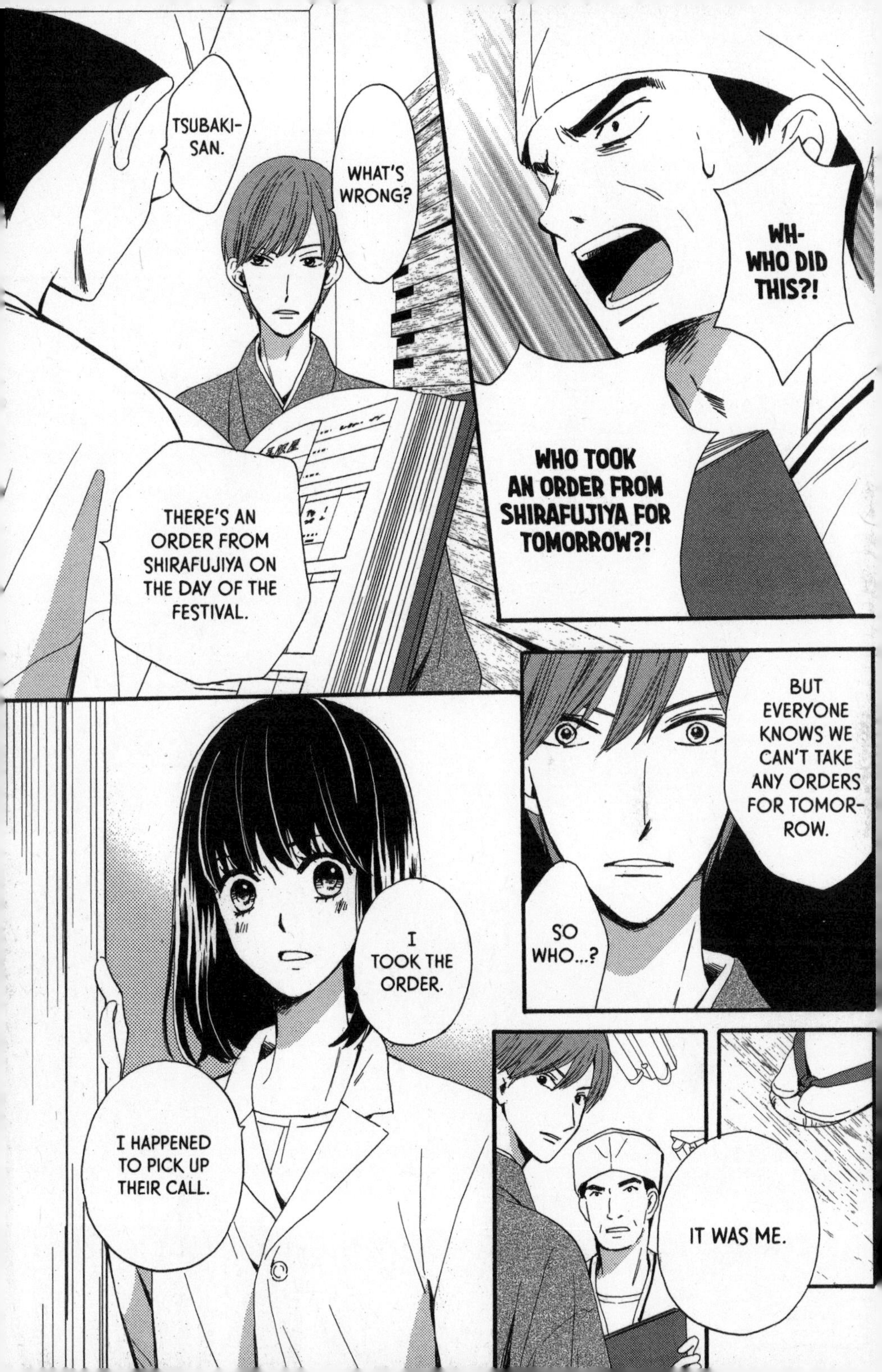
WH-
WHO DID THIS?!
WHO TOOK AN ORDER FROM SHIRAFUJIYA FOR TOMORROW?!
TSUBAKI-SAN.
WHAT'S WRONG?
THERE'S AN ORDER FROM SHIRAFUJIYA ON THE DAY OF THE FESTIVAL.
BUT EVERYONE KNOWS WE CAN'T TAKE ANY ORDERS FOR TOMORROW.
SO WHO...?
IT WAS ME.
I TOOK THE ORDER.
I HAPPENED TO PICK UP THEIR CALL.

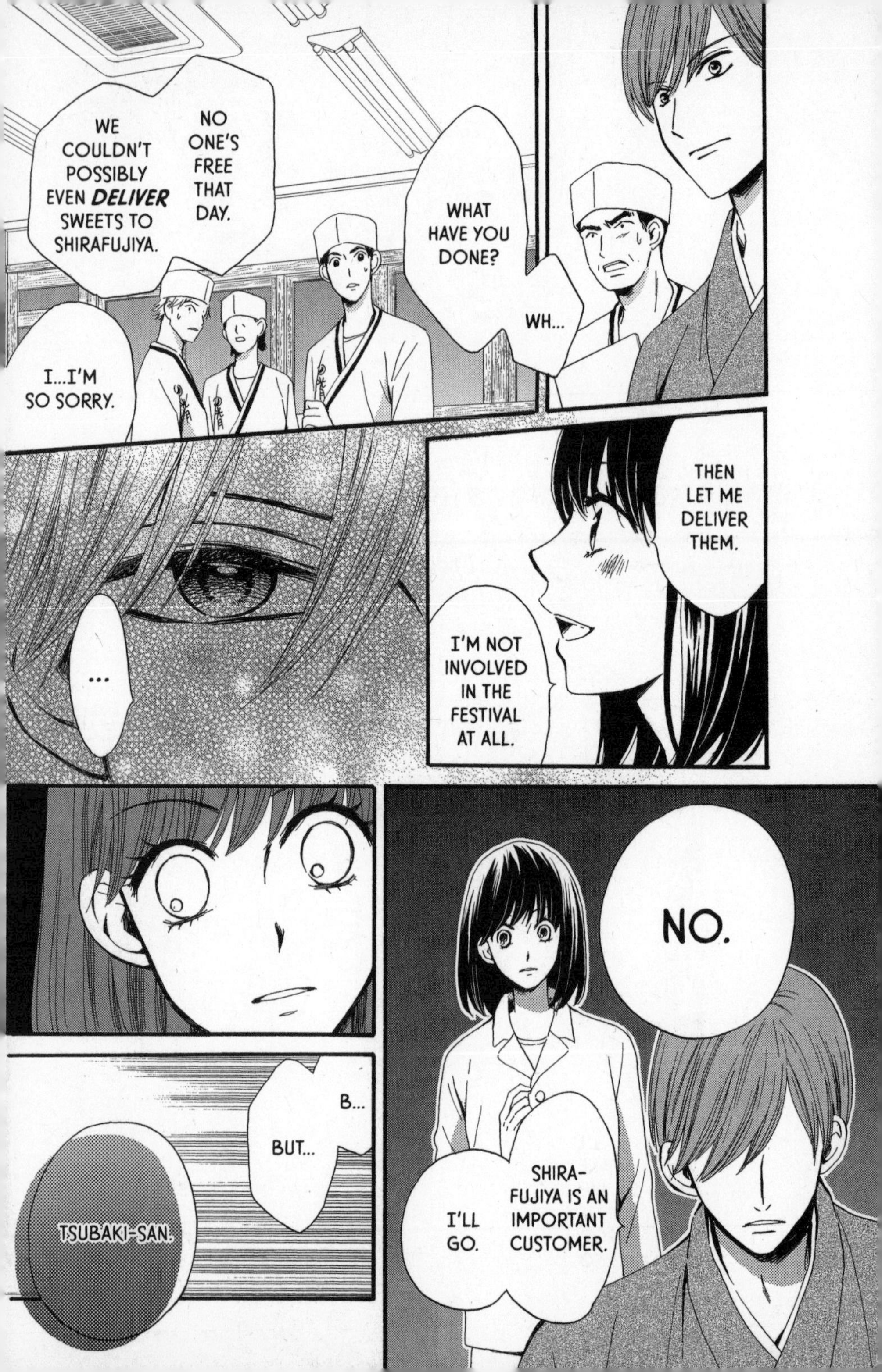
WHAT HAVE YOU DONE?
WH...
NO ONE'S FREE THAT DAY.
WE COULDN'T POSSIBLY EVEN **DELIVER** SWEETS TO SHIRAFUJIYA.
I...I'M SO SORRY.
THEN LET ME DELIVER THEM.
I'M NOT INVOLVED IN THE FESTIVAL AT ALL.
...
NO.
SHIRA-FUJIYA IS AN IMPORTANT CUSTOMER.
I'LL GO.
B...
BUT...
TSUBAKI-SAN.

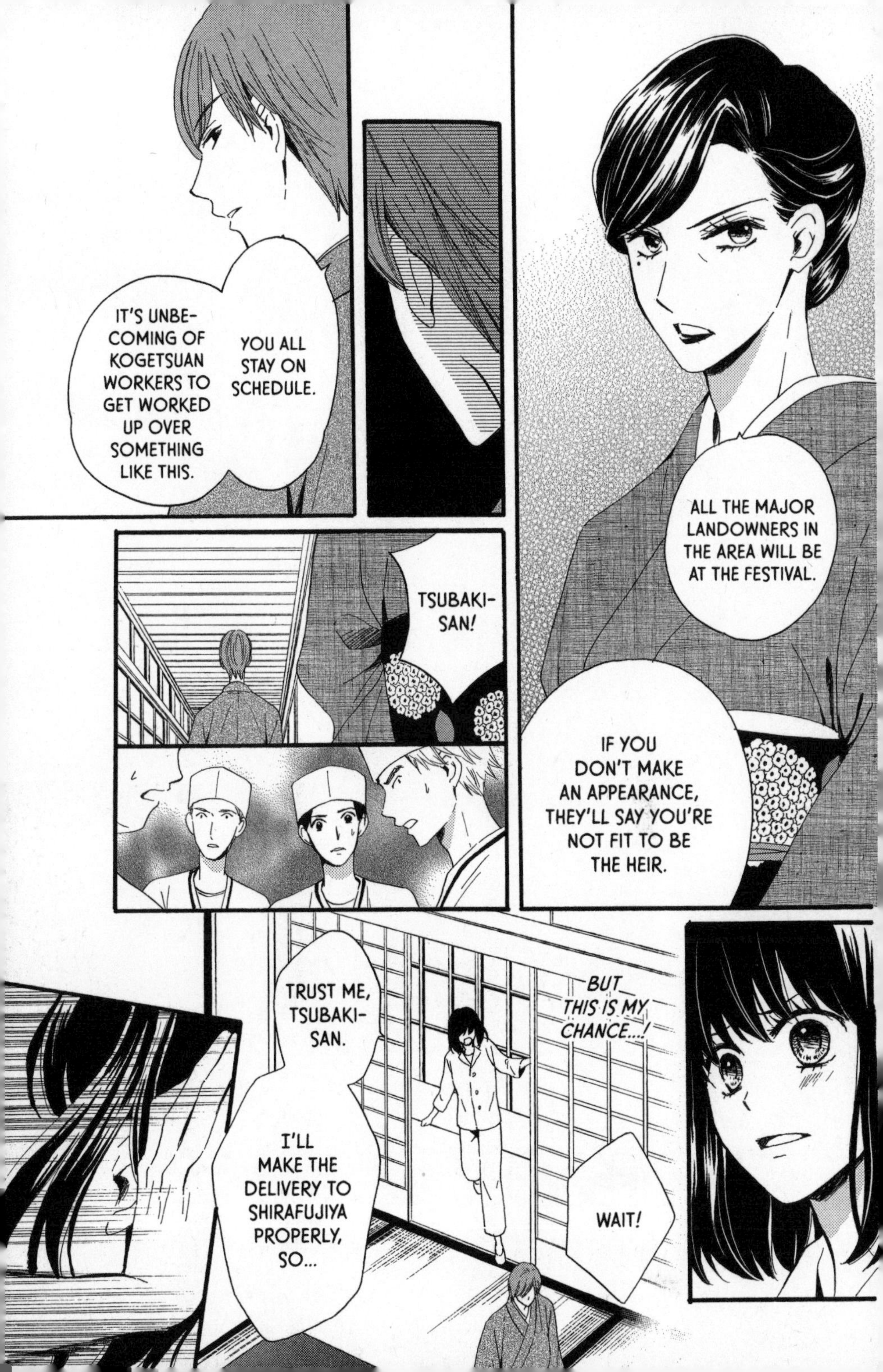
ALL THE MAJOR LANDOWNERS IN THE AREA WILL BE AT THE FESTIVAL.
IF YOU DON'T MAKE AN APPEARANCE, THEY'LL SAY YOU'RE NOT FIT TO BE THE HEIR.
YOU ALL STAY ON SCHEDULE.
IT'S UNBE-COMING OF KOGETSUAN WORKERS TO GET WORKED UP OVER SOMETHING LIKE THIS.
TSUBAKI-SAN!
BUT THIS IS MY CHANCE...!
WAIT!
TRUST ME, TSUBAKI-SAN.
I'LL MAKE THE DELIVERY TO SHIRAFUJIYA PROPERLY, SO...

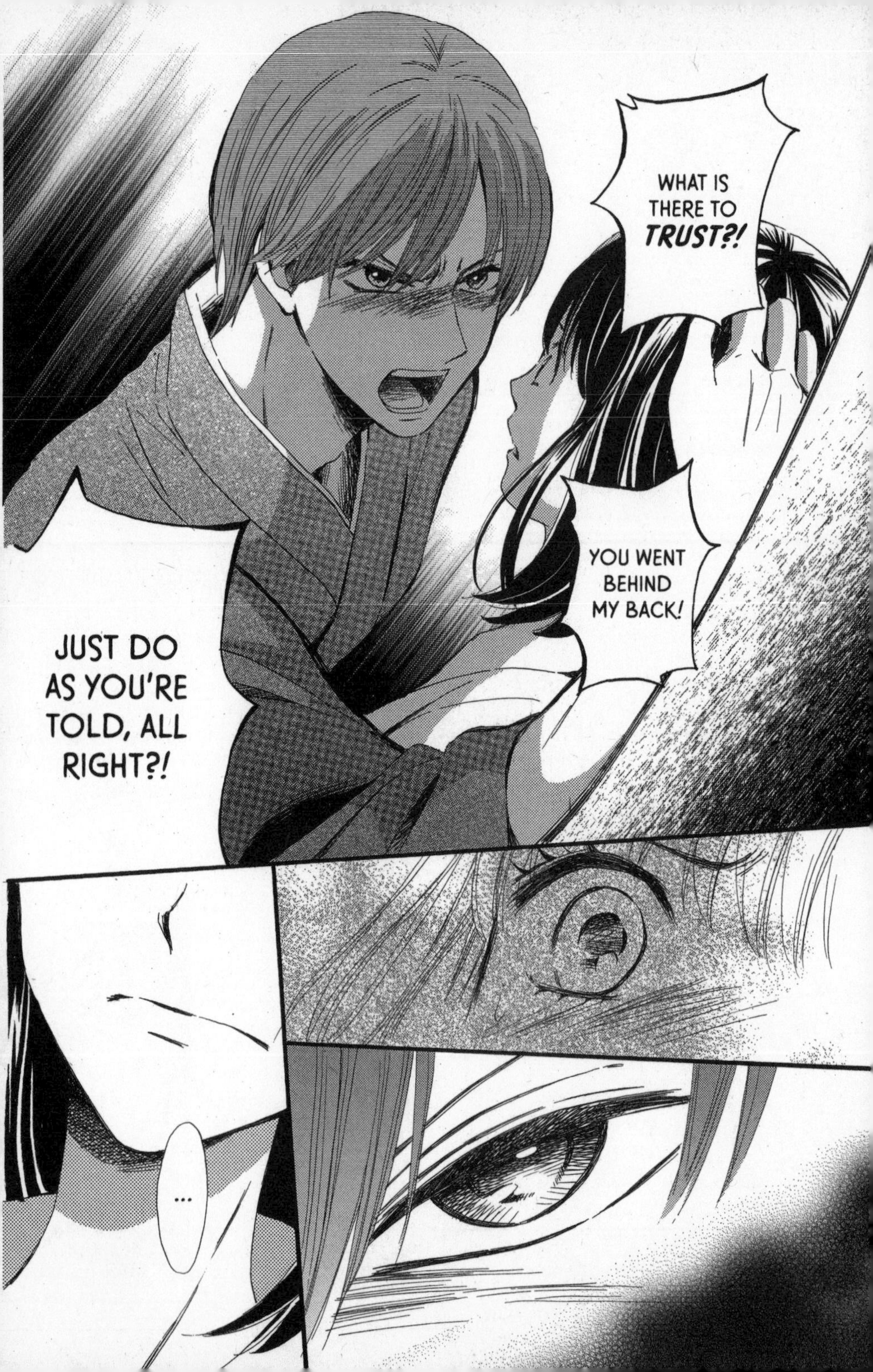
WHAT IS THERE TO TRUST?!
YOU WENT BEHIND MY BACK!
JUST DO AS YOU'RE TOLD, ALL RIGHT?!
...

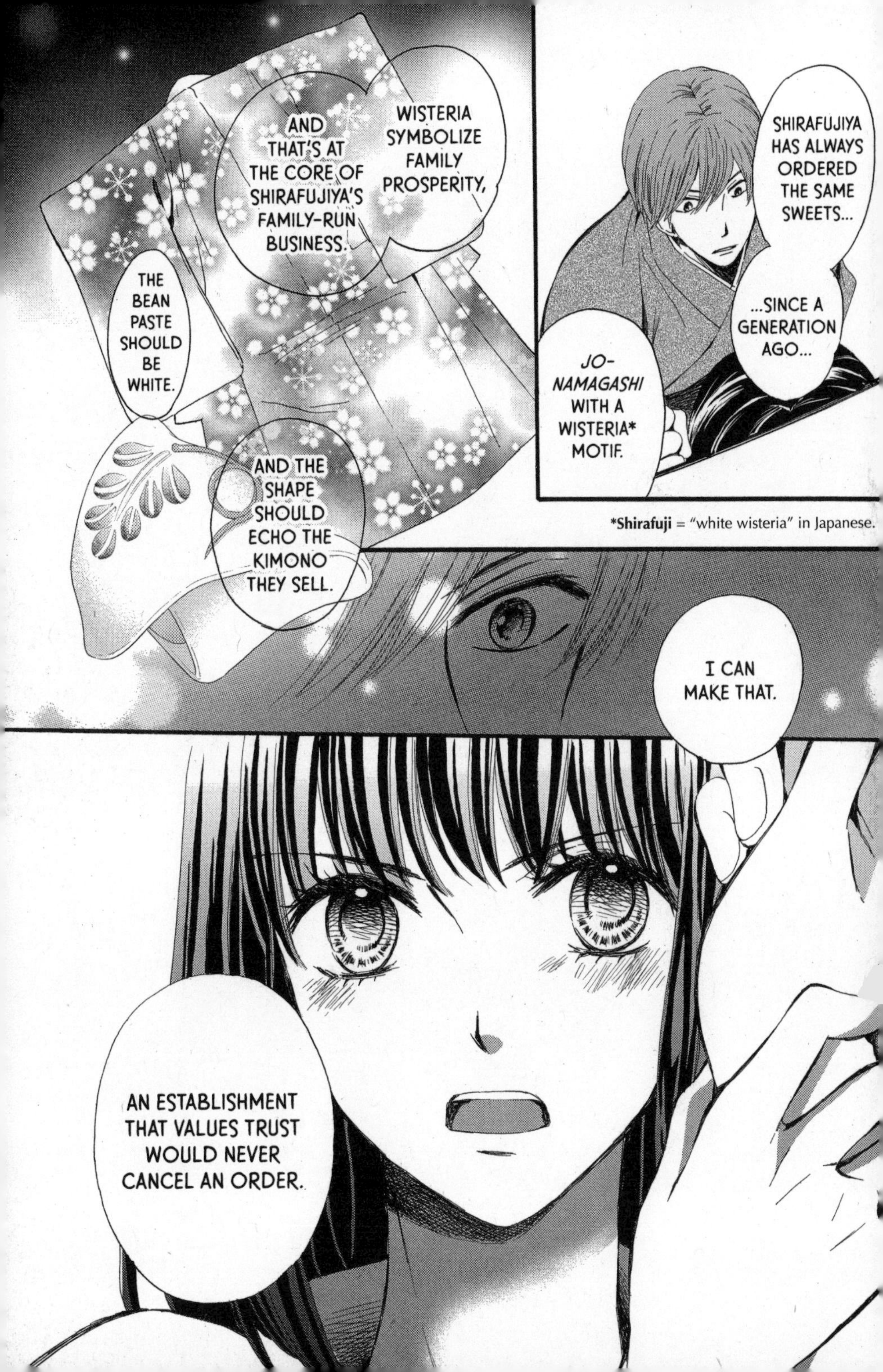
SHIRAFUJIYA HAS ALWAYS ORDERED THE SAME SWEETS...
...SINCE A GENERATION AGO...
JO-NAMAGASHI WITH A WISTERIA* MOTIF.
WISTERIA SYMBOLIZE FAMILY PROSPERITY,
AND THAT'S AT THE CORE OF SHIRAFUJIYA'S FAMILY-RUN BUSINESS.
THE BEAN PASTE SHOULD BE WHITE.
AND THE SHAPE SHOULD ECHO THE KIMONO THEY SELL.
I CAN MAKE THAT.
AN ESTABLISHMENT THAT VALUES TRUST WOULD NEVER CANCEL AN ORDER.

***Shirafuji** = "white wisteria" in Japanese.

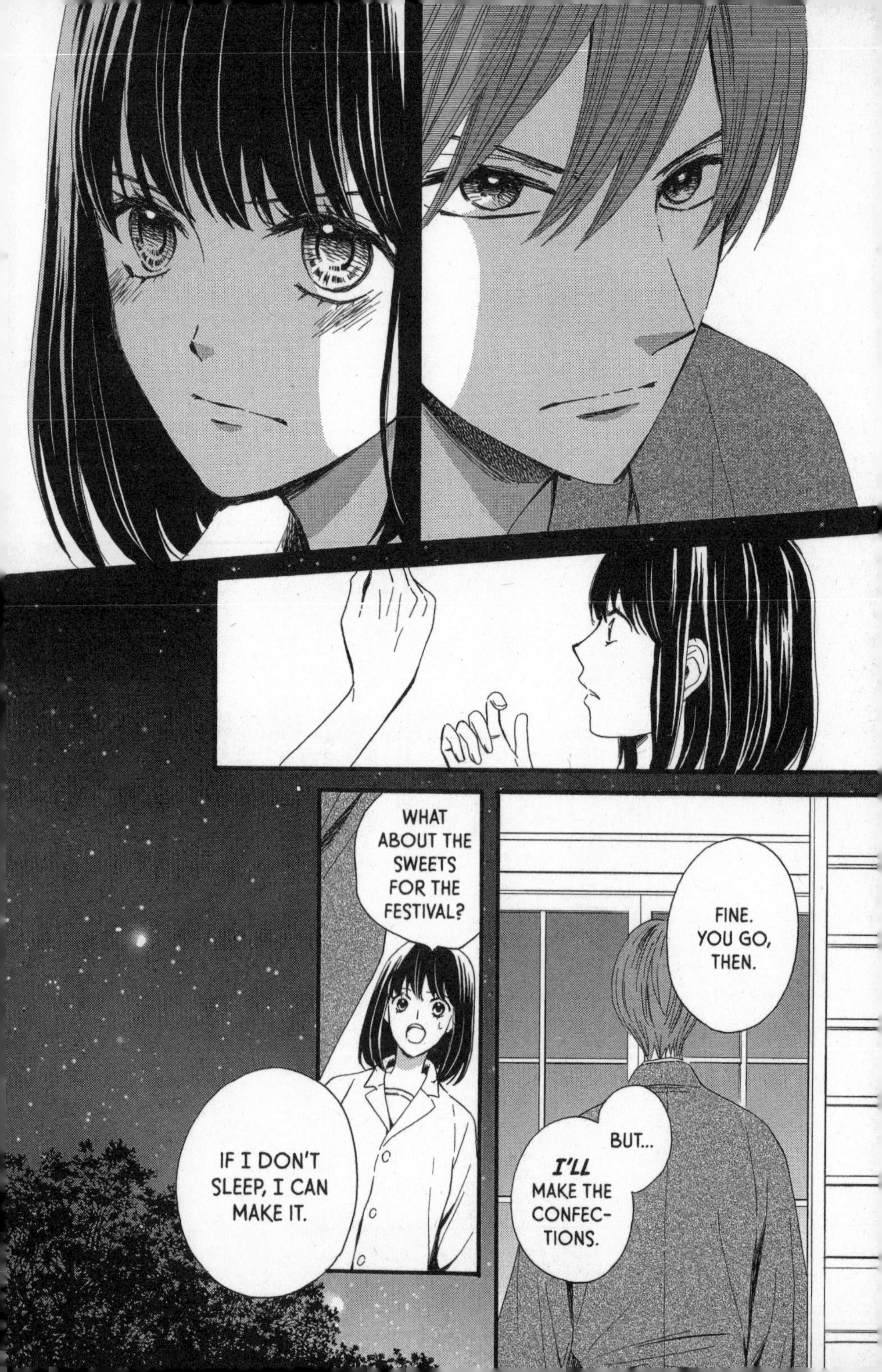
FINE. YOU GO, THEN.
BUT...
I'LL MAKE THE CONFECTIONS.
WHAT ABOUT THE SWEETS FOR THE FESTIVAL?
IF I DON'T SLEEP, I CAN MAKE IT.

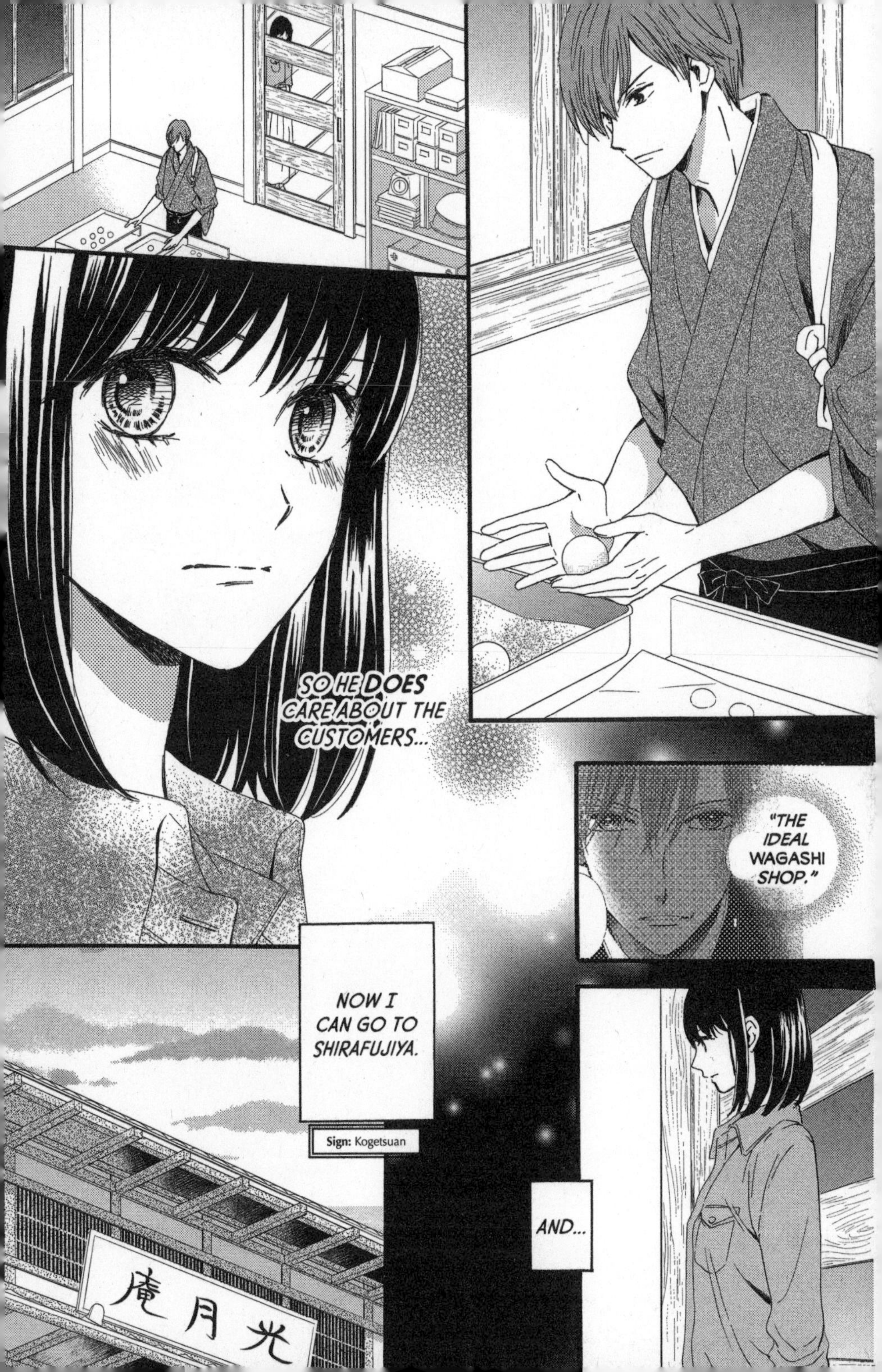

SO HE DOES CARE ABOUT THE CUSTOMERS...
"THE IDEAL WAGASHI SHOP."
NOW I CAN GO TO SHIRAFUJIYA.
Sign: Kogetsuan
光月庵
AND...

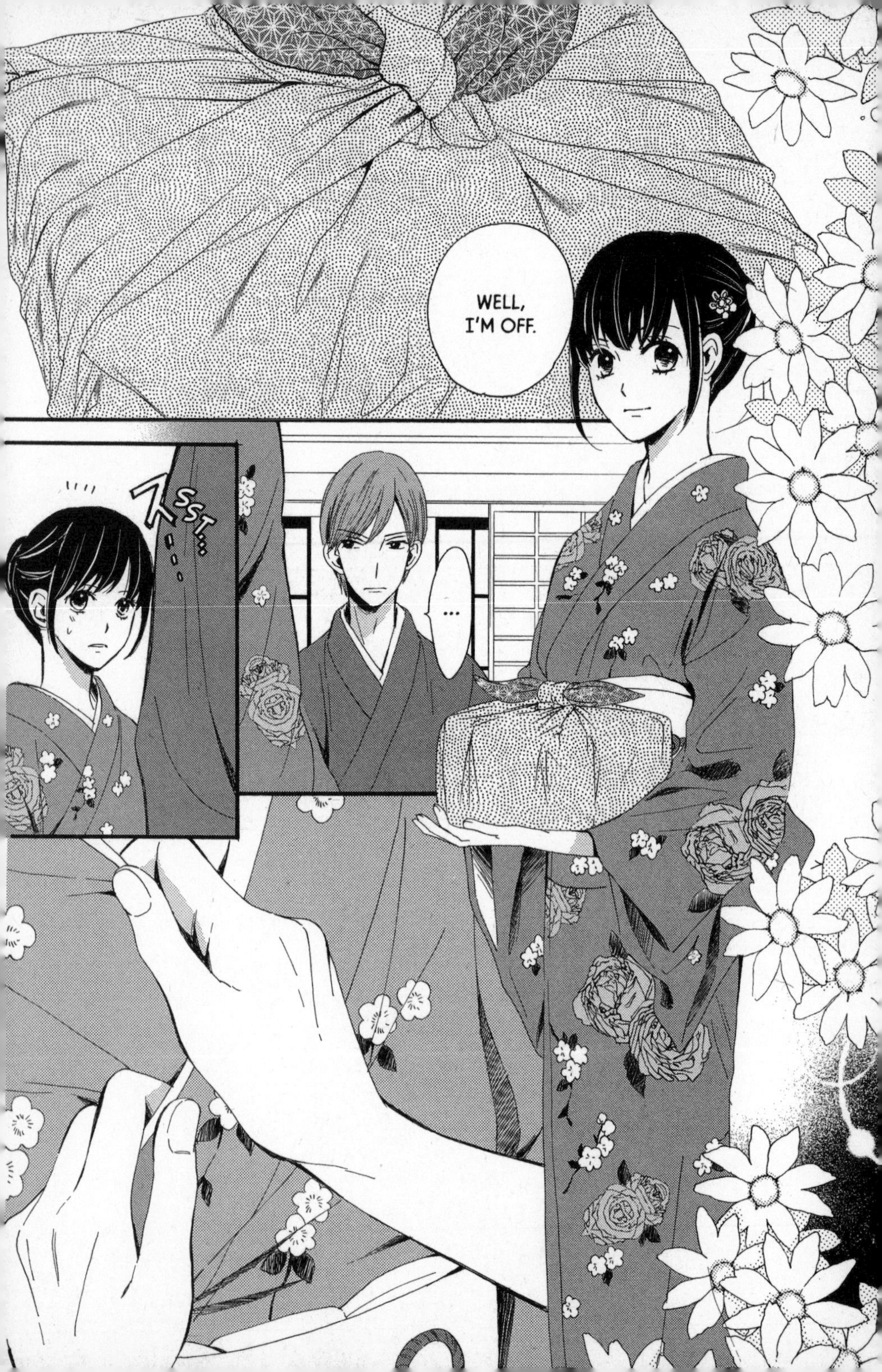
WELL, I'M OFF.
...
SSST..

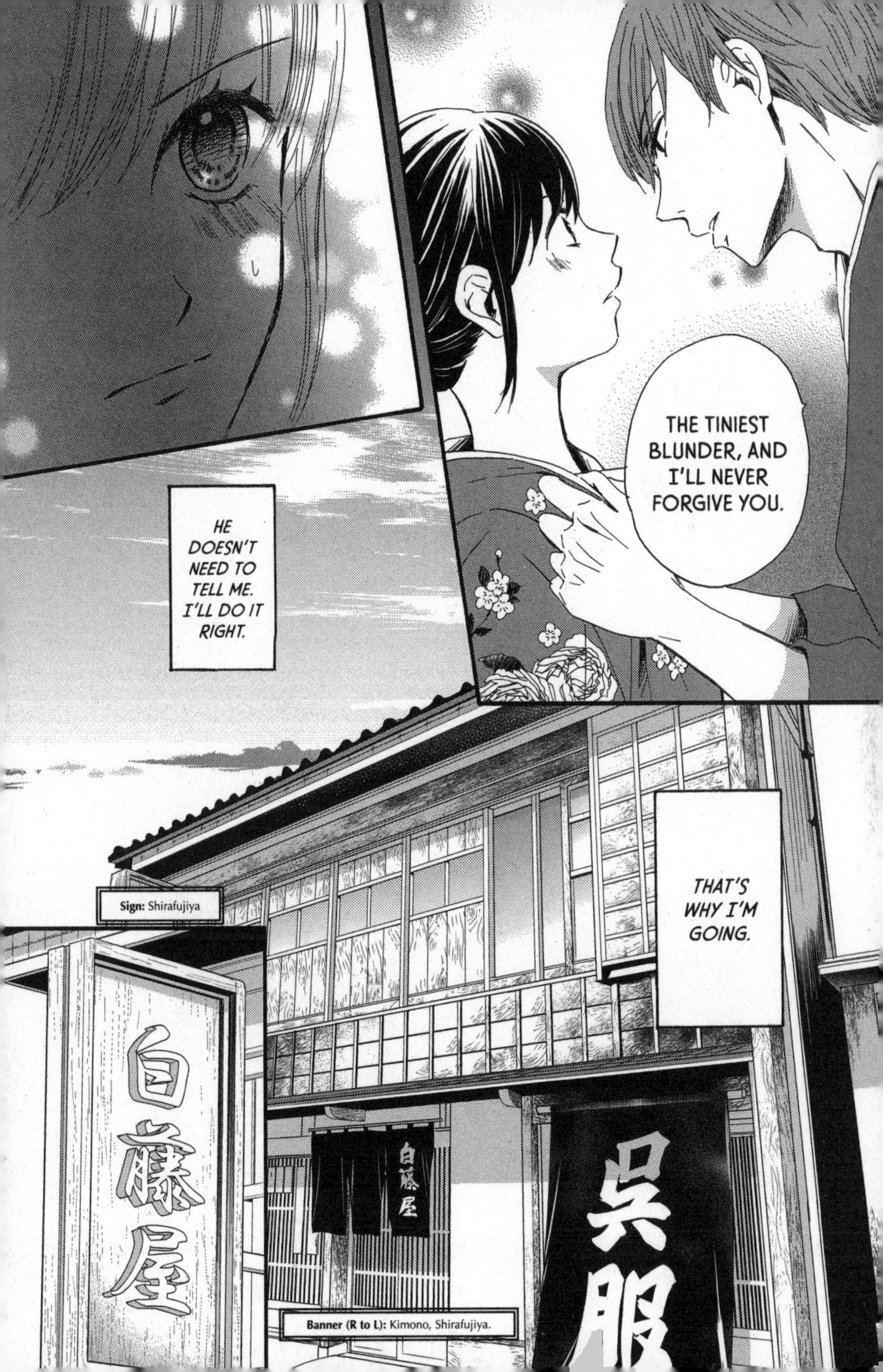
THE TINIEST BLUNDER, AND I'LL NEVER FORGIVE YOU.
HE DOESN'T NEED TO TELL ME. I'LL DO IT RIGHT.
THAT'S WHY I'M GOING.
Sign: Shirafujiya
白藤屋
呉服
白藤屋
Banner (R to L): Kimono, Shirafujiya.

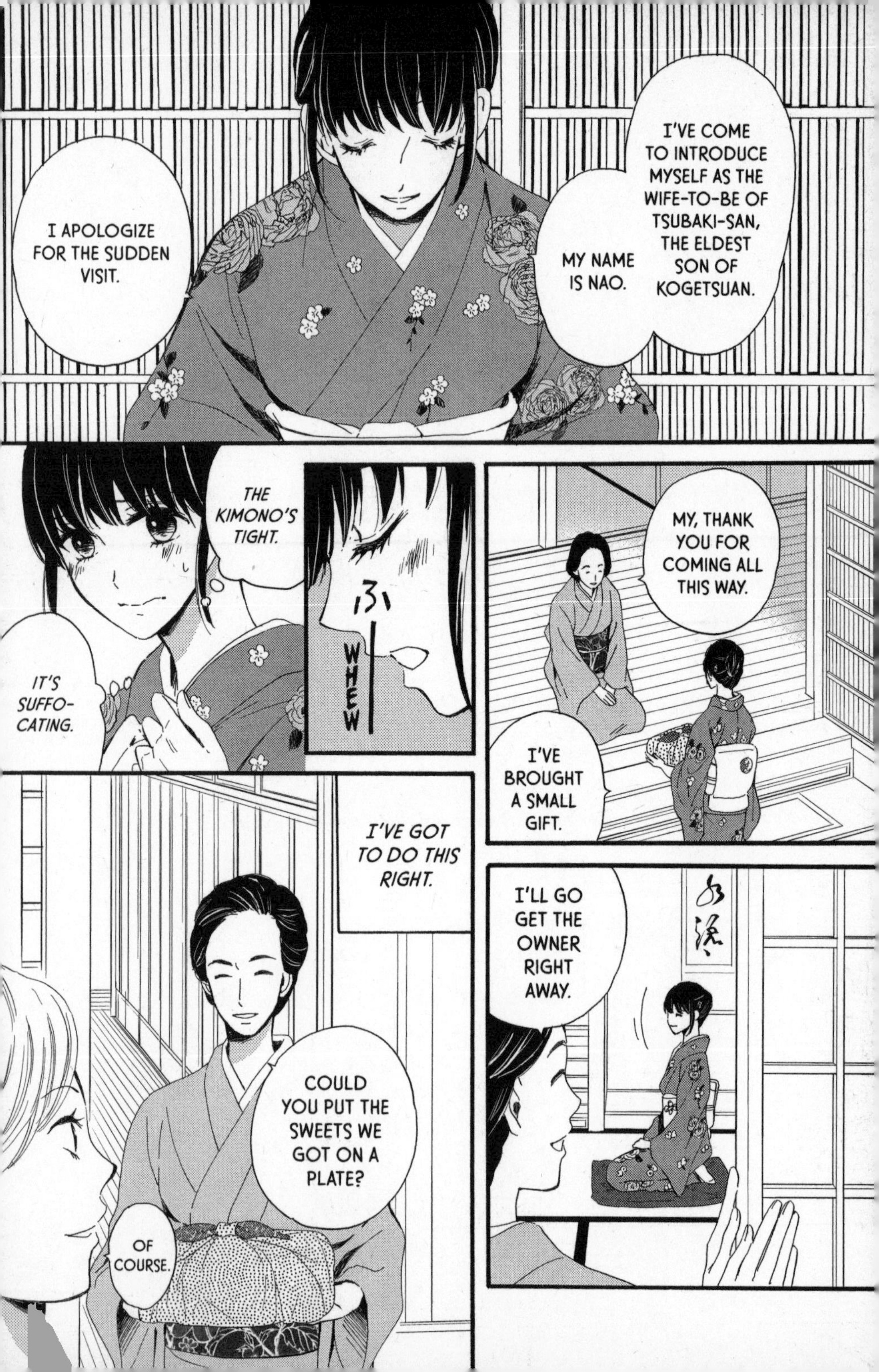
I'VE COME TO INTRODUCE MYSELF AS THE WIFE-TO-BE OF TSUBAKI-SAN, THE ELDEST SON OF KOGETSUAN.
MY NAME IS NAO.
I APOLOGIZE FOR THE SUDDEN VISIT.
MY, THANK YOU FOR COMING ALL THIS WAY.
I'VE BROUGHT A SMALL GIFT.
ふ
WHEW
THE KIMONO'S TIGHT.
IT'S SUFFO-CATING.
I'LL GO GET THE OWNER RIGHT AWAY.
I'VE GOT TO DO THIS RIGHT.
COULD YOU PUT THE SWEETS WE GOT ON A PLATE?
OF COURSE.

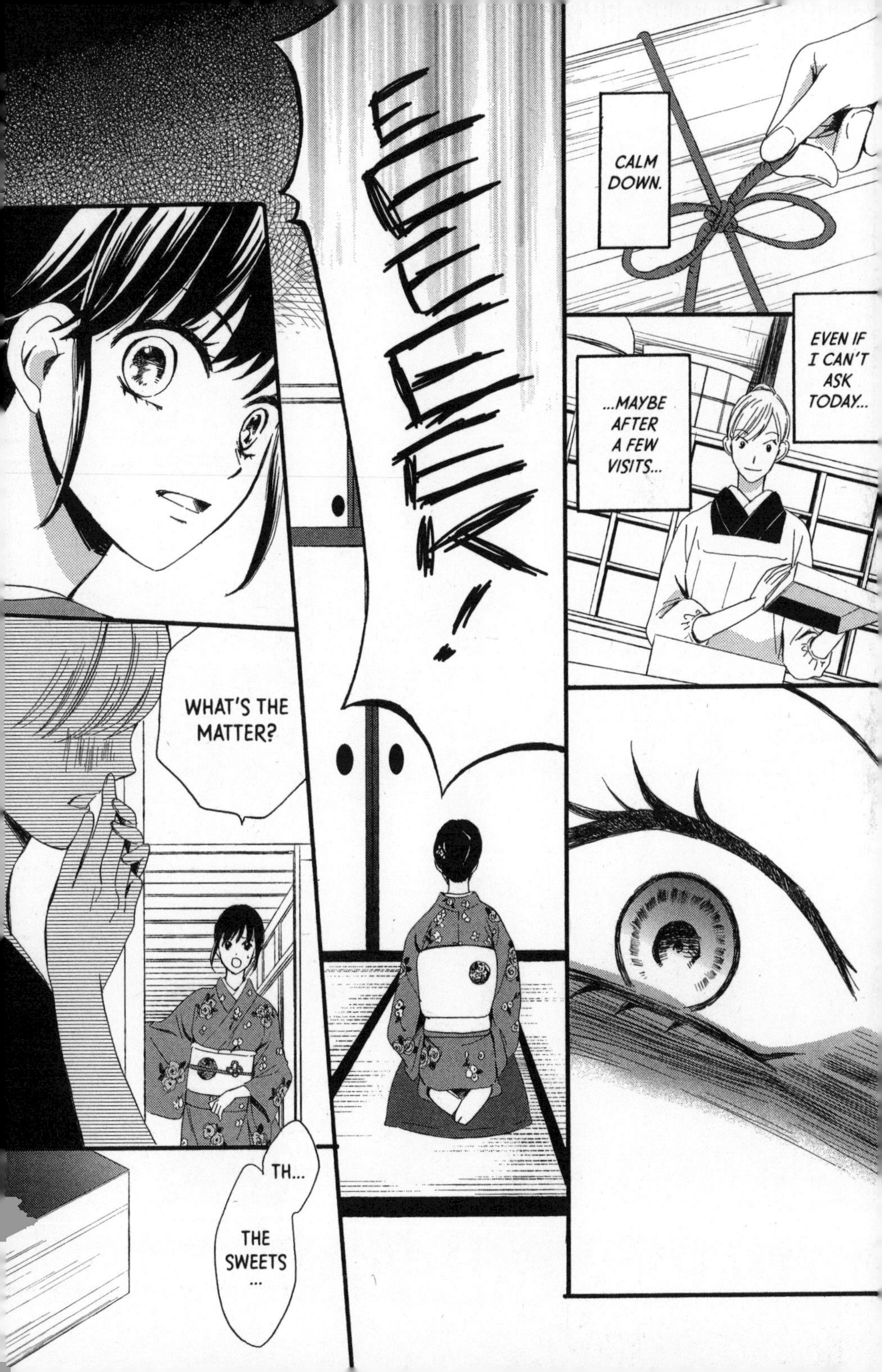
CALM DOWN.
EVEN IF I CAN'T ASK TODAY...
...MAYBE AFTER A FEW VISITS...
EEEEEEEK!
WHAT'S THE MATTER?
TH...
THE SWEETS ...

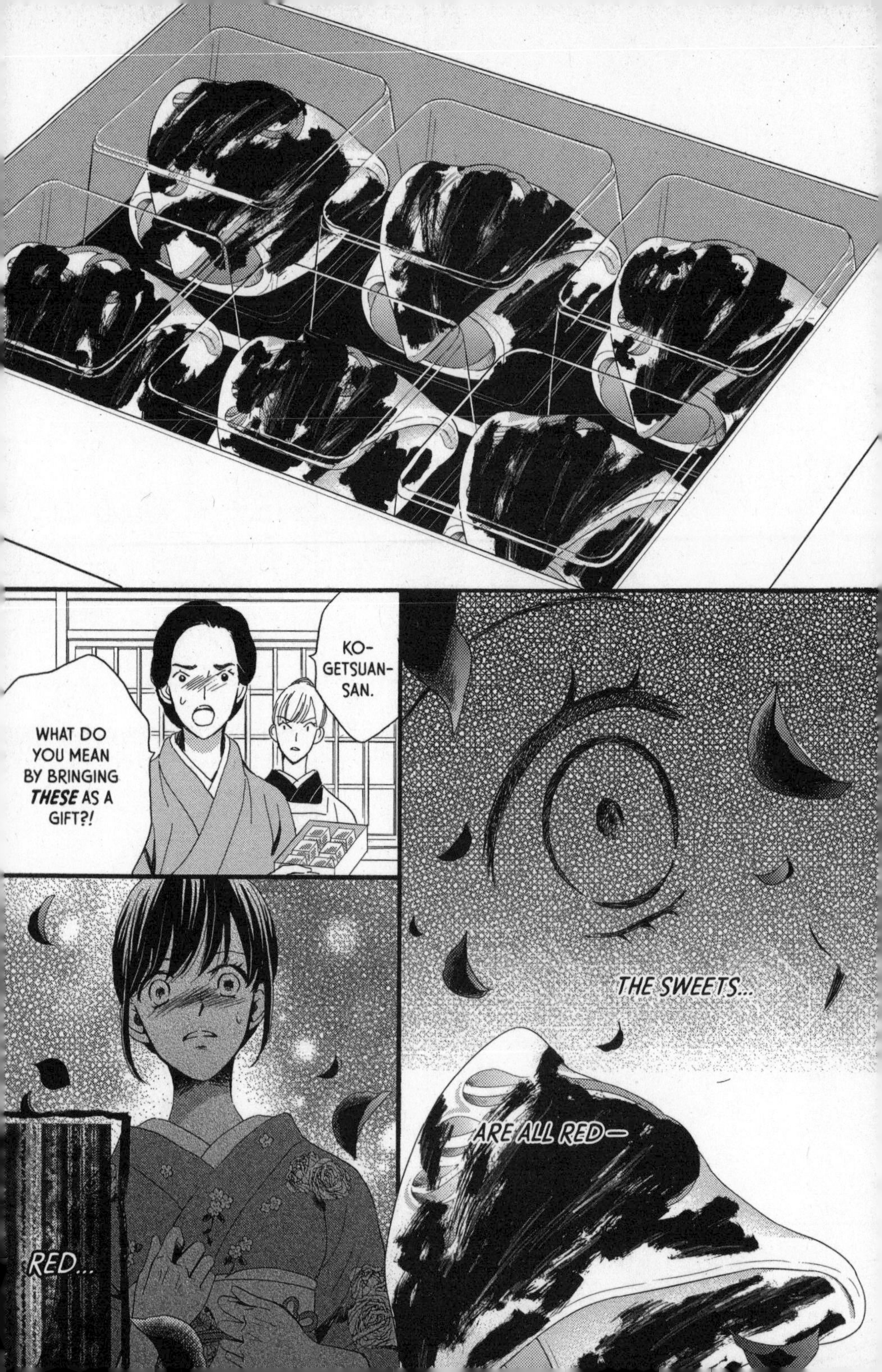
THE SWEETS...
ARE ALL RED—
KO-GETSUAN-SAN.
WHAT DO YOU MEAN BY BRINGING THESE AS A GIFT?!
RED...

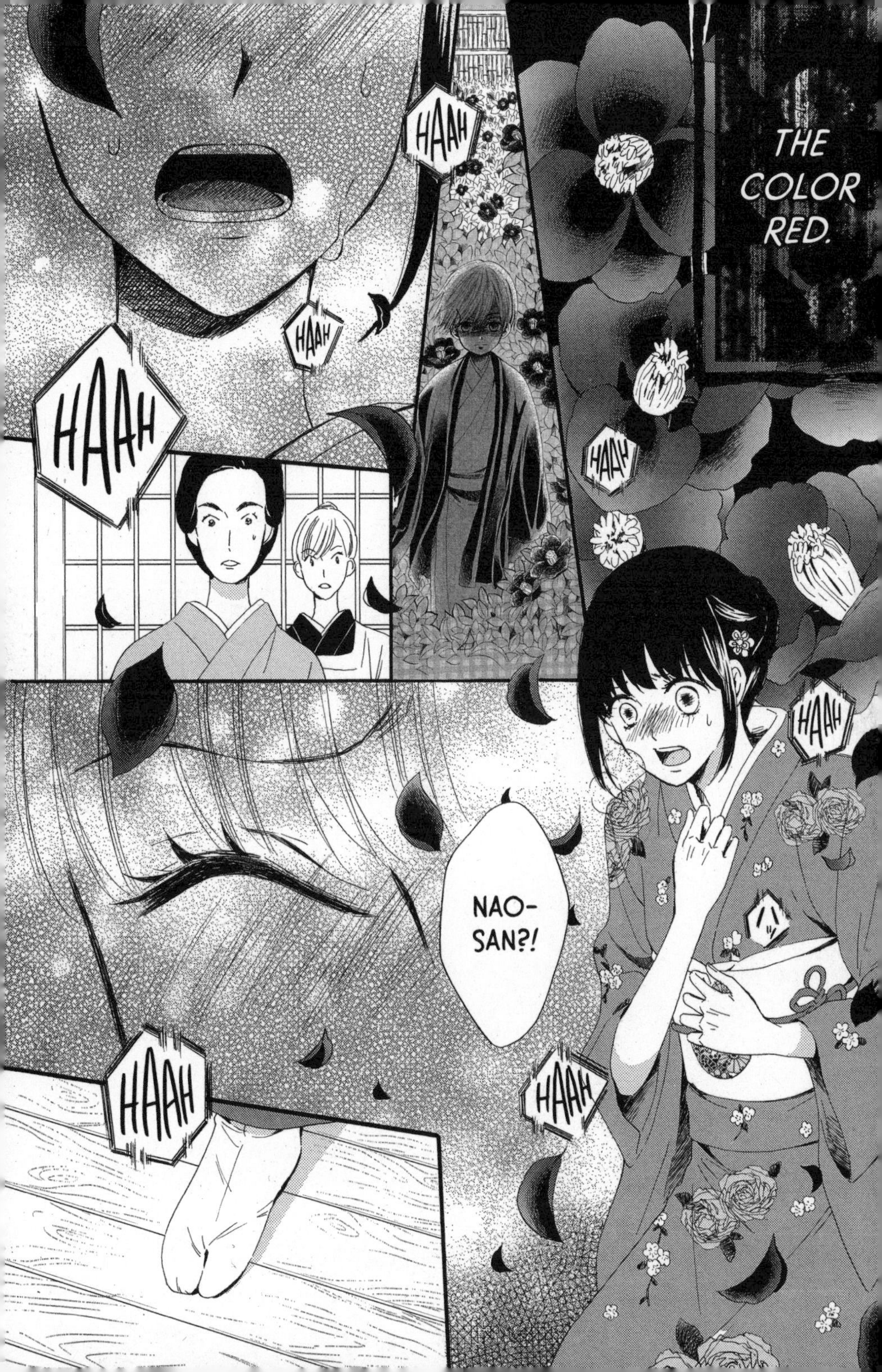
THE COLOR RED.
HAAH
HAAH
HAAH
HAAH
HAAH
NAO-SAN?!
HAAH
HAAH

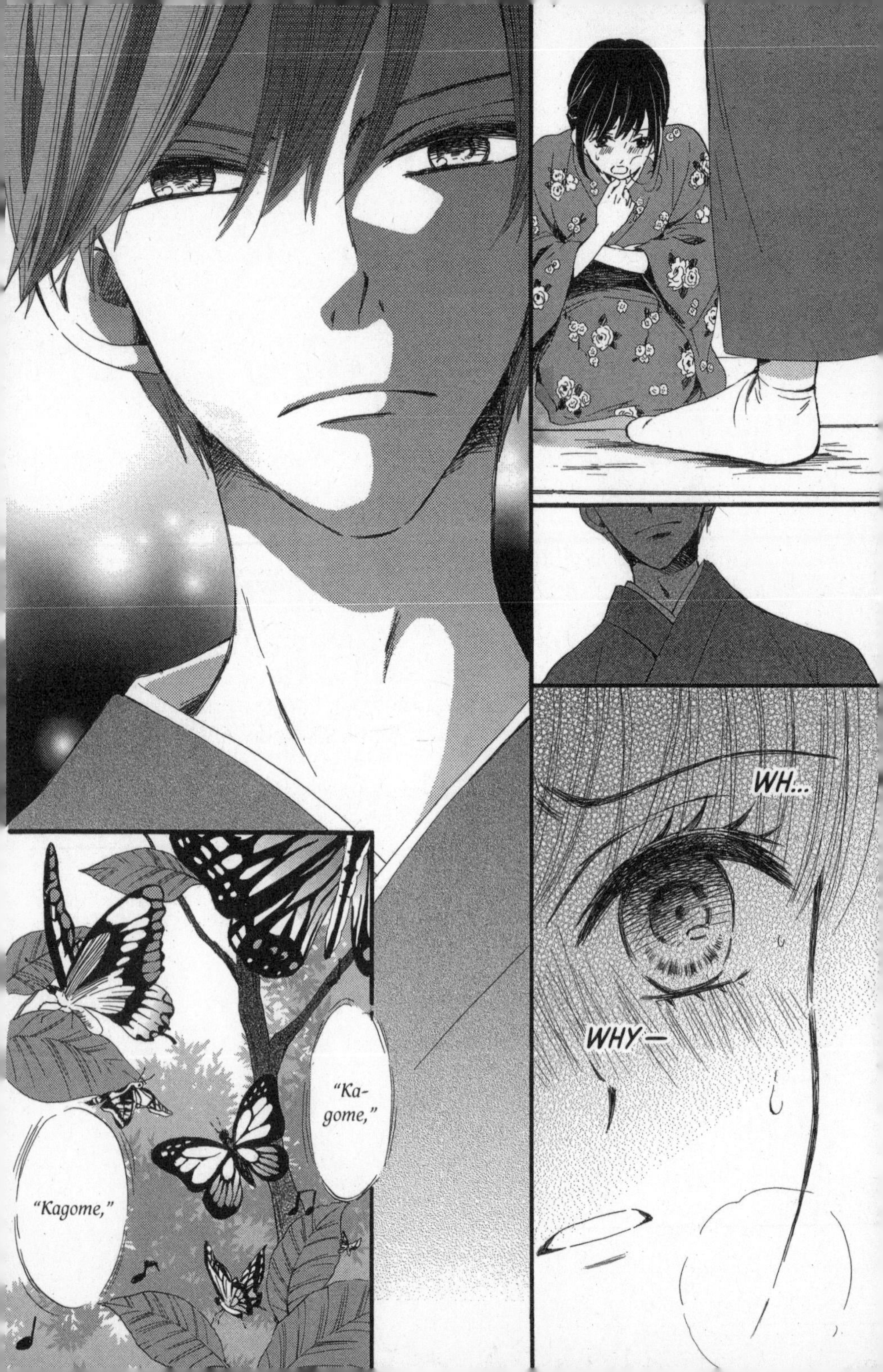
WH...
WHY—
"Ka-gome,"
"Kagome,"

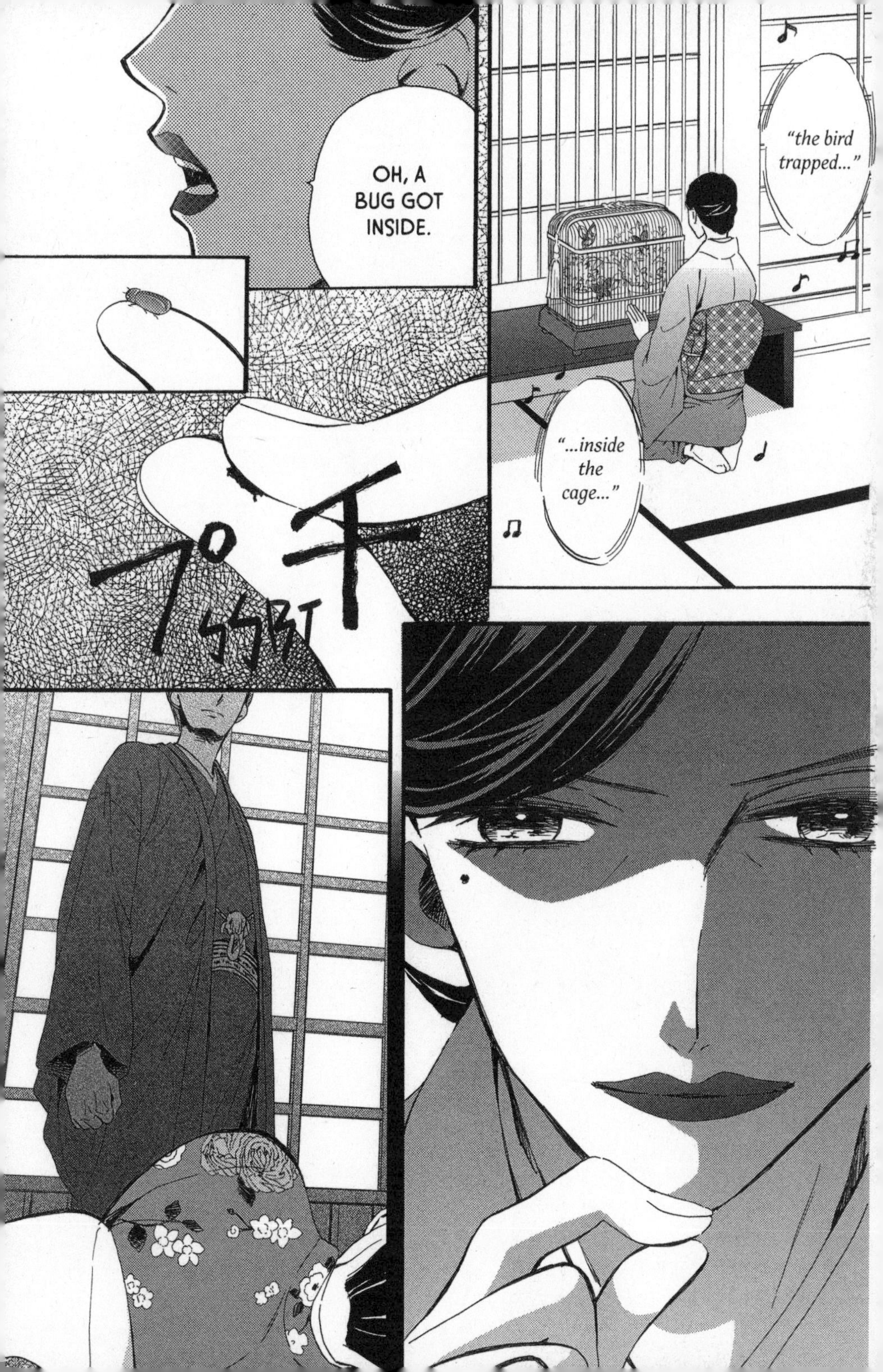
"the bird trapped..."
"...inside the cage..."
OH, A BUG GOT INSIDE.
プチ
SSBT

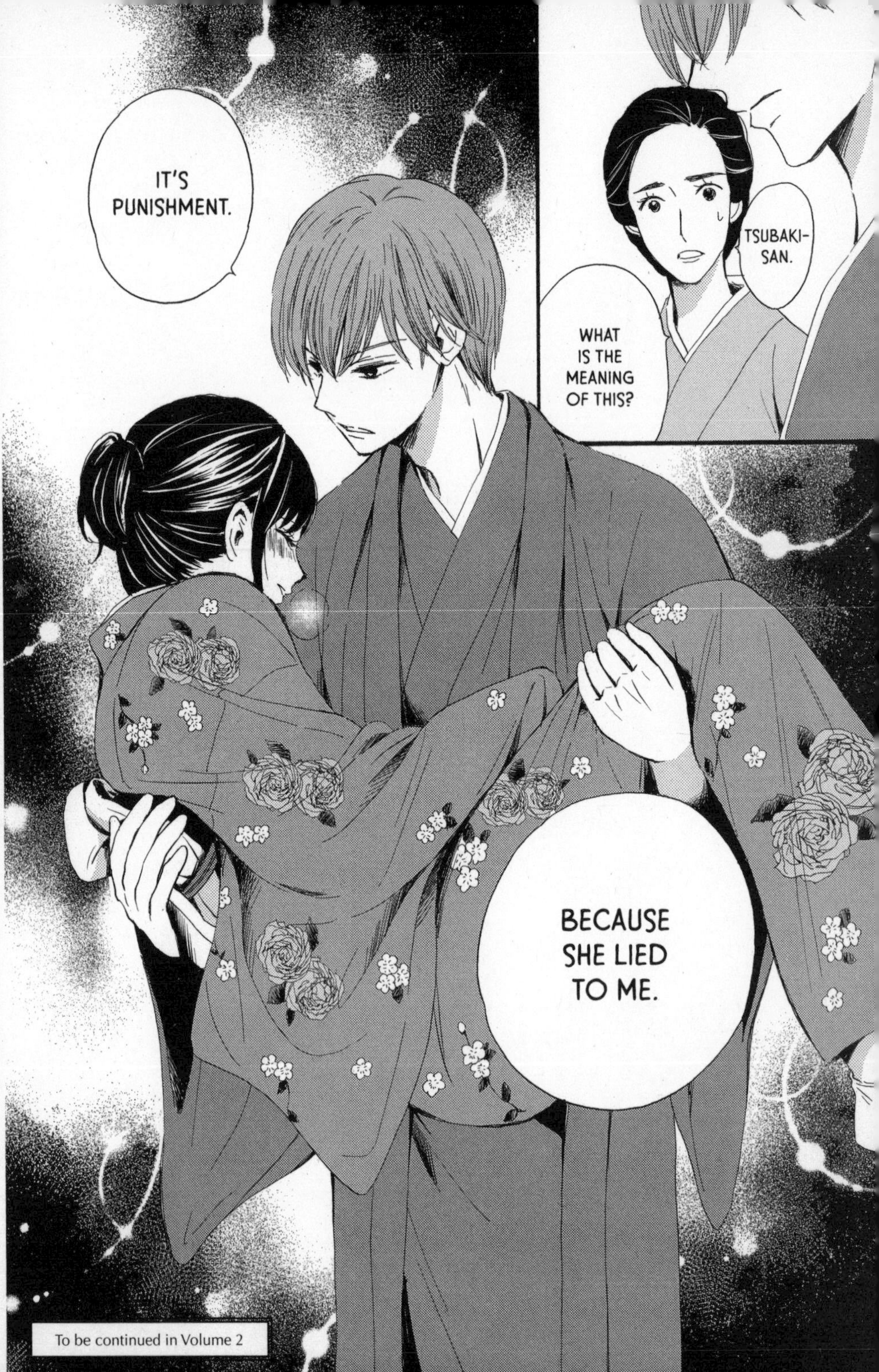
TSUBAKI-SAN.
WHAT IS THE MEANING OF THIS?
IT'S PUNISHMENT.
BECAUSE SHE LIED TO ME.
To be continued in Volume 2

Something's Wrong With Us

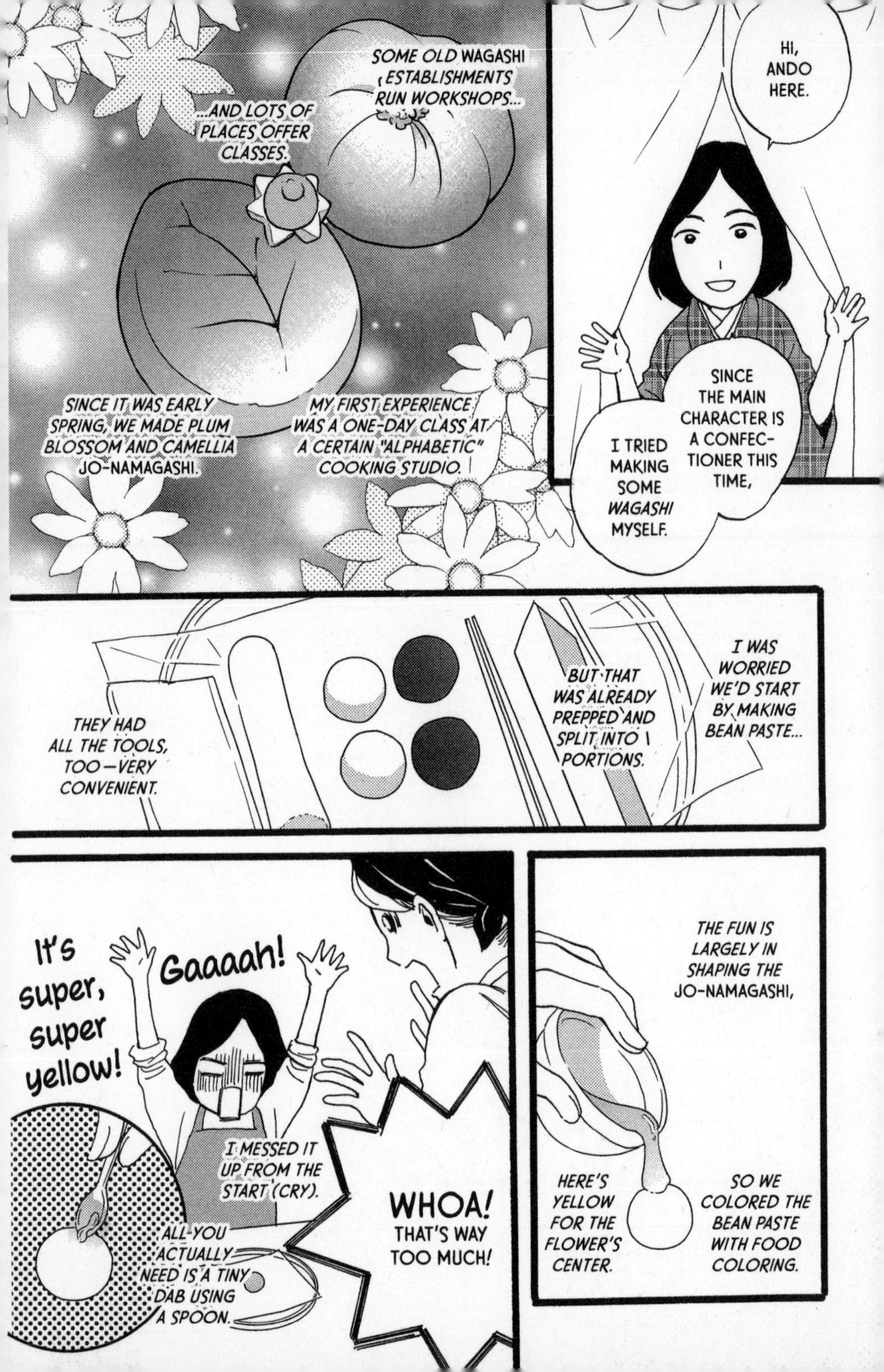
HI, ANDO HERE.
SINCE THE MAIN CHARACTER IS A CONFECTIONER THIS TIME,
I TRIED MAKING SOME *WAGASHI* MYSELF.
SOME OLD WAGASHI ESTABLISHMENTS RUN WORKSHOPS...
...AND LOTS OF PLACES OFFER CLASSES.
MY FIRST EXPERIENCE WAS A ONE-DAY CLASS AT A CERTAIN "ALPHABETIC" COOKING STUDIO.
SINCE IT WAS EARLY SPRING, WE MADE PLUM BLOSSOM AND CAMELLIA JO-NAMAGASHI.
I WAS WORRIED WE'D START BY MAKING BEAN PASTE...
BUT THAT WAS ALREADY PREPPED AND SPLIT INTO PORTIONS.
THEY HAD ALL THE TOOLS, TOO—VERY CONVENIENT.
THE FUN IS LARGELY IN SHAPING THE JO-NAMAGASHI,
SO WE COLORED THE BEAN PASTE WITH FOOD COLORING.
HERE'S YELLOW FOR THE FLOWER'S CENTER.
WHOA! THAT'S WAY TOO MUCH!
Gaaaah!
It's super, super yellow!
I MESSED IT UP FROM THE START (CRY).
ALL YOU ACTUALLY NEED IS A TINY DAB USING A SPOON.

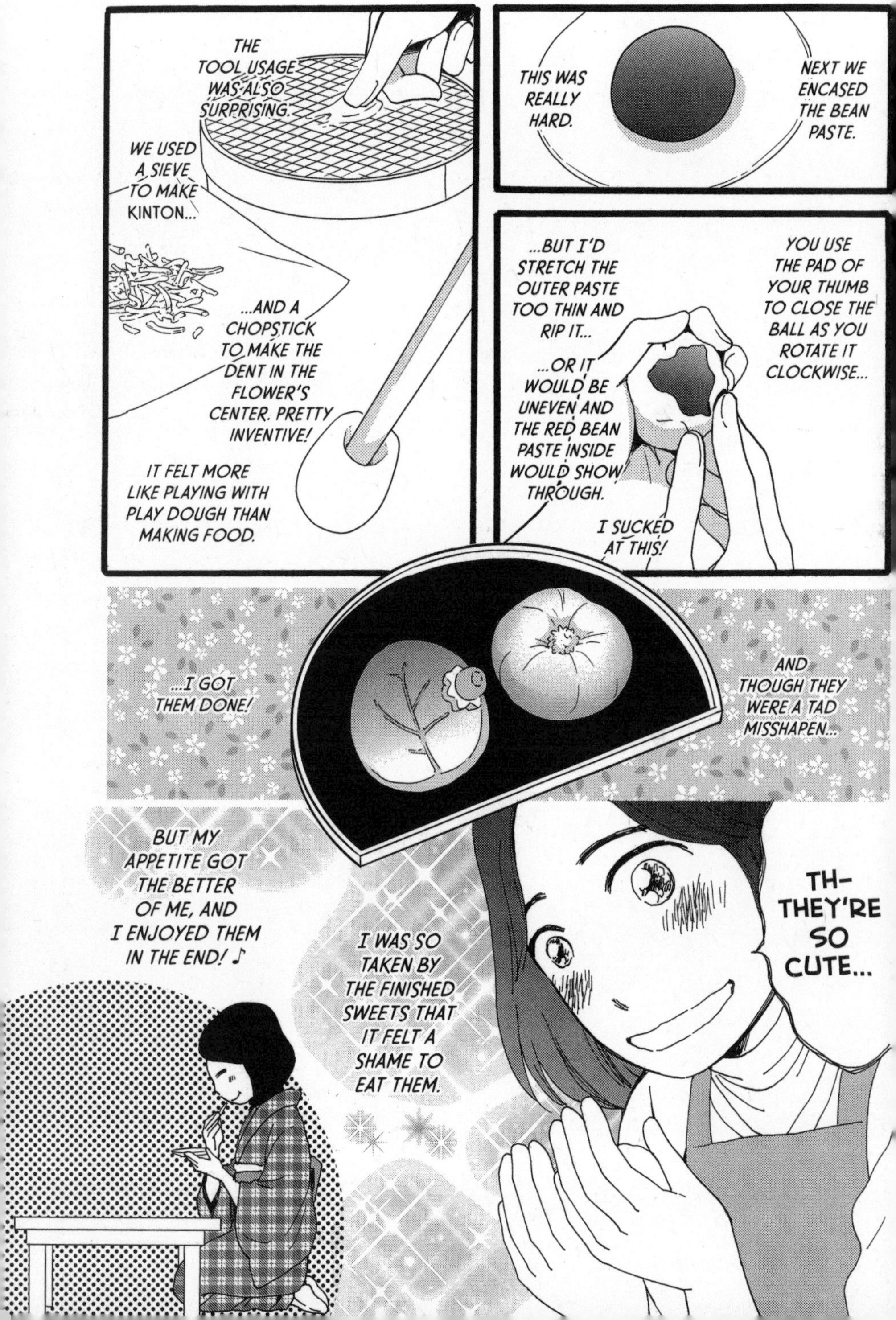
NEXT WE ENCASED THE BEAN PASTE.
THIS WAS REALLY HARD.
YOU USE THE PAD OF YOUR THUMB TO CLOSE THE BALL AS YOU ROTATE IT CLOCKWISE...
...BUT I'D STRETCH THE OUTER PASTE TOO THIN AND RIP IT...
...OR IT WOULD BE UNEVEN AND THE RED BEAN PASTE INSIDE WOULD SHOW THROUGH.
I SUCKED AT THIS!
THE TOOL USAGE WAS ALSO SURPRISING.
WE USED A SIEVE TO MAKE KINTON...
...AND A CHOPSTICK TO MAKE THE DENT IN THE FLOWER'S CENTER. PRETTY INVENTIVE!
IT FELT MORE LIKE PLAYING WITH PLAY DOUGH THAN MAKING FOOD.
AND THOUGH THEY WERE A TAD MISSHAPEN...
...I GOT THEM DONE!
TH- THEY'RE SO CUTE...
I WAS SO TAKEN BY THE FINISHED SWEETS THAT IT FELT A SHAME TO EAT THEM.
BUT MY APPETITE GOT THE BETTER OF ME, AND I ENJOYED THEM IN THE END! ♪

NEXT VOLUME PREVIEW

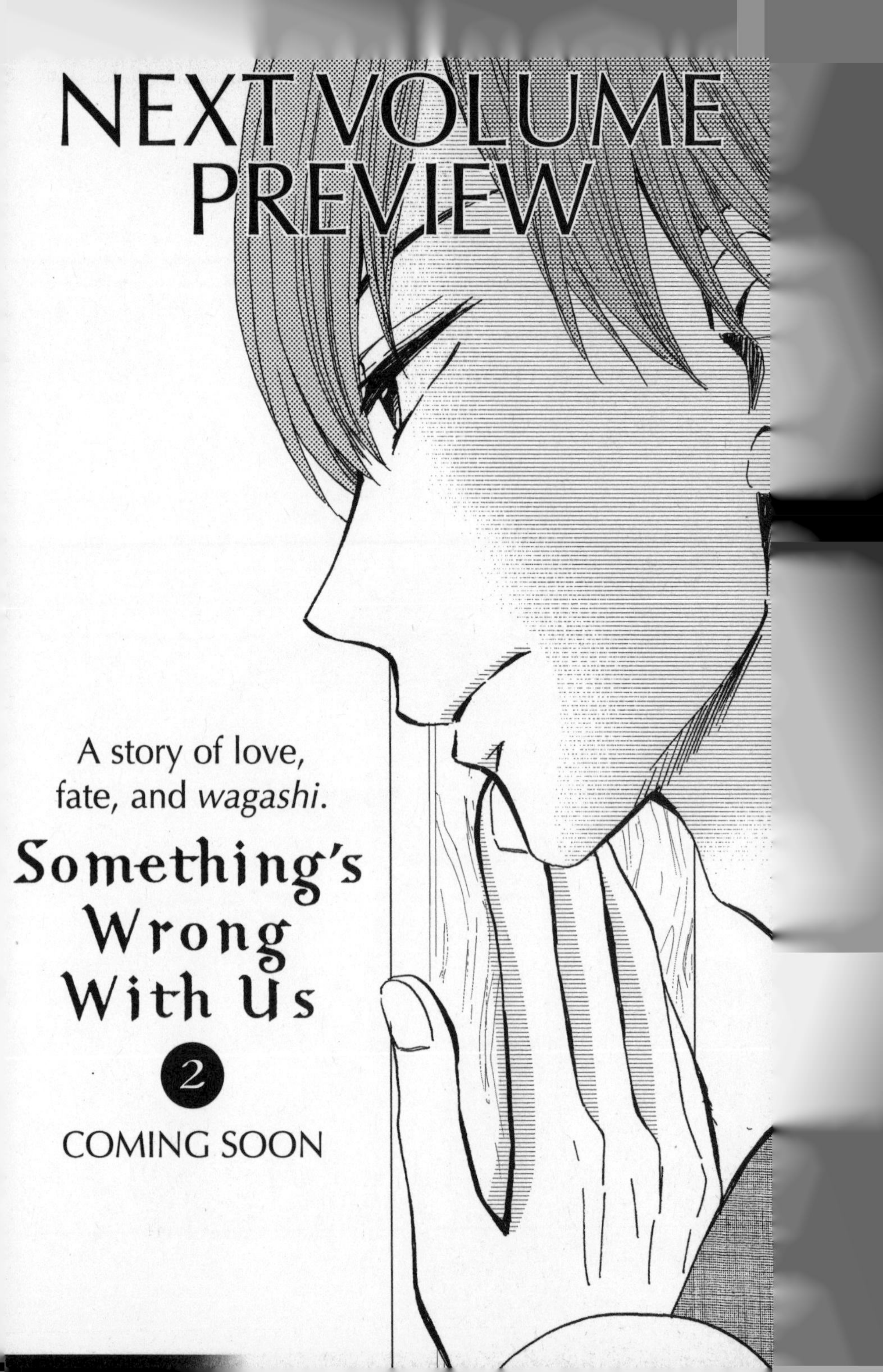

A story of love,
fate, and *wagashi*.

Something's Wrong With Us

2

COMING SOON

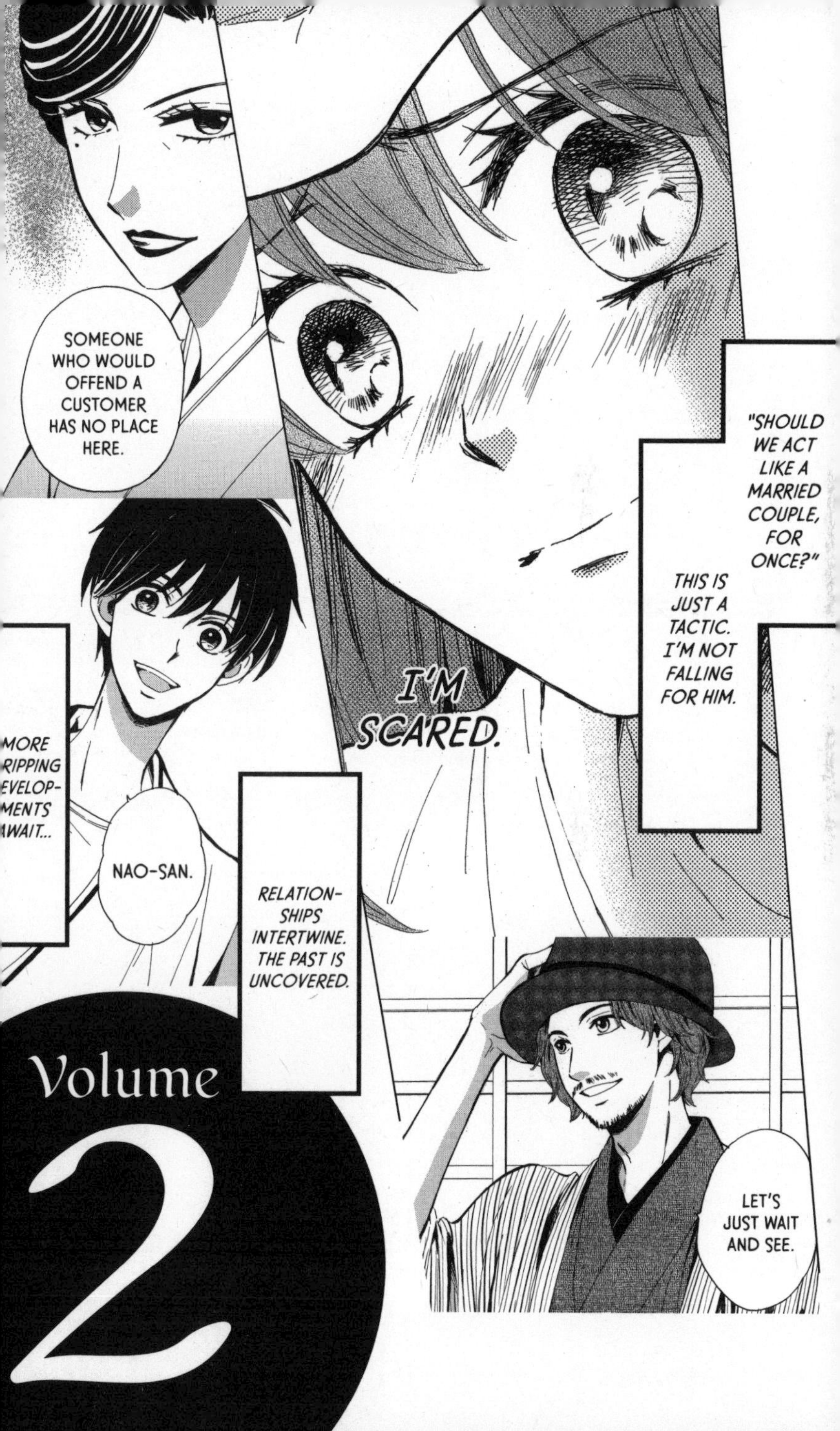
"SHOULD WE ACT LIKE A MARRIED COUPLE, FOR ONCE?"
THIS IS JUST A TACTIC. I'M NOT FALLING FOR HIM.
I'M SCARED.
SOMEONE WHO WOULD OFFEND A CUSTOMER HAS NO PLACE HERE.
RELATION-SHIPS INTERTWINE. THE PAST IS UNCOVERED.
NAO-SAN.
MORE RIPPING EVELOP-MENTS AWAIT...
LET'S JUST WAIT AND SEE.
Volume 2

Natsumi Ando

I've had the chance to visit a lot more old *wagashi* establishments recently, though I very rarely used to go in them before. There's a distinct atmosphere in these shops as soon as you walk in.

I feel like my character is under scrutiny, like I should stand up with my back straight.

I imagine that the protagonist Nao feels that way, too.

Something's Wrong With Us

Translation Notes

wagashi, page 5
Traditional Japanese confections.

Sayama-ryu, page 22
The formal Japanese Way of Tea is split into various "*ryuha*," or "schools," each practicing their own style of the traditional Japanese tea ceremony.

hanaikada, page 30
A spring *wagashi* motif that represents sakura blossom petals flowing down a river, like tiny rafts.

manju, page 33
A bite-sized bun with sweet filling, usually bean paste.

kintsuba, page 33
A block of sweet red bean paste with a thin coating of grilled batter.

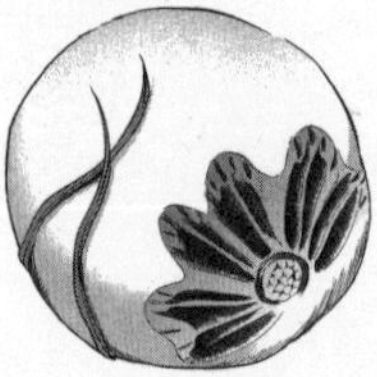

Usuzumi-zakura, page 59
A solitary sakura blossom tree that has stood in Gifu Prefecture for over 1,500 years, known for the unusual color change that its flowers go through. *Usuzumi* means "pale ink."

"I head home under green sakura trees, and season fish with salt." page 73

A haiku by 20th century poet Ayako Hosomi, about how, now that the petals have fallen and the leaves are out on the sakura blossom trees, life is back to ordinary with the usual salted fish for dinner.

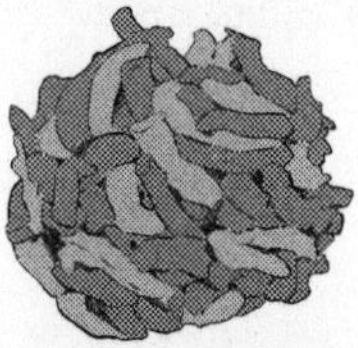

natane, page 85

A yellow and green spring motif of a field of *natane* (rapeseed) plant flowers.

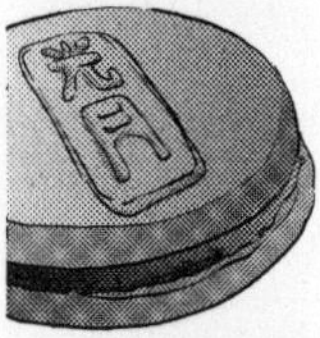

monaka, page 85

Two crispy wafers made of rice flour with a sweet filling (usually bean paste) sandwiched in between.

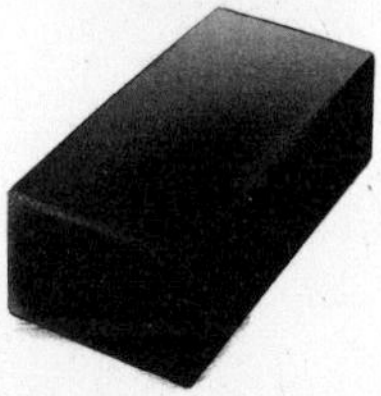

yokan, page 103

A smooth, jellied sweet made of bean paste and agar. The most common type is made of red bean paste and is a very dark brown—almost black.

The color black, page 103

Black in a wedding gift is inappropriate because it is thought to represent misfortune. In Japan, auspicious colors for weddings are red and white.

betrothal, page 111
Traditionally, when two people get engaged, the two families hold a formal betrothal ceremony where they exchange gifts, often in the form of money. Although this has become less extravagant in recent years, the gifts would involve thousands of dollars, even for normal households. A marriage between two prestigious households like the ones here would likely involve a small fortune.

Tsubaki-san, page 113
In very formal households like the Takatsuki family, the mother will often address her children with the "-san" honorific. "-san" is akin to "Mr., Ms., Mx." etc. Additionally, the honorific "-sama" is at a higher level of respect, akin to "Master" or "Lord." For example, the father-in-law on page 119 would be referred to with the "-sama" honorific.

rakugan, page 120
Delicate, pressed sugar candies made with *wasanbon* sugar (a fine-grained sugar with a distinctive taste used for *wagashi*) and starch. They're made using traditional wooden molds and come in all kinds of colors and shapes.

shibukiri, page 144
Literally "cutting the bitterness." The process of pouring away the water once the *azuki* beans come to a boil. This is repeated several times to remove the bitter taste from the beans.

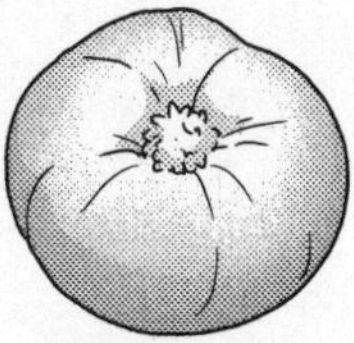

bikkurimizu, page 144

Literally "surprise water." The process of adding cold water to rapidly cool down a boiling pot.

jo-namagashi, page 155

Fresh, artistic *wagashi* that are made with specific (usually seasonal) motifs.

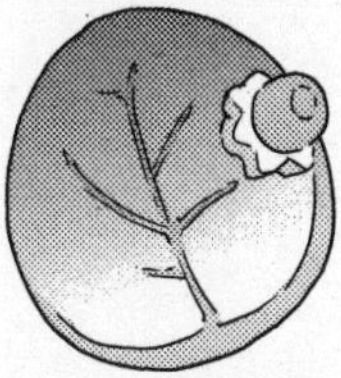

Kagome, kagome, page 164

A nursery rhyme used in a children's game, where a blindfolded child has to guess who stands behind them at the end of the song.

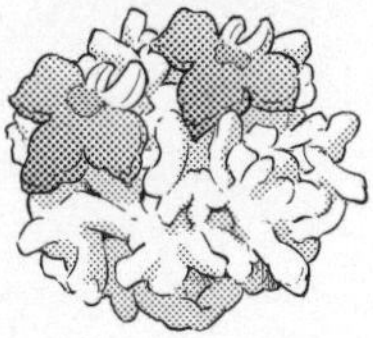

kinton, page 169

A popular type of *jo-namagashi* that involves a ball of bean paste covered in strands of colored bean paste, giving it a "fuzzy" appearance.

Acclaimed screenwriter and director
Mari Okada (*Maquia*, *anohana*) teams up
with manga artist Nao Emoto (*Forget Me
Not*) in this moving, funny, so-true-it's-
embarrassing coming-of-age series!

When Kazusa enters high
school, she joins the Literature
Club, and leaps from reading
innocent fiction to diving into
the literary classics. But these
novels are a bit more...*adult* than
she was prepared for. Between
euphemisms like fresh dewy
grass and pork stew, crushing on
the boy next door, and knowing
you want to do that *one thing*
before you die—discovering
your budding sexuality is
no easy feat! As if puberty
wasn't awkward enough,
the club consists of a
brooding writer, the
prettiest girl in school,
an agreeable comrade,
and an outspoken prude.
Fumbling over their
own discomforts, these
five teens get thrown
into chaos over three
little letters: S...E...X...!

O Maidens in your Savage Season

Anime
coming
soon!

Mari Okada   Nao Emoto

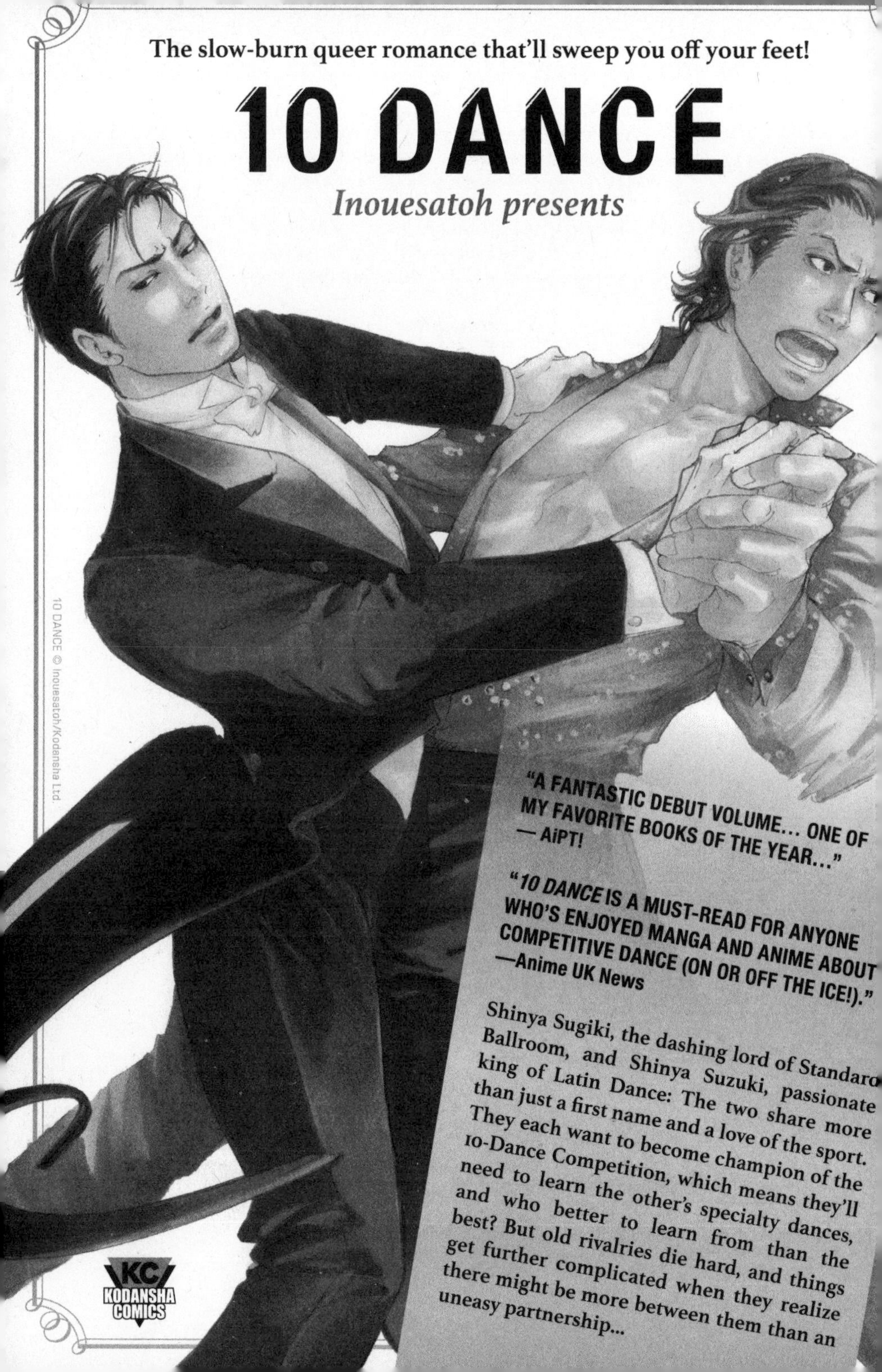
The slow-burn queer romance that'll sweep you off your feet!
10 DANCE
Inouesatoh presents
"A FANTASTIC DEBUT VOLUME... ONE OF MY FAVORITE BOOKS OF THE YEAR..."
— AiPT!
"10 DANCE IS A MUST-READ FOR ANYONE WHO'S ENJOYED MANGA AND ANIME ABOUT COMPETITIVE DANCE (ON OR OFF THE ICE!)."
—Anime UK News
Shinya Sugiki, the dashing lord of Standard Ballroom, and Shinya Suzuki, passionate king of Latin Dance: The two share more than just a first name and a love of the sport. They each want to become champion of the 10-Dance Competition, which means they'll need to learn the other's specialty dances, and who better to learn from than the best? But old rivalries die hard, and things get further complicated when they realize there might be more between them than an uneasy partnership...
10 DANCE © Inouesatoh/Kodansha Ltd.
KC KODANSHA COMICS

A Kodansha Comics Trade Paperback Original
Something's Wrong With Us 1 copyright © 2017 Natsumi Ando
English translation copyright © 2020 Natsumi Ando

All rights reserved.

Published in the United States by Kodansha Comics, an imprint of Kodansha USA Publishing, LLC, New York.

Publication rights for this English edition arranged through Kodansha Ltd., Tokyo.

First published in Japan in 2017 by Kodansha Ltd., Tokyo as *Watashitachi wa doukashiteiru*, volume 1.

ISBN 978-1-63236-972-7

Printed in the United States of America.

www.kodanshacomics.com

9 8 7 6 5 4 3 2 1
Translation: Sawa Matsueda Savage
Lettering: Sara Linsley
Editing: Haruko Hashimoto
Kodansha Comics edition cover design by Matt Akuginow

Publisher: Kiichiro Sugawara
Managing editor: Maya Rosewood
Vice president of marketing & publicity: Naho Yamada

Director of publishing services: Ben Applegate
Associate director of operations: Stephen Pakula
Publishing services managing editor: Noelle Webster
Assistant production manager: Emi Lotto, Angela Zurlo
Logo and character art ©Kodansha USA Publishing, LLC